DIRT TRACK DREAMS
The Tunis Speedway Chronicles

Welcome
RACE FANS
TUNIS SPEEDWAY
Enjoy
Coca-Cola

Compiled and Edited by Jim Volgarino
Illustrations by Steve Hunter

Dirt Track Dreams--The Tunis Speedway Chronicles

ISBN 978-0-692-54274-3

This book is a work of non-fiction. Names, characters, businesses, organizations, places, events and incidents are, to the best knowledge of the author, true though some recollections by those offering the stories and facts, may have been embellished slightly as the years have passed.

There is no intent to present erroneous information and it is hoped readers will understand this is an attempt to gather not only images but information related to the operation of the former Tunis Speedway in Waterloo, Iowa from 1948 - 1983 in the best way possible.

Further information can be obtained at:

www.tunisspeedway.com

www.facebook.com/groups/tunisspeedway/

Cover design and chapter illustrations by Steve Hunter, Cedar Falls, Iowa

DEDICATION

What started as simple curiosity grew into an obsession as I discovered the story of Tunis Speedway including more interesting elements than I could have imagined.

Barbara Higgins, Judd and Marie Tunis's granddaughter, allowed me to look over the scrapbooks Judd kept during the years the race track operated its weekly programs,

I knew then this was going to involve more than a quick overview of just one of thousands of dirt tracks that sprang up around the country following World War II.

1948
1983
Waterloo
T
IOWA
TUNIS SPEEDWAY
CORDES
2
32
35 Years of Racing

With Barbara's blessing I took those scrapbooks which included envelopes packed with pictures and proceeded to work on identifying who was actually in the pictures. Judd, who obviously knew all the people pictured, only wrote the years on each envelope and that began my research in earnest.

I'm fortunate to have had so many people willing to help with this entire effort. More than 1200 photo images were gathered from sources all over the country. Fans, families of drivers, drivers themselves and people who worked at the track all provided images going back to the earliest races.

I began this project some 30 years after Tunis Speedway ran its last race on the property located between Waterloo and Cedar Falls, Iowa. Amazingly there were hundreds of people who shared their pictures and memories and I am forever grateful for thie help and encouragement.

I didn't talk with anyone who didn't think Tunis Speedway was the greatest thing since sliced bread. Everyone seemed to have a story to tell, from fans sharing about heading to the track every Sunday afternoon to drivers sharing their experiences as novice racers.

I've attempted to capture just some of the stories and I know I missed many other good ones. I apologize to those who I failed to reach and I thank those who took the time to revisit all they could remember about the track during its 35 year history.

Let me finally dedicate this entire effort to J.L. (Judd) Tunis and his wife Marie, who agreed to have this crazy mix of race car drivers ripping around their property all those years. Promoting a race track probably looked like great fun, but it was hard work (just ask Claus Stricker!). Judd and Marie always worked hard to make sure the fans and the drivers got the very best effort they had. And I want to think Waterloo and the surrounding area were better for it.

FOREWARD

This project began as a simple search to find information about a dirt track racing facility that operated in my hometown of Waterloo, Iowa for 35 years.

As a youngster I could well remember my trips to the track on my bicycle, ducking under a back fence and watching in awe as cars roared around this sometimes muddy, sometimes dusty oval, smacking into each other on occasion and even rolling over, most times to the delight of the crowd.

The track was pretty well known, not only in the local area, but within the Midwest region as many drivers from other communities would travel to compete on the oval in hopes of taking home both a trophy and some prize money.

Auto racing was born of the natural human inclination for competition. In the auto industry's formative years, as builders vied to prove their products were superior to others, the sport of racing generated innovative and technical advances in an exciting, highly visible environment.

Racing in America—

The Henry Ford Museum

The above quote, taken from a historical account of early U.S. auto racing, sets the stage for the chronology of events that occurred at Tunis Speedway, carved from a former agricultural field on the western outskirts of a growing city.

Competition moves people to do things they might not ever have thought of trying before. Almost to a person, the drivers interviewed for this perspective said they saw somewhere an actual race and thought, "I want to do that". Or at least that same thought in similar words.

That competitive spirit, mixed with a generous dose of ingenuity and an even larger measure of courage, produced weekly events that fans, even now some 30 years after the track closed, still remember with fondness and awe.

Some might call that "courage" a crazy disease, something caught the first time a driver smelled the acrid mixture of tire rubber and gasoline. Others were drawn by the prospect of speed, that tangible rush of adrenalin that came from moving an object faster than it probably was meant to move.

But it was the racing and the racers that made the track thrive, bringing in droves of families, race helpers and support staff. And while Judd Tunis, who built the track at the urging of local racing enthusiasts, learned how to promote this crazy synthesis of speed, metal and dirt, the competitive industry that grew from these formative years became one of the country's most popular entertainment venues.

These are the stories…the chronicles if you will, of the men and women who found excitement, devotion and a lifetime of memories on this little dirt oval. There is a rich history here that reflects much of what the American dream is all about. And I hope you'll enjoy it.

Chronology and Facts About the Track

1941—Judd Tunis purchases 52 acres of land with money borrowed from his daughter Lorene.

The property sat on the outskirts of Waterloo at that time and he paid $200 per acre to acquire it.

"Everyone called me a damned fool."

1942—Builds home and accessory buildings on the land.

1947—Judd uses part of the land to build a track to race and exercise horses. This was a ½ mile track. Judd wanted a track closer than Waverly where he could run his own horses.

1948—Judd is convinced by his son-in-law, Bill Higgins, and local midget car racer, Ira "Speed" Chumley to build a ¼ mile track inside the ½ mile track for midget racing. First unofficial motorcycle races on the track were sponsored by the local Black Hawk Motorcycle Club.

1949—First midget races are held. Judd decides auto racing has some promise.

1950—The first full sized auto races are held.

1966—Judd sells a portion of the land to Welles Department Store to build a retail store. He also leases the track to Jim Cordes, Roger Beck and Bill Zwanziger who take over promoting the races. The track is renamed Cordes Speedway, but just for one year when Judd took back promotion the following year.

1974—Claus Stricker takes over promotion and management of the track.

1975—The track is expanded from ¼ mile to 3/8 mile.

1979—Judd decides to stop running weekly racing events despite efforts to convince him otherwise.

1983—The final race is held September 25, an Enduro Race promoted by Keith Knaack of Vinton and sponsored by The Deery Brothers.

Track would seat 5000 spectators in the stands and many times did just that. Largest crowd was over 8,000.

Admission was $1.00 to $2.50 per person throughout the time the track was operating. (1949-1979)

No race car driver was ever killed on the track. A thrill show performer was killed when a dynamite trick did not work correctly and a young boy died when he fell from a horse while on the track. There were also at least two heart attacks at the track, one a driver who drove off track but didn't hit anything, and a car owner who died just after his driver won and collected his winnings and trophy.

Judd conditioned the track himself. Each spring the track surface was rebuilt. He was quoted in 1965 (Des Moines Register, May 24) as saying "It takes a good rich soil on top of clay to make a good running surface. You can't do it with sandy soil. You need soil that will knit together. We go below the frost line every spring and plow it up and then repack it with sheep-foot rollers."

Marie Tunis was involved in operating the track, coordinating ticket sales and as a bookkeeper.

More than 50 people manned the staff of the track during weekly races. This included car parkers, ticket sellers/takers, gatemen, pitmen, infield workers, race car pushers, judges, flagmen, tow truck operators, track waterers and security staff (normally off duty policemen).

In addition the concession stands were manned with even more people, some of whom walked among the spectators selling peanuts, popcorn and cold drinks.

Insurance for race events was $600 per event. Prize money typically was about $3000 per race date.

In 1975 there were five dirt tracks attracting drivers between Webster City and Dubuque along Highway 20. The Tunis track was the first of those tracks to be built.

1895
Durgea Motor Wagon Company
EVANSTON
CHICAGO
5
NO USE FOR HORSES.
Springfield Mechanics Devise a New Mode of Travel.
Ingenious Wagon Now Being Made in This City for What the Makers Claim Great Things.
PACO SPEEDSTER BODY
FOR FORD CARS
A FEW GOOD FEATURES
PACO
PEORIA ACCESSORY COMPANY, Peoria, Illinois

Dirt Track Racing—The Beginning

In 1895 the United States experienced its very first viewed and recorded automobile race. It happened in Chicago, Illinois and included just six vehicles and was actually sponsored by the Chicago Times-Herald in an effort to bolster the exposure of a budding American auto industry.

It must have been successful on all fronts because winner Frank Duryea, driving a self-built gas-powered horseless carriage fairly common to the era, not only won the 50-mile trek from Chitown to Evanston, Illinois (in a blinding snowstorm at an average 7.5 miles per hour in 10 hours flat).

Frank also went on to sell 13 of his (and his brother's) Duryea named Motor Wagons which turned out to be more than any other car maker in the country at that time.

The Chicago Times Herald reported, "The progress of the preliminary trials has been watched by thousands of potential manufacturers in every part of the world and there is no doubt that there will be a great interest in the manufacture of these horseless carriages now that it has been demonstrated what can be done with them."

As soon as automobiles began plying the roads all over the world in the late 1800s and early 1900s, drivers were enthralled with seeing who could best who in speed, endurance and daring. Organized and unorganized contests cropped up on roads, in farm fields and on roughly constructed tracks where if the dirt didn't slow you down, the ruts and holes would probably swallow your race car or some important component before you could make all the required laps.

But drivers slowly became racers and those racers captured the imagination of a growing audience of race enthusiasts in all parts of the country. The very earliest race cars sported no fenders and skinny wheels, piloted by a driver usually perched directly behind an engine that could self-destruct at any moment.

The race courses, depending on what part of the country they were located, were flat, curved, banked or any combination of those designs and typically had dirt surfaces. Some went so far as to apply gravel or rock or sand to the surfaces and in some parts of the country, clay was a major ingredient of the track surface.

But in Iowa, it was just good old black dirt which, when it was wet, was slimy as grease and when it was dry would blow into every crevice it had even a remote potential to reach.

From the early 1900s to just shortly after World War II, the racing industry languished some. There were tracks being built and racers making the regular journey to the dirt ovals to rev their engines and try to beat their racing comrades.

But it was soon after the war, when GIs returned home that racing fervor really took off and tracks began popping up everywhere.

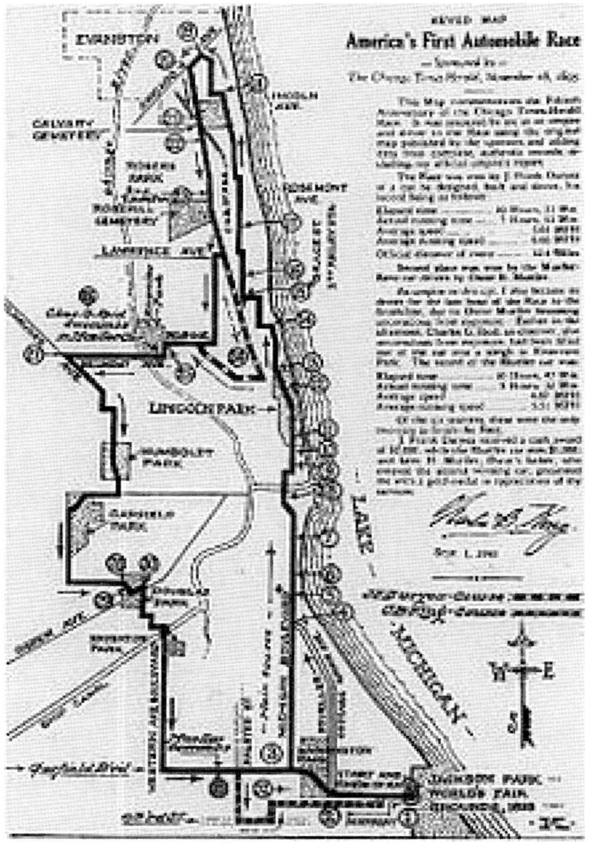
America's First Automobile Race
EVANSTON
LINCOLN PARK
HUMBOLDT PARK
GARFIELD PARK
LAKE
MICHIGAN

And of course it made things even more interesting when Bill France Sr. created NASCAR in 1948 following his own exploits as a closed car "jalopy" racer. France had discovered that audiences would come in large numbers to see cars with a stock appearance speed around a track and he went to work creating the largest automotive racing sanctioning body in the world. But that's another story.

Among thousands of tracks that were being built throughout the country, Iowa was not to be left behind. One of the most recognized tracks in the world, Knoxville Raceway in Knoxville, Iowa, was actually constructed in the late 1800s at the Marion County Fairgrounds as a horse racing facility.

Much like that fairgrounds track, county fair boards began realizing there was a specific interest in local racing and proceeded to either convert former horse race tracks to automobile racing or built a track from scratch.

NASCAR managed to grab just enough news space that the interest in stock car racing grew with former GIs in many cases, putting their mechanical talents to work modifying cars for their once a week forays on the dirt ovals.

In the southern U.S., racing grew from former prohibition drivers deciding it was best to get off the roads and onto the track. In the Midwest the tracks many times grew with farm boys and girls grabbing onto a growing number of dilapidated vehicles to speed around the dirt ovals.

Remember, the country was emerging from a war that had virtually stopped the auto industry and people were keen to buy up the newest vehicles Detroit could produce.

This helped increase the number of race candidates that had probably run their course on the streets, but were plenty ready for some rowdy crashing and banging.

So began a racing venue that even today remains an ever popular way for a speed crazy audience to get their fix. Though the numbers of local dirt tracks has probably decreased, the interest continues to be strong and though safety and technology factors have changed, fans still find dirt track racing exciting.

Without those earlier racers just wanting to see who could beat who, it's possible dirt tracks might not have caught on.

The story of Tunis Speedway is one mirrored at tracks throughout the nation. And for 35 years it showed the local racing community just how it was done.

INDEPENDENCE
Lorene
12/1917
J. L. Tunis Hamburger
and Sausage
Cadillac

The races at Tunis Speedway drew an average of 5000 people per race with drivers receiving 40% of the gate. The stands held 5000 people so the overflow sat behind the half-mile track in their cars or put out blankets on the banks. Admission was $1.00 for adults, 50 cents for children 6 to 12 years, and free for younger children. People with disabilities were granted free admission.

Initially the track was distant from housing, but as Cedar Falls and Waterloo expanded, homes were built adjacent to the track. The noise and dust were significant.

The City of Waterloo had indicated that the track would be allowed as long as it was owned and/or operated without interruption by Judd Tunis and he took complete charge of conditioning the track. It was rebuilt each spring by plowing up the track below the frost line and repacking with rich soil that knit perfectly with the clay base.

Family members worked in all aspects of the Speedway. Lorene organized ticket sales, washed the ticket-selling aprons, and was the Secretary and Treasurer. On Saturdays, Lorene and Bill would roast peanuts and bag them in small brown paper sacks to sell on Sundays. Peanuts were not commercially available in small quantities at that time. If there were rain cancellations, they'd have to remove the peanuts from the bags and re-roast the next week.

Bill did all the ordering and preparation for concession stand sales and for those who sold food in the stands and on the grass bank of the half-mile track. He bought Kleen Maid hamburger and hot dog buns from Alstadt and Langlas Baking Company, hot dogs from Rath Packing Company, and hamburger from J. L Tunis Hamburger and Sausage.

Bill also bought a variety of soft drinks in glass bottles from The Coca Cola Company in Waterloo and iced them in large galvanized vats.

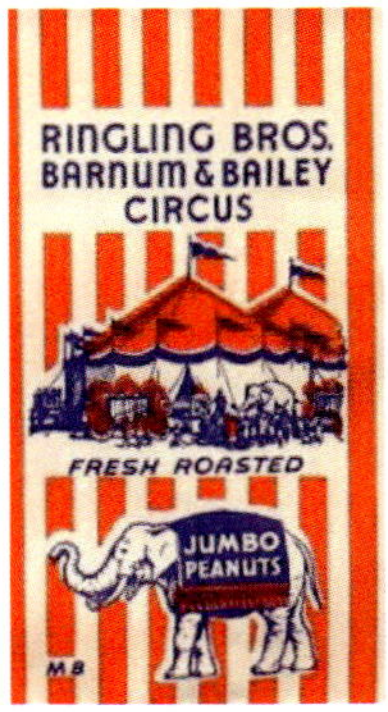
RINGLING BROS.
BARNUM & BAILEY
CIRCUS
FRESH ROASTED
JUMBO
PEANUTS

Marie sold tickets and helped count money from ticket sales and concession proceeds. Hazel Fish and her friend Emaline Ratcliff from Cedar Rapids operated the popcorn stand. Barbara and Jim Higgins as well as Kevan and Steve Cortright were among those who sold peanuts, popcorn, and fudgesickles. In 1952 peanuts were 5 cents a bag, popcorn was 10 cents, and ice cream products were 15 cents. The sale of 20 packages of peanuts from a galvanized pail netted the seller a ten cent commission.

On Mondays Lorene and Marie would complete the payroll and bank statements and do a large laundry consisting of concession stand aprons, rags, and change aprons from those selling food in the grand stands. All the wash went through a ringer washing machine and was hung on outside lines as clothes dryers weren't available then. Bank tellers from the National Bank and Waterloo Savings Bank would also sell tickets on Sundays and holidays. Judd employed off-duty police officers, parking attendants, and staff for the concession stands.

Ringling Brothers Barnum and Bailey Circus was hosted at Tunis Speedway, one of the last times the three rings were under one Big Top. The famous clown, Emmett Kelley was a performer at that circus event.

Judd wanted to have events that whole families could enjoy. He allowed no beer or liquor and would physically remove violaters with a stern warning.

He sponsored not only the car races, but also sponsored thrill (Joey Chitwood) and stunt shows, powder puff and demolition derbies, ostrich and chuckwagon races, hosted Johnny Cash in his early days, and sponsored wrestling matches. Ringling Brothers Barnum and Bailey Circus was hosted at Tunis Speedway, one of the last times the three rings were under one Big Top. The famous clown, Emmett Kelley was a performer at that circus event. Admission for horse races was free to the public.

Judd had his routine on event days. He would fill the water wagon multiple times, watering the track and adding 60-pound bags of sodium chloride to keep down the dust. He always wore his longjohns, overalls, billed cap and heavy work shoes, caked with mud and horse manure. He chewed and spat tobacco.

Judd wanted to ensure that the John Phillip Sousa marches were on the broadcast system from four o'clock on. He especially liked "Stars and Stripes Forever". He would head to the house, take a bath, put on Old Spice, clean clothes, a long-sleeved shirt, generally a bolo tie, and a brimmed straw hat. He tucked three cigars into the breast pocket of his shirt. Judd would carry a roll of twenty $20 bills in his pocket on race nights, just in case.

Since no one could vacation in the summers, Marie and Judd would travel in the fall to visit their 560 acre century farm in Plankinton, South Dakota, given to Lois and Judd by their relatives, the Irwins. Their visits were unannounced but the farmers who were managing the farm figured out after a couple of times that they could anticipate a visit in September or October each year.

The Tunises also traveled to California for a couple of months in January and February. They would arrive unannounced and plan to stay with Marie's relatives, Nellie Fish Cartwright and her husband, Andrew, and her sister, Lorene Fish Scanlon and her husband, Edward. Sometimes they would take other friends with them to California and Arizona.

Both Marie and Judd were great conversationalists. Once, when there was another couple with them, they stopped for gas. Marie initially had not wanted to use the restroom facilities but later changed her mind. Judd, talking with his friend, assumed Marie was still in the back seat and drove off. He was surprised when a highway patrol officer pulled him over many miles away from the gas station, with Marie in the patrol car, embarrassed and fuming.

Judd liked his Cadillacs and had a series of them. The most showy of them was finger-nail polish red with a white top and white and black seats. He purchased his cars from Tate Cadillac and Olds on West Fifth Street.

He didn't sell his old Caddy when he bought a new one, but recycled it into the vehicle he used to drive to the barns. As Judd got older, he would encourage friends to drive him to horse-racing events and county fairs and use those Cadillacs.

During the week he spent most of his time at the barns with his friend and fellow horse-lover, Frank Nanke. They would curry their animals and talk away the morning. Marie would ring a large bell mounted on a post to call him to dinner at noon.

They continued to operate the butcher shop in the basement of their home into the 1960's. Then the business was sold to S and S Meats, relocating the business to West Fifth and Allen streets in Waterloo.

Judd worked during the week picking up the grounds from the Sunday races and caring for his animals. He liked to keep things up and would personally mow the grass and grade the track. He also liked a thick layer of white wash on fence posts and rocks every year.

Judd employed an elderly man of 84 who helped drive the old Ford tractor. With a stick with a nail at the end, George Pagel would pick up the litter on the grounds. George couldn't see well and didn't drive his own car, so Judd would pick him up at his home in the morning and take him back in the evening.

The Hesse brothers lived on a farm at the northwest corner of what is now University Avenue and Cedar Heights Drive in Cedar Falls. They worked many summers at Tunis Speedway.

When people got hurt at the track, Judd would visit them in the hospital. Unbeknownst even to family members, Judd would support deserving families who were down on their luck by giving them groceries and buying a car if necessary.

Judd contributed to the Shrine Hospital, never a thought to its being a tax deduction. He knew when people would come to the pit area during the week and would often greet and talk with them.

There was one young man who always worked hard on his car, but Judd had observed had never won any money in a race. Judd awarded his persistence and industry by giving him $100 on several occasions.

Judd was a very hard worker and put in long days throughout the racing season. He slept little, insisting that "When you are asleep, you're dead."

His typical day began about 5:30 a.m. He would turn on KXEL or KWWL and listen to his "spots" on the radio.

Judd would occasionally join the victors down in front of the crowd when they were awarded trophies during the races, but he didn't insist on it.

Judd listened to the news and read The Des Moines Register. Judd made a pot of coffee for himself and added a fair amount of cream and sugar. He would eat cookies or rolls that were kept in a covered metal container on the counter. Judd poured the coffee mixture onto white Wonder Bread in a saucer and added pats of butter as an extra treat. It was a time that was uniquely his, uniquely quiet.

Then he would head downstairs from the kitchen to the basement that housed his wholesale meat business during weekdays, put on his overalls, coat, and cap and head toward the barns to feed the horses and muck stalls.

Right after breakfast Judd would hoist the American flag on the tall pole located in the front yard; he brought the flag in every evening, folding it carefully and respectfully.

Marie and Judd enjoyed dining out two to three times a week once they retired from their wholesale meat business. They tried to patronize restaurants that had traded with them in wholesale meats: Bishops, Steamboat Gardens, Tip-i-Tin Inn, the Purple Parrot, the Colony Club, the Chesterfield Club, Rollinger's, the Hickory House, both downtown Maid-Rites, and both east and west side Morg's and Porky's.

Their favorite was Freeman's Café on Falls Avenue. In the late 50's, one could purchase a complete dinner including drink and dessert for 90 cents. Most of the wait staff had been with Freeman Moser for 20-30 years.

People who knew Judd and Marie also knew them to be outspoken and to use colorful language. One evening Judd apparently offended a waitress at Freeman's and was asked by Mr. Moser not to come again to his restaurant. After a hiatus of 15 years, Mr. Moser wrote a letter to the Tunises asking them to return, which they did, happily. No more words; no more incidents.

After supper, Judd would read The Waterloo Courier and smoke a cigar before falling asleep in his chair about 9 p.m., sometimes charring the paper with the cigar. Marie would wait until something was about to burn before giving him a sharp reprimand.

Every Tuesday, he would fastidiously cut out all the advertising for the Sunday or holiday racing event that was in the Courier or the Register, add the write-ups of the races or other events, document the attendance and weather/temperature on race day and meticulously glue those newspaper articles into the large burgundy volumes The Waterloo Courier provided.

Judd was active in the High Twelve Club, Sports of Sorts, and Bethany and White Shrine lodges in Waterloo and Cedar Falls.

Judd loved to give rides to friends and relatives in the various buggies, carts, surreys, sulkies, and sleighs he owned, no matter the season or the temperature. He regularly went to the Waverly Horse Auction where he bought some of his animals and was a frequent customer of the Jerald Sulky Company.

There was always the ritual of cleaning up the horses, currying their coats, combing their manes, removing stones from their hooves, and carefully harnessing them for the drives. There was a raised cement platform near the barns. One day when he was putting gas into the Ford tractor he used to haul trash , he tripped over the platform and broke his leg. The doctor set it and warned him not to walk on the cast. Two days later, he was carrying the motor from the Ford tractor, against medical advice.

Judd seldom went to the doctor and did not complain when he was ill. The family had a long relationship with Dr. Donald Bickley who continued to make house calls until Marie died. Judd was diagnosed with colon cancer in 1968 and underwent Cobalt treatments, the maximum that could be given. In 1983 he was diagnosed with testicular cancer and went to Mayo Clinic in Rochester, Minnesota where he underwent surgery and many rounds of chemotherapy. Near the end of his life he was in the Hospice unit at the former Schoitz Memorial Hospital for about six weeks.

Judd died in the hospital on April 24, 1985, just shy of his 89th birthday. Marie had to relocate from University Avenue as an access road was to be developed that would go through the lots their home occupied.

Marie died in her home on Elmridge on December 9, 1993 at age 94. Both Marie and Judd are buried in Waterloo Memorial Park Cemetery next to Will and Corda Fish.

Lois Tunis died in September, 1994 and was buried with her parents in the cemetery at the intersection of Old Highway 20 and the Quasqueton Bypass just east of Independence.

The 52-acre property was reduced in size by the Department of Transportation's development of Greenhill Road to the south and the expansion of Highway 218 (University Avenue) and its frontage road.

The large flat grassed area that had been used for general admission parking was sold to Food 4 Less. Osco Drug purchased the four acres where the Tunis home was located, which coincidentally was the initial site of the Hannah homestead and the highest point in Black Hawk County. When Osco did not succeed, John Deery, Sr. purchased the land and building and donated them to Exceptional Persons, Inc.

In 1998 the land where the half mile and three-eighths mile tracks lay was sold but never *developed.

If you look really hard and listen carefully, you can see the tracks and remember.

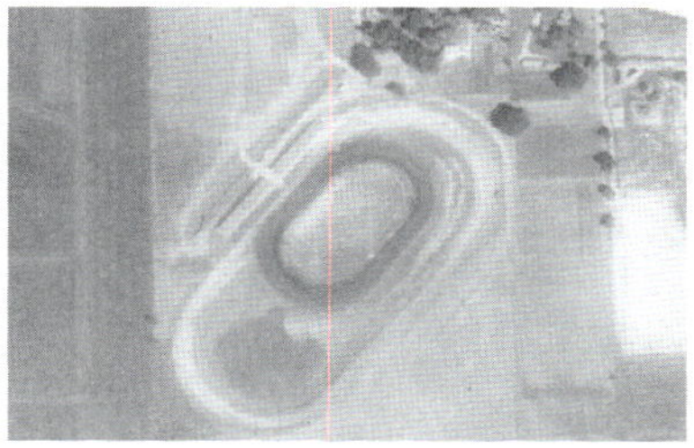

* The property development began in 2014.

JUDD AND MARIE TUNIS - Recollection by *Barbara Higgins

It was from humble beginnings that this local entrepreneur came. Judd Lorenz Tunis was born May 2, 1896 in a home on Main Street in Independence, Iowa, just two doors from the Wapsipinicon Mill on the west bank of the Wapsipinicon River. His father, August Tunis, worked for Standard Oil and delivered home heating oil with a horse-drawn rig. His mother, Charlotte "Lottie" Tunis maintained the home for the family. A sister, Lois Anna Tunis, was born September 15, 1898.

Judd apparently had been in ill health as a child and quit school after the second grade. In the late summer of that year, he was given a small number of chickens to tend. Judd wandered through the neighborhood in the fall, asking for table scraps for the chickens. He then proceeded to sell the chickens to those same neighbors for Christmas dinner, several times a week,

Charlotte Tunis would dress Judd and Lois in their Sunday clothes and have them ride the train between Independence and Center Point selling popcorn and candy to the passengers. Lois's big brown eyes and long black rag curls were certain to bring a sale. When Judd was 10, the Tunis family moved from Independence to Waterloo. He became employed as a delivery boy for a local butcher shop. By the time Judd was 14, he had been working as a butcher's apprentice for two years.

Marie Eleanor Fish was the oldest of four sisters, born December 2, 1899 in Waterloo, Iowa. Her father, Will E. Fish, was employed as a carpenter building mausoleums throughout Iowa and Minnesota. He would be gone during many weeks of the year, but kept up a lively correspondence with his wife, Corda Duke Fish, and his daughters who were living in a home on West Sixth Street. The sisters, Marie, Nellie, Hazel, and Lorene were known affectionately as "The Four Fighting Fishes" as they were strong-willed women.

Judd and Marie always liked parades. When Marie was 17, Judd noticed her standing by the Fourth Street bridge with her friends and decided that she was the woman he wanted to marry. They courted , Judd's coming by with horse and buggy, and were married in December, 1917. Their only daughter, Lorene,was born in 1918.

To support the family, Judd continued working as a butcher for Wittock Meats in Waterloo. Family and money pressures arose. When Lorene was a baby, Judd strayed; he and Marie divorced. Judd moved to Pasadena, California. He worked as a butcher and continued writing letters to Waterloo and "his girls", asking that Marie and Lorene come to visit him.

Judd had saved enough money ($350) to open his own butcher shop. When Lorene was two, Marie and Lorene arrived in California, but Marie decided she didn't want to live there. Judd and Marie remarried; the three of them moved back to Waterloo into a house on Leavitt Street.

*Barbara Higgins is the granddaughter of Judd and Marie Tunis

After graduating from high school, Lois Tunis moved to Kansas City, Missouri and worked for the Jones Store Company (later Allied Brands) for 62 years. She never married but was the top salesperson for the entire company, selling clothes in the junior department. She won many trips and took her great niece and nephew to many parts of the United States and Canada. After Lois's mother died, her father moved to Kansas City.

She took care of him until he required more attention and supervision. He then returned to Waterloo to live with Marie and Judd until he died one Christmas morning. Marie's father, Will Fish, also lived with them for several years. Lorene was a teen and able to assist in his care. He was diagnosed with "hardening of the arteries" and dementia. He died on Lorene's birthday.

Judd continued to operate a series of butcher shops called J. L. Tunis Hamburger and Sausage: one on West Fourth Street where the Sullivan Brothers Convention Center is now located; another shop on West 5th Street where Baltimore intersects; and finally in the basement of their home on Falls Avenue.

All family members worked in the shop or delivered a variety of meats to individual households and businesses. Marie was a very talkative person; sometimes the deliveries to homes would last into the evening. They sold Rath Packing Company meats in their shops – cuts of beef and pork delivered in wooden crates to be cut into smaller portions.

Tunis also sold eggs, chickens, and turkeys; a large wooden barrel on the side of the counter contained dill pickles. Marie's sister, Lorene, and her daughter "Little Lorene" were three years apart in age and played together as children. For fun, they would use the sawdust in the meat market that was used to clean floors, put it on a wooden ironing board, and slide down. Other days they made ham sandwiches, took pickles from the barrel, and walked to a park for a picnic. Judd and his employees made their own pork sausage, link and bulk, and ground beef.

When MacDonald's first opened its restaurant on University, selling hamburgers for 15 cents and fries for 10 cents, they approached Judd Tunis about making their beef patties – sixteen to a pound. Any self-respecting butcher would have refused doing that to good hamburger and Judd was no exception!

After their daughter, Lorene, graduated from West High School in 1935 she started working for the The Rath Packing Company. In 1941 Judd borrowed money from Lorene to buy the 52-acre parcel of land on Falls Avenue (later University Avenue) between Waterloo and Cedar Falls.

He constructed a house, three garages with attached storage sheds, barns, a chicken coop, a corn crib, and developed a half-mile horse track to exercise his animals. There were fenced pastures near the homestead for his horses to graze.

Judd had a life-long love of horses, maintaining race horses, a Morgan driving mare, and several ponies when his grandchildren came along. The Waterloo Courier noted in an article that in 1948 Judd Tunis sponsored the first horse race that had occurred in Iowa for fifty years.

Judd, much to the chagrin of his wife and daughter, continued to sponsor horse races. In the 1950's he expanded the size of the two main barns and added a metal storage barn to be able to accommodate 72 horses on racing days. The rest of the year, the additional barn held the equipment used in maintaining the tracks.

With no parimutuel betting allowed, it was all for sport and sportsmen as the horse races were never profitable. Judd would put up the purses for the races and generally lost between $3000 and $5000 each horse-racing event. Fans would come from all over the state to watch the pacers and trotters. Judd seldom hosted races with jockeys. Although he never drove the horses in the races, he did send his horses to other Iowa communities to be trained.

Lorene Tunis and William Henry Higgins (Adding Machine Sales and Service, later aka Iowa Business Machines) were married August 14, 1941. Bill was drafted to serve in the U.S. Army during World War II. While he was in the United States, Lorene accompanied him to his stations in Neosho, Missouri and Denver, Colorado. Later Bill was sent to New Caledonia as part of the medical corp. He and Lorene corresponded but did not see each other during wartime. During the war Lorene was working for William Hinson at Hinson Manufacturing; it was he who helped determine where Bill Higgins was stationed as that information could not be conveyed in writing. When the war ended, Bill was on leave.

When Bill returned to Waterloo, he and Lorene lived in the upstairs dormer apartment of the Tunis home on Falls Avenue. A daughter, Barbara Lorene, was adopted in 1947 and a son, James William, in 1951 through Catholic Charities of Dubuque. With four people the dormer apartment was tight, so the Higgins family bought a new home on Terrace Drive in Waterloo.

It was Bill Higgins along with John Gerber of Davenport, a promoter of midget car racing in Davenport and Cedar Rapids, who suggested a switch from horses to midget car racing then to modified stock cars no older than 10 years. Judd then put a quarter-mile track inside the half-mile track later adding lights and bleachers. That track was subsequently modified to a banked three/eighths mile track. Sunday nights and holidays from mid-May through Labor Day in September, Tunis Speedway operating in partnership with the Cedarloo Racing Association, was the hub of entertainment for people in Waterloo and the surrounding communities.

T
TUNIS
SPEEDWAY
July 12, 1949
Waterloo Daily Courier
3,000 See First Cycle Races Here
A crowd of 3,000 persons saw Sunday afternoon's first motorcycle races at the new Tunis Speed bowl.
They watched Freddie Leatherby of Rockford, Ill., register the day's best time when he rode to victory in the four mile expert finals in four minutes, 20.19 seconds.
BLACK HAWK MOTORCYCLE CLUB
Official Program
10c
MIDWEST
Tunis Speed Bowl
West on Hiway 218 - Waterloo, Iowa
TUNIS SPEEDWAY
5A
121

Build a Race Track. They Will Come.

Just imagine what it would be like today if Judd Tunis, who really knew little about auto racing when he decided to build a race track, attempted to build a track that could compete in a world where everybody has 10 things to do on any Sunday evening… and then there's the weather.

Even in 1948 when Tunis Speed Bowl was first planned, Judd was taking a pretty big gamble because there were no active racers in or around Waterloo, Iowa at that time. He was dependent on what he was hearing from his son-in-law Bill Higgins, who happened to know a midget racing buddy over in the Quad Cities, and Ira "Speed" Chumley, who had raced midget cars at one time and owned a used car lot in Waterloo.

Ira "Speed" Chumley

The discussion had to be an interesting one because Judd was not one to do anything just half way. He was known for being pretty shrewd in his business dealings so Speed Chumley and Bill Higgins had plenty of work ahead to convince Judd he should build that ¼ mile track inside his already established ½ mile oval.

Midget car racing was big in the Midwest at that particular point in time. There were tracks popping up in neighboring Illinois, but none were in Iowa that catered to the midget racing faithful. These little power demons had tiny little cockpits with giant steering wheels and exposed tires. Though they didn't run nearly as fast as full sized vehicles, they still could claim some exciting speeds when you put a bunch of them on a ¼ mile circuit and the spectators were enthralled, at least for a short time.

Once the decision was made, it is reported Judd spent nearly $50,000 to actually construct the track surface, build the additional grandstands and put necessary buildings in place to handle an automotive racing event. This was very different from the sulky-style horse racing Judd was used to hosting.

Building the track required not only materials, but labor and Judd managed to find some manpower in the form of the Black Hawk Motorcycle Club.

Members of the club agreed to build the grandstands if Judd would provide the materials. The catch was Judd needed to agree to let the club host its own motorcycle racing events on the newly minted track. Judd agreed and the stands were raised.

The very first races on the ¼ mile were motorcycles in 1948. The events were not sanctioned or even formal in some cases, but the club was given the opportunity to try their racing skills and they took full advantage.

An article in the Waterloo Daily Courier in July 1949 described a sanctioned race that drew riders from other states and over 3000 spectators. Judd's track was on its way to becoming a racing destination.

Also in 1949 the midget racers showed up with the very first race on June 14 with not one driver from the Waterloo area. On August 14 of that year, however, the midget racers included Vic Ellis from Waterloo as one of the participants. No record, however, on how Vic did in the event.

Stock Car Races
As Seen Through the Camera's Lens
by Morris L. Bailey, Dike, Iowa
Vol. 1 - No. 1
Spore Wins Try-out on Muddy Track
Arnold Spore of Waterloo
Hawkeye Racing Association, Inc.
Car No. 161
Owner Al Runyan
May 18, 51
1st Event
2nd Event
3rd Event
4th Event
5th Event
6th Event
24
7up
DON
2nd heat - Hilmer, Droste
Final - Spore, Droste

The Drivers--Rough Riders of the Dirt Track

In May 1935, Popular Mechanics Magazine featured a story about the "Rough Riders of the Dirt Track" with a quote from "Wild" Bill Cummings who had just set a new speed mark at the speedway (116.901 mph) that answered a rhetorical question from a fan..."You must be all worn out!"

Cummings, who listened to the fan talk of driving 500 miles in less than 5 hours said, "On the contrary. Driving that race was comparatively easy." Cummings went on to say, "It's the short dirt tracks that really wear out the drivers!"

"Finishing races is important, but racing is more important."

--Dale Earnhardt

Obviously its the drivers who are the cowboys of the oval, shoving their mechanical steeds at the fastest speeds possible, all the while trying to avoid a crack up so they can make it to the finish line before anyone else.

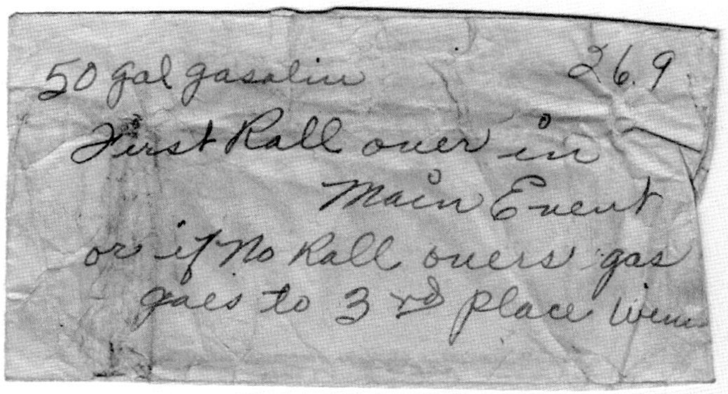
50 gal gasolin
26.9
First Roll over in
Main Event
or if No Roll overs gas
goes to 3rd place Win

Payout Envelope

Without the drivers, there was no race. Who wants to see a bunch of machines just twirling around when drivers will make the entire performance so much more interesting!

This chapter of the Tunis Speedway chronicle should include stories from every driver who ever came through the gates. But that would be impossible.

Judd Tunis knew how important the drivers were and treated them with respect. He was concerned about their safety, wanted to help them when he could and even tossed in some dollars once in awhile when he saw drivers who were working hard, but not getting into the winning ranks.

Tunis Speedway, much like the hundreds of dirt tracks that dotted the American landscape, attracted all sorts of drivers. Some were short lived, making the effort to bring a car out onto the track only to find that it was a bit more complex (and maybe frightening) then they expected.

Other drivers managed to not only survive that very first attempt, but flourished in some cases, making the rounds on the Tunis track a proving ground for their eventual foray into races at other facilities across the Midwest.

Nearly every driver contacted said the same thing when describing their first introduction to auto racing. They attended a race, watched the cars tearing around the track and thought, "I can do that!" And for some a driving career was born. Following are just a few of their stories.

Remembering Red Droste

By Kyle Ealy

In the 1980's pro wrestler Rick Flair used a famous catchphrase; "To be the Man, you gotta beat the Man!"

77
UNITED
AUTO-MATIC
TRANSMISSION
EXCHANGE

It could have very well been the catchphrase that LaVern "Red" Droste used throughout the 1960's. Starting in the early 50's and ending somewhere around the mid 1970's, Droste was by far the most dominant stock car driver in Eastern Iowa and probably the Midwest.

You either loved him or hated him, but you always respected his driving ability and innovation that consistently put him in the winner's circle.

Simply put; Red Droste was the man in Eastern Iowa racing circles and he dared anyone to beat him. Hundreds of drivers tried and hundreds of drivers failed.

It has been said many times that when Droste pulled into the pit area at a Eastern Iowa track on any given night, the rest of the field knew they were running for second place. He was that great of a driver.

Hawkeye Racing News' Keith Knaack was once quoted as saying, "I really do believe Droste wins 50 percent of his races by mental power over other drivers when he drives through those pit gates. He's that good…"

Red Droste was born and raised in Waterloo, Iowa. Like a lot of kids, Droste attended school but after his parents split up, he was forced to quit school

after his parents split up, he was forced to quit school after the eighth grade to help the household.

To earn money, he ran the dairy farm of a neighbor and was the man of the house from the time he was age 14.

Married at age 17, Droste and his wife, Eleanor "June" lived in Tripoli, Iowa but drove every day to Waterloo for their jobs.

In 1947, Droste started Red's Auto Service in Waterloo, eventually moving to town. Barely subsiding on their incomes, the couple lived in a small trailer with no running water while working on cars, something for which Red showed a natural ability.

The shop grew and he added more stalls to accommodate his business. Race car drivers from near and far began coming to Droste to have him work on their engines.

RED'S

"It was the city's first real speed shop," recalled Rich, the oldest of the Droste children.

Droste began building engines for race cars and then moved on to building whole cars. It's because of working on race cars that Droste himself decided to take up racing, competing in cars he built himself.

Droste started his legendary career around 1951 or 1952, racing at his hometown track of Tunis Speedway.

He would have immediate success…

Droste started his legendary career around 1951 or 1952, racing at his hometown track of Tunis Speedway. Even starting out at a young age, Droste established himself fairly quickly and because of his aggressive nature on the track, immediately became the villainous driver that he would portray for the next 20 plus years.

In 1953, promoter Judd Tunis quickly capitalized on his new star driver's appeal by staging a special grudge match between Droste and one of the more popular fan favorites at Tunis, Arnold Spore.

It was a true novelty act, with both men driving ancient, but drivable cars. Spore won when Droste's car left the track with a broken wheel. His car rolled coming out of the second turn and landed on its top.

Droste scrambled out, made a quick trip to the ambulance for first aid, then jumped in his regular car and went on to win the feature that night.

A star was born…

Back then, if you wanted to be up front and make money at the end of the night, sometimes you had to be a little "assertive" on the track. That, as it would turn out, would never be a problem for Droste for unseen years to come.

Later that same season, Red's overaggressive style sent another fan favorite, this time Chub Liebe of Oelwein, Iowa tumbling off the track at Tunis. It so incensed area race fans, letters to area newspapers were being written right and left, complaining about the "dirty tactics" that were being employed by the young hot shoe.

SUNDAY NIGHT, MAY 31st
STOCK CAR RACES
ADDED ATTRACTION - - - GRUDGE RACE
ARNOLD SPORE vs. RED DROSTE
TIME TRIALS 7:00 P. M. — RACES 8:00 P. M.
FREE PARKING
Adm.: Adults $1.00, incl. tax
Kids 10 to 12, 50c. Children under 10 FREE when accompanied by parents!
TUNIS SPEEDWAY
ON HIGHWAY 218 BETWEEN WATERLOO AND CEDAR FALLS

This advertisement found in the May 27, 1953 edition of the Waterloo Courier, promoted the grudge match between the "villain" Red Droste and the "hero" Arnold Spore.

One upset race fan wrote a letter to the Oelwein Daily Register; "Red Droste will never qualify for public relations chairman at the Tunis Speedway. The stock car racer has a few dirty tricks that even in fighting would be called "below the belt."

"It was his shenanigan that threw Chub Liebe of Oelwein off the track on Labor Day night. We saw the whole thing develop and there was no question. Probably he resents the impertinence of anyone outside Waterloo using his track."

Years later, Droste himself admitted he didn't fool around on the race track. "Things were different in those days," he said. "And we ran a little bit rough."

Droste would prove to be as tough as he was rough. September 19, 1954 was the season championships at Tunis Speedway. The program was highlighted by a special 100-lap feature. It would be one of those rare hot, steamy days for September.

Those hot temperatures took their toll on man and machine that day and with 20 laps left, it came down to Droste and Gene Petersen of Waterloo. They battled back and forth for the remaining circuits but on the final lap it was Droste who came in for the checkered flag. He pointed his car for the infield, pulled up to victory lane, got out of his car and then blacked out for about 10 minutes, the time it took to revive him.

Once on his feet, Red was sipping a cold one and smoking a cigarette as he accepted the championship trophy.

Red Droste started his racing career in in early 1950's piloting this car, competing in the Hawkeye Racing Association at Tunis Speedway.

Even when he didn't have a properly working race car, Droste would find a way to muster up a victory. In a 1957 race at Tunis, Red had issues with shifting during his heat race. Upon further inspection, he discovered that the transmission had thrown second gear. Not a problem...

Droste, racing in low gear for the entire feature, came from dead last, sped past point leader Bob Hilmer of Dysart, Iowa and Bill Zwanzinger of Waterloo to win that evening.

It wasn't just stock cars that Ol' Redhead excelled in either. Red proved that if it had four tires and a steering wheel, he could win in just about anything.

245

In 1958, Droste got behind the wheel of a midget and soundly beat the 1957 California State Midget Champion, Barney Flynn of Carlsbad, Calif., at Tunis Speedway. Droste, driving a midget he built himself, also took the time trials, the trophy dash and the first heat.

With more winning, came more hatred from the fans. But instead of being bitter, Droste took a lot of humor in the fact he was so despised. At one point, in the mid 1960's, Red printed up a 1,000 t-shirts that said, I Hate Red Droste" on the back, and made sure they found their way into the people's hands.

WIEHE

One night after a race at Hawkeye Downs, he made an infrequent trip to the beer pavilion. There, seated at a table next to his, was a group of people wearing their "I hate Red Droste" t-shirts.

One woman, in particular was talking in a very loud voice and using foul language in discussing "that damn Red Droste". Droste sat and quietly listened for a while and then ordered a round of beers for the table.

He then went over and asked the woman, "Lady, this Droste guy you keep talking about – who is he?" After about two words, the woman recognized who she was face to face with. Droste simply pulled up a chair, bought a round of beers, talked it all out and the group, Droste said, walked out as his newest fans.

245

"It's easy to hate somebody when you don't know them," he summed up later. Apparently Red Droste was also a prophet.

Despite his rough and tumble reputation, Droste did have his stable of fans. In 1967, Droste, in a dispute with then promoter Homer Melton at Hawkeye Downs, decided to boycott the track that season.

There were hundreds and hundreds of pleas from race fans, including numerous letters to the Cedar Rapids Gazette, pleading for him to return.

Even Gazette sportswriter Gus Schrader mentioned in one of his columns how missed Droste was; "Someone mentioned the words Red Droste. This was as popular as serving gefulte fish at an Arab unity dinner.

Droste has been kindling a few fires under Homer and the fair board — all from the relative security of Waterloo, of course. Red isn't racing in Homer's Saturday night events at Hawkeye Downs this year.

He's dissatisfied with the financial terms. Everybody misses him — the 50 percent who come to cheer his exciting brand of driving and the 50 percent who come to see him crowded off a curve, or at least be defeated by the Good Guys in the White Hats."

The mere mention of the name Red Droste could spark a lively debate over whether he was unfairly deemed a villain. But no matter which side of the fence one came down regarding Droste, one thing that couldn't be argued, and that was Droste's impressive statistics.

During a span of 11 years, from 1960 to 1970, while racing at Cedar Rapids, Dubuque and Independence, Red Droste won 29 out of a possible 33 track championships. In 1970, racing at Darlington, Wis., he won every single feature race that season.

In addition to those three tracks, Droste would also "step out" once in awhile and terrorize the competition at Davenport, Farley, Independence, Mason City, Monticello, and Tipton. If there were features to be won and money to collect, you could count on the 'Ol Redhead to show up.

Phil Roberts, a long-time motorsports journalist and track announcer here in Eastern Iowa, remembered Droste well; "I began watching races from the bleachers at Davenport Speedway when I was in my early to mid teens. Then, in 1965 at age 16, I began helping out on the pit crew of a Novice Division car at the track."

RED'S AUTO SERVICE
UNITED AUTO-MATIC
TRANSMISSION EXCHANGE

"During those years, Red Droste competed now and then in Davenport Speedway's late model division, and I saw him turn many laps. He was one of the finest drivers I've ever seen and, though I didn't know him, he also appeared to be a nice guy."

"Red wasn't a regular competitor at Davenport, but you knew when he showed up there was going to be a heck of a feature race. Red Droste is one of those special people who has made racing from that era so memorable."

As fine as a driver Droste was, he was also an innovator in stock car racing. Red built the cars he raced and even built cars for his fellow competitors. "One year at Tunis, there were only seven cars NOT using my engines," Droste was quoted as saying.

Red wasn't too proud to scrounge ideas from other people either, especially if it meant more victories under his belt and more money in his pocket. An idea he borrowed from

Texas sports car driver, Jimmy Hall, was incorporated in Droste's 1957 Chevrolet right before the 1966 season.

"We're going to use an automatic transmission in this car," he was quoted in the April 3, 1966 edition of the Cedar Rapids Gazette. "It will do several things for me; eliminate much of the weight of a standard gearbox, free myself from having to shift during a race, and make it easier to stop in case of an accident."

According to Droste, it marked the first time that an automatic transmission was used in a late model or modified stock car in the area. Droste also took a page out of a local racer's handbook by mounting the steering wheel towards the center of the car.

"It's very similar to the little Chevrolet coupe that Charlie Moffitt of Stanwood drove several years ago," Droste said. Droste also lowered the entire chassis, "so it would handle better."

When asked why he had made all of the revolutionary changes on his already fast Chevy, his answer was straight to the point.

"I had a bad season last year. I only finished second." For Droste, though, experimenting with new and innovative creations was often short-lived. "I tried a lot of things over the years but usually they were banned for the next," he said with a laugh.

Darrell Dake, one of Droste's chief rivals in the 60's, was once quoted saying, "Droste would try almost any gimmick he thought might give him a small edge in the competition. Red always told everyone that he had his steering column moved towards the middle so his car would balance better. I told Red I thought the real reason he moved his wheel over was for safety features. He always got his cars so light that he wanted to get as far away as possible from that plastic left door on it."

As much as Droste understood that horsepower was an important thing in racing, it wasn't what he spent most of his time with. His attention to driving details was the reason for most of his success.

"My whole deal was always trying to figure out how to get around the track quicker than the next guy," he once said. "How to get through corners quicker and how to "finesse" the car to turn laps a little quicker was what I thought about most."

The career of Red Droste started in the 1950's, peaked in the 1960's and lasted until the mid-70's, competing on a number of different tracks in the Midwest. As his career started to wind down, Droste would always state that he raced more for the money than titles. "Winning a championship used to mean a lot to me, but I really don't have a lot to prove any more," he was quoted as saying in a 1973 Cedar Rapid Gazette column.

After Droste's remarks, Al Miller, the racing editor for the Gazette summed it up best about Red, saying, "That's hard for most of us to believe, especially because of the reason given. Naturally, Red races to make money, but anyone who knows Red Droste well knows he has a tremendous desire to excel, even after 20 plus years of racing. And, we suspect, until the day he's through with racing, he will attempt to maintain his No. 1 status."

You'll always be #1 with us, Red.

Thanks for the memories…

The Petersens

Harry Petersen, Junior to friends and family, won the very first track championship in 1952. Brother Eugene followed that up in 1961 with a track championship of his own.

13

Harry Petersen after winning that first Tunis track championship in 1952. His wife still has the trophy (below)

PETERSEN TUNIS KING

Waterloo's Gene Petersen sped to a 30-lap feature race victory at Tunis Speedway here Sunday night before 6,252 Fa-

events at Tunis.

Petersen, who also copped the "B" semi-main race, was one of two double winners Sunday. Tuffy Myers of Big Rock gar-

Zwanziger placed second and Moffett third.

First Heat (15 laps)—1. Tuffy Myer, Big Rock; 2. Chuck Smith, Onalaska, Wis.; 3. Wayne Young, Dubuque; 5:06.

Second Heat (15 laps)—1. Bob Posek-

Gene

Harry Peterson Wins Main at Tunis After 2 Seconds

H. Petersen Wins as 3,140 See Stocks Race

Harry (Junior)

TUNIS
SPEEDWAY
WATERLOO

100
99
113

The checkerboard top was the coat of arms for the Petersen brothers and they competed as one of several brother combinations during the Tunis years. #100 Babe Marquand (half brother), # 99 Gene Petersen and #113 Junior Petersen (Harry).

99 Dixie Cream

113

Gene and Babe doing some last minute tuning.

Gene Petersen's original helmet and goggles.

Zwanziger: The Driver's Driver

Bill Zwanziger had an incredible smile. He could probably charm just about anybody, but his smile was for real and he wasn't afraid to provide a grin at any moment.

Something else Zwanziger could do. He could drive. When he was out front, it was a major chore just to keep up. The car would do just what he wanted it to do. And if he had a good car, watch out. The night was about to be his.

2

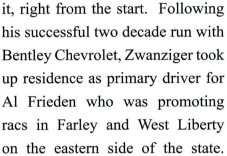

Bill Zwanziger, like many other local drivers, started his career at Tunis Speedway at the tender age of 17. He admitted he wasn't much for the wrenching and tuning. He just wanted to drive.

And for 20 years he was the primary driver for Bentley Chevrolet in Fairbank, Iowa. Zwanziger said the decision to drive was pretty easy. "I had a friend who was building a car to run on this new track in town (Tunis Speedway) and he wanted to know if I would drive it, " he explained.

Of course Zwanziger said yes and a nearly 50 year racing career was begun. He estimated he won more than 100 features during his career, though some figure he won way more than that.

"We raced mostly '39 and '40 coupes early on," he said. "Big heavy cars you had to wrestle around the track."

Later Zwanziger got into some pretty quick Chevys, courtesy of his Bentley Chevrolet sponsorship and his number 35 became a regular at the winner's podum.

Zwanziger remembered having 35-40 cars each night and racing side by side with the likes of Red Droste, Bob Hilmer, Verlin Eaker and Darrell Dake.

"Those were great times."

All of these drivers became part of the racing lore that was northeast Iowa racing. Zwanziger was right in the thick of it, right from the start. Following his successful two decade run with Bentley Chevrolet, Zwanziger took up residence as primary driver for Al Frieden who was promoting racs in Farley and West Liberty on the eastern side of the state.

This was the 1970s when Zwanziger and Frieden managed to cover quite a bit of ground in the state, hitting tracks like Hawkeye Downs in Cedar Rapids on Friday night, then heading to Eldon Speedway on Saturday with a trip over to Freeport, Illinois to round out the weekend on Sunday.

"That's where the money was, so that's where we went," said Zwanziger while reminiscing about those years of nearly full time racing.

He always worked regular jobs except for a three year span in the late 60s when he raced five days a week.

The Frieden partnership was a good one, however, and led the pair to think seriously about taking on bigger and better opportunities and several times they showed up at tracks as far away as Florida and Canada.

Toward the middle of the 1980s, Frieden wanted to get into promoting and Zwanziger thought it might be a good time to get out of the driving as well.

But he never really quit and continued to drive well into the late 1980s after Tunis Speedway had stopped being a weekly racing venue. And while Frieden headed for the promotion side of racing, Zwanziger remembered his own foray into the promotions, partnering for two years with Waterloo car dealer Jim Cordes to promote the Tunis events in 1963 and 1964.

CORDES FORD

"Didn't really like that too much," he said when asked how that experience was, particularly for a driver who was still active on the local circuits.

"You just couldn't make enough money with all the headaches," he said. "In those years it seemed like there was so much racing that revolved around tempers, so I had to be pretty careful when I stepped into a car for a Tunis event."

Always the diplomat, Zwanziger said he many times would start at the back of the pack, no matter what number he drew. "Then, if I won, I won. No questions asked."

As the 1980s came to a close Kathy Root, who owned International Motor Contest Association located in Vinton, Iowa, called Zwanziger to see if he might consider becoming the group's competition director.

He took up the challenge and was back into racing full time, but was now helping to direct events and laying the groundwork for growth that IMCA later experienced under Keith Knaack.

"Keith did some great work with IMCA and I definitely enjoyed my time with the assocation," he said. "of course, the racing was what really made me happy and I tried my hand at a lot of it over the years."

Though Zwanziger probably left his biggest mark in the stock car ranks in the midwest, he raced a srprint car at Knoxville for two years in the 1960s (owned by Cordes Ford in Waterloo) but found it was getting in the way of his stock car racing.

"You could only run once a week (at Eldora) and it was keeping me from running the late model where I could win a lot more races."

He also tried midget cars for a time, racing in Davenport and at Blue Grass Speedway in Illinois. He also traveled down to Florida to race the midgets and spent some time there with the Frieden team in the late models.

Biggest disappointment? "Easily the World 100 held at Eldora Speedway in Ohio (1972)," he said. "I was there with teammate Verlin Eaker (both racing for Frieden at that time) and led the race for 90 laps."

Zwanziger actually had lapped the entire field when his steering broke and he was out of the race. "Verlin went on to win, which was great," he described. "But, boy, I was unhappy with that one."

Sadly Bill Zwanziger passed away November 18, 2013. We're all going to miss that smile.

35 BENTLEY'S
NEW & USED
CARS
RILEY BROS.
THAT'S OIL

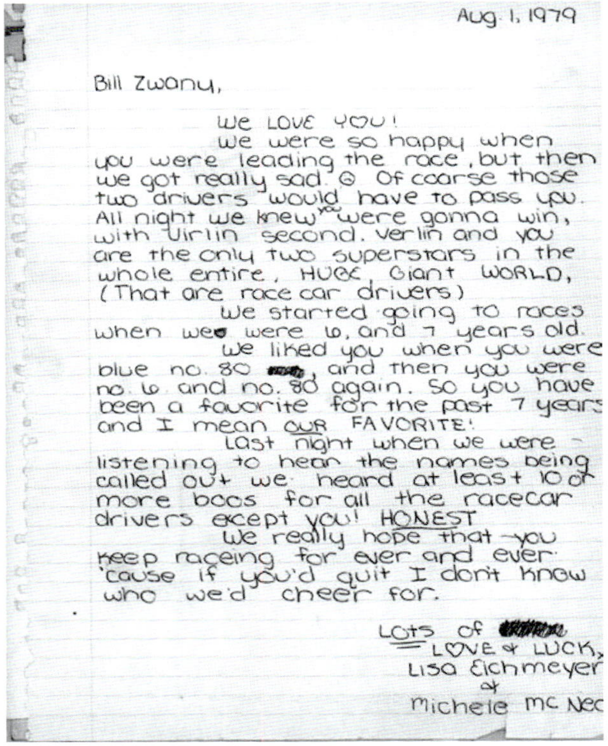

Aug. 1, 1979

Bill Zwany,

We LOVE YOU!

We were so happy when you were leading the race, but then we got really sad ☹ Of coarse those two drivers would have to pass you. All night we knew you were gonna win, with Virlin second. Verlin and you are the only two superstars in the whole entire, HUGE Giant WORLD, (That are race car drivers)

We started going to races when we were 6, and 7 years old. We liked you when you were blue no. 80, and then you were no. 6 and no. 80 again. So you have been a favorite for the past 7 years and I mean OUR FAVORITE!

Last night when we were listening to hear the names being called out we heard at least 10 or more boos for all the racecar drivers except you! HONEST

We really hope that you keep raceing for ever and ever 'cause if you'd quit I don't know who we'd cheer for.

Lots of LOVE & LUCK,
Lisa Eichmeyer
&
Michele Mc Nee

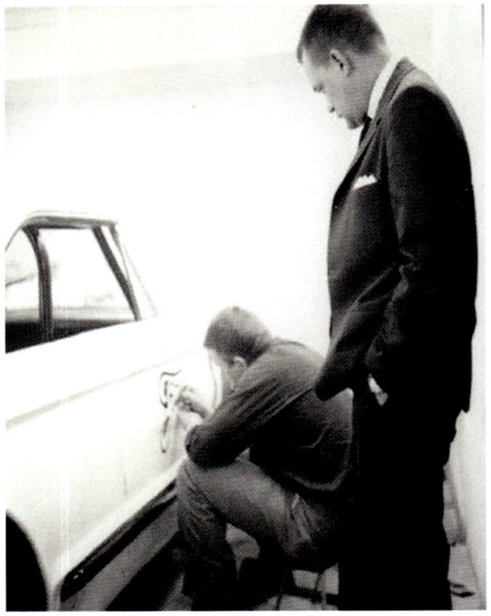

CHEVROLET
35

CHEVROLET
V8
35

35

BUD & LEE'S
64

USED CAR OFFICE
1
JIM
CORDES
Ford

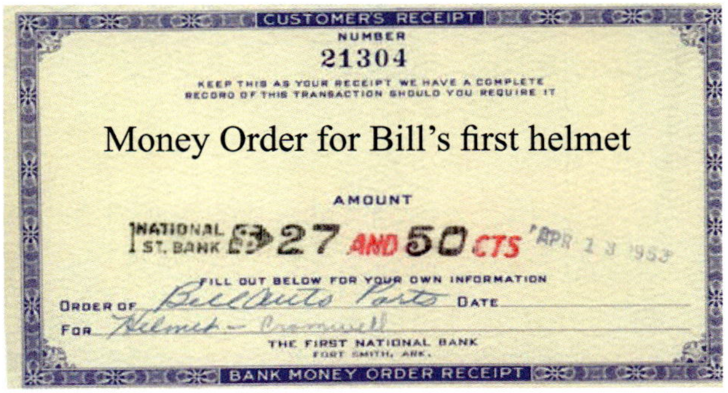

CUSTOMERS RECEIPT

NUMBER
21304

KEEP THIS AS YOUR RECEIPT WE HAVE A COMPLETE RECORD OF THIS TRANSACTION SHOULD YOU REQUIRE IT

Money Order for Bill's first helmet

AMOUNT

NATIONAL ST. BANK $27 AND 50 CTS APR 13 1953

FILL OUT BELOW FOR YOUR OWN INFORMATION

ORDER OF Bell Auto Parts DATE

FOR Helmet – Cromwell

THE FIRST NATIONAL BANK
FORT SMITH, ARK.

BANK MONEY ORDER RECEIPT

Carroll Jensen

HOOK'S RADIATOR
11

Carrol Jensen Wins Stock Car Race as Bob Hilmer Has Engine Trouble

Carrol Jensen was the big winner in Thursday's Memorial Day stock car races at Tunis Speedway. He won the feature and second heat and placed second in the first semi main.

Engine trouble kept last Sunday's winner, Bob Hilmer, from placing. Al Runyon won the first heat and class A semi main.

Red Droste was limited to a first in the class C semi main and a second in the second heat, after developing steering trouble in his back-seat driven car.

Several cars failed to place when they bogged down in the wet infield and an even greater number lost out on the turns when they slipped over the top and into the mud outside the track.

A crowd of 1,710 also saw Walt Lang win the junior novice race.

The next races at Tunis' are set for Sunday at 7:30 p. m.

FIRST HEAT (10 laps)—
1. Al Runyan, 121; 2. Chuck Halligan, 7-0; 3. Dale Hickman, 61; 4:25.

SECOND HEAT (10 laps)—
1. Carroll Jensen, 11; 2. Red Droste, 77; 3. Gene Peterson, 99; 4:06.

THIRD HEAT (10 laps)—
1. Vic Payton, 63; 2. Arnold Spore, 555; 3. Bob Ledje, 66; 3:85.

CLASS A SEMI (15 laps)—
1. Al Runyan, 121; 2. Carrol Jensen, 11; 3. Chuck Halligan, 7-0; 4. Gene Welch, 62; 5. Elmer Bradley, 51; 6. Ron Hutchens, 5-D; 6:10.

CLASS B SEMI (15 laps)—
1. Arnold Spore, 555; 2. Jack Hickman, 64; 3. Bill Zwanziger, 35; 4. Carrol Hilmer, 18; 5. Bob Ledje, 66; 6. Dick Kronick, 111; 5:50.

CLASS C SEMI (8 laps)—
1. Red Droste, 77; 2. John Mullink, 27; 3. Vern Weber, 10; 2:84.

FEATURE (15 laps)—
1. Carrol Jensen, 11; 2. Carrol Hilmer, 18; 3. Bill Zwanziger, 35; 4. Dick Kronick, 111; 5. Chuck Halligan, 7-0; 6. Gene Welch, 62; 7:05.

NOVICE—1. Walt Lang, 46; 2. Ernie Sommerfelt, 44; 3. Irv Venier, 71; 4. Jerry Clark, 18; 5. Jerry Lang, 40; 6. Don Heldeman, 56.

18

Jensen Wins Micro Feature

Carroll Jensen won his second straight micro-midget race feature here yesterday afternoon at Airline Speedway.

Dick Hinton crashed into the east fence on the first lap of the main event Hinton, who had changed a broken axle earlier in the day, hurtled the car of Junior Stephens. After a restart Stephens and Jim Hook collided on the second lap.

Hinton won the time trials.

Jensen also won the second heat and one of the semi-mains.

Bill Zwanziger finished second in the feature.

As an added feature, motorcycle races were included on the card. Jim Flockhart won the feature after cracking up and being thrown 20 feet in an earlier race.

The attendance was 550.

Tropny dash—1. Jim Hook, 2. Carroll Jensen, 3. Dick Hinton.

First heat—1. Junior Stephens, 2. Kenny Rugg, 3. Jim Porter.

Second heat—1. Carrol Jensen, 2. Bill Zwanziger, 3. Don Schmidt.

A semi—1. Junior Stephens, 2. Bill Zwanziger, 3. Les Toothman.

B semi—1. Carrol Jensen, 2. Dick Hinton, 3. Don Schmidt.

Feature—1. Carrol Jensen, 2. Bill Zwanziger, 3. Don Schmidt.

CYCLE RACES.

First heat—1. Bill Lynch, 2. Jim Smith.

Second heat—1. Tom Moe, 2. Jim Flockhart.

Main — 1. Jim Flockhart, 2. Jim Smith, 3. Bill Lynch, 4. Tom Moe.

Carroll Jensen...yes, it's spelled with two "L"s...was another of the very early racers who spent nearly 30 years in and around the racing community. He was also active and very successful racing micro midgets.

20

11
RAMBLERS

Charlie Moffit

32
RED'S AUTO SERV

Charlie Moffit may have been best known for the little screaming 6-cylinder GMC engine he ran in his '32 Ford coupe. You have to believe Charlie loved playing havoc on all the V-8s the other racers were using. And yes, his name was always misspelled.

Moffett Nips Zwanziger in 50-Lapper Before Over 7,000

By ROGER MATZ
Courier Staff Writer

Charlie Moffett replaced Bill Zwanziger as the Tunis Speedway mid-season champion here Sunday night and broke Zwanziger's time record in the process.

Moffett, from Stanwood, raced to a record 15.70 with Zwanziger, last year's mid-season and season champ, rubbing bumpers with him all the way. Zwanziger's time last year was 15.75.

Track owner Jud Tunis said the paid attendance was 5,164, in addition to some 2,000 children admitted free.

ONE OF THE men who was considered among the favored contenders wasn't in the line-up. Gene Petersen, who has won several features this year, broke a connecting rod behind.

After traffic thinned out, Moffett stretched his lead to about a car length for a few laps, until Zwanziger, one of the top Waterloo drivers competing at Tunis, again closed in within inches.

One mistake on Moffett's part would have put Zwanziger into the lead and a similar mistake on Zwanziger's part would have put Moffett out of reach for certain.

NEITHER DRIVER overstepped a corner. They seemed to be attached to each other by an invisible cable.

On at least two occasions, Zwanziger was able to pull up alongside, but Moffett always slid ahead again.

Other top finishers in the race were Jim Hoerman of ...

... in the first 10-lap event, John Mullink, of Iowa City, in the second, and Moffett in the third.

Bob Posekany of Cedar Falls was knocked unc... scious and suffered an ear ... jury when the car he w... driving rolled seven times ... the third heat.

Posekany was leading ... race when Moffett, in seco... tried to go by on the ins... of a seventh lap-turn. T... two cars bumped slightly a... Posekany began his roll alo... the turn.

MOFFET, who said, "I h... my brakes on and was slidi... all the way" at the time ... the accident, went inside ... wrecked car to retrieve Po...kany after track attenda... had difficulty freeing the ... jured driver because ... jammed doors.

... borrowed a novice car for the midseason race but had a flat tire.

Willie Kleinfurs, of Waverly, won the novice race and ...

Moffett Leads Tunis Speedsters

Charlie Moffett of Stanwood will be out for his third straight feature win as the stock cars roll again tonight at 7:30 on the Tunis Speedway oval.

His two wins boosted him into the point total lead among Cedarloo Racing Assn. drivers at Tunis and he will have challenges from second-place Red Droste and third-place Bill ...

CHARLIE MOFFETT

. . . seeks third straight

Moffett Cops Tunis Feature

Charlie Moffett of Stanwood raced to his second feature victory in four days at Tunis Speedway here Sunday night. He also won the main event Memorial Day.

Moffett's victory came before 4,758 stock car fans. Tha... brought the total attendance fo... three racing dates in the pas... eight days to 15,200.

Red Droste of Waterlo... placed second to Moffett in th...

7
HOOK'S
WATERLOO, IA.

Moffett Gets Trophy

Moffett Extends Stock Car Streak to Four

By ROGER MATZ
Courier Sports Writer

MOFFETT COPS MID-SEASON CORDES TITLE

New 10-Lap Mark; Moffitt Wins Feature

John Moss Ends Moffett's String

3,544 See Broken Axle End Moffett's Bid

Rapid Robert Indeed

Bob Hilmer appears to be one of those people who simply can't slow down. It is part of his DNA. He pushes forward at the fastest speed possible and makes no bones about wanting to get to a destination first. And in racing circles, Hilmer made sure all the other drivers knew he was there, particularly if he was behind them.

Hilmer remembers 1949 as the year that put him in the driver's seat. He describes, as many of the former Tunis drivers described, going to watch the races and thinking that would be something he wanted to do. From that point on, Rapid Robert started making his mark on the racing community, going faster than anyone else and winning so many times he simply lost count over the course of his career.

"At one point I think I had 57 wins in a row," Hilmer said. "Now those weren't all features, but heat races as well. If I raced, I was winning." Hilmer started getting so successful he even talked his younger brother Carroll into joining the ranks and the two brothers many times competed against each other on the track.

"My first car was a '37 Ford sedan, much like what a lot of other drivers were using," he explained. "But the big break came when I started driving a '50 Olds for Lyle Shriver in Waterloo." Hilmer was working at the Shriver Oldsmobile dealership and was helped by fellow mechanics Leo and Roger Beck. "Somehow Lyle (Shriver) managed to get a 3-carb setup for the new J1 engine that Olds had just introduced and that was one fast car!"

Oldsmobile had just introduced their new V-8 engines and began giving the flathead racers fits. In stock form the Olds V-8s were producing 135 horsepower, compared to only 100 horsepower for the tried and true flatties. "We raced that car for quite awhile," Hilmer said. "We even towed it to Minot (South Dakota) and Louisiana to race."

Hilmer recalls being the first Iowa driver to race against Floridians Cotton Hodges and Jim Millard who were traveling up to Iowa to race. "With three tracks running weekly (Independence, Tunis and Cedar Rapids), this was a great place to race. We probably had some of the best racing on that three track circuit of anywhere in the country."

Shriver Oldsmobile kept the wheels rolling on Hilmer's race cars and in 1955, driving a new 1955 Rocket 88 Olds, Hilmer became the first driver in the world to break the 30 second mark for stock cars running on a half mile flat dirt track.

35
SHRIVER CADILLAC-OLDS CO

The record breaking time was set in Sioux Falls, South Dakota and Hilmer wheeled the powerful Olds around the track in 29:70 seconds. "I even started in last position in that race," Hilmer recalled and drove 15 laps in only 7 minutes and 30 seconds.

Rapid Robert was on a roll.

By 1965 Hilmer had moved to Chevrolets when brother Carroll, who was service manager for Van Wechel Chevrolet in Grundy Center, Iowa, managed to get one of the very first 396 cubic inch engines Chevrolet introduced that year.

“If I remember right my brother (Carroll) contacted Kunzman Chevrolet in Guttenberg because he had heard about this new engine and that Kunzman had been able to get one.

22

” The dealership was owned by the father of Lee Kunzman who also was a racer and eventually went on to race in IMCA, USAC and CART series, becoming general manager of the former Hemelgarn Racing Team which won the Indy 500 in 1996.

OFFICIAL RECORD CERTIFICATE
OF THE
INTERNATIONAL MOTOR CONTEST ASSOCIATION

Chicago, Ill., December 1 1955

This Is to Certify That
Bob Hilmer - Dysart - Iowa
is holder of the following IMCA OFFICIAL RECORD for
Stock Cars - One-Half Mile Flat Dirt Track

Distance 1/2 Mile Time :29.38
Oldsmobile Date September 5, 1955
West Missouri State Fair - Bethany, Missouri

INTERNATIONAL MOTOR CONTEST ASSOCIATION
Frank Harris
Secretary

“When we started running the big block Chevys, we could run most anywhere and we traveled all over the Midwest,” Hilmer said. “Those were great racing years.”

Bob Hilmer spent 30 years racing, finally retiring in 1979, the same year Tunis Speedway stopped its weekly racing events. “I learned a lot on the Tunis track which was one of the tougher tracks in the area,” Hilmer said.

RAPID ROBERT

Throughout the process of gathering the information from former Tunis drivers for this chronicles, those contacted would be asked who was the toughest competition? Invariably the answer would be Bob Hilmer…Rapid Robert. He always ran as fast as he could and he hated being in the back of the field.

RAPID ROBERT
35
SHRIVER CADILLAC-OLDS CO.
WATERLOO IA.

Rapid Robert made the Tunis era of racing the best.

The Saga of Fast Eddie

Ed Sanger never imagined he would build a career out of stock car racing.

"I was working at Feldman-Evans Pontiac in Waterloo as a mechanic in 1964 and started helping out one of the sales guys, Dick Hagen, with a race car," he describes. "Morris Feldman had agreed to sponsor a car for Hagen and he ran, I think, two races when he decided that this kind of racing wasn't for him."

"Morris Feldman came to me and asked if I had any interest in buying the race car. When I told him I didn't have any money to do that, he said 'just go down to Waterloo Savings Bank and ask them for a loan.' So I did just that."

Sanger says he found out later that Feldman had co-signed the loan. "But I think he just wanted to get rid of owning a race car!" Feldman proved to be good for Sanger, however, and continued to provide space where he could wrench on the car during the following season.

BEN

"I started out the 1965 season racing in the third heat against some of the toughest drivers around…Droste, Hilmer, Swanson. It was just a 10-lap race but those guys lapped me at least a couple of times each, which gives you an idea how fast I was," he laughed. That lack of speed didn't last long.

For the next 40 years Sanger would not only race, but he became known as the guy to go to if you wanted a race car that could win races.

Winning over 500 features himself during that 40 year career was impressive enough, but his building may have been his crowning achievement in a sport that can swallow drivers and owners up in pretty quick fashion.

"I was fortunate to have a bit of common sense in 1980", he describes. "I started salting away my winnings and made better use of what I had to race, which taught me how a race car could be built to endure an entire season."

Sanger built cars started to show up at regional tracks, notably under the driving expertise of Curt Hansen who managed to win 33 features the very first year he raced a Sanger built racer.

"I looked at cars over the years and thought I could do a better job of making them a bit more durable and dependable," he said.

"I came up with the idea of creating crash zones (later called crush zones) so if a driver got into a tangle, the entire car wasn't destroyed and could be repaired in just the area where damage might occur."

"In 1976 I managed to win 46 total features during the season, which at the time was unheard of, but I was learning how to make the cars last." Sanger took to racing full time in 1970, showing up at tracks all over the Midwest. "I was racing a Monte Carlo at that time and won over $100,000 during '70 and '71."

The Stable--Ed Sanger, Stan Stover, Larry Wasserfort, Doc Mayner, Red Dralle, Gary Crawford

With expenses topping out about $6000 per year, Sanger knew he was on to something and in 1973 he built a Chevelle for himself along with six more cars, all driven by other drivers with their own crews. The Sanger dynasty began in earnest.

BENTLEY CHEVROLET
94

"I think I really raced at my best in those years," he remembers. The race seasons were long and arduous, but Sanger kept at it until the 1980s when he started dealing in Howe chassis, building cars for the likes of NASCAR Sprint Cup Series star Bobby Allison.

"Bobby made some special appearances in Cedar Rapids in '83 and '84 and I even built a car for his son, Davey for the '84 season."

In 1985 Sanger got the chance of a lifetime, going to work for Helen Rae Smith of Ames, Iowa who put together a NASCAR Sprint Cup Series team with Sanger as the crew chief.

"We had three drivers (Phil Barkdoll, Sterling Marlin and Morgan Shepherd), but I got a chance to drive in a race at North Wilkesboro Speedway in North Carolina."

Sanger said the driving was meant to educate him a bit about how the cars worked on the track and says he learned plenty from that race. "Qualified at 29 for the race and finished 26th, still running the car to the end," he said. "I learned plenty and we spent a lot of time after that experience re-working the cars so they could be more competitive."

Sanger eventually moved to the team's engine department and he continued with them until 1990. "But I had to get back to Iowa," he explained. "My farming operation was growing and needed my full time attention." Sanger dropped from the circuits for a couple of years, returned part-time in 1992 and raced in over 60 races by 1997.

In 2005 he suffered a serious accident that slowed him down, but he's kept his nose in the business ever since, now more as a spectator than anything else.

"Those early days at Tunis Speedway really helped me to gain the racing understanding I needed to really be successful." Sanger said the Tunis track was a "must stop" for those wanting to move onto a bigger stage of competition. "We had some of the very best drivers in the country racing at Tunis Speedway," he said.

"When I think about Red Droste, for instance, I think about how he was simply one of the very best there was. He was as good as anyone, anywhere. And I got to race with him and so many others who taught me what racing was all about.

Inspired to Race

Like many racers, Curt Hansen's Dad inspired him to race. "He loved racing," Hansen said and there were times he would accompany his Dad to see races twice a day. "Ernie Derr was my hero," Hansen said in describing his own fascination with the sport and in 1964 he went out onto the oval himself to begin a career that spanned nearly 30 years.

"I told my Dad when I was 16 that I was going to race," he explained. That first race in 1964 was in Nashua and Curt said his Dad managed to see him just one time. "He got me started and I've always looked back at that time when racing was so fascinating for me. I'll always be thankful for Dad's interest and enthusiasm when it came to watching racers on the dirt tracks."

During that first Nashua track race Hansen broke the front end of the car and flipped it in turn two. "I just about quit over that," he said.

Within two years Hansen, who is a native of Dike, Iowa, managed to move into the late model division and by the early 70s he was winning regularly and by 1978 had won no less than four track titles in a single year, something very few drivers were able to do.

"In 1978 I ran all four tracks…Tunis, Iowa State Fairgrounds, Hawkeye Downs (Cedar Rapids) and the track in Oskaloosa. And I'd do it in a single week, racing Wednesday through Sunday!" 1978 proved to be a banner year for Hansen as he not only won four track points championships, but some special races during the year that sealed his reputation as one of the great drivers in the Midwest.

"I raced the Falstaff 100 at Hawkeye Downs which had a purse of nearly $10,000 with the winner pocketing $2300."

Hansen was driving an Ed Sanger car (another legend of the circuit) and he managed to take the lead at the very start of the race, never looking back at the field of 27 who followed him in the 100-lap feature.

"Over 7,000 showed up to watch that one," he described, but he was done after that first place finish. He went on to compete at the Wapello County Fairgrounds (Eldon, Iowa) in a super ½ mile competition dubbed the Pepsi-Mountain Dew Special.

He won over Ed Sanger in that one along with 39 others who were vying to break Hansen's streak of winning.

Hansen admits Tunis Speedway was easily one of his very favorite tracks and that one played a part in that memorable 1978 performance as well. Tunis held its annual Coke Special and Hansen won the first heat, drawing him to the pole, where he blew everyone else away during the 40-lap feature.

"I did like the bigger tracks," he said, "but Tunis kept you more alert because it was a short track and really tested a driver's ability." Tunis holds a special place in Hansen's memory because so many drivers he watched growing up and later raced against called Tunis their home track. "The crowds were simply amazing at Tunis," he explained, "compared to the other tracks. They had such enthusiasm and you could feel it when you raced there."

In all during his career, Hansen managed over 300 feature wins along with wins in multiple specials and invitationals both in Iowa and as far away as Florida and Canada.

"Things changed over the years I raced," Hansen said. "We made a lot of our own parts including wheels and we raced as long as the car was ready." Hansen said he feels blessed to have been able to race during an era when it was "absolutely the best time for racing."

"Today's racers now can only race when they can afford it, which makes it pretty tough to put a full season together for many racers." Hansen, though he "officially" retired in 1981, got called back a few times over the years, racing one last time in 2001. "I got to race in five separate decades," he said. "Not many drivers get to do something like that."

In 2015 Hansen, along with Red Droste from Waterloo, was inducted into the National Dirt Model Hall of Fame, one of nine Iowans who have been named to the prestigious group. "I am so honored to be among such a great group of drivers. It just can't get any better."

Payoff System Changed Back

Hansen Takes Tunis Feature

By LARRY D. SPEARS
Courier Sports Writer

Dike's Curt Hansen moved from the third starting position into the lead on the ninth lap Sunday night and left the field behind to win the 25-lap feature race and Tunis Speedway's first and last $500 winner's purse.

The purse, which had been raised from $300 to $500 just last week in an attempt to bring back more and better drivers to Tunis, instead drew the ire of the steady Tunis runners, who felt that the top-heavy pay-off system cut into their profits unless they won.

A post-race discussion between promoter Keith Knaack and several of the quarter-mile track's top drivers found many of the drivers threatening a boycott of Tunis in favor of

The one-night $500 purse did have its effects on the quality of racing, however, as some 20 drivers made the feature and fans were treated to the hardest running of the season on the dirt oval.

Hard Races

Numerous spinouts, two collisions and a fire failed to slow ...

pushing the slower cars and Hansen succeeded in working through the pack while the second and third place cars got caught behind the tail-enders.

Hansen opened up a ten car length lead before the other contenders could lap the slower cars and no one could even get near the hard-charging

never relinquished it. Sanger started all the way back in the eighth spot and steadily worked his way up to fourth behind Burger and Hansen on the sixth circuit.

Buger spun on the seventh round advancing both cars and Sanger bypassed Hansen on the back straight of the eighth lap

Hansen runaway mid-season victor

By JIM FICKESS
Courier Sports Writer

Curt Hansen's victories are becoming increasingly impressive as his Tunis Speedway late model stock car feature winning streak grows.

classes' point leaders.

John Weers led from start to finish in the 25-lap sportsman title race. Weers, driving Jim Wyant's race car, topped second place Mike Krall and third-place finisher Greg Kastli.

Weers, like Sanger, sold his machine earlier this season.

ROGER PATTERSON defeated Scott Braun in a virtual two-car duel for the roadrunner mid-season honors.

Despite showers throughout the day Sunday, including a littelight drizzle a half hour before race time, the Tunis track was in excellent condition for the mid-season races.

Curt Hansen ends drought at Tunis with late model victory

By JIM FICKESS
Courier Sports Writer

Curt Hansen, second-leading money-winner going into Sunday night's stock car races at Tunis Speedway, finally won his first late model feature of the year at that track.

Hansen earned the victory by getting by Ed Sanger on the low side during the 23rd of 25 laps. Sanger, the top Tunis cash earner, also is the owner of Hansen's race car.

Sanger wound up second, an exceptionally good finish considering a couple of problems he had in the feature. Ed hit the retaining barrier on the back straightaway during a fourth-lap accident but was able to keep his car going.

He's the sixth feature winner in eight nights of racing.

Greg Kastli, driving Tim Swope's car, captured the 15-lap sportsman feature, which was marred by five restarts. Swope is out with of action with a broken hand. Kastli also easily won the second sportsman heat.

Roger Patterson's five race roadrunner winning streak came to an end Sunday. Scott Braun won that class' feature. Patterson lost a wheel early and couldn't recover the ground he lost while fixing it.

Tunis promoter Claus Stricker banned late model driver Red Dralle from the track for the rest of the season after Dralle tried to dump a bucket of water on

Hansen Nips Sanger in One-Two Daytona Finish

(COURIER NEWS SERVICE)

DAYTONA BEACH, Fla.—A pair of Waterloo area drivers proved here Thursday night that Northeast Iowa features some of the country's finest stock car racing.

Curt Hansen of Dike and Ed Sanger of Waterloo, both in Florida for the Daytona Speed Weeks program, opened the dirt track portion of the activities with a one-two finish in a 50-mile event, besting 22 drivers from throughout the United States.

Sanger, last summer's season champion at Waterloo's Tunis Speedway, and Hansen, one of his closest competitiors, made the final race by working their way through a time trial field of 93 cars.

The top 24 from those time trials went into Thursday's race and Hansen and Sanger ran away from the pack.

Hansen jumped into an early lead and was never challenged by anyone but Sanger, the pair taking the checkered flag less than a car length apart and almost a full lap ahead of the rest of the field.

Two more dirt track events are on the Daytona schedule and the Iowa duo will rank as favorites for both races, scheduled for Friday and Saturday night.

The Daytona 500 will conclude speed weeks activities Sunday.

Curt Hansen
John Deery
Olds-Datsun
Cedar Falls, Ia.
9

Flippin' and Racin'

Bob Piper isn't sure if he holds a special record for flipping his race car at Tunis Speedway, but he did pick up a nickname the 88-year-old still answers to from time to time.

FRAZER

A young Bob Piper with his first "official" sponsor, Howard Boslough, the local Kaiser-Fraser dealer.

"I think By Gosden (well known KXEL Radio broadcaster and Tunis track announcer at the time) gave me the name "Flip" after one race where three separate times I managed to turn over the race car," Piper explained.

"I flipped the first one, got into a second car, flipped it and then in another race turned over again. The Flip nickname stuck from that time on and I still hear it occasionally when I talk with old friends."

Piper can remember his first trip to the dirt oval in 1949. "I managed to win the time trials, so I thought I was on to something," Piper said. He was an active motorcyclist at the time, a member of the local Black Hawk Motorcycle Club and a hillclimbing enthusiast. He said his brother-in-law worked at Boslough Motors, the Cedar Falls Kaiser-Fraser dealer, and managed to get a car from them to turn into a race car.

"It was a four door Ford sedan," Piper said, "and we cut off the front fenders and stripped away as much of the car as we could to get it ready."

He said the car lasted several races before he decided he should move to a two-door coupe. The auto dealer provided space for him to work on the car and helped with painting and putting numbers and sponsor information on it. "They really couldn't afford to give me money as a sponsor, but I appreciated what I got and it allowed me to go racing."

Piper described his racing exploits as fairly straightforward. "I won some, lost some but managed to most of the time finish the races," he said. "I learned a lot during those years and I think a lot of the other guys racing from this area learned a lot as well.

He said when Florida drivers Cotton Hodges and Jim Millard came to Tunis to race, they dominated the events. "They had cars with engines that were balanced and set up specifically for racing. We just had stock motors and didn't really know anything about setting up a car to run on a track."

Over time other drivers began to get information about what needed to happen and the cars started to be more competitive.

"You knew the Florida guys were doing things that were probably not really legal in our part of the country, but we tried to talk with them as much as possible and they filled us in on a lot of ideas we could put into our own cars."

Piper said the early years produced some good racers and also some interesting "bending of the rules". He said some cars that appeared to be not particularly fast would come in and run away from the field of cars with everyone wondering how they managed to be so fast.

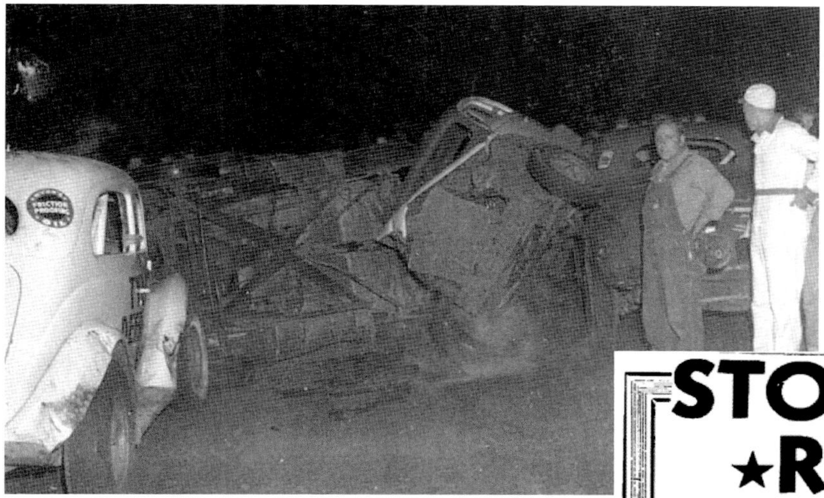

Bob Piper is under there somewhere!

"We had one guy who won numerous races," he explained, "and eventually we found out he was modifying the camshaft of the car to give it a bit more valve lift." That valve lift translated into more power and Piper said the racer never did get caught.

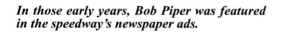

STOCK CAR
★RACES★
TUESDAY
8:15 P. M.
Time Trials at 7 P. M.
Thrills!
Chills!
Spills!
FREE PARKING!
ADM.: ADULTS $1.00 Inc. Tax
CHILDREN UNDER 12 FREE
When Accompanied by Adults
BUS SERVICE
Busses leave Waterloo at 7 and 8 P. M. There will be special bus service at the grounds after the races!
TUNIS SPEEDWAY
HIGHWAY 218 Between WATERLOO and CEDAR FALLS
TUESDAY IS FAMILY NIGHT!
Bring every member of the family and sit in the privacy of your own car and watch the rip-roaring stock car races!
Come Early for Best Seats!
FLEET OF 34 STOCK CARS!
• Bob Piper and Don Dennis, C. Falls
• Bill Chumley and Bob McIlrath, Waterloo
• George Bare, Cedar Rapids
• Cotton Hodges and Jim Millard, Davenport.

In those early years, Bob Piper was featured in the speedway's newspaper ads.

In early Waterloo Courier advertisements, Piper is listed as one of the highlighted racers who were expected to be part of the field. And his finishes in those early years pushed him into faster and more race ready vehicles. "Eventually I got out," he said. "Family obligations started to change for me and I knew racing was going to have to be just a spectator sport for me."

Howard Boslough offering some advice to his young driver.

Sometimes Bob got a pretty good view of the track.

"I often wonder though, if I had been able to get a good sponsor who could put me in a good car, just what I might have been able to do as a driver."

Doc Mayner...Free Spirit Extraordinaire

To describe Alfred Emory Mayner M.D. (also known as Doc for any of us who followed racing in the 60s and 70s) as a free spirit would probably be understating the Doc's passion for life and his pure thrill of living.

Doc Mayner began his racing career sometime in 1967 and a news article in September of that year described his 5th place finish in a stock car race at Independence.

A.E. (Al) Mayner, better known as Doc,was a physician from Winthrop, Iowa. Doc loved speed and he loved the competition of racing.

It's not known if this was indeed his very first race, but on October 26, 1966, the Doc placed a want ad in the Waterloo Courier looking for a used go kart, which could be presumed was for his own use. Possibly a speed demon was born at that moment.

So many stories swirl around the Doc and the fans simply had to love his tenacity. When he was on the track, everyone knew he was there and he always gave it his all. As a physician, of course, he was a bit unusual in his choice of hobbies, but as described earlier, the Doc didn't allow much of anything to slow him down.

In September 1971 he was clocked by an Iowa Highway Patrol airplane (yes, an airplane) going somewhere north of 120 miles per hour. Patrolmen on the ground couldn't catch him and for the surrounding area gearheads, he sealed his legacy as the ultimate speed guy.

Eventually the highway patrol tracked him down, served him with a warrant and he ended up spending five days in jail, but on five consecutive weekends only. Makes you wonder if the judge didn't love him as well.

An article in the mid-1970s published by the Des Moines Register described him. "There are race car drivers and then there is Dr. Al Mayner." The article went on to describe Doc Mayner's daughter's wedding, which occurred in Oelwein.

Daughter Alexa was marrying Mark Hunt of Winthrop at 7 p.m. that particular evening. Of course it was a Saturday evening and there were races to attend so the Doc managed to not only leave the wedding by 7:15, but make it to the track just as racing started at 7:30.

He told the reporter he really did obey the speed limits on his trip to Independence as it was "only 14 miles away" and fortunately he won that evening because he neglected to tell his wife he was headed out the door.

Wife Linda let it be known that he'd better win, once she found out about his exit. Everything went well as he won the feature and a heat race, but he had to slip back into his wedding suit upon returning to the church because "I'd forgotten about the wedding pictures."

Doc describe his beginnings into racing this way… "About 10 years ago (when he was in his early 30s) some friends took my wife and me to the races."

Wife Linda said to the Doc, "Gee, those guys (drivers) are neat." That was all it took as he thought "Hell, I can do that!"

He admitted it wasn't quite as simple as it looked and said he made $14,000 in 1973 racing, which still didn't cover his expenses.

"I'm a little limited," he said. "I don't get to all the tracks because my work keeps me close to home." He was a practicing physican, after all.

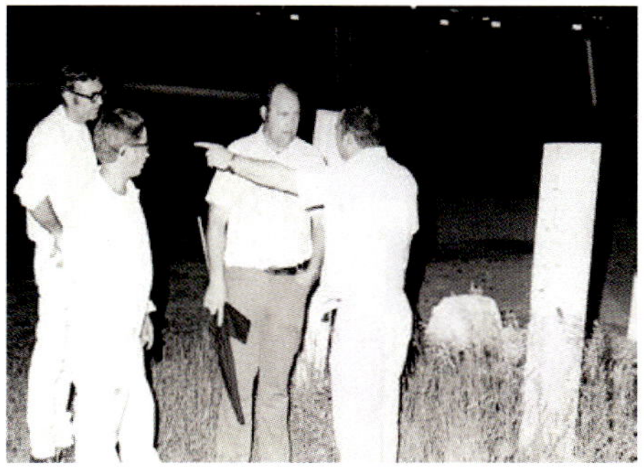

Doc wasn't timid about providing his opinion on the track. Here he has a friendly discussion with promoter Claus Stricker about an on track incident.

Doc Mayner provided a lot of extra excitement to the local racing scene and the stories still abound about how he approached life…full of passion and enthusiasm.

The Doc died too young at the age of 47 in 1984. He's still greatly missed by his family and the great many friends he made over the years.

(Quotes and some details come via Des Moines Register archives)

Morris "Beetle" Bailey

Though he wasn't a driver and and it's not even certain if he ever actually sat in a race car, much less drive one, Morris "Beetle" Bailey played an important role

in the growth of Tunis Speedway, particularly in its early years when he would act as the "official" track photographer.

Beetle would show up at each race, putting his life in danger most of the time as he worked to capture images of the races and then he would make black and white prints available, most of the time for $1 each , to both fans and drivers.

People gobbled up the images and many still reside in people's scrapbooks or tucked into boxes and bags in attics and basements.

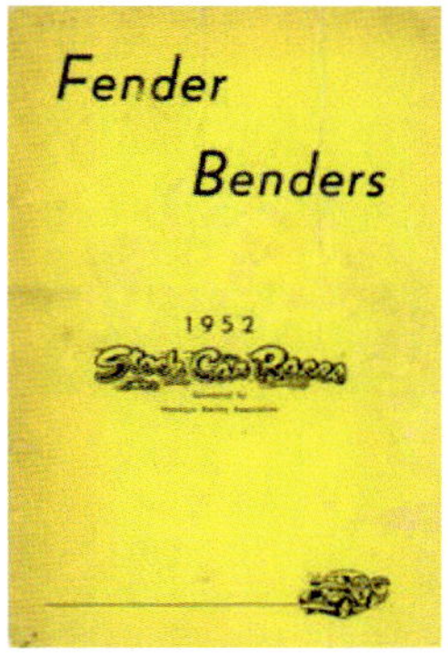
Fender
Benders
1952
Stock Car Races

Beetle also produced for two years a publication called Fender Benders which wrapped up the racing season providing profiles of the drivers who sped around the dirt oval at Tunis. Reproductions can be found later in this book.

He also provided a weekly news publication for fans called Stock Car Racing as Seen Through the Camera's Lens.

"Beetle" Bailey died of heart failure on May 19, 1994. The Boone, Iowa resident was 80-years-old. With a memorable name and abilities to match, Bailey carved himself a permanent place in the memories of race fans and drivers through his photography and publishing contributions to motorsports journalism.

Fuzzy Racing

MaryAnn Liddell can remember when she and her husband, Fuzzy, went to the races in the early 1970s. "He decided he liked racing and he wanted to do it himself," she said, remembering how exciting it was to sit in the stands and cheer on their favorite drivers.

TOP ROADRUNNER — Fuzzy Liddell of Waterloo, Iowa, won the season point championship in the Roadrunner division at Tunis Speedway in 1976.

In 1975 Liddell began racing in the Roadrunner division and stayed with it through 1976, winning that division's season championship. He got so good, MaryAnn said, "they called him the King of the Roadrunners!"

He obviously didn't want to just rest on his laurels, however, and purchased a car from fellow racer Jack Mitchell and moved into the Sportsman division which provided some needed experience before he made the final move to Late Models.

Using some of the aluminum panels that were being built by Scott Braun, Liddell started building his own Late Model race cars and MaryAnn said he worked tremendously hard to make them as competitive as possible. It was obvious he enjoyed the sport, but as with many young married drivers, the Liddells were faced with expenses related to raising three young daughters and in 1981 it was decided they couldn't really afford to keep racing.

MaryAnn described a couple of things she most remembers about Tunis Speedway that made it such a special time for her family.

"At one point the track was sponsoring some special events that included a wheelbarrow race," she recalled. "Mike Krall, one of Fuzzy's buddies, told him they should build a wheelbarrow and race it." He was certain the two of them could win it."

"So with Mike pushing and Fuzzy riding, they went out and won the race," she explained, "and it was so fun watching them do it!" The prize, a keg of beer, was tapped and brought into the pits after the racing where it was shared with everyone that participated that evening.

"We (the wives) were always told that no one was to be in the pits except the drivers and crew," MaryAnn said. "I was never sure if it was a rule or not. Sometimes I think the guys just told us that to keep us away from the pit area."

"But we wives were pretty happy to be sitting up in the stands together, cheering on our husbands and rotting them on to victory. We had so many good times at Tunis. It was really hard to see it shut down."

And that name…Fuzzy? MaryAnn said her husband's real name was Donald, but when he was two years old he managed to get some bubble gum tangled into his hair.

"His mother shaved his head and when the hair started to grow back in, it was real fuzzy so his older brothers started calling him Fuzzy. And the name stuck even up

27
HARMON
GLASS
WATERLOO

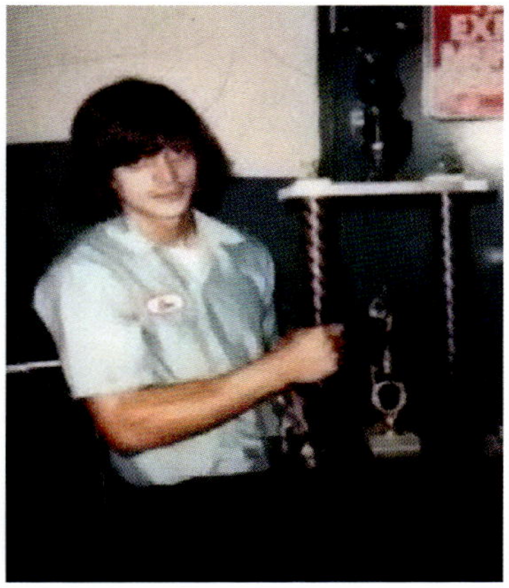

Boots Sweerin

BLOCK MASONRY CO.
115
Ph 9834

Boots Sweerin remembers his racing days at Tunis Speedway fondly, though he didn't race nearly as long as many of the drivers that tried their hand at circling the dusty oval.

"One of the things I remember is how rough and tumble it was in those days," he recalled. "If you got tangled up out on the track you could probably count on a fight back in the pits," he laughed.

But something that made that time different, he thought, was even if a fight occurred, it was a different kind of battle.

"Back then, if you punched a guy and he went down, you let him back up again," he described. "Not so sure that happens today."

So what about those cool white wall tires you ran on your race cars, Boots?

"We'd go back behind the Cadillac dealer and grab the take offs," he explained. "For us, they were perfect. And who wouldn't want those white walls!"

"I Knew I Had to Have It"

Merlin Benning's racing story began simply enough. His uncle, Tom Hicks, had a race car and the young Benning was fascinated with watching the races. "Just like all the other kids, I wondered what it would be like to be out there on the track," Benning describes. "I just knew I had to have a race car."

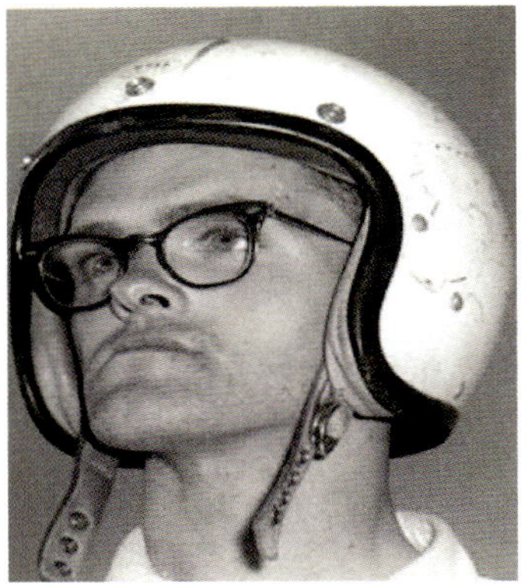

So on July 4, 1959, Merlin Benning showed up at Tunis Speedway with a 1940 Mercury he purchased from Aikey's Salvage in Cedar Falls for $20. "I stuck another 20 bucks in it," he said, "so for $40 total I was racing!"

17

Was he scared that first time out on the track? "You bet," he explains. "I can't imagine anyone wouldn't be a little bit scared." And wouldn't you know it, Benning rolled that Mercury and the damage was enough that he couldn't race it any longer.

17

"I knew the Hesse boys (Tunis racers Lloyd and Bob Hesse) and I bought Lloyd's 1933 Ford coupe with a flathead engine in it for $300, which was a lot of money in those days." He dragged the coupe home (and no, his dad was not pleased) and before long he was out on the track again, learning the ropes and finding his place among the dirt track racing fraternity.

"I raced at other tracks in the area in addition to Tunis," Benning said. "I tore up that coupe numerous times, sometimes tearing it up so bad you couldn't quite tell if it would ever be able to move on its own again."

17

17

But the little coupe did indeed keep racing and for three seasons Benning pushed it each and every week to make the events, sometimes pulling it home with bashed in sides and top and fractured suspension only to be chained to a tree so he could pull it back into shape, do some welding and get it back on the track.

"It saw a lot of wrecks," he recalled. And pictures he kept of the coupe are testament to its rough life. In 1963 Benning retired the coupe.

"That was the last year for flathead engines at the tracks," he explained, "when the overhead valve V-8s began to dominate the short track racing."

Eventually Benning moved to a 1955 Chevrolet and later got into racing contemporary Camaros, filling in time during a 40 year racing career flagging for races at such places as the Big 4 Speedway, Midway Downs and at the track in Nashua, Iowa.

"I stopped racing in 1999," he said, "but I still miss it." But 40 years was probably enough and today Benning can still enjoy dirt track as his son Dana operates the track located in Vinton, Iowa.

And the little coupe? Why, Benning still has it in a shed on his Century Farm located outside Waverly, Iowa. It looks much like it did back in 1959 when he started racing it. It still carries the scars of those years…the dents and bent components and gutted interior. But when he pulls it from the shed where it rests, it fires right up, the crude headers blasting smoke and rust skyward and bellowing much like it did in its heyday.

"Still runs pretty good," Benning says. Yes, it still runs pretty good.

The little coupe took a lot of abuse during it's four seasons of racing.

Benning spent 40 years racing, finally retiring in 1999. He said that was "probably enough."

Merlin and son, Dana, who is active as a manager and promoter in dirt track racing.

“Without Tunis? Not Sure Where I’d Be”

Like a lot of kids, Scott Braun admits he loved the excitement of racing. The noise, the speed, the competition…it all worked for him and he enjoyed many visits to Tunis Speedway with his friends to watch the racers tear up the dirt on a weekly basis.

Little did he know at the time that this interest would change his life and become a career that would touch dirt track racers all over the country.

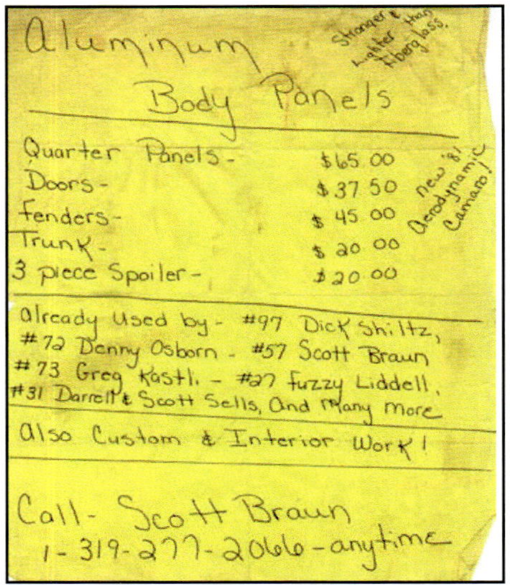
Aluminum Body Panels
Stronger & lighter than fiberglass.
Quarter Panels - $65.00
Doors - $37.50
Fenders - $45.00
Trunk - $20.00
3 piece Spoiler - $20.00
new '81 aerodynamic Camaro!
already used by - #97 Dick Shiltz, #72 Denny Osborn - #57 Scott Braun #73 Greg Kastli - #27 Fuzzy Liddell, #31 Darrell & Scott Sells, and many more
also Custom & Interior Work!
Call - Scott Braun
1-319-277-2066 - anytime

The simple “flyer” Scott Braun scrawled on a yellow sheet and passed around to his fellow Tunis drivers.

“I watched the races in high school,” Braun explains. ”Me and my buddies would head to the track and watch our heroes race. It was a great time.”

At some point Braun decided maybe building and driving a race car might be in his future. “I convinced my buddy Pat Loy to help me buy an old Camaro, weld some gas pipe into it for a roll cage and we headed out to the track.”

Heading to the track meant pulling the tired Camaro behind a pickup truck with a log chain, but the two managed to get the Camaro entered into the Roadrunner class and in 1976 Scott Braun became a race car driver. “I was out of high school, working in my Dad’s shop, so I was ready to do a little racing.”

Braun raced that beat up Camaro for two years finally rolling it and essentially destroying his trusty vehicle. “I moved to a ’67 Chevelle next,” he describes, “and put a bit more into the engine to pick up some speed.” The engine seemed to work but Braun found himself caught up in a rule after one race where he nearly lost his car.

“The rule was if you won in the Roadrunner class someone could “claim” your car for $350,” he explained. “Well, I had been winning (three times before this happened) and the rule was meant to keep racers from investing too much in the race car, but I had more than $350 invested. I wasn’t about to give it up!”

So Braun forfeited the race (and the prize money) and the right to race the car at Tunis in the Roadrunner class again. He ended up changing the car, however, placing a Nova body on the chassis and painting it a different color. “I had started racing down in Cedar Rapids and at Marshalltown so the Nova was put together in 1979.

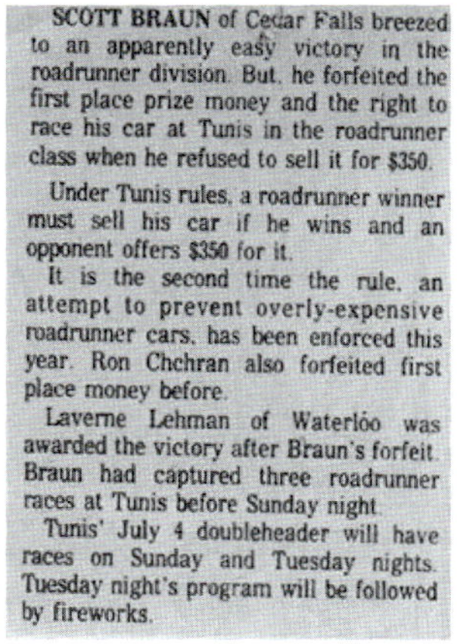
SCOTT BRAUN of Cedar Falls breezed to an apparently easy victory in the roadrunner division. But, he forfeited the first place prize money and the right to race his car at Tunis in the roadrunner class when he refused to sell it for $350.

Under Tunis rules, a roadrunner winner must sell his car if he wins and an opponent offers $350 for it.

It is the second time the rule, an attempt to prevent overly-expensive roadrunner cars, has been enforced this year. Ron Chchran also forfeited first place money before.

Laverne Lehman of Waterloo was awarded the victory after Braun's forfeit. Braun had captured three roadrunner races at Tunis before Sunday night.

Tunis' July 4 doubleheader will have races on Sunday and Tuesday nights. Tuesday night's program will be followed by fireworks.

Braun was working in his Dad’s heating and cooling business and part of what he did was bend sheet metal to create the various venting and air ducts needed to complete installations. He found he could make panels for race cars as well and began selling those panels.

"I sold my first panels to racer Fuzzy Liddell and other racers found out about them and asked if I might bend them some panels as well," Braun said. "I was doing steel panels and found I could also bend and create aluminum panels which were cheaper and lighter so I started making more of those. This was in 1980."

57
B&G

"It didn't take too long and more racers started using them. Before I knew it, I was getting all kinds of requests and I decided this might be a good way to make some money and help to pay for some of my racing expenses," he explained. "I created a handwritten flyer I passed out at the races I would attend and the orders started coming in."

An ad in the 1982 issue of Stock Car Magazine proved to be the start for what became Performance Bodies and Braun, along with his racing buddy, Pat Loy, began seriously producing body panels for more and more racers, taking phone calls and delivering panels to racers all over the Midwest.

Today the company not only produces body panels, but has a full catalog of items specific to racers and their need to have product in hand as fast as possible.

"I learned early on that racers needed things as quickly as possible, so we worked to get orders turned around as fast as possible."

The company grew and expanded, now occupying a new facility in the Cedar Falls, Iowa industrial park where Braun has gathered a crew of dedicated racers and enthusiasts to meet the needs of racers nationwide.

"I'm convinced that without Tunis Speedway I wouldn't be doing what I am today and this company would not exist," Braun explains.

"I started out as a kid wanting to go racing and ended up creating a company around a sport I love. It is, and continues to be, a great ride."

Welcome
RACE FANS
TUNIS SPEEDWAY
Coca-Cola

Curt Hansen, Gene Ehlers, Scott Braun

Red Dralle

Ed Sanger, Dralle Win Season Championships

Two Waterloo-Cedar Falls metropolitan area stock car drivers won late-model season championships Sunday on other tracks while Stan Stover of Reinbeck was winning the 50-lap finale at the Tunis track here.

Ed Sanger of Waterloo won the season's crown at the Dubuque Speedway Sunday afternoon.

Dike's Curt Hansen finished a close second to Sanger as he was on the Dubuque late-model point leader's tail throughout most of the 50-lap captured the sportsman season championship at Dubuque.

Evansdale's Red Dralle was crowned the season champion at Fountain City, Wis. Sunday. Dralle was unsuccessful in his attempt to make it back to Waterloo in time for the Tunis season championship later in the day, however.

The Evansdale stocker, who was fourth in the Tunis point standings, would have started on the outside of the second row for the championship race.

Hansen scores, Dralle banned at Tunis

WATERLOO, Ia.—Curt Hansen of Dike became Tunis Speedway's sixth late model feature winner in eight nights of racing last Sunday when he scored his first Tunis main event victory of the season.

Hansen, the second-high money winner going into Sunday night, passed Ed Sanger on the 23rd lap of the 25-lap event.

Tunis has two open competition nights of stock car racing planned for the Fourth of July Weekend. A total purse of $9,00 is being offered for Sunday and Monday's open competition cards.

Bob Hilmer led the first four laps of Sunday's main, but dropped out with apparent mechanical problems at the race's first of five restarts.

A second red flag on the fourthe lap sent Sanger in to the fence off turn No. 2, but he was able to keep going.

Jack Mitchell then grabbed the lead and held it until the 12th lap, when Wanger overtook him. Sanger nearly spun out and lost the lead temporarily to Dan Nesteby on the 14th lap.

Sanger got first place back from Nesteby, only to lose it to Hansen, on the 23rd lap. Sanger wound up second with Nesteby third and Roger Klingfus fourth.

Klingfus won the late model semi-main while Sanger and Bob Hilmer captured the 10-lap heats.

Red Dralle was banned from Tunis for the rest of the season by promoter Claus Stricker when he tried to dump a bucket of water over pit steward Dick Hinz' head. The action came in front of the judges' stand when Dralle apparently thought Hinz was going to black flag Schiltz, who was driving a Dralle car, for taking on water to cool off during a restart.

Dralle ran from the pits to the judges' stand but slipped as he started to douse Hinz.

'Fun night' for Dralle

By DON KRUSE
Courier Sports Writer

When Red Dralle of Evansdale arrived at the pits Sunday night at Tunis Speedway, he announced that he was there for the fun.

Fun and all, Dralle certainly got more "than he bargained for as he copped the top prize in the late model 50-lap championship race.

The big race, the late model 50-lapper, was pushed up on the program by Tunis promoter Claus Stricker when dark clouds started moving in early in the evening.

Stricker turned out the winner on that one when high winds and rain ... their seats early when the race, slated last on the program, was moved up.

Oddly, though, Nesteby was the first to go as only nine of the 15 cars finished the race, and Sanger ended in third when it was all over.

Nesteby, exercising his option to take the outside start just as he did last year when he won this race, was in the lead after eight laps when his car came too strongly into the third turn and went over the bank, flipping over once before coming to a stop on its side. His gas pedal apparently stuck after bolting the backstretch.

The popular Nesteby waved to the crowd's applause as he rode on the ...

Red Dralle
GT-1
OIL
24
7up

JAX
24

Dralle Nips Ed By Half Length

By LARRY D. SPEARS
Courier Sports Writer

Tempers among the late model drivers at Waterloo's Tunis Speedway were considerably more subdued Sunday night than they were two weeks ago, but action was just as furious as Evansdale's Red Dralle scored one of the narrowest victories of the year.

Dralle, who powered his red No. 24 Chevelle into the front spot on the 12th lap of the 25-lap feature, had Tunis points leader Ed Sanger, center of the track's controversy two weeks ago, on his heels the entire distance, but refused to give any ground.

who edged Waterloo's Jo... Schaefer for the second hea... victory, edged him again fo... the No. 6 spot in the feature. Larry Wasserfort of Waterlo... was eighth and Dave Bedar... of La Porte City finished nint... after being involved in a pai... of accidents that caused th... only restarts in the race.

Eighteen-year-old Mike O... born, subbing for his dad, Dal... in the No. 72 '57 Chevy, starte... on the pole and out-maneuvere... the field for 11 laps before lo... ing the top spot to Dralle. H... finally finished 12th. Dr. A. I... Mayner of Winthrop, winner ... the first heat, dropped out ... the feature due to mechanic...

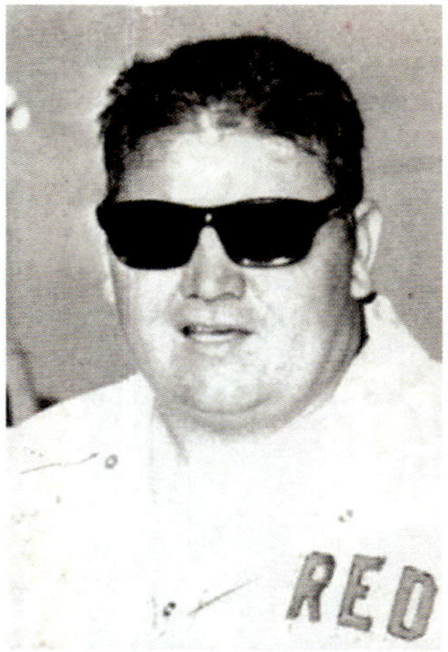

RED

Red Dralle
ALL-CAR TRANSMISSION
FRIEDLEY
4
Lincoln MERCURY CEDAR FALLS
IOKABOOS Lounge WATERLOO, IA.

SPEEDWAY
FLEXI-FLYERS
NEED Midwest DEALERS
4

“Here’s $5. I’m goin’ racin’”

In 1960 Roger Klingfus came to Waterloo to go to work for a local commercial roofing company. Like a lot of drivers at Tunis, he was fascinated at the prospect of driving at the track and for $5 purchased his first “race car” from the former Behrens Buick in Waterloo.

“It was a 1948 Buick Roadmaster with a smashed front end,” he said. “I paid a co-worker $15 to weld roll bars inside the four door sedan and went racing in the novice division.”

By the fall of that year Klingfus had won the season championship and remembers getting a trophy that “seemed like it was half the size of the Buick.” He says he still has that trophy and thinks it was probably the very best one he won during his racing career.

Klingfus moved to a 1941 Buick coupe next as he was moved into the modified class in 1961. He said he rolled the car about mid-season and ended up sitting out the remainder of the year.

In 1962 Klingfus says he started using Chrysler products for his racing efforts and had a 1959 Dodge that began the season with a 383 engine, eventually moving to a 426 wedge and then a 426 hemi. He continued to be competitive each season and in 1966 decided to build a 1963 Plymouth convertible with an automatic transmission and power steering. “That was the first time anybody tried power steering on a race car, but it wasn’t long and most everybody was using it,” he said.

R&M

Win for Klingfus

Roger Klingfus of Waterloo won the first feature race of his career Monday night at Tunis Speedway, edging out Red Droste of Waterloo.

Klingfus, who has been racing for over three years at Tunis, also won the first heat and placed third in the A-semi.

Walt Broton of Dunkerton won the special roll over derby, turning his car over two and one-quarter times.

The season championship race will be the main feature on the racing card next Sunday, the final night of racing at Tunis. Total purse for the evening will be $3,000 with $500 going to the winner of the 50-lap title race. Two 20-lap novice races and a [illegible]

[illegible] City), 2. Rich Krafka (Dysart), 3. Cal Swanson (Remoreck), 4. Jensen, 5. Fitzpatrick, 6. Droste.

Consolation—1. John Webb (Independence), 2. Claus Stricker (Waterloo), 3. Karl Sanaer (Waterloo).

Feature—1. Klingfus, 2. Droste, 3. Swanson, 4. Nesby, 5. Donovan, 6. Wurst.

Cadet No. 1—1. Chuck Larsen (Waterloo).

Cadet No. 2—Rick Albright (Waterloo).

KARLSON

From 1966 to 1972 Klingfus raced several different body styles and engines until his brother Don built a 1968 Chevelle that he described as “perfection”. “Don was a perfectionist, so everything had to be clean and in order all the time,” Klingfus said. “Don almost always had the best looking car and perfect attendance at the races, even after a major wreck from the night before.”

“Don would work and do whatever it took to go back out with the car all fixed up like nothing happened,” Klingfus described and he raced that car up until 1979 when Don passed away.

In 1977 Klingfus set a class record at Tunis of 15 seconds flat for the then 3/8 mile oval and no one ever managed to beat that record before the track finally closed in 1983.

Klingfus’ wife Alyce also got involved in the racing, doing three Powder Puff events, winning her final one in 1965.

Dysart's "Dick" Rich Krafka

By Kathy Krafka Harkema

From the farm where he was born south of Dysart, Iowa, Rich "Dick" Krafka raced his way into history at Tunis Speedway in Waterloo, Iowa.

The young farmer drove to the Tunis Speedway Season Championship in 1957, at only 19 years old.

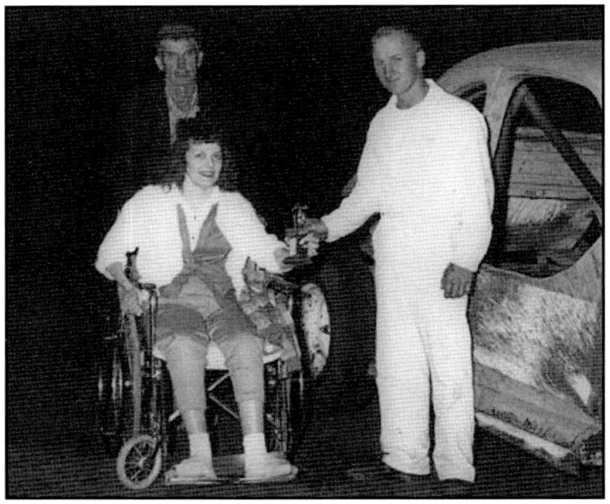

And the young Krafka's engine, powered Knoxville, Iowa's Kenny Crook to the championship in the race that today is known as the famed Knoxville Nationals.

That engine propelled "Dick" Krafka into stock car racing. In exchange for loaning that engine to Crook for the super modified race in Knoxville, Crook built Krafka a stock car, a remarkable five-window 1934 Ford coupe. Krafka raced that car to the season championship at Tunis Speedway.

Crook, who owned a body shop in Knoxville, raced under number 23. And that's how Rich "Dick" Krafka became number 24, awarded to him by his racing friend, Kenny Crook.

In the late 1950s and '60s,Krafka competed at Hawkeye Downs in Cedar Rapids on Friday nights, Independence Motor Speedway on Saturday nights and Tunis Speedway on Sunday nights.

Even though Krafka won track season championships at Hawkeye Downs, and Tunis, Tunis quickly became his favorite because of the outstanding way promoter Judd Tunis managed the show.

"Judd Tunis was the best. He was very organized. He took great care of the track. He knew how to advertise and how to promote. He hired good help and ran a good, professional organization, and put on a tremendous show for the fans and treated the drivers very well and always with respect," Krafka recalls. "No one could compete with Judd Tunis as a promoter."

"Judd and his crew were fair. His word was always good. They had rules and they stuck with them to provide for good, clean, fair competition. When you won at Tunis, you knew you were the best anywhere," Krafka recalls with pride.

"The flagman, Speed Chumley, was fair with everyone, too. Tunis was ahead of its time, and set the standard for how racetracks and races should be run," Krafka said.

Krafka started racing at Tunis Speedway when he was 17. "Tunis attracted all the good drivers and Tunis paid real well, real real well!" Krafka said.

24

In the '50s and '60s, drivers were paid right after the races in cash. "You could easily take home $500 to $800 every Sunday night from a weekly race at Tunis, which was more than what you would take home even if you won it all at other shows," Krafka said.he put that money back into his stock cars, and to provide for his family.

"Judd Tunis was real good to drivers, because Judd paid drivers a percentage of the grandstand gate proceeds in the weekly purse," Krafka recalls. "Many nights there would be thousands of fans in the grandstands, and hundreds more honking the horns in their cars before we took the green and cheering us on from their blankets on turns three and four. The more people that were at the race, the more money the drivers made which made for a winning combination," Krafka said.

Krafka 1st Leader in Point Standings

Although a couple of exciting personal duels for honors between Bill Zwanziger and Red Droste, both of Waterloo, caught the fans' interest at Tunis Speedway Sunday night, another driver stands at the top of this week's point standings.

Dick Krafka, of Dysart, racked up 57 points on the basis of wins in the first heat and "A" semi-main and a fourth place finish in the feature. Krafka has a seven point lead over Droste and Zwanziger who are tied for second with 50 points apiece. Droste's total came from the feature win and a second in the "B" semi. Zwanziger scored on a second place finish in the feature, three in the "B" semi and on a third in the third heat. Gene Petersen of Waterloo has 46 points and Tuffy Meyer of Big Rock 38 to round out the leaders.

The use of point standings by the Cedarloo Racing Association eliminates the necessity of determining starting positions by time trials. Without the time trials the balance of the season. Racing cards for the modified stock cars will get underway at 7:30 p. m. Sundays and holidays.

Two of the long-time favorites of the Tunis track fans, Cal Swanson of Waterloo and Charlie Moffett, of Stanwood, plan to be back this Sunday night. Both missed last Sunday's racing because of engine trouble. Swanson hold the 10-lap record set last year at Tunis.

That approach meant drivers helped recruit their friends and family members into the Sunday night shows and occasional specials like "media races" where local news celebrities took their turn behind the wheel to get a feel for racing, and in turn, carry it in their news coverage.

Everything Judd Tunis did was done well, Krafka recalls. From the ads he ran to promote the races, to the results he meticulously provided to the radio stations and newspapers each week, Judd Tunis took pride in promoting Tunis Speedway.

That's why drivers like Krafka, Ed Sanger and Curt Hansen often considered it their favorite track, and recalled the memories of Tunis at the Tunis Racing Reunion at Performance Bodies in Cedar Falls October 5, 2013, flipping through Judd Tunis' detailed scrapbooks and reliving the memories of their racing careers and years competing at Tunis Speedway.

Krafka recalls when Hansen, of Dike, and Sanger, then of Waterloo, and now of Postville, got their start at Tunis. "Curt Hansen is a good fellow and was a well-respected driver, he always ran well," Krafka said.

And what about Sanger, who earned the term "Cap'n Crunch" painted on a rear quarter-panel of his stock car in his early years? "He was wild, real wild when he got started, but he got it straightened out, and went on to be one of the best in the country," Krafka said.

Krafka Sets Record to Win Season Stock Car Championship

By ROGER MATZ
Courier Sports Writer

Dick Krafka took home the Hawkeye Racing Assn. season championship trophy Saturday night after clinching the 75-lap stock car title race on the 35th lap at Tunis Speedway here. Krafka also set a new track record of 23.97 minutes for 75 laps when he kept up top speed throughout the race even though he said afterwards he thought he had it won. Carroll Hilmer was second, Cal Swanson third and Carroll Jensen fourth.

Krafka was the only one of the race's three leaders who didn't drop out while in the No. 1 spot. Bob Hilmer, starting on the pole, led the race until a transmission or clutch failure forced his 22B out on the 23rd lap. Bill Zwanziger then took over and kept the lead until the 35th when a broken spindle caused his car to lose a front wheel. That left Krafka out front, and his little flathead Ford coupe withstood the endurance test.

THE TOP FOUR in the Hawkeye Racing Assn. point standings, Hilmer, Zwanziger, Red Droste and Krafka, moved out in front of the pack soon after the green flag fell. Droste moved up to second on the seventh lap ahead of Zwanziger but Bill overcame him on the next lap as Droste's car began to lose steam. Krafka took over third on the 10th lap as Droste continued to lose ground.

The trio of Hilmer, Zwanziger and Krafka stayed in that order for about 15 laps although Zwanziger nearly stole the lead from Hilmer twice. Then Hilmer dropped out, followed 12 laps later by Zwanziger. After that, Krafka moved in for the duration.

Both Hilmer and Droste went into the feature with some misgivings. Hilmer's car wasn't handling very well after last Sunday's accident that damaged the front end. Droste and Krafka had come together in the third heat and the jolt knocked the petcock from Droste's radiator. Red had to solder shut the half-inch hole but it was still leaking at race time.

JACK HICKMAN won the special 25-lap consolation by a comfortable margin when his nearest competitor, John Hill, blew a tire and was forced to leave the race. Hickman had won the second heat while Hill was the first heat winner. Zwanziger took the third heat.

Lloyd Hesse won the novice race in a spectacular finish that brought the crowd of 2,816 to its feet. Hesse tailed Don Heideman for about three laps, and on the last lap Red Morgan appeared out of the pack to join the chase. The trio came into the final turn three abreast but somehow Hesse spurted out in front as the cars crossed the finish line. Heideman was second, Morgan third.

Hesse then hooked Heideman's bumper and slid broadside into Red Morgan's oncoming car. Morgan rammed Hesse's novice in the middle, the impact flipping Hesse's 22A several times. It came to rest on its side against the fence in front of the grandstand. Hesse was slightly shaken up by the accident and was taken to the hospital later in the evening. Hesse had no apparent fractures or severe injuries and his condition was described as good.

The novice race for the season's championship will be the highlight of next Sunday's open competition night.

First heat (10 laps)—1. John Hill (8), 2. Chub Liebe (18), 3. Bob Domer (20B); 3.22.

Second heat (10 laps)—1. Jack Hickman (10), 2. Harry O'Dean (16), 3. Elmer Bradley (51); 3.23.

Third heat (10 laps)—1. Bill Zwanziger (33), 2. Dick Krafka (24), 3. Carroll Hilmer (23); 3.20.

Novice (20 laps)—1. Lloyd Hesse (22A), 2. Don Heideman (6), 3. Red Morgan (9A), 4. Bob Heimlund (10), 5. Howard Ingles (76), 6. Don McGraw (72).

Consolation (25 laps)—1. Jack Hickman (10), 2. Harry O'Dean (16), 3. Bob Domer (20B), 4. Chub Liebe (18), 5. Jerry Sherbon (3D), 6. Keith Knack (4).

Championship (75 laps)—1. Dick Krafka (24), 2. Carroll Hilmer (23), 3. Cal Swanson (8), 4. Carroll Jensen (5), 5. Vern Weber (16), 6. Lyle Johnston (68), 7. Red Droste (77), 8. Gene Peterson (9), 9. Bill Kemp (?), 10. Al Runyan (3D); 23.97.

Krafka, a lifelong competitor who focuses on being the best, enjoyed his time racing. He looks back on photos, of his racing career with pride. Photos like those taken by track photographer Morris "Beetle" Bailey, who peered through his Coke-bottle thick glasses to take dramatic photos of cars in action. In the days before good track lighting, long camera lenses, digital photography and flashes with much range, Bailey got daringly close to stock cars to take fabulous photos. "Beetle Bailey was absolutely one of the best photographers in racing. He would get right out on the track to capture the cars at the best angles and capture the action," Krafka said.

When he was in the winner's circle at Tunis Speedway, Krafka recalled the trophies were "heavy suckers, works of art made of marble and metal" not the cheap plastic kind given away today.

"Dick" Krafka, wasn't the only one in the family to win trophies at Tunis. His wife, "Carol" Caroline Krafka, who helped launch Hawkeye Racing News with family friend Keith Knaack as an early racing reporter, earned Powder Puff Derby trophies there, too. "She pushed it hard. She drove like hell and drove it hard," he recalls.

One night, she drove it a little too hard. "She lost it and she rolled it," Krafka recalls of his hard-charging wife's powder puff racing days. "She was out of the car before the wheels even stopped rolling, because in those days, there were no front wheel brakes," he said.

Luckily, Caroline Krafka wasn't hurt. But her pride was. "She was quiet, real quiet," her husband recalls when he and the wrecker came to her rescue.

Were there words between the racing couple? "Not many," Rich recalls. "I wasn't happy, because I drove that car for five years and never rolled it. She rolled it her first time out with it," he said. It was a quiet ride home to Dysart that Sunday night, and one the Krafka's made weekly in many happier, more talkative many times during Rich's racing career.

During those days, the pits were dark, so men wore whites to be seen. Rich raced with a red handkerchief to keep the dirt out of his nose and mouth as he donned goggles and an open-faced Bell helmet.

Caroline appliquéd red stripes and a red 24 on his racing shirt and pants and soaked them after each race to restore them to their bright white freshly-pressed condition. There were no racing shoes, so Rich wore worn out slip-on leather shoes with a thin sole to get a feel for the accelerator.

In those days, women weren't allowed in the pits until after the races were run. And you didn't make unnecessary trips. So when their daughter, Kristi, was born Labor Day weekend in September 1964, her first stop out of the hospital was Tunis Speedway, before she ever made her first trip home to the family farm at Dysart.

"Dick" Krafka retired from racing the first time in the late 1960s to devote his focus to his three daughters, Kathy, Kristi and Kerri, as they began raising and showing sheep competitively to state and national championships across the USA in 4-H and FFA. Once the girls completed their outstanding 4-H and FFA careers showing livestock, Krafka came back out of racing retirement, buying a modified in his 50s and returning to racing at Vinton, Iowa, under the alias of "Speedo Shepherd" in the familiar 24—a tribute to the family's sheep showing success. Caroline passed away in 2003, her memory living on in the racing movie "Fever Heat" in which she had a cameo role and did racing reporting for Hawkeye Racing News.

Still actively farming and raising seed corn, hay, soybeans and livestock today, Rich finally retired from racing, and now sits in the stands as a fan at racetracks and at livestock shows, where he enjoys watching his granddaughters earn championships at the county fairs and State Fair, just as he did in his younger days.

The Legend of Tony Conrad

Ethan Thomas Akin has a need for speed. Growing up in Waterloo, he made use of city streets to feed that need, at one point managing to accumulate 56 individual traffic tickets and having his license suspended no less than three times.

Even when he graduated in 1954 from Orange High School in Waterloo, he and a buddy lined up outside the front entrance of the school on the last day and powered away, creating plenty of noise and smoke to enthrall the kids and exasperate school officials.

But Tom Akin wasn't a bad kid. He just liked going fast and it was sometimes tough to get that desire satisfied as easily as he liked.

76

Akin's dad knew about the need as well and warned him that his traffic troubles were going to jeopardize his life, in more ways than one. The elder Akin had a thriving business in Waterloo catering food every day to the various John Deere locations where workers could pick from a vast array of snacks and food items. And Tom had his role in making that business function, driving a truck daily to meet up with Deere workers and share drinks and vittles.

Akin worked across the street from Wayne's Skelly (later Hedge's Skelly) where Ed Hedges built engines, many of them slated for installation in race cars.

The local racers knew Ed, who raced himself, and counted on his expert advice and building expertise to provide the proper engines for racing at tracks in the area including Tunis Speedway.

Akin's dad had made it clear that Tom was, in no uncertain terms, to be racing...on the street, on the track… no where. He was adamant. He needed him driving those daily rounds and besides, Tom had gotten married and begun his own family, so dad figured it was time for the boy to stop doing "boy things."

Ed Hedges knew about Tom's penchant for speed and one day while he was talking with some fellows about a race car he had just installed an engine into, the conversation turned to who in the area might be available to drive that car.

The 1935 Chevy coupe had belonged to another Tunis Speedway racer, Jack Hickman, and he had sold it to three guys out of Greene, Iowa…Jerry Hagerty, Dean Brinkman and Clarence Jensen. Hedge's built a modified 292 cubic inch six-cylinder GMC engine for the car and it was meant to go plenty fast. None of the owners wanted to drive it.

Hedges suggested a possibility in young Tom and decided to ask the kid if he might get behind the wheel. Akin accepted immediately, but with just a simple request. He couldn't race under his own name. What with his dad and all, the effort would need to be done under another identity. And Tony Conrad was born.

When asked how he came up with the name, Akin said it was a combination of then famous actors Tony Curtis and Robert Conrad, a couple of his favorites. So the deal was set and Akin became the driver of the little coupe.

GREENE IOWA
76
BARTH
CHEVROLET
B&H

And he did pretty well for a couple of years. Neighbors and his wife and kids would pile in the car on Sunday afternoons to head over to Tunis where "Tony Conrad from Greene, Iowa" would join in with the 40+ racers that would show up each week to tear around the ¼ mile Tunis oval.

In 1963 "Tony" managed to get into a spin out on the Tunis track and crashed into some fencing, flipping the car over and generally tearing it up pretty good.

Tunis Feature To Ninth Winner

Now there are nine feature winners.

A crowd of 5,746 Monday saw Tony Conrad of Greene cop the held-over feature that was postponed because of rain Sunday and seven races later watched Darrell Dake of Cedar Rapids win the regular Monday feature in only his second try this year at Tunis Speedway.

Conrad was an easy victor in the opening event as Dake, a veteran driver who appeared here Sunday for the first time this season, finished fifth. Conrad's best finish after that was third in the A semi-main while Dake finished fifth in the B semi before winning a close race in the second feature.

In nine features this season there have been as many winners. Next Sunday's feature will be the 50-lap, mid-season race, named in honor of the late Speed Chumley, with the top 20 cars starting in the order of their current season point standings.

Tunis program

He said he emerged from the car in a bit of a daze, but wasn't really hurt. The track events were being managed by Ira "Speed" Chumley of Waterloo, a local used car dealer who had been influential to build the ¼ mile inside Judd's ½ mile horse track.

Chumley's wife also helped out at the events and was one of the first over to the wreck as Akin crawled from the wreckage. She was checking him over and produced some paperwork that was handed to all the drivers who might be hurt, allowing the track to get them transported to the local hospital to be checked over.

"No way," Akin said and proceeded to explain to Mrs. Chumley that his name wasn't really Tony Conrad and he wasn't really from Greene, Iowa.

"You can't do that," she said and started ripping young Akin up and down for deceiving her and everybody else at the track. He said he shrugged and walked away and managed to come back later in a "new" car, a 1955 Chevy that replaced the '35.

Akin said he got away with the Tony Conrad persona for a couple of years before one night when he came into the pit area after a final race and someone walked up to tell him someone was looking for him.

As he looked toward the gate leading into the pit area, who did he see but, you guessed it, his dad. Akin said his dad simply motioned to him to come his direction and he knew the days of Tony Conrad were probably ended.

But it didn't actually end Akin's racing career and he continued to race for a short time at Tunis, but at the

the same time taking up a brand new interest…drag racing.

In 1966 Akin said he was sometimes racing at the local NEITA Raceway in Cedar Falls in the mornings and then hitting the Tunis track in the evening, which proved to be pretty tiring. As a drag racer he showed his prowess at the start line where he could beat most anyone with his quick reflexes, allowing him a head start before many racers could get their car to move.

Eventually the drag racing took over his race career and he went on to win a number of national championships, at one point piloting a full size Chevrolet station wagon that he specially ordered and had modified to compete against cars half its size.

It was a long but fruitful journey for the speedster from Waterloo and he reflects fondly on his exploits in racing. Even son Rich continues to race today, back on the dirt ovals that are within driving distance of Waterloo and keeping the Akin name active in the sport. That need for speed never quite goes away.

LEAD SLED

Tom Akin, alias Tony Conrad, went on to national prominence in drag racing piloting his now famous Lead Sled 1969 Chevrolet wagon.

How Many Can You identify?

For several years pictures were taken annually of regular drivers and various class winners at Tunis Speedway. Below are just some of those drivers.

Left to right front row, Vern Weber, Red Dralle, Karl Sanger, Joe Schaefer, Ed Sanger, Curt Hansen. Back row is Bonnie Hartwell (promoter), Dan Nesteby, Marv Shafer for Bill Barthelmes, Larry Wasserfort, Harold Cox for Dave Bedard, Glen Martin, Jack Hunt and Keith Knaack.

Bob Posekany

Bob Posekany Heads Cedarloo Race Assn.

Bob Posekany was elected president of the Cedarloo Racing Assn. at its annual meeting here this weekend. The group conducts weekly stock car races at Tunis Speedway here during the summer.

Other officers for the 1966 season will be Guy Rich, vice president; John Hill, secretary; Cal Swanson, treasurer; Jerry Sherbon, sergeant-at-arms, and Gale Card, Glenn Martin and Ed Sanger, trustees.

Other members of the board of directors are Dick Krafka, Stan Stover, Vern Weber and K. L. Kober, legal counsel.

Bob Posekany spent over 20 years racing and helping to promote racing at Tunis Speedway and throughout Iowa.

He headed up the Cedarloo Racing Association in 1965 and helped implement many new safety guidelines for the racers under his guidance.

AFTER FAST 50—Bob Posekany, left, president of Cedarloo Racing Assn., presents the season's championship trophy to Bob Hilmer of Dysart after he won the 50 lap stock car feature race at Cordes Speedway Sunday night in his car No. 22.

POSEKANY
CONST.
CEDAR FALLS
8

THOMAS'
8

POSEKANY CONSTRUCTION
CEDAR FALLS
8

Cal Swanson

Tuning Up for Title Race

Cal Swanson, point leader of the Hawkeye Racing Association, is pictured tuning up his car for Sunday night's 50-lap mid-season championship stock car race at Tunis Speedway here. Swanson, 21 years old, is from Dike and is employed as a truck driver. On the race track he drives No. 5-9. Time trials start at 7.

Cal Swanson began racing pretty much by accident. In 1949 he was attending a race in Cedar Rapids and a driver who was scheduled to race didn't show up. Cal stepped into the driver's seat with no previous experience and found out he was pretty good. Like a lot of drivers, it became a passion.

Cal Swanson Ends Season in First Place

Cal Swanson Sunday eliminated any question concerning the season point standings leader in the Hawkeye Racing Association this season.

Swanson, from Dike, copped the main Sunday night at Tunis to end the season in first place. Red Droste, Waterloo, finished second in the point standings and Bob Hilmer, Dysart, finished third.

The drivers will line up in order of their point standing finish in the 50-lap season championship race next Sunday afternoon.

Only 984 chilled fans watched the stocks race.

Hilmer had the fastest time trial at 19.97.

Results:

Time trials—Bob Hilmer (35), Dysart 19.97.

First heat (10 laps)—Al Runyan (A) Waterloo; Bob Ledtje (141), Gladbrook; Carrol Hilmer (247), Dysart, 3.47.

Second heat (10 laps)—Bob Posekeny (555), Oelwein; Bob Hilmer (35), Dysart; Carrol Hilmer (35A), Dysart, 3.4[illegible]

Third heat (10 laps)—Cal Swanson (5-9), Dike; Gene Peterson (99), Waterloo; Red Sanderson (142), Gladbrook, 3.4[illegible]

Novelty (10 laps)—Mark Kustir (19), Waterloo; Carrol Hilmer (247); Ledtje (142), 3.44.

Semi main (12 laps)—Sanderson (142); Peterson (99); Posekeny (555); Max Taylor (94), Waterloo, 4.32.

Main event (25 laps)—Swanson (5-9); Bob Hilmer (35); Ledtje (141); Gene Hultman (711), Waterloo; Peterson (99); 5.00.

Swanson Wins 50 Lap Race

Cal Swanson, the Hawkeye Racing Association point leader, took off from his pole position and never was headed in winning the 50-lap season championship stock car race before 1,692 fans at Tunis Speedway Sunday afternoon.

Swanson's only serious challenge as he copped the 12½ mile event was from Don Graham, who finished second.

A rough track made the race hazardous, but only one roll over resulted in the feature. Frank Lago of Oelwein went out of control and sommersaulted midway in the event.

Most interesting contest was the neck and neck battle between Arnold Spore and Bob Hilmer well back in the field of 20 starters. At one point they both went over the steep bank on the first turn, but they managed to return to the track and both completed the race. Spore was fifth and Hilmer seventh.

Red Droste, No. 2 in the point standings who started in the position next to Swanson, had trouble with spinouts and fell back to ninth.

Bill Zwanziger, on leave from the service, raced car No. 247 to an eighth place finish.

Time trials—Bob Posekeny (555), Dike: 20.31.

First heat (10 laps)—Al Runyan (33), Waterloo; Bob Hilmer (35), Dysart; Arnold Spore (64), Waterloo; 3:45.

Second heat (10 laps)—Don Graham (121), Waterloo; Harry Peterson (113), Waterloo; Gene Hultman (711), Waterloo; 3.47.

Third heat (10 laps)—Cal Swanson (5-9), Dike; John Hill (89), Marshalltown; Bob Ledtje (141), Gladbrook; 3.44.

Feature (50 laps)—Cal Swanson (5-9), Dike; Don Graham (121), Waterloo; Bob Posekeny (555), Dike; John Hill (89), Marshalltown; Arnold Spore (64), Waterloo; Gene Hultman (711), Waterloo; Bob Hilmer (35), Dysart; Bill Zwanziger (247), Fairbank; Red Droste (245), Waterloo; Carrol Jensen (11), Waterloo; 16.91.

Courier Sports

WATERLOO, IOWA, WEDNESDAY, JULY 22, 1953 — PAGE SEVENTEEN

Swanson Wins; Almost Sure of Pole Position

Cal Swanson, Tunis Speedway stock car driver from Dike, virtually clinched the pole position for the midseason championships scheduled for here next Sunday night, when he won both the time trials and the feature Tuesday night.

Swanson drove the fastest time trial in 19.63 seconds, and then took the feature in to build a substantial point lead over Red Droste of Waterloo.

In the trophy dash Carrol Hilmer, Dysart, won honors under new association rules which eliminates all two-time winners from the dash. Bob Posekeny won the semi-main event.

Russ Steffans of Waterloo was the winner of the rooster race after the dust cleared in the 10-lap much-publicized novelty event. Tuesday's races, which drew 1,725 fans, were rained out last Sunday.

The results:

Time trials—Cal Swanson (5-9), Dike: 19.63.

Trophy dash (6 laps)—Carrol Hilmer (35A), Dysart; Dick Hinton (Circle 4), Waterloo; Russ Steffans (4), Waterloo 2.04.

First heat (10 laps)—Don Graham (45), Cedar Falls; Cal Swanson (5-9), Dike; Don Isley (1), Cedar Falls; 3.36.

Second heat (10 laps)—Bob Hilmer (35) Dysart; John Hill (89), Marshalltown; Carrol Jensen (11), Waterloo; 3.47.

Third Heat (10 laps) — Frank Lago (199x), Oelwein; Harry Peterson (113), Waterloo; Don Isley (00), Cedar Falls; 3.40.

Novelty (10 laps)—Russ Steffans (3), Waterloo; Red Droste (245), Waterloo; Bob Reid (1), Waterloo.

Semi-main (15 laps) — Frank Lago (199x), Oelwein; Bob Posekeny (555), Oelwein; John Hill (89), Marshalltown; Bob Ledtje (141), Gladbrook; (no time, roll over).

Main event (20 laps)—Cal Swanson (5-9); Carrol Jensen (11), Waterloo; Carrol Hilmer (35A), Dysart; Bob Ledtje (141), Gladbrook; Gene Peterson (100), Waterloo; 6.61.

Swanson and Droste Duel for Point Lead

First place in the Hawkeye Racing Association point standings will be at stake Sunday night when Cal Swanson of Dike and Red Droste of Waterloo duel in the stock car races at Tunis Speedway with only a slim ten-point margin between them at the start of the program.

Droste, three time winner of the main, has racked up a season point total of 202 points to Swanson's 192. Cal has won the

Cal Swanson, left, picks up a trophy at the judges' stand as Dale Randall, track announcer, talks with Swanson.

main twice and has been time trials winner five times thus far this season.

Officials of the speedway on Highway 218 between Waterloo and Cedar Falls said recently that Swanson has been coming up rapidly in the past few weeks and stands a good chance of passing Droste in the races Sunday.

Started in 1949.

Formerly of Cedar Falls, Cal Swanson began racing almost by accident. In 1949 Swanson happened to be at the track in Cedar Rapids when one of the drivers failed to show up. Still in his teens, Cal volunteered to take over the driver-less car.

He had never raced before but turned in a good performance and has been racing ever since. He is employed as a truck driver.

Fireworks Display.

Sunday's card will be high-

Swanson Cops Tunis Feature

Cal Swanson of Reinbeck won the feature race at Tunis Speedway Sunday night despite placing only third in the third heat race.

Second place went to Red Droste of Waterloo who also won the B-semi event. Beverly Harberts of Waterloo won the special powder puff derby.

Total purse for the evening was $1,600.

First heat—1. Bob Nesiby (Dubuque), 2. Kale Tibbits (Waterloo), 3. Derrell Sells (Waverly).

Second heat—1. Rich Krafka (Dysart), 2. Roger Klingfus (Waterloo), 3. John Hill (Cedar Falls).

Third heat—1. Bill Zwanziger (Waterloo), 2. Mert Williams (Rochester, Minn.), 3. Cal Swanson (Reinbeck).

A-semi—1. Krafka, 2. Ty Burger (Waterloo), 3. Nesiby, 4. Karl Sanger (Waterloo), 5. Curt Hansen (Dike), 6. Tibbits.

B-semi—1. Red Droste (Waterloo), 2. Ed Sanger (Waterloo), 3. Glen Martin (Waterloo), 4. John Connelly (Delhi), 5. Chub Liebe (Oelwein), 6. Williams.

Consolation—1. Dave Noble (Blooming Prairie, Minn.), 2. Dave Worthen (Oelwein), 3. Dick Helden (Cedar Rapids), 4. Don Donovan (Brandon), 5. Claus Stricker (Waterloo), 6. Willie Klingfus (Waterloo).

Feature—1. Swanson, 2. Droste, 3. R. Krafka, 4. Connelly, 5. Nesiby, 6. Martin, 7. Hill, 8. Worthen, 9. Zwanziger, 10. Noble.

Cadet—1. Ron Plum (Waterloo), 2. Chuck Larsen (Waterloo).

Powder puff derby—1. Beverly Harberts (Waterloo), 2. Gaye Ryan (Waterloo).

SATURDAY AT INDEPENDENCE

First Heat—1. Don Donovan, Brandon; 2. Roger Kress, Independence; 3. Bob Hartman, Cedar Rapids.

Second Heat—1. Curt Hansen, Dike; 2. Bill Zwanziger, Waterloo; 3. Dave Worthen, Oelwein.

Third Heat—1. Dick Helden, Cedar Rapids; 2. Dick Nesiby, Dubuque; 3. Paul Fitzpatrick, Rochester, Minn.

A Semi—1. Worthen; 2. Donovan; 3. Kruse; 4. Hansen; 5. Hartman; 6. Roger Klingfus, Waterloo.

B Semi—1. John Webb, Independence; 2. Zwanziger; 3. Rich Krafka, Dysart; 4. Red Droste, Waterloo; 5. Chub Liebe, Oelwein; 6. Nesiby.

Consolation—1. Ed Sanger, Waterloo; 2. Ty Berger, Waterloo; 3. Stan Stover, [illegible]; 4. Karl Sanger, Waterloo; 5 [illegible]

Brakes? Who Needs Brakes?

Like many young boys of his generation, 15-year-old Dale Osborn was fascinated with cars. Not just the look or design, but the speed and the power of the machines.

Today the 80+ year-old still remembers that first time he was allowed inside a car to do just one thing…go fast. And it changed his life from that moment on.

APCO

Dale Osborn

"I was hanging around the pits at Tunis Speedway in Waterloo," Cedar Falls resident Osborn explains. "I was at the track working, picking up rocks off the track so they wouldn't get tossed into the crowds during the races."

Osborn says he was standing trackside watching the racers doing hot laps or practicing on the race course. "Red (John) Broline, who owned a few cars and sponsored drivers, was nearby," Osborn says, "when he came over and said, 'you should try that!' pointing out a well-worn 1937 Ford sedan.

Osborn said this was 1953 so the race cars were big and heavy and the car Broline pointed out to the young kid looked especially huge to the would-be racer.

72

"I jumped in", he explains, "and headed out onto the track." Osborn was suddenly part of the racing world.

"I got out there and discovered a couple of things. The steering was so bad that you had to turn the wheel nearly a half turn before the car would even respond in either direction and there were no brakes."

Osborn pulled up into the crowd of vehicles taking their laps and promptly got mixed into a minor fender bender with several cars. Back into the pits he came.

"What's the matter?" Broline yelled as the kid jumped out, the car slowly rolling to a stop. "The steering is shot and there aren't any brakes!" Osborn shouted.

"Brakes? Who needs brakes?" Broline is claimed to have said, peppered with a bit of salty language for emphasis. "You don't need brakes! You have that pedal over there on the right side (describing the throttle pedal). That's all you need!"

John Broline

Osborn said after that experience he was hooked, even though he admits that being out on the track among all that machinery was frightening. "I'm certain that is when I got the bug to race and it's never completely gone away."

DALE
72
McINROY
SPECIAL

D. Arthur Nesteby

Nesteby laps eight cars enroute to Tunis victory

By JIM FICKESS
Courier Sports Writer

D. Arthur Nesteby had to repeatedly execute one of stock car racing's most potentially dangerous maneuvers—lapping an opponent—during Sunday night's Tunis Speedway late model feature and came out of it unscathe with the checkered flag.

Nes' ... ing point-... lappe... cars ... the 2... Me...

the second place car is gaining on you.

"The guys I lapped tonight were real cooperative and let me by," praised Nesteby.

That fact, which reduced the odds of Nesteby getting in pileup while trying to get around a slower-moving machine, was just one of three reasons the Waterloo driver enjoyed a large margin of

Tim Swope won the tightly contested first heat with Willy Klingfus (second) and Tom Moore (third) close on his tail. Marshall Hilmer scored his second heat win in as many weeks in the second preliminary before Roger Klingfus was a comfortable winner in the third 10-lapper.

PATTERSON took the lead

(Oysart); 2. Jim Buhlman (Waterloo); 3. Tom Bartholomew (Waterloo).

THIRD HEAT—1. Roger Klingfus (Waterloo); 2. Bob Hesse (Waterloo); 3. Bob Hamer (Dysart).

FIRST SEMI—1. Wayne Hesse (Waterloo); 2. Dave Plum (Waterloo); 3. Tom Hamilton (Jesup); 4. Kenny McCombs (Waterloo).

SECOND SEMI—1. Arthur Nesteby (Waterloo); 2. Darrell Sells (Waverly); 3. Jack Mitchell (Cedar Falls); 4. Denny Osborn (Cedar Falls).

CONSOLATION—Duane Van Deest (Grundy Center).

FEATURE—1. Nesteby; 2. Bartholomew; 3. Osborn; 4. B. Hilmer; 5. Hamilton; 6. Sells; 7. M. Hilmer; 8. Plum; 9. Karl Sanger (Waterloo); 10. Buhlman.

14 Waterloo Courier Fri., Aug. 22, 1975

Nesteby chooses outside; wins

By JIM FICKESS
Courier Sports Writer

A pre-race decision appears to have spelled the difference between first and second place for Tunis Speedway late model season champion D. Arthur Nesteby Sunday night.

Nesteby exercised his option as point leader before the 50-lap title race and chose to run on the outside instead of the ... first row.

...ision was crucial, ...e least," smiled ...o took advantage ... high groove and ...rl Sanger for the ...n-finale to claim a ... victory and the ...

...most had to wait ...ake a mistake on ...tonight," asserted

...S right on my tail ... race, that's for ... Waterloo stocker

...ouldn't see him for ...half of the race. A ...aud flew up and

flawless race which was totally free of any restart-causing accidents. Sanger was equally as brilliant.

"Dan couldn't be beat the way he was driving tonight," commented Sanger. "It was a one-groove track all the way.

"I MANAGED to get my inside the back of his car in the corners, but then I'd hit some grease (wet dirt which has no traction) and almost lose control," said Sanger. "I could catch him on the straights but he could pull 100 feet on me in the corners," continued Karl, whose car is set up primarily for a half-mile. Nesteby's machine is strictly a quarter-mile car.

The first half of the race was a three-car battle. Evansdale's Red Dralle kept right on Nesteby's and Sanger's tails early but fell off the pace some and managed to take third place by a wide margin.

Tom Bartholomew of Washburn finished fourth as just eight cars out of the starting

overcome four restarts and a field of 24 cars for his title.

Nesteby won the semi-main earlier in the evening. The eventual champ took the lead from Waterloo's Dave Auringer after an eighth-lap restart and widened his margin for the remainder fo the contest.

Auringer bounced back and won the consolation event, getting by leader Tom Moore on the homestretch of the final lap in the most thrilling race of the evening.

Denny McCombs and Bob Hesse scored relatively easy victories in the two late model heats.

The Tunis title furthered Nesteby's outstanding winning string. The five-year late model veteran won three features—his seventh straight main event at Boone Friday night and his second Independence 25-lapper of the season Saturday—as well as Tunis Sunday. He's now claimed five features in the six programs he competed in over the past three weekends.

Jim Fickess'
column

Nesteby, Sanger to battle in 50-lapper

NO TWO STOCK CAR races will probably every by exactly the same, even if the same cars, starting order and track are used. Too many variables come into play—differing mechanical performances, drivers' ability and a big factor in most races, just plain luck—to allow any race, much less a season championship event, be a carbon copy of a previous one.

Although the same will more than likely hold true for Sunday's 50-lap late model title race at Tunis Speedway, several similarities could lead to the same drivers placing high that did last year.

D. Arthur Nesteby

The main repeating feature of this year's race is the top two point leaders.

D. Arthur Nesteby and Karl Sanger, both of Waterloo, are once again No. 1 and 2 going into the championship night and will occupy the front row of the starting grid.

Nesteby, who will be on the inside pole Sunday, virt... year's race before ... moter Claus Strick... a choice of starting ... outside of the fron... now-defunct quarter-mile track.

D. Arthur, who came into his own as a late ... 1974, realized the track had just one good gr... high—and began on the outside of Sanger. Ka... stick on Nesteby's trail the entire race and w... to capitalize on a costly mistake which never c...

THE NEW THREE-EIGHTHS mile track ... differences this year. It has proven to be mo...

Nesteby running checkered laps; lean years gone

By JIM FICKESS
Courier Sports Writer

In stock car racing as in any other sport, there is a fine, often times undefinable, line which seperates the few outstandings performers from the multitude of also-rans.

Waterloo stock car driver Dan (D. Arthur) Nesteby ...

ber Heiberger said: "But it just doesn't make sense. We know we aren't set up to run the big tracks, so why switch while you're winning?

"We realize our limitations."

And, Gerst has a reply to those drivers who condemn

D. Arthur Nesteby
...ry's
F... OOD DRIVE-INS
9

2nd Tunis feature to Nesteby

By JIM FICKESS
Courier Sports Writer

Losing full control after getting up too high on the track proved costly in Sunday night's late model stock car feature at Tunis Speedway.

Defending track champion ... Nesteby became ...river to win two ...s at Tunis this ... a pair of leaders ...lves out of conten-...

...anaged to stay in ...-mile's high grove ...ng his brakes on

...Sells of Waverly ... 25-lapper on the ...the first row and ... grabbed a wide ...e other 17 cars. ...inued to build his ...til a three-car ...e 13th lap necessi-...art.

SELLS AGAIN pulled away from the pack off the restart but went too high on the fourth turn of lap No. 13. Bill Barthelmes led six cars down under Sells before he was able to regain full speed.

Barthelmes led for the next seven laps before going off the track's high groove on the second turn of lap 19, where Nesteby took over.

Nesteby held off a charge by Glen Martin and won the $400 first place check by a full car length.

"I lost my brakes the lap after that restart," Nesteby recalled. "Luckily I was out of the traffic by then. If I wouldn't have been, I probably would have caused a wreck before I could have controlled it."

Barthelmes wound up third

See TUNIS
Continued on page 15, col. 8

Arnie Spore

Spore Seeking Second Victory

Arnold Spore, who has one leg on the new traveling trophy awarded the feature race winner, will attempt to cut into Red Droste's point lead and take another step toward retiring the trophy in Sunday night's stock car races at Tunis Speedway.

Spore won last week's feature after Droste won the first three this year in succession.

The time trials as usual start at 7 p. m. Sunday with the first of seven races at 8.

First Stock Car Title to Spore

Arnold Spore of Waterloo won the season's first stock car main before 927 opening day fans at Tunis Speedway Sunday afternoon on a heavy track.

He outraced 15 rivals in the 20-lap windup event for his second victory of the day. Spore won the third heat after finishing third behind Red Droste and Al Runyon in the time trials. Droste won the second heat.

A total of 24 cars drove in the trials.

One of the early "driver feuds" that helped fuel spectator interest...Arnie Spore and Red Droste--1954

▼▼▼▼▼▼▼▼

Spore Wins Again in Stock Car Races at Tunis Track

Arnold Spore still is the only driver to win a feature stock car racing event at Tunis Speedway here.

Sunday he won his second straight feature in as many Sundays of racing as 1,214 fans looked on.

Bob Hilmer and Gene Peterson finished second and third. Spore had finished third behind Peterson and Carroll Jensen in

"ARNIE"
FORD 121

2531 FALLS AVE. • WATERLOO
ARNIE
JIM
CORDES
FORD
INC.
CARS
TRUCKS
SIGNS
21

7
HOOK'S
WATERLOO, IA.

Jerry Sherbon

300

3

EVANSDALE SHELL SERVICE
300

99

"You Got a Ride!"

For Larry Wasserfort, he was in the right place at the right time to begin his racing career.

"I started racing in 1970 in late model," he explains. "My first race ever was at Tunis is car #2, a car I had helped Denny Hankes build during the winter before that 1970 season."

Wasserfort said when the car was all done, all that was left was to "set the seat" for the driver. "I don't remember who the driver was supposed to be, but he told Hankes he was too busy to come over to get that last part of the car done."

Wasserfort went on to say that Hankes was mad about that and turned to him saying "you got a ride." "I had told him I was interested in sometime trying my hand at driving, so here was the chance."

"I didn't think much about it at the time but I went out and won several feature races that first year." Not only did Wasserfort win features, but was named Rookie of the Year at the Independence track and then managed to pick up a driving opportunity with Ed Sanger's stable of cars.

Wasserfort enjoyed success at both Tunis and surrounding tracks for a number of years and admits he had some great memories of racing against great drivers and in many memorable races.

Second Year Driver Takes Downs Feature

Big Win for Wasserfort

By Al Miller
Gazette Sports Writer

Larry Wasserfort is in only his second year of stock car racing, but that's difficult to believe after watching him perform in the All-Iowa fair races Friday night at Hawkeye Downs.

The 26-year-old late-model pilot from Waterloo capped his biggest night in racing by running off with the 25-lap feature on the quarter-mile dirt track before an estimated crowd of 6,500.

It was simply no contest for Wasserfort. He started his 1967 Chevelle on the pole in the 18-car finale, maintained the lead through the first lap and won going away.

He finished nearly half a lap ahead of Ed Sanger of Waterloo ('70 Monte Carlo) and pocketed $400 for the victory. Larry also copped the 15-lap semi and placed second in the second heat.

LARRY WASSERFORT

He was, to say the least, surprised at his good fortune.

"The car was working pretty good," Wasserfort explained, "but not as well as in the past when I didn't win. I didn't think I was getting all the horses I should tonight.

badly before he lost a right-rear tire and faded fast. Dave Trower came in second and in the process regained the point lead from Becker.

Becker went into the race with only a 10-point margin over Trower.

Frank Neustel of Central City finished third, with Bill Wright of C. R. fourth and Jim Stodola of Shellsburg fifth.

LATE MODEL

Feature (25 laps): 1. Larry Wasserfort, Waterloo; 2. Ed Sanger, Waterloo; 3. Bill McDonough, Cedar Rapids; 4. Don Nesteby, Waterloo; 5. Chub Liebe, Oelwein; 6. Red Oralle, Waterloo; 7. Bill Barthelmes, Troy Mills; 8. Bill Zwanziger, Waterloo.

Semi (15 laps): 1. Wasserfort; 2. Joe Schaefer, Waterloo; 3. Cal Swanson, Reinbeck; 4. Bill Beckman, Lisbon; 5. Barthelmes; 6. Dale Snyder, Cedar Rapids.

Fast-car dash (10): 1. E. Sanger; 2. Oralle; 3. Liebe; 4. McDonough; 5. Dr. Al Mayner, Winthrop; 6. Curt Hansen, Dike.

1st heat (10 laps): 1. McDonough; 2. Zwanziger; 3. Hansen; 4. Dr. Mayner.

2nd heat (10 laps): 1. Swanson; 2. Wasserfort; 3. Snyder; 4. Nesteby.

SPORTSMAN

Feature (15 laps): 1. Ron Fisher, Cedar Rapids; 2. Dave Trower, Cedar Rapids; 3. Frank Neustel, Central City; 4. Bill Wright, Cedar Rapids; 5. Jim Stodola, Shellsburg; 6. Max Overturf, Cedar Rapids.

"One of my most memorable races was driving the Mile Track in Springfield, Illinois," said Wasserfort as he recounted some of those memories. "Started 36th and finished 3rd!"

"I had so many memorable moments, made so many friends, had so much fun, it is hard to pick out the highlights. Racing, for me, was truly one of the greatest highlights of my life."

WHEELS BY Tournier
AYR-WAY
2

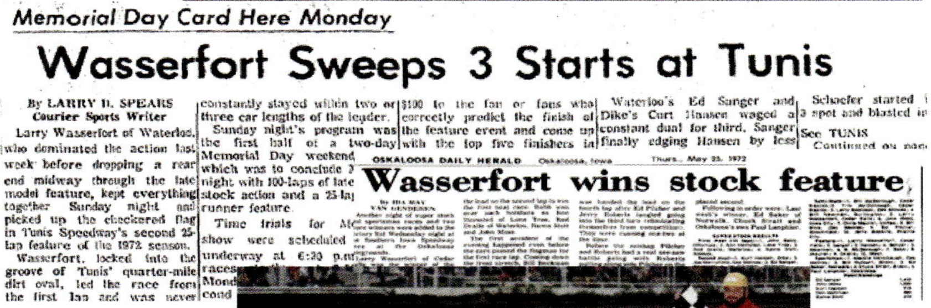

Memorial Day Card Here Monday

Wasserfort Sweeps 3 Starts at Tunis

By LARRY D. SPEARS
Courier Sports Writer

Larry Wasserfort of Waterloo, who dominated the action last week before dropping a rear end midway through the late model feature, kept everything together Sunday night and picked up the checkered flag in Tunis Speedway's second 25-lap feature of the 1972 season.

Wasserfort, locked into the groove of Tunis' quarter-mile dirt oval, led the race from the first lap and was never constantly stayed within two or three car lengths of the leader.

Sunday night's program was the first half of a two-day Memorial Day weekend which was to conclude ... night with 100-laps of late stock action and a 25-la... runner feature.

Time trials for M... show were scheduled ... underway at 6:30 p.m... races... Mond... cond...

$100 to the fan or fans who correctly predict the finish of the feature event and come up with the top five finishers in

Waterloo's Ed Sanger and Dike's Curt Hansen waged a constant dual for third, Sanger finally edging Hansen by less

Schaefer started ... 3 spot and blasted in

See TUNIS
Continued on page

OSKALOOSA DAILY HERALD Oskaloosa, Iowa Thurs., May 25, 1972

Wasserfort wins stock feature

49

Herman Wenzel

121

In 1950 Herman Wenzel decided to go racing. Like any young guy, he was attracted to the excitement and wanted to be part of the growing racer community.

At the same time he applied to become a fireman with the Waterloo Fire Department. He managed to achieve both of his dreams except, the fire department really didn't want to have one of their finest tangled up in a race car.

The story goes that Wenzel at one point was called into a superior's office and told he would have to give up compeititve driving. And he did.

OMOTIVE

Gary Kaune

76
The Dugout

1978 POINT LEADERS ROADRUNNERS
Ben Cunningham, Gary Kaune, Scott Braun (leader).

76

Gary Kaune was Roadrunner track champion in 1970.

Like Son, Like Father

Families were involved throughout the Tunis years and many brother combinations became active participants in the dirt oval contests.

The Hesse family was just one of many but the patriarch, Henry, arrived at racing in the opposite way most people began their speedy exploits.

BOB'S
DX
22
Lloyd and Henry Hesse

Lloyd Hesse began racing at the tender age of 17 after working at the track for Judd Tunis (and also in Judd's butcher shop). Like all novice drivers, he saw the excitement and challenge and won two times, once in 1957 and the other in 1958. And while it is likely most drivers pestered their fathers to drive, that wasn't the case with Lloyd. It was Dad Henry who pestered him.

Bob Hesse

After seeing Lloyd race three times he asked Lloyd if he, Henry, could drive in a race. Lloyd refused so Henry went out and bought his own car, showing up the following week to race.

In the meantime Lloyd was experiencing some financial problems that pushed him to sell his own race car, but he wasn't worried because he figured he'd just drive Dad's car.

Not so fast, said "Pops", the name the track denizens attached to Henry once he got started. Lloyd wasn't driving Dad's car. No how, No way.

Brother Bob Hesse soon joined the racing ranks and the Hesse family began racing in earnest, finding they could roll over and burn through engines with the best of them. At one point the three calculated they had destroyed no less than 12 engines in a three seasons of racing. Oh, well. That's racing.

Bob Hesse kept his racing career going well into the 1970s taking on the likes of some of the bigger names of the era.

Bob Hesse comes from 5th to win

By DAVE PAXTON
Courier Sports Writer

Bob Hesse came from a fifth row starting position to take the lead in the Tunis Speedway late model feature Sunday in the sixth lap and was never really challenged after that as he cruised for the 25-lap victory.

In the position following Hesse, however, Karl Sanger, Roger Klingfus and Dan Nesteby fought it out and finally ended up 3rd, 4th and 5th respectively.

Before his big win Hesse had managed only a third place finish in his late model heat and didn't place in the top three in either of the semi-main events.

Hesse, who currently stands before he crossed the finish line for the flag.

Mike Krall won the sportsman heat and John Duwa finished second in the sportsman feature.

In the only roadrunner race of the eveining Dave Frost picked his way through three major pile-ups and two red flags to capture that 10-lap feature race.

Total point standings for the Tunis Speedway show D. Arthur Nesteby leading the pack by a comfortable 180-point margin with 2,385 points.

Nesteby is followed by Glen

LATE MODEL

FIRST HEAT—1. Dave Beard (LaPorte City); 2. Kim Swope (Raymond); 3. Greg Kasti (Waterloo).

SECOND HEAT—1. Jim Decker (Winthrop); 2. Tom Hamilton (Jesup); 3. Kenny McCombs (Waterloo).

56

Hesse, Dralle win at Tunis

By JIM FICKESS
Courier Sports Writer

Tunis Speedway's three-eighths of a mile stock car track got off to a rousing debut Sunday night. The largest crowd in several years watched Waterloo's Bob Hesse and Red Dralle of Evansdale win late model features in a program which featured some of the season's best racing.

Hesse captured the first race ever on the lengthened remodeled track, a 25-lap feature rained out the previous Sunday. Dralle's triumph came in a 30-lap Fourth of July weekend main event.

A total of 4,848 spectators paid their way into Tunis Sunday. That marks the largest paying gate since 5,100 turned out for Tunis four years ago when Keith Knaack of Vinton was the promoter.

Knaack, the publisher of Hawkeye Racing News, was at Sunday's races and guessed the total crowd was greater than the night he drew 5,100. Knaack agreed with other observers who unoffically estimated the crowd was in the 7,000-neighborhood.

HESSE AND Dralle drove different styles of races for their victories.

Dralle took the lead from Waterloo's Roger Klingfus on the eighth lap after starting on the outside of the second row. The Evansdale pilot added to a comfortable lead throughout the remaining 22 laps for his second Tunis win of the season.

Glen Martin of Independence edged Hesse out of second place on the next-to-last lap of the 30-circuit race. Hesse was third and Bill Barthelmes of Walker fourth.

Hesse held off a late Barthelmes charge to win the evening's initial race.

Actually, Hesse's first feature win of 1975 spanned a week. He led when the race was stopped by an accident a week earlier. It started to rain before the track's guard rail could be repaired that night.

The red-headed Tunis veteran, therefore, started on the pole for Sunday's 24 remaining laps. He was challenged early by Cedar Falls' Jim Burger before Barthelmes made his move.

BARTHELMES overtook Burger on lap No. 18 and immediately went for Hesse.

He was door-to-door with Hesse and appeared to be almost around him a couple times in the final few laps.

Hesse found that elusive something extra and pulled to a car-length margin at the checkered flag.

Sunday's large slate of racing was shortened by an accident in the first of two scheduled roadrunner heats.

Three cars collided in front of the flagman's stand with Dave Rice flipping his machine. Rice was uninjured but another driver involved,

See TUNIS
Continued page 15, col. 2

Les Schmitz

LES
SCHAEFER'S
TAVERN
WASHBURN
IA.
218

777

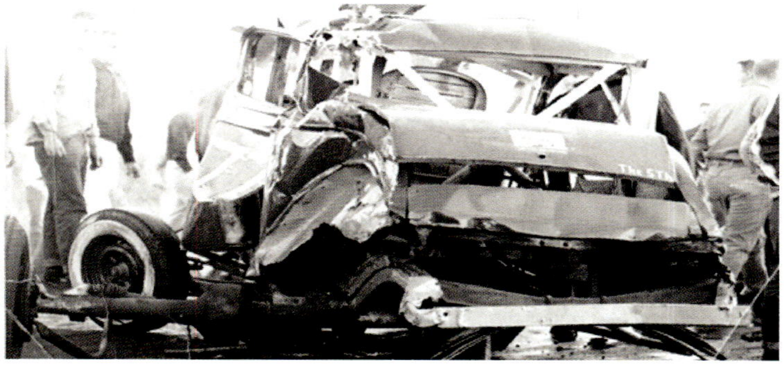

Willy Klingfuss

Reninger CONST.
CEDAR FALLS, IA. 266-3930
Evergreen
LOUNGE
Challenger

Buick 440 cu
26
WILLY
CEDAR
HIDEAWAY TAVERN
FALLS

6
PLYMOUTH

26

Gene Hultman

Summer Sunday nights as a kid were spent at the race track. Because Dad raced we would get there early.

We always sat in the same section of seats just to the right of the main entrance facing the race track about one third of the way up.

My Aunt Joyce (Jensen) and her three boys along with Mom and her three girls comprised the core group. Others would join us from race to race.

Dad and my uncle Carroll Jensen were sponsored by Hook's Radiator.

--Rebecca (Hultman) Schildroth

Stan Stover

49
STEPHANS
REINBECK
IOWA

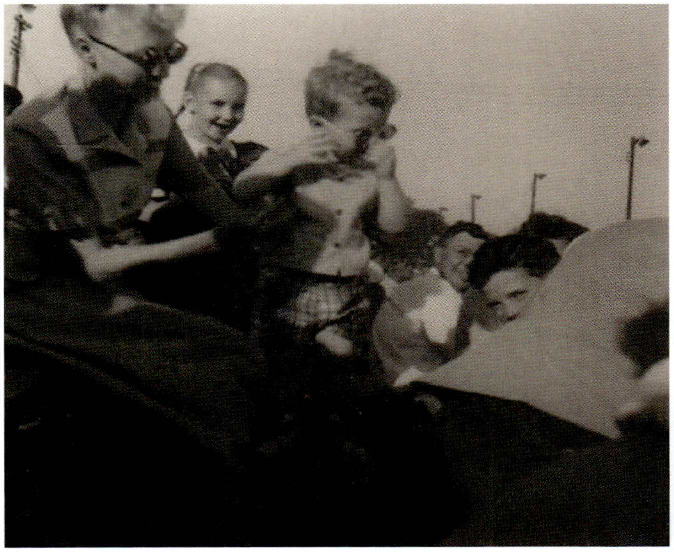

For a lot of families, spending Sunday evening at the races was just a part of their weekly, warm weather routine. Sitting in the stands, rooting on your favorite drivers, particularly if they were friends or family, really made these times extra special and memorable!

3,500 Bikini Night Fans

Stover Takes Feature

By LARRY D. SPEARS
Courier Sports Writer

Spurred on by a whole bevy of bikinied beauties, a newly-crowned Tunis "Bikini Queen," and the largest crowd of the 1972 season, Tunis Speedway's stock car drivers put on one of the finest racing shows in Iowa history Sunday night.

Whether the 44 drivers present were inspired by the crowd of approximately 3,500 or merely fired up after their duties as judges in Tunis' first Bikini Contest isn't known, but they recovered from a pair of lackluster late model heat races to put fans on their feet numerous times with outstanding high-speed, bumper-to-bumper and fender-to-fender racing action.

Both the 20-lap roadrunner feature, finally captured by Marshalltown's Earl Pruitt, and the 25-lap late model main, taken by Reinbeck's Stan Stover, were the most hotly contested of the year.

Stover, who's first feature win of the season completed a sweep of races for the evening, was constantly in jeopardy during the 25 circuits of the quarter-mile dirt oval. Six other cars, all running flat out, were within easy striking distance, ready to take advantage of any mistake by the leaders.

Drive Train Goes

And, Stover didn't have a free ride into the top spot. Jim Burger of Cedar Falls started in the No. 1 spot in the feature and blasted out of the pack and by Joe Schaefer on the third lap. Burger, his No. 21 Camaro running harder than it has all year, quickly opened up a wide lead over the rest of the cars, still tangled in the pack, but disaster struck on the eighth circuit.

With the engine still screaming, his drive train let go down the front straight and he was forced to pull off the track letting Schaefer, from Waterloo, regain the lead.

By that time, Stover had moved up from his No. 5 starting position and was right on top of Schaefer with Tunis points leader Ed Sanger close behind.

Those three cars, along with Red Dralle of Evansdale, already back after a serious roll-over Saturday night at Independence, jockeyed for position without a change in order until the 19th lap, often barreling through the turns as many as three abreast.

Goes Low

Then, on the 20th circuit, Schaefer slipped too high and Stover got by on the underside. Taking advantage of Schaefer's loss of control, both Sanger and Dralle passed as well, going on to a one-two-three finish five laps later.

Schaefer got passed one more time, winding up in fifth behind Karl Sanger of Waterloo, but still stayed within four lengths of the winner.

Larry Wasserfort of Waterloo, Curt Hansen of Dike and Bob Hesse of Waterloo were tightly packed about three lengths further back, while Arnie Braland of Boone, Roger Klingfus of Cedar Falls and Dave Plum of Waterloo all finished on the same lap as the leaders.

Plum was also involved in one of the year's most thrilling finishes in the consi. Starting in the No. 2 spot in the six-lapper, Plum had built up a lead of almost eight lengths coming into the final turn of the race.

But, he got a little too high and Independence's Gary Crawford highballed through the No. 4 turn in a desperate catch-up bid. The maneuver worked as the two cars streaked down the final straight side-by-side, sparks flying high into the air from the scraping metal and Crawford taking the checkered flag by two feet.

Klingfus Takes First

In earlier action, Klingfus edged Schaefer by less than a length for the first heat win; Stover ran away with the second heat; and Hanson fought off Hesse for the semi victory.

Pruitt survived three early field-reducing restarts in the roadrunner event, then outdueled Chuck Larson of Cedar Falls for the victory, his first of the year.

Tunis promoter Claus Stricker, Stan Stover and Gary Kaune, 1973.

Hultman Takes Feature for First Major Win of Season

Gene Hultman of Waterloo scored his first major victory of the season here Sunday night when he won the main event of the stock car races at Tunis Speedway before 3,043 fans.

He beat out Carrol Jensen of Waterloo in the feature to finish a night of racing that included four crashes.

One of the accidents sent Bob Roe to the hospital, but he was released after x-ray examination. He was shaken up in a tangle [illegible]

Gene
HOOK'S RADIATOR
711

STAN STOVER
HOOK'S
ERFORMANCE
NGINEERING
49

Point-Leader Stover Wins

By JIM FICKESS
Courier Sports Writer

Tunis Speedway's 25th consecutive year of stock car racing ended on a chilly, but thrilling, note as Stan Stover of Reinbeck won the late-model season championship Sunday.

Stover, who gained the pole position for the 35-lap title race by virtue of being the [illegible]

mechanical problems on the 13th lap of the roadrunner.

THE SUNDAY twilight program was marred by three roll-overs as none of the drivers involved were seriously injured.

Denny Osborn of Cedar Falls had the dubious honor of the most spectacular roll-over of the day as his machine [illegible]

liminary and Hilmer the third.

Waterloo's Carroll Jensen enjoyed an easy win in the consolation event.

The Hare 'N' Hound mini-demolition derby was called off since one of the cars had a ruptured gas tank.

One of the smallest crowds of the season was on hand to [illegible]

Don Feckers

DON
244

DON
24

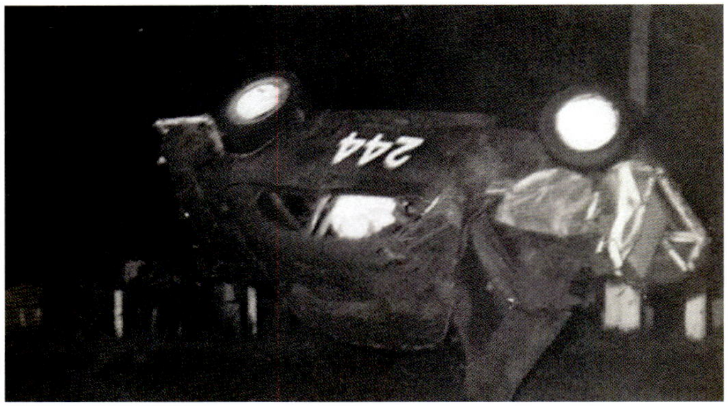

244

218

244

ED'S SKELLY

Darlene Feckers

DON
244

ZIP
GAS
144

Dick Feckers

Racing to Fulfill a Dream

From 1953 to 1968 John Hill devoted a lot of time to fulfilling his dream of being a race car driver. He was good friends with Dale Osborn, another driver yearning to get out on the track, and the two youngsters bought a couple of topless cars and headed for Tunis Speedway to try out their talents.

Unfortunately the speedway soon outlawed using cars with no tops and the two novice drivers headed out to Hill's family farm where they tore around the fields in the jalopies until they could scrape together the needed funds to field a real race car.

That happened soon enough and Hill was on the Tunis and Vinton tracks on a regular basis, racing the number 89 until passing it off to Lee Kunzman of Guttenberg when Hill took a couple years off during the mid 60s.

He came back as car number 71, racing until 1968 when he finally decided racing was getting too hard for a young family man to continue and sold his 1966 Chevelle to an aspiring A.E. (Doc) Mayner of Winthrop who went on to become a legend of sorts within the racing community of Northeast Iowa.

John Hill's son Scott said his Dad was friends with many of the drivers who continued to race at Tunis and in the local area for many years after he decided to hang up his goggles and helmet for good.

71

71

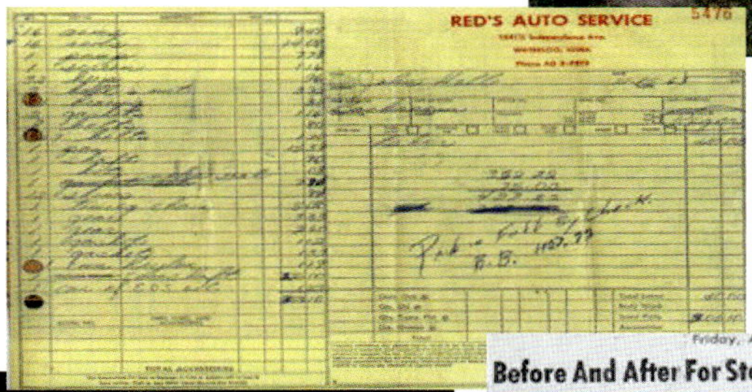
RED'S AUTO SERVICE

Friday, April 28, 1967 Cedar Falls Daily Record

Before And After For Stock Car . . .

71
DIKE OIL CO.

Here's the before and after sequence of four enterprising racing enthusiasts who bought this wrecked car in February and with many long hours of hard work came up with this flashy hard-top stock car racer which will get its first test May 6 at Independence. The four proud men who accomplished the miracle are owners Stan Hermansen, Dike, Ronnie Nie, Waterloo, and John Hill, Cedar Falls, who is also the driver, and Hill's son, Scott, who serves as the head mechanic. The four will race the car on the Independence Racing Association circuit which includes Monticello, and Waterloo too. First showing of the racer in Waterloo will be May 14. The car is a 1966 Chevrolet with a 427 cubic inch engine in it.

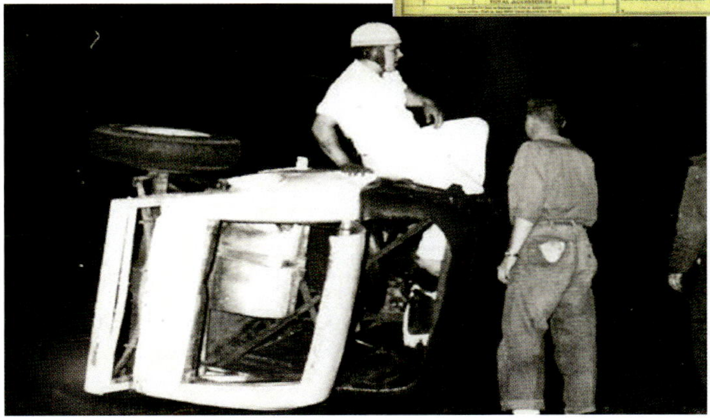

144
DIKE OIL CO.

Jensen, Lahre Capture Season Titles at Tunis

Waterloo's Buss Jensen and Joan Lahre of Manchester won season championships in their respective races at Tunis Speedway here Monday night.

Jensen raced to the novice season championship, defeating Mike Plumm of Waterloo, who placed second. Jack Wentworth, also of Waterloo, wound up third.

Lahre edged Judy Neithe and Betty Halligan of Waterloo for the Powder Puff derby season championship.

In the 20-lap feature John Connely of Delhi placed f i r s t, followed by Waterloo's Bill Zwanziger. Verlin Eaker of Austin, Minn., who won the third heat and "B" semi. was third in the feature.

First heat (10 laps)—1. Whitey Minnecus, Cedar Falls; 2. Reber, Waterloo; 3. Chuck Smith, Owatonna, Minn.; 3:46.
Second heat (10 laps)—1. Bill Borgbohn, Waterloo; 2. S. Slover, Reinbeck; 3. Leonard Carlson, Waterloo.
Third heat (10 laps)—1. Verlin Eaker, Austin, Minn.; 2. Bob Hilmer, Dysart; 3. Cal Swanson, Cedar Falls; 3:06.
"A" Semi (15 laps)—1. Chuck Smith, Cedar Falls; 3. Merlin Benning, Waverly.
"B" Semi (15 laps)—1. Verlin Eaker, Austin, Minn.; 2. John Connely, Delhi; 3. Bob Hilmer, Dysart.
Consolation (15 laps)—1. Tom Hughes, ... 2. Mike Plumm, Waterloo; Jack Wentworth, Waterloo.
Powder Puff—1. Joan Lahre, Manchester; 2. Judy Neithe, Waterloo; 3. Halligan, Waterloo.

Betty Halligan, above and below

Powder Puff

Like many race tracks, Tunis Speedway made room for the ladies to get out on the track and churn up some dirt and battle for some trophies. Though it wasn't a regular weekly event, it was often enough that the fans enjoyed the special races reserved for many a male racer's companion, friend or family.

ED'S SKELLY

'Powder Puff Derby' Slated At Tunis Sun.

The season's firt Powder Puff Derby — a chance for the ladies — will come off this Sunday night at Tunis Speedway.

The track reports that quite a few entries have been received for the distaff derby.

Women to Drive Stock Cars at Tunis Speedway Tuesday

Women drivers will be behind the wheel for the first time at Tunis Speedway this Tuesday when they'll take over for one event in the holiday stock car races.

Mrs. George Bare and Mrs. Bill St. Clair of Waterloo are expected to drive against women from Cedar Rapids and Davenport, and track officials hope to line up a field of more than 10 women and cars.

Dottie Harris, who won the women's race at Cedar Rapids two weeks ago, is scheduled to be on hand. Any other women over 21 years of age interested in driving may contact the Tunis Speedway so that cars for them to drive can be obtained.

Time trials are set for 7 p. m. Tuesday night, with the first race at 8:15, and rivalry is expected between stock car drivers of Waterloo and Cedar Falls and those from Cedar Rapids and

BIG 64
CARLSPLACE

135

Woman in Runaway Car Causes Racing Officials Problem; Moffett Wins 6th

Charley Moffett finally won his sixth modified stock car feature of the season and Betty Hulligan won the Powder Puff Derby, but it was Bess Albertson who caused the greatest excitement at Tunis Speedway here Monday night.

Mrs. Albertson, a Powder Puff contestant, ran wild in a runaway novice car for a good 10 minutes before Cedarloo Racing President Speed Chumley corraled her with a jeep.

The trouble started when an accident early in the race forced starter Vinton Jones to halt the cars with a red flag. As Jones waved the flag, all the cars stopped—except a green No. 7, with Mrs. Albertson inside. As Jones waved the flag, Mrs. Albertson waved back and continued around the track at near top speed.

THE NEXT TIME around, Jones waved the flag and she waved back again. Jones didn't think it was so funny this time, and when she came around again he jumped out in front of her, violently shaking the flag. This time she didn't wave back but she didn't stop either. Jones jumped.

It was then apparent that the throttle must be stuck, so officials began shouting, "Shut off the key!" That was no solution since the car didn't have a starter switch but was wired directly.

Several times the cars rode up on two wheels on the verge of rolling, but each time Mrs. Albertson brought it down again. At times, the car would go into a slight skid sideways, which would reduce its speed a bit. During one of the skids, Jones made a running leap for the car, thinking he could ride the running board while reaching inside to jam it out of gear. He missed and landed in the mud.

OWNERS AND crews of other cars entered in the derby tried to get out on the track to remove their cars. Each time Mrs. Albertson sent them scattering with her careening car.

Finally Chumley began chasing her with a jeep. After several laps he worked into position and when she started into a skid entering the backstretch turn, he drove the jeep in front of her car. Mrs. Albertson hit the jeep sideways, skidding to a stop as she pushed the jeep along in front of her. Mrs. Albertson was removed from the car unhurt, but shaking and tearful.

Moffett's feature win was a walkaway as he gained the lead on the second lap and was never challenged. His time was 6.28, compared to the record of 6.23. A crowd of 2,680 attended.

DON DONOVAN of Brandon was removed to Schoitz Memorial hospital after his car broad... running second in the race when he blew a tire and slid in front of Donovan. Donovan had a bad gash on the forehead and a possible fractured rib.

Larry Sommerfelt won the novice race that was shortened to 16 laps when Rich Somers rolled.

Gene Petersen was the night's only double winner, taking the third heat and the class A semi.

The annual 75-lap season championship race is scheduled for next Sunday night at the Speedway. Race time is 7:30 p. m.

First heat (10 laps)—1. Bill Reser... tremont (127), 2. Gene Welch (64), 3. Darwin Reber (18); 2.46.

Third heat (10 laps)—1. Gene Petersen (82), 2. Bill Zwanziger (35), 3. Harry Petersen (113); 3.33.

Class A semi (15 laps)—1. Dale Osborn (72), 2. Jim Hoerman (12), 3. Bill Kemp (66), 4. Darwin Reber (18), 5. Boots Ellery (21); no time, accident.

Class B semi (15 laps)—1. Gene Petersen (82), 2. Bill Zwanziger (35), 3. Cal Swanson (11), 4. Jack Hickman (70), 5. Charley Moffett (52); 4.85.

Junior Novice (16 laps)—1. Larry Sommerfelt (1), 2. Bob Holmlund (20), 3. Don Fleming (16), 4. Lloyd Hesse (22), 5. Ronnie Sells (44); no time, accident.

Consolation (15 laps)—1. John Moss (27), 2. Les Schmidt (218), 3. Jerry Sherbon (300); 4.88.

Feature (20 laps)—1. Charley Moffett (52), 2. Gene Petersen (82), 3. Bill Zwanziger (35), 4. Cal Swanson

Alice McInroy, left, Joyce Jensen and Lois Johnson are three ladies who raced in the various Powder Puff races over the years. They came to the Tunis Reunion in October 2013.

POINT LEADERS SPORTSMAN 1978
Gene Ehlers, Larry Schmidt, Greg Kastli, Fuzzy Liddell, **Bernie Juliar, Mike Krall, Tim Swope.**

Glen Martin and Miss Tunis Speedway 1970

Checkered top. Yup, a Petersen racer.

Cal Swanson

Top Money Winners for 1967, back row left to right, Droste, Hughes, Liebe, Hilmer, Swanson, Williams and Beck; front row left to right, Fitzpatrick, Krafka, Sanger, Nesetby, Kruse

POINT LEADERS LATE MODEL 1978
Stan Stover, Curt Hansen (Leader), Ed Sanger. Dick Schiltz, Darrell Sells, Denny Osborn, Tom Bartholomew, Dan Nesteby, Karl Sanger, Al Freiden for Bill Zwanziger.

Al Runyan

FRONT ROW L-R: Dick Feckeers, Bob Hilmer, unknown, Harry Petersen, Jerry Sherbon, Cal Swanson, Bob Posekany, Don Feckers. STANDING BACK ROW L-R: Arnie Spore, Jack Hickman, Harry O'Deen, Gale Card, Bill Zwanziger, Tuffy Meyer, Jim Hoermann, Bob D., Charlie Moffett, John Moss

Roger Bucholz, Karl Sanger

OIL CO
144

Dick Feckers, Marty Robinson, Stan Hermansen

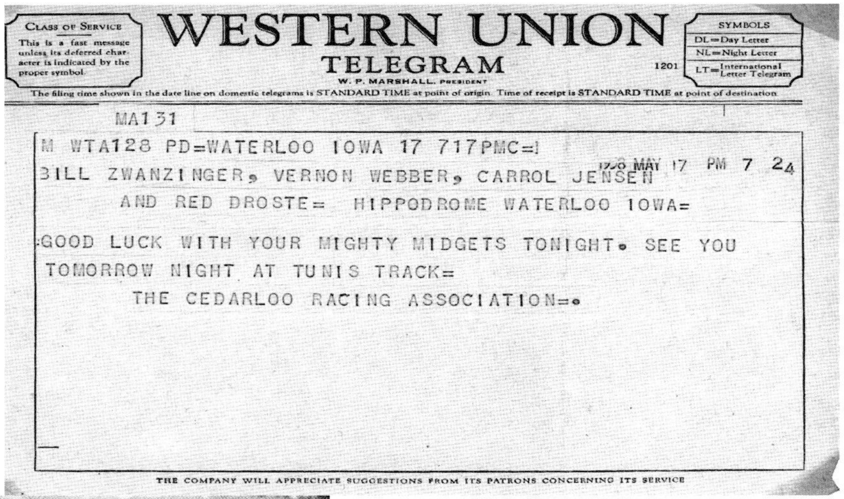

CLASS OF SERVICE
This is a fast message unless its deferred character is indicated by the proper symbol.

WESTERN UNION
TELEGRAM
W. P. MARSHALL, PRESIDENT

1201

SYMBOLS
DL=Day Letter
NL=Night Letter
LT=International Letter Telegram

The filing time shown in the date line on domestic telegrams is STANDARD TIME at point of origin. Time of receipt is STANDARD TIME at point of destination

MA131

M WTA128 PD=WATERLOO IOWA 17 717PMC=|

BILL ZWANZINGER, VERNON WEBBER, CARROL JENSEN 1958 MAY 17 PM 7 24

AND RED DROSTE= HIPPODROME WATERLOO IOWA=

GOOD LUCK WITH YOUR MIGHTY MIDGETS TONIGHT. SEE YOU TOMORROW NIGHT AT TUNIS TRACK=

THE CEDARLOO RACING ASSOCIATION=.

THE COMPANY WILL APPRECIATE SUGGESTIONS FROM ITS PATRONS CONCERNING ITS SERVICE

Carroll Jensen

Don Isley

Eugene Petersen

Harry O'Deen

Top Money Winners for 1967, back row left to right, Droste, Hughes, Liebe, Hilmer, Swanson, Williams and Beck; front row left to right, Fitzpatrick, Krafka, Sanger, Nesetby, Kruse

Cy Bohr, Judd Tunis, Ed Sanger, Debbie Bohr

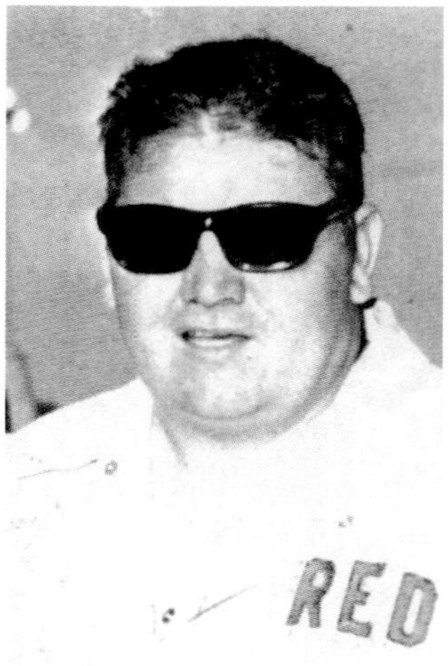
RED

Red Dralle

Dave Bedard

Al (Doc) Mayner

Bob Hilmer

PINT'S
BODY SHOP
1
REX TOLLE CHEVROLET
ALLISON IOWA

Chuck Smith

CHUB
0
IOWA MOTOR CO.
FORD MERCURY
LINCOLN

Chub Liebe

Curt Hansen

08

Dave Trower

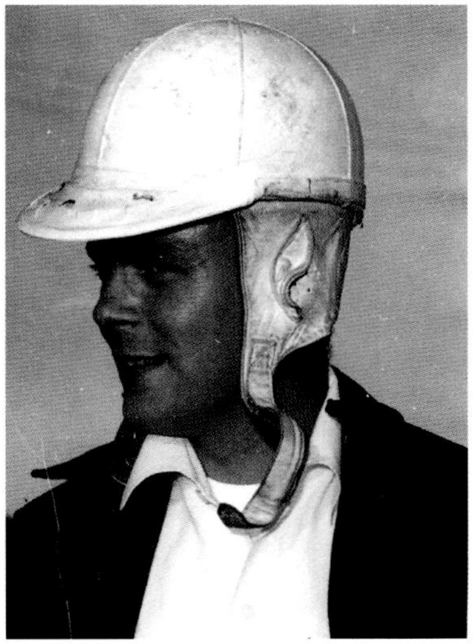

Bill Zwanziger

CONCESSION STAND
32
RED'S AUTO SERV

Charlie Moffett

95
BENTLEY

Ed Sanger

72

Denny Osborn

Jerry Sherbon

DON

Don Feckers

Gene Hultman

Harry Petersen

Barth Steere
31

Scott Sells

Jack Hickman

52
IOWA CITY

Vern Weber

Jimmie Krogh

Mark Kustic

Red Sanderson

Red Droste

Mark Taylor

Larry Wasserfort

BACK ROW STANDING L-R: First four, unknown, Bob Hilmer, Carroll Jensen, John Hill, Dick Feckers, Arnie Spore, Bob Posekany, John Moss, Charlie Moffit

FRONT ROW L-R: Tuffy Meyer, Dale Osborn, Jerry Sherbon, Les Schmitt, Harry Petersen, Cal Swanson, Bill Zwanziger, Gene Petersen

POINT LEADERS SPORTSMAN 1978
Gene Ehlers, Larry Schmidt, Greg Kastli, Fuzzy Liddell, Bernie Juliar, Mike Krall, Tim Swope.

BILL ZWANZIGER
ONE OF IOWAS
FINEST
CIRCLEBURNERS
FROM THE
WATERLOO FANS

Ira Chumley Stricken at Wheel, Dies

Funeral services tentatively are set for Friday at 2 p. m. at First Methodist church for Ira W. (Speed) Chumley, 59, of 707 South St., Waterloo car dealer, who died of a heart attack, suffered in his car one mile north of Washburn on Highway 218 at 7 p. m. Tuesday.

Mr. Chumley was dead on arrival at Schoitz Memorial hospital. Friends may call at Kearns-Dykeman Chapel after 6 p. m. Wednesday. He was born in Waukee, the son of Peter S. and Mary Sroufe Chumley on June 23, 1905. His death occurred on his 59th birthday.

Chumley

He had resided in the Waterloo area for 38 years, coming here from Emmetsburg. He married Kay Byrne on Oct. 11, 1954, in Sioux City, S. D. Mr. Chumley was owner-operator of the Chumley Auto Market for 35 years. He was a member of the Waterloo Chamber of Commerce; member of the Loyal Order of the Moose Lodge No. 328; and manager of the Cedarloo Racing Association, Inc. He was likewise widely known throughout the state for his racing activities.

Surviving are his widow; one son, William G. of 511 Progress Ave.; one daughter, Mary L. of Torrance; Calif.; two brothers, Ray of Walker, Minn.; Warren of Encino, Calif.; one sister, Mrs. Harry Hansen of Humboldt; and three grandchildren. He was preceded in death by his parents, one sister; and one brother.

Gene Petersen

Claus Stricker, Dan Lake, Cy Bohr

Herman Wenzel

Bill
HALUPNICK
Hudson
IA.

Bill Halupnick

9

Betty Halligan

22

Bob Hilmer

SILVER
FRONT
21

Arnie Spore

ROY
SERVICE

Al Runyan

3

Bill Hopp

GENE
127

Bob Piper

Claus Stricker, Dave Frost, Rick Swartz, Mike Krall, Duane Van Deest

Cindy Bohr, Don Berg, unknown, Kathy Messer

Gordon Bentley, Tiny Russell, Bill Zwanziger, Guy Rich

Jon Wiers, Roger Bucholz, Chuck Moore, Steve Auringer

Dave Rice, Roger Bucholz, Roger Klingfus, Bob Hesse, Tom Bartholemew, Jack Mitchell, D. Arthur Nesteby

Claus Stricker, Leroy "Tiny" Russell, Earl Jensen, Casey Tucker, Roger Patterson, Fuzzy Liddell

71

John Hill, Stan Hermanson, Marty Robinson, Ronnie Nye

Claus Strciker, D. Arthur Nesteby, Karl Sanger

127
BACHTELL'S
STATION

Bob Roe

MODIFIED Car No. 15

THIS CERTIFIES THAT

Bud Graham

IS A MEMBER IN GOOD STANDING OF THE

INDEPENDENCE RACING ASSOCIATION, Inc.

Independence - Waterloo

98

1969

Secretary

BUD GRAHAM
15

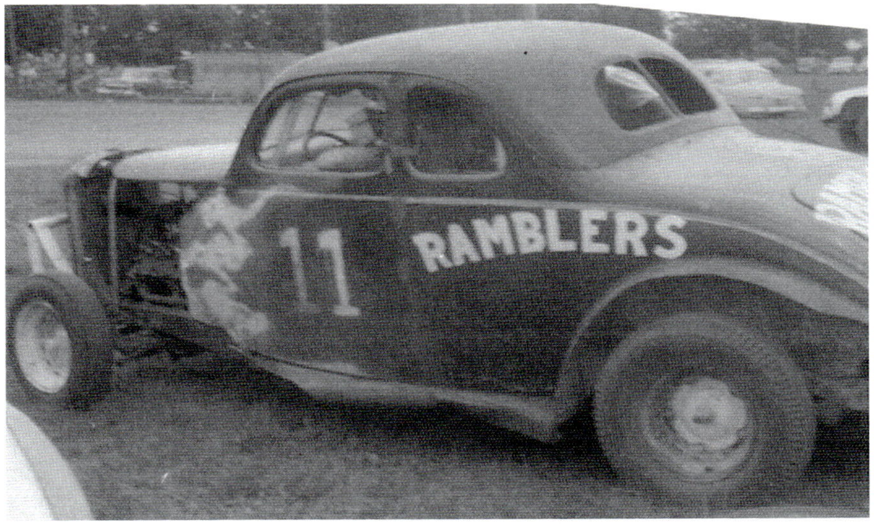
11
RAMBLERS

Carroll Jensen

POSEKANY CONSTRUCTION
CEDAR FALLS
8

Bob Posekany

OLDSMOBILE
Mobil
7

Bob Hilmer

34

Bud Slater

32

Charlie Moffit

DALE
DEEP ROCK
13
LUCKY

Dale Osborn

DON
244

Don Feckers

D.J. FLEMING
NOR

D.J. Fleming

10

Gale Card

BOBS
CITGO
DIKE
7

Curt Hansen

DON
HAZLET'S-DX
1901 LOGAN
AD 2-9525
02

Don Fentle

12
HEINE
CLARKSVILLE, IA.

Jim Hoerman

John Connelly

100

Eugene Petersen

CORDES
Ford

Leo and Roger Beck

ZERO

Jack Mitchell

GO
SCHUKEI
CHEVROLET
WATERLOO, IA.
GO
29

Red Droste

John Proctor

STAN STOVER
HOOKS
ERFORMANCE
ENGINEERING
49

Stan Stover

Tom Bartholomew, Waterloo

Denny's
44

Gene Ehlers

Roger Kruse

Russ Steffens

RED DRALLE
APPLETON
FLEXI-FLYERS
NEED 'Midwest' DEALERS
4
ICKABODS
Lounge

Red Dralle

66

Mert Williams

Don Graham

WHEELS BY Journier
2
AYR-WAY

Larry Wasserfort

Here's Some Statistics

Waterloo native Darren Kopache not only went through literally every Waterloo Courier published during the history of the former Tunis Speedway, copying articles from microfiche to satisfy his own curiosity about the track, but he also did a little figuring to determine some statistics that few reading this probably know about.

Darren claims these aren't "official" so read them for your own enjoyment, but they are probably real close to what the actual numbers would have been if someone had been keeping track during all those years.

Point Champions (different from track champions)

1948-51 No driver associations were formed yet

1952	Bill Zwanziger
1953	Cal Swanson
1954	Bob Hilmer
1955	Carroll Hilmer
1956	Carroll Hilmer
1957	Bob Hilmer
1958	Bill Zwanziger
1959	Charlie Moffit
1960	Bill Zwanziger
1961	Bill Zwanziger
1962	Red Droste
1963	Bill Zwanziger
1964	Red Droste
1965	Red Droste
1966	Red Droste
1967	Red Droste
1968	Red Droste
1969	Curt Hansen
1970	Ed Sanger
1971	Ed Sanger
1972	Ed Sanger
1973	Stan Stover
1974	Dan Nesteby
1975	Dan Nesteby
1976	Ed Sanger
1977	Curt Hansen
1978	Curt Hansen
1979	Ed Sanger

Total Race Events	**581**
Rain Outs	**88**

First Place Finishes--Features

1) Bill Zwanziger	60
2) Bob Hilmer	48
3) Red Droste	47
4) Ed Sanger	46
5) Curt Hansen	40
6) Gene Petersen	26
7) Cal Swanson	22
8) Mert Williams	17
9) Charlie Moffit	15
Stan Stover	15
10) John Moss	12
Karl Sanger	12
11) Verlin Eaker	10

First Place Finishes--Semi Main

1) Bill Zwanziger	47
2) Bob Hilmer	34
3) Red Droste	30
4) Cal Swanson	26
5) Gene Petersen	21
6) John Hill	19
7) Arnold Spore	17
8) Mert Williams	15
9) Chub Liebe	14
10) Bob Posekany	11
11) Harry Petersen	10
Charlie Moffit	10

Track Champions

1952	Harry Petersen
1953	Cal Swanson
1954	Red Droste
1955	Carroll Hilmer
1956	Bob Hilmer
1957	Dick Krafka
1958	Bill Zwanziger
1959	Bill Zwanziger
1960	John Moss
1961	Gene Petersen
1962	Red Droste
1963	Red Droste
1964	Mert Williams
1965	Chub Liebe
1966	Bob Hilmer
1967	Red Droste
1968	Red Droste
1969	Chub Liebe
1970	Ed Sanger
1971	Ed Sanger
1972	Curt Hansen
1973	Stan Stover
1974	Dan Nesteby
1975	Red Dralle
1976	Ed Sanger
1977	Curt Hansen
1978	Curt Hansen
1979	Ed Sanger

The **Waterloo Courier** played a big role in the success of Tunis Speedway. Not only was it the primary advertising vehicle for the track, but the newspaper provided excellent coverage of the racing events, even in its slow years when competition became more prevalent around the Midwest.

From 1948 to 1983, the newspaper had two different sports editors--Roger Matz and Russ Smith--and had various writers assigned to cover the racing. The most prominent writers, however, were Jim Fickess and Larry Speares, who authored specific sports columns devoted to racing.

SUNDAY NIGHT, MAY 31st
STOCK CAR RACES
ADDED ATTRACTION - - - GRUDGE RACE
TIME TRIALS 7:00 P. M. — RACES 8:00 P. M.
FREE PARKING
TUNIS SPEEDWAY
Jim Fickess' column
Stricker to operate Tunis; Races will start May 19
"Have a good day."
Enjoy Coke
WELCOME TO
Every SUNDAY Night
TUNIS SPEEDWAY
Waterloo, Iowa
Home of Iowa's Best Late Model Drivers
1972 Official Program 25¢
TUNIS SPEEDWAY PRESENTS
"CONTEST OF RACING KNOW-HOW"
LARRY LANGE FORD
Largest Dealer in Eastern Iowa
TUNIS SPEEDWAY NEWS
Waterloo, Iowa
VOLUME 1 NUMBER 1--JULY 1972
Receive this free by mail— Subscription blank on page 4
Massive Mid-season Championship set
ED SANGER of Waterloo is a strong hopeful for this year's Mid-Season Title
Who Will Be This Year's Champion?
KARL SANGER of Waterloo
Schedule
GLEN MARTIN of Independence is another hopeful for this year's crown.
CURT HANSEN of Dike
AUTO DAREDEVILS
CHITWOOD
AUTO DAREDEVILS
RACING ASS'N. INC.
EVERY SUNDAY NITE
TUNIS SPEEDWAY
Stock Car Races
TUNIS SPEEDWAY
SUNDAY NIGHT
Races at 7:30
GATES OPEN AT 6:00 P.M.
LATE MODEL — SPORTSMAN and ROADRUNNER
Admission: Adults $3.00
Bargain Gate $2.00
Children 6 to 12 Yrs. Both Gates $1.00
Under 6 Yrs. FREE
BEER and FOOD AVAILABLE
(No Coolers Please)
Located HiWay 218 Between Waterloo and Cedar Falls

The Promoters--Gettin' The Fans in the Gate

Ask anyone involved in the operation and promotion of a small dirt track anywhere in the United States about what it takes to make the track "work" and you will probably get a long sigh and an invitation to sit a spell while they detail the process.

Dirt track promotion has changed dramatically, like most everything else, since the days when Judd Tunis walked out his back door, climbed on the grader he used to condition the track and had to make some decisions that could be wiped out when the threat of rain appeared above his 52 acre plot.

WATERLOO SAVINGS BANK

It wasn't unusual in the 1950s to have the local bank promote an event or organization in its front window. Here is one for Tunis Speedway in the window of the former Waterloo Savings Bank.

Probably no one really told Judd the work would be hard, but he wasn't one to walk away from a difficult challenge and Tunis Speedway, in all of its 35 years, had an incredible record of not only drawing strong crowds, but also an impressive array of drivers.

Judd handled the vast majority of management and promotion over the years, hand picking assistants who would do things like carefully painting all the white washed barriers and posts around the track, picking rocks and debris out of the track itself before that residue could do damage to race cars and spectators alike and concessions.

Judd started at an advantage and a disadvantage. He relied on Speed Chumley to guide him through some of the initial contacts and expectations when the track first hosted midget racers. But he had to work his way through advertising the races, producing posters to hang around town, getting ads put together for the local newspaper and having regular announcements on the radio stations that surrounded the Waterloo-Cedar Falls area.

Much of that was new to him though he had done some advertising for his own business J.L. Tunis Hamburger and Sausage.

Dirt track racing began growing in popularity all over the country in the early 1950s. Southern states had their own recipe for racing while out on the west coast the racers started out on the dry lake beds before deciding that an oval surrounded by bleachers might be a bit more exciting to watch.

As the popularity grew, of course, the competition started to make the process of managing a successful weekly racing event just a bit more complex. Tunis Speedway was hosting better drivers, faster cars and larger crowds, but the expectations were being compared to what other tracks might be offering that were well within driving distance for both fans and drivers.

Through the 1950s dirt track racing grew, both in the number of drivers and the number of spectators willing to go where there was action and excitement. Judd Tunis had a great opportunity to build on that building interest and promoted his track and its events aggressively. And the crowds responded. It wasn't unusual to have 3,000, 4,000, 5,000 fans and there were times the track was overflowing with over 7,000 spectators to see drivers battling around the ¼ mile oval.

STOCK CAR
RACES
TUNIS
SPEEDWAY
WATERLOO
EVERY
TUESDAY NITE
TIME TRIALS 7 P.M. – RACES 8 P.M.

By the mid-1960s, however, things were changing and Tunis recognized the difficulties of staging weekly events that were competing not only for spectators, but also for some of this area's very best drivers. Other tracks were also growing their event schedules and purses. The drivers were noticing and weren't afraid to do a bit of traveling to compete where the money seemed to be.

In 1966 Waterloo auto dealer Jim Cordes, who had been sponsoring cars for driver Bill Zwanziger, decided to partner with Zwanziger and lease the track from Tunis, who indicated he wanted to retire from the weekly grind of putting together the races.

(Courier Photo)

New Proprietor Takes Over From Old

New proprietors, left to right, Roger Beck of Hudson, Bill Zwanziger and Jim Cordes, and retiring Jud Tunis gather around the car Zwanziger will drive when the newly refurbished Cordes Speedway opens its stock car racing season Sunday night. Several changes in the layout, including a new entrance about two blocks nearer downtown Waterloo, new parking facilities and bleachers on both sides of the track instead of just the west side, have been made. Cordes leased the track this year from Tunis who has operated auto racing there the past 18 years. Racing programs will start at 7:30 p.m. both Sunday and Monday, Memorial day, this week.

Cordes took up the challenge with Zwanziger, renamed the track Cordes Speedway, and began the process of not only promoting the track schedule, but also made some changes to things like parking, entrances and adding bleachers to increase seating for spectators.

But the experienced racer and the auto dealer found out fairly quickly the issues that had to be addressed weekly just to keep the track operating so both drivers and spectators could have a good experience.

Some years later Zwanziger lamented that one thing he didn't enjoy was being a promoter. "Too much work!" he said. He thought the job of a promoter would be simpler than what he found during that year and by the end of 1966, he and Cordes had had enough. The track operation returned to Judd Tunis and Zwanziger got to focus on his driving and Cordes his auto dealership.

For many years the Tunis track rules were governed by driver associations, put together to provide some guidelines for the types of vehicles being raced and giving the drivers some safety regulations that would make the racing a bit safer. Cars were starting to go much faster and it was necessary to set up some procedures so everyone could compete on a level playing field.

In 1967, after the Cordes Speedway experience, the track became involved in a three-track circuit made up of Tunis in Waterloo, the track in Independence and a third track in Monticello.

Lyle Shriver, another Waterloo auto dealer who had been involved for many years sponsoring race cars (Bob Hilmer, specifically), teamed up with another Waterloo resident, Vern Weber, who had racing experience himself and would later go on to operate tracks in other parts of Iowa. The idea was to better coordinate efforts and allow all three tracks to draw drivers and spectators without damaging each other's business.

COMPETITION FOR DRIVERS

RUSS SMITH'S COLUMN

A STOCK CAR war? Perhaps it was bound to happen with the mushrooming growth of the sport.

Tunis Speedway in Waterloo appears to have gone into a bidding war with the Hawkeye Downs in Cedar Rapids for drivers and cars for its Fourth of July program here Friday —at least that's the way they see it in Cedar Rapids, according to Cedar Rapids Gazette racing writer Al Miller.

There are races every Friday at the Downs but, because it is a holiday, Tunis has scheduled a race card for that night, as well as its usual Sunday night, and is offering purses of $3,250 for both nights, compared to the $1,200 purses that are normal at Tunis.

Many drivers who hit the Friday (Cedar Rapids), Saturday (Independence) and Sunday (Tunis) circuit will have to choose between Cedar Rapids and Waterloo Friday and the deciding factor may be the prize differential. Cedar Rapids is guaranteeing its usual $2,400.

The drivers who belong to the Independence Racing Assn., which encompasses Waterloo and Independence, may also risk losing their membership by passing up the Waterloo card.

Miller says: C. R. had been racing on Saturday nights, but (the late Frank) Winkley moved the program to Friday so as not to conflict with Indee (on Saturday) and thus make more cars available to C. R. The marriage was a good one—that is, until Tunis pulled the latest funny.

"Even Ed Sanger of Waterloo, who is the secretary of the IRA, was apologetic last week.

" 'It's none of my doing,' said Sanger, who is the Downs point leader. 'You may still see me back here on Friday, although I may not be secretary up there any longer.'

"(Hawkeye Downs promoter Nick) Nachicas said he already had '24 signed entries for the Fourth of July. They are expected to be honored and if they race somewhere else they will be penalized. I'm not sure yet what the penalty will be.' "

So for the next three years Tunis Speedway worked under an agreement for the three-track circuit, but that didn't end the competition for both drivers and spectators. Hawkeye Downs in Cedar Rapids was also running racing events on the weekends and as purses began rising, the bidding wars began.

Tracks were trying to attract the best drivers and many of those had begun their careers in Waterloo, though that didn't necessarily stop them from heading to the track with the biggest purses.

Once the leasing agreement with the three-track Independence Racing Association ended, Judd Tunis was right back in the thick of the competition and made the necessary moves to keep his track fully attended. The July 4 racing in 1969 proved to be a harbinger of what was to come for stock car racing at small tracks all over the Midwest.

Keith Knaack

The holiday weekend happened to include a Friday night and Tunis decided to not only run the usual Sunday night races, but also on Friday night, upping the guaranteed purse to push Hawkeye Downs, also running a Friday night event, out of the picture.

Drivers who were associated with both the Independence Racing Association, but had committed to race at Hawkeye Downs on that Friday had a tough decision to make as they could be penalized by choosing either one of the two venues.

By 1970 things had become even more competitive as more drivers found themselves traveling all over the Midwest to vie for points and dollars, putting promoters in a position where they had to work out alliances that would keep those drivers close to home.

Keith Knaack, who founded the Hawkeye Racing News in Vinton, Iowa in the late 60s, formed CarPac, Inc. to promote racing and took over the reins at Tunis Speedway in 1970, hiring driver Claus Stricker of Waterloo as his right hand man and the guy who would do most of the leg work to bring the track up to some new standards as the track entered another decade of racing.

CarPac, Inc. became part of the Greater Iowa Racing Association which joined together Tunis Speedway and the tracks at Cedar Rapids and Independence. Together the groups offered purses of $6500 for combined point earnings at all three tracks in addition to regular purses for winners at the individual ovals. At Tunis the first place season point winner was paid $1200 with second and third getting $900 and $700 respectively.

Knaack, Stricker and CarPac jumped right into the fray, offering fans a demolition derby, late model stocks (1969-70 years), junior stocks and some specialty racing events that were meant to keep the crowds entertained and coming to Tunis Speedway on a consistent basis.

Knaack had been instrumental in elevating the coverage of stock car racing throughout Iowa and the Midwest through his Hawkeye Racing News and later got involved in the purchase and re-development of the International Motor Contest Association (IMCA).

The IMCA was founded in 1915 and was the oldest active sanctioning body in the United States before falling on hard times in the mid to late 1970s. Knaack stepped in, purchased the organization and moved it to Vinton, Iowa where it still operates one of the most successful sanctioning bodies in the racing industry.

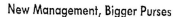

New Management, Bigger Purses

AND, SPEAKING OF TUNIS, the Waterloo dirt oval is under new management this season and boasts a larger prize fund. Keith Knaack, new at the Tunis helm, has announced that the track will join Independence and Cedar Rapids in the Greater Iowa Racing Assn. The three tracks feature a combined point fund of $6,500.

First place to the season point winner pays $1,200, with second and third getting $900 and $700 respectively and the rest receiving amounts descending in $100 steps.

The May 10 opener will feature a demolition derby and late model racing and the follow-up, slated for Sunday, May 17, will feature 1969-70 late model stocks and junior stocks, all after the $400 winner's share of the guaranteed $2,000 purse being offered by Car Pac, Inc., the Tunis promoters.

Drivers should also note that if they file for their Tunis numbers before May 12 they will not have to pay the regular $10 entry fee. The gift fee idea is designed to save time and aid in setting up programs and press releases as well as saving the drivers $10.

During those first years of promoting Tunis Speedway, Knaack recognized the challenges ahead for the racing community, both for the drivers and the fans. The rebound for Tunis was going to slow and steady and he reflected on the challenge early on.

"It has taken a lot of hard work," said Knaack at the time. "But we are seeing the fruits of our labor." Knaack and Stricker, who had first-hand knowledge of the costs involved in racing as a driver and car owner, knew it would take some creative changes to overcome the new problems tracks faced with increased expenses in racing equipment which forced drivers to travel to find the biggest purses to fund their racing lifestyle.

Claus Stricker

Knaack and Stricker began seeing fans who had been traveling to other tracks to watch the best action coming back to Tunis Speedway to see not only a stronger field of Late Model competitors, but also the popular Sportsman cars and the mini stocks, Roadrunners and Powder Puff racers.

"Stock car racing is entertainment," said Knaack, "and that is the product we are in the business of selling. Give the fans a good action program, without delays, and it's not long before the word gets around that there is something going on at the track (Tunis) that should not be missed."

Knaack staged a full 10 race program on every Sunday night with a new policy of finishing by 10 p.m. and working to have not less than 60 cars in attendance for every event.

Knaack said he wanted Tunis Speedway to return to its former glory and be the "action track of late model racing."

Stricker was staying busy during this time as well, not only providing the support to Knaack to handle track management, but also racing himself, not passing up the opportunity to get into the competition as well.

At the time he was hired by Knaack, Stricker was driving for a car owner in Independence and even drove for Karl Sanger during the 1972 season.

Stricker had begun racing at Tunis Speedway in 1961, not long after he arrived in Waterloo to work at John Deere. Like many drivers he owned and raced many of his own vehicles, but also stepped into the driver seat for other owners. He was well known within the driver community.

"When Keith hired me in 1970 I had just returned to work at Deere but I just didn't want to end my racing," Stricker explained. "There were times when I would work at the track every single day, even though I was also working full time at Deere."

The two worked together up until 1972 when Knaack suffered a heart attack that would alter his racing involvement and ultimately push Sticker to become even more involved. Knaack had a heart transplant in Texas in the spring of 1973 and dropped completely away from his promotional duties, leaving Tunis Speedway without a full time promoter again.

Moyer Taking Court Action

Tunis Returns Tonight

By JIM FICKESS
Courier Sports Writer

Today's cards at NEITA Raceway and Tunis Speedway could quite easily comprise the best Northeast Iowa auto racing weekend of the season.

Tunis is scheduled to celebrate the grand opening of its 25th consecutive year of racing with a $2,750 purse this evening while NEITA is slated to host an American Hot Rod Assn. Record Run during today's program.

Tonight will mark Judd Tunis' return to stock car promoting as he and Claus Stricker have taken over the management of the quarter-mile dirt track from Iowa International Raceways, Inc., which promoted the first two races of the season.

If IIR president Bill Moyer is successful in court, tonight's Tunis card may be the last one at the quarter-mile track for a while.

Moyer, who filed a damage suit against Judd Tunis claiming a breach of contract in district court Friday, said yesterday that he plans to file an injunction against Tunis promoting any further races if no agreement is reached by next Sunday.

Moyer planned to file an injunction against Tunis for tonight's program, but indicated there wasn't enough time to go through the necessary legal procedures.

Tunis' reasons for taking over was that the IIR lacked experience and the drivers were complaining about the way the races were being run.

"I think we did a great respectable job!" exclaimed Moyer. "Sure we had some areas that needed improvement, but others agreed with us, that we were doing a good job.

"The way I look at it, you need to do three things to successfully promote a stock car race — get people out to the race, get plenty of drivers to compete and get the program over in a relatively-short period of time. We did a great respectable job doing all three!

"Tunis didn't take over the track at the first of the year because he was afraid he couldn't get the drivers. He let

See NEITA
Continued on page 22, col. 5

Stricker stayed on to help Judd Tunis with maintenance and track preparation when Bill and Carl Moyer, two brothers involved in racing in the Des Moines area, approached Tunis about handling the track promotion and management. An agreement was made (though there wasn't a signed contract) and Tunis Speedway was ready to take on the 1973 season with new management, again.

Stricker said the Moyer experience didn't turn out quite as good as Judd Tunis had hoped with drivers complaining almost from the first day about how things were being handled.

Bill Moyer was the primary organizer for his Iowa International Raceways, Inc. organization and had promoted stock cars only one other time before taking over the Tunis track.

Moyer made some changes including running the first racing event with both the Late Model and Sportsman classes running together and changing how purses were to be paid. That immediately rankled drivers who complained loudly enough that he adjusted again for the second season event the following week.

But it wasn't enough and Stricker, who had remained to assist Judd Tunis, said when Moyer called the drivers together at the end of the racing for the payouts, Tunis went into the meeting and fired Moyer on the spot. "Judd knew the drivers were unhappy with what was going on and he wasn't one to not take action immediately," Stricker said. "So Moyer was out after just two nights of racing."

Stricker had stopped racing himself in 1972, so when he and Tunis talked following the Moyer incident, Tunis asked him if he would consider working together and they would take over promotion.

So for the rest of the 1973 season, Stricker worked with Tunis to promote and stage racing events.

As the 1973 season came to an end, a number of issues were facing the racing industry including the shortage of gas that was occurring across the country. This made racing one of the targets of those who were looking for ways to conserve gas which was in short supply and was making it tougher for consumers to travel. Judd Tunis was painfully aware of what the gas shortage would do to attendance and had to make some decisions about how the track could operate.

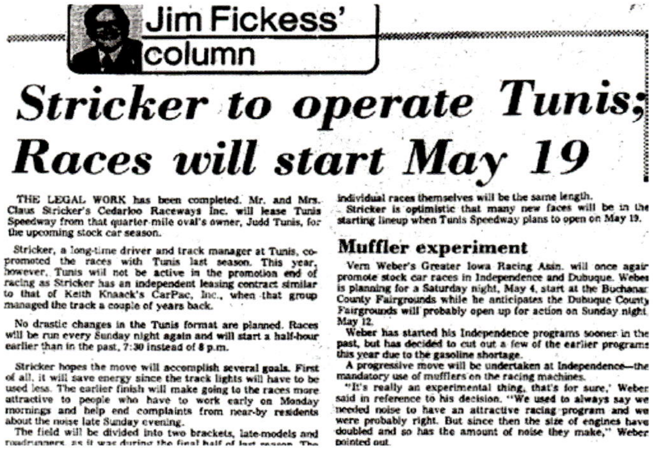

Jim Fickess' column

Stricker to operate Tunis; Races will start May 19

THE LEGAL WORK has been completed. Mr. and Mrs. Claus Stricker's Cedarloo Raceways Inc. will lease Tunis Speedway from that quarter-mile oval's owner, Judd Tunis, for the upcoming stock car season.

Stricker, a long-time driver and track manager at Tunis, co-promoted the races with Tunis last season. This year, however, Tunis will not be active in the promotion end of racing as Stricker has an independent leasing contract similar to that of Keith Knaack's CarPac, Inc., when that group managed the track a couple of years back.

No drastic changes in the Tunis format are planned. Races will be run every Sunday night again and will start a half-hour earlier than in the past, 7:30 instead of 8 p.m.

Stricker hopes the move will accomplish several goals. First of all, it will save energy since the track lights will have to be used less. The earlier finish will make going to the races more attractive to people who have to work early on Monday mornings and help end complaints from near-by residents about the noise late Sunday evening.

The field will be divided into two brackets, late-models and roadrunners, as it was during the final half of last season. The individual races themselves will be the same length.

Stricker is optimistic that many new faces will be in the starting lineup when Tunis Speedway plans to open on May 19.

Muffler experiment

Vern Weber's Greater Iowa Racing Assn. will once again promote stock car races in Independence and Dubuque. Weber is planning for a Saturday night, May 4, start at the Buchanan County Fairgrounds while he anticipates the Dubuque County Fairgrounds will probably open up for action on Sunday night, May 12.

Weber has started his Independence programs sooner in the past, but has decided to cut out a few of the earlier programs this year due to the gasoline shortage.

A progressive move will be undertaken at Independence—the mandatory use of mufflers on the racing machines.

"It's really an experimental thing, that's for sure,' Weber said in reference to his decision. "We used to always say we needed noise to have an attractive racing program and we were probably right. But since then the size of engines have doubled and so has the amount of noise they make," Weber pointed out.

But even in what was considered a very difficult time, Claus Stricker still had racing in his blood and convinced his wife, Marlene, to form up a whole new organization, Cedarloo Raceways, Inc., and work out a lease arrangement with Tunis for the track. It would be hard work with a myriad of challenges, but Stricker was convinced he could overcome those obstacles and bring new life to the racetrack.

"I had learned early on that promotion meant hard work," Stricker said when asked about how he approached this new phase in his own racing career. "I went all out trying to get the word out to people, taking posters out to areas within 75 miles of Waterloo to let people know the track was holding some of the best racing they could attend."

WATERLOO
T
IOWA
TUNIS SPEEDWAY

Stricker also made some other changes to get past some issues that had been dogging the track for many years, one of which was noise. He changed the start time to 7:30 p.m. on Sunday instead of 8 p.m. This would allow the events to end earlier in the evening, which would please those who complained about the noise, but also save the additional expense of using the track lights.

He also figured it would make it easier for people traveling to get home by a decent hour for getting to work on Monday. He also split up the field into two brackets which he and Tunis had tried during the previous season with good results. Now the track would run late models and roadrunners.

With such racing stalwarts as the Daytona 500 and other major NASCAR venues trimming down race lengths, he looked closely at keeping race lengths shorter, which helped to stay within the total event time schedules.

Costs were even escalating for such things as tires for the race cars and Stricker worked with the other track promoters to determine what types of tires could be used with success and keep costs in line. His racing background came in handy throughout his time managing the track in being able to understand the racers' concerns and addressing them in a logical, reasonable manner.

It even got to where other tracks were considering having race cars run mufflers, most specifically at both Independence and Dubuque where promoter Vern Weber implemented an experimental program to require mufflers on all race cars saying with the increase in engine sizes has come an increase in the noise. Stricker never formally implemented a muffler requirement, but knew many cars coming to his track would have them installed if only because they were required at other venues.

So for the next five racing seasons, Claus Stricker, along with his wife Marlene, and even the couple's children, became heavily involved in not only promoting but managing the track facility with Stricker carefully following many of the processes Judd Tunis had established over the years to make the track the best racing surface possible.

Judd Tunis and Claus Stricker

In 1975 Stricker changed the track layout slightly and lengthened the oval to 3/8 of a mile with the front straightaway widened to allow drivers a bit more room and give the fans more vehicles coming around turn four right in front of them. At the same time the lighting system was revamped to better serve the wider track and certain areas of the track were re-tiled so groundwater could be controlled and the track would suffer less from rain and the constant potholes that seemed to appear during the racing season.

Stricker made even more changes in how information was distributed, implementing a newsletter for the track and a new logo that was placed in ads and in the new color programs. Spectator numbers began increasing as people came to not only enjoy the racing, but to vie for free prizes given away to lucky program number holders, to see things like the driver wheelbarrow races or the hare and hound events where Stricker himself would jump in a car and have drivers try to catch him on the track.

The food selections were expanded in the concession stand and Stricker added beer to the offerings. Parking areas were better managed and entry and exit from the track was made smoother so people could come and go without a lot of waiting and inconvenience.

Stricker made end of year driver banquets much more formal, giving drivers a chance to relive the past season and get together with track employees and management.

All the efforts began paying dividends as more drivers began showing up to race at Tunis Speedway and the spectator numbers grew as well. Stricker said he even went so far as to work with city officials to address noise issues and he said they were able to come up with ideas that helped to decrease the number of complaints in that area.

For many people these five years from 1974 to 1979 may have been some of the speedway's best years. There was a large group of very talented drivers who would show up to race providing great shows for the spectators.

As the racing industry matured and vehicles became faster and more sophisticated, Tunis Speedway was able to keep up with what was happening and continue to maintain a strong reputation as one of the best tracks in the state of Iowa, if not the Midwest.

But, as with all good things, an end was coming and Stricker knew that things couldn't continue with much of the infrastructure of the aging track needing attention. "I was constantly having to repair things like the grandstands and the support buildings and other areas that simply were wearing out," he explained.

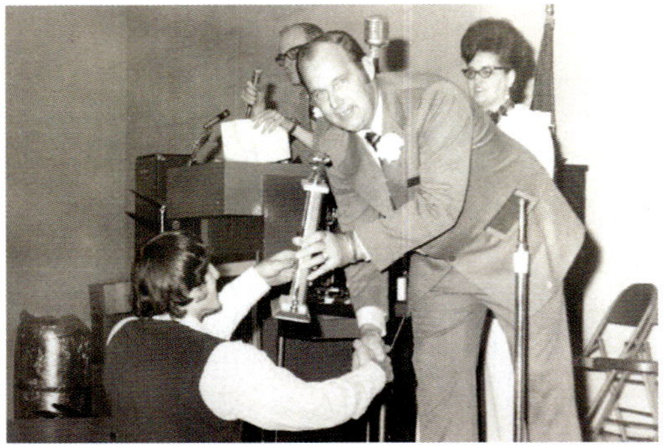

Claus Stricker made a huge effort to improve not only the spectator experience but that of the drivers as well.

"It was getting harder and harder to stage races when much of the facility was needing serious attention, so I knew there would come a time when those repairs would no longer be enough."

Seize the hop-portunity!
HOLDIMAN MOTOR
University Ave.
Cedar Falls 277—1210
TUNIS SPEEDWAY
Bicenntenial Souvenier Program
WATERLOO
Every
Sunday
Night
7:30 p.m.
1976
30¢
Between Waterloo and Cedar Falls on Highway 218
PROMOTER: CLAUS W. STRICKER
Best Drivers in the Midwest
Read all about it in the
Waterloo Courier

Even the programs played a part in drawing in the spectators with color graphics and sponsorships coming from a wide range of local businesses.

Add to that the fact that Judd Tunis was now in his mid-80s and Stricker knew the time would come when he and the track owner would have to make some difficult decisions.

The time finally came in 1979 at the end of another successful racing season and Judd Tunis decided it was time to stop. "Many people think that somehow he was forced to close things up, but that wasn't the case," Stricker said. "I had a good working relationship with the city at that time and the noise issue was not really one we couldn't work around."

But the track facilities were aging and needing some major investment to bring it up to more modern standards. "I was pretty concerned about the safety of such things as the grandstands which had been standing in some cases over 30 years," Stricker said. "Our repair work just wasn't going to be enough and Judd said he wasn't interested in investing more into the property at this stage of his life."

Stricker said he and Tunis talked at length before the final decision was made to end regular weekly racing events.

"It was a tough decision and many people tried to convince Judd to keep the track going," Stricker said. "I even tried to work out a way to purchase the property, but Judd would have none of it and once he made the decision to stop, you weren't going to change his mind."

So the final weekly racing ended in 1979, though there was a sprinkling of events that occurred over the next four years, culminating in the very last event held on September 25, 1983, promoted by none other than Keith Knaack who convinced Tunis to run just one more event, this one a 250 lap endure race where the one racer who could last all 250 laps won all the marbles.

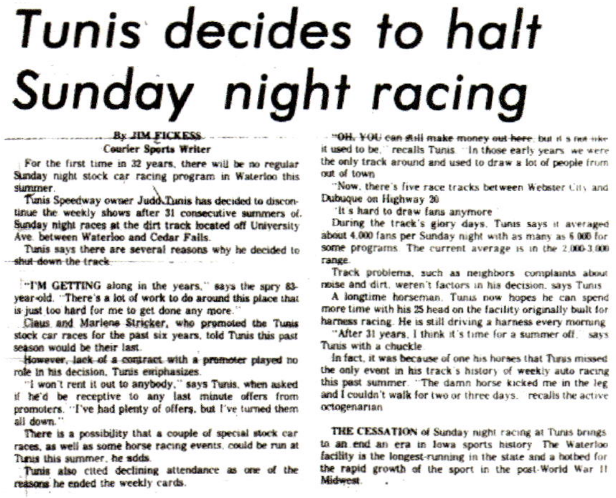

Tunis decides to halt Sunday night racing

By JIM FICKESS
Courier Sports Writer

For the first time in 32 years, there will be no regular Sunday night stock car racing program in Waterloo this summer.

Tunis Speedway owner Judd Tunis has decided to discontinue the weekly shows after 31 consecutive summers of Sunday night races at the dirt track located off University Ave. between Waterloo and Cedar Falls.

Tunis says there are several reasons why he decided to shut down the track.

"I'M GETTING along in the years," says the spry 83-year-old. "There's a lot of work to do around this place that is just too hard for me to get done any more."

Claus and Marlene Stricker, who promoted the Tunis stock car races for the past six years, told Tunis this past season would be their last.

However, lack of a contract with a promoter played no role in his decision, Tunis emphasizes.

"I won't rent it out to anybody," says Tunis, when asked if he'd be receptive to any last minute offers from promoters. "I've had plenty of offers, but I've turned them all down."

There is a possibility that a couple of special stock car races, as well as some horse racing events, could be run at Tunis this summer, he adds.

Tunis also cited declining attendance as one of the reasons he ended the weekly cards.

"OH, YOU can still make money out here, but it's not like it used to be," recalls Tunis. "In those early years, we were the only track around and used to draw a lot of people from out of town.

"Now, there's five race tracks between Webster City and Dubuque on Highway 20.

"It's hard to draw fans anymore."

During the track's glory days, Tunis says it averaged about 4,000 fans per Sunday night with as many as 6,000 for some programs. The current average is in the 2,000-3,000 range.

Track problems, such as neighbors' complaints about noise and dirt, weren't factors in his decision, says Tunis.

A longtime horseman, Tunis now hopes he can spend more time with his 25 head on the facility originally built for harness racing. He is still driving a harness every morning.

"After 31 years, I think it's time for a summer off," says Tunis with a chuckle.

In fact, it was because of one his horses that Tunis missed the only event in his track's history of weekly auto racing this past summer. "The damn horse kicked me in the leg and I couldn't walk for two or three days," recalls the active octogenarian.

THE CESSATION of Sunday night racing at Tunis brings to an end an era in Iowa sports history. The Waterloo facility is the longest-running in the state and a hotbed for the rapid growth of the sport in the post-World War II Midwest.

December 6, 1979

The race was well attended and sponsored by The Deery Brothers of Cedar Falls who continue today to sponsor short track racing events around the Midwest.

On April 25, 1985 Judd Tunis died at the age of 88 in Waterloo. He had long been retired from the meat cutting business and he and his wife Marie had moved into a different single story home in Waterloo. Marie continued to own the Tunis property following Judd's death and toward the end of 1985 was approached by former Tunis driver Bob Hilmer of Dysart and Vic Frey, a race driver from Waterloo, about reopening the track.

The city of Waterloo had passed an ordinance in 1982 that would have required that mufflers be installed on any race cars being raced within the city limits, so the two would have been faced with that possibility if Marie Tunis had agreed to sell the property.

But nothing more was published about the proposal and in 1998, after Marie Tunis had passed as well, the property was sold by the family to a real estate developer in Marion, Iowa. Nothing was actually built on the property until 2014 when the developer began the process of building 12-plex apartment buildings directly south of the former track which is still visible in aerial photos.

Judd L. Tunis

Services for Judd L. Tunis, 88, of 3715 University Ave., will be 1 p.m. Saturday at Memorial Park Chapel with burial in the Memorial Park Cemetery.

Judd Tunis

Waterloo Lodge 105 AF & AM will conduct public Masonic services at 7:30 p.m. Friday at O'Keefe & Towne-Carter & Waychoff Funeral Home, where friends may call after 2 p.m. Friday.

He died at 12:35 p.m. Wednesday at Scholtz Hospice Unit.

Mr. Tunis was born May 2, 1896, at Independence, son of August and Charlotte Lorenz Tunis. He married Marie Fish in 1917.

At the age of 10, he was employed by Wittick Meats. In 1923 he and his wife opened a butcher shop in the location presently occupied by Con-Way Civic Center. In 1942, he opened a wholesale meat outlet in the family home on University Avenue.

Mr. Tunis developed and operated Tunis Speedway for 32 years, an enterprise begun in 1950. He sponsored or supported numerous entertainment events: horse racing, midget car racing, stock car racing, car stunt shows, circuses and parades.

He was an expert horseman.

He was active in Waterloo Masonic Lodge No. 105, served as an officer in the White Shrine Lodge of Jerusalem No. 9 of Cedar Falls, and a long-time member of the High 12 Club.

Survivors include his wife; a daughter, Lorene C. Higgins of Waterloo; a sister, Lois Tunis of Kansas City, Mo.; two grandchildren; and three great-grandchildren.

The family will receive friends at the funeral home from 7:15 to 9 p.m. Friday.

Memorials may be made to Shrine Crippled Children's Hospital or the Scholtz Hospice Unit.

TUNIS SPEEDWAY OCTOBERFEST
WATERLOO, IOWA
Presented by
THE DEERY BROTHERS
John Deery Oldmosbile-Datsun
Dan Deery Pontiac Dodge
TUNIS
ENDURO 250
Waterloo, Iowa
SUNDAY, SEPTEMBER 25th
2 P.M. Gates Open
Race at 4 P.M.
2 P.M. Gates Open Enduro Practice
3 P.M. Mandatory Drivers and Scorers Meeting
3:30 Practice
4 P.M. Line-Up and Introductions
4:15 Race Begins
6 P.M. (Approx.) Awards Ceremony
TUNIS SPEEDWAY
3715 UNIVERSITY AVENUE
WATERLOO, IOWA

The very last race--
September 25, 1983

May 1982

Stock car races return to Tunis Monday

Courier News Service

Waterloo stock car racing fans haven't had their hometown track, Tunis Speedway, running regular weekly programs for three summers now.

But, weather permitting, there should be plenty of racing action Monday night in the John Deery Memorial Day special on that banked three-eighths mile dirt oval.

Knaack also predicts he'll have an outstanding field of cars, including most the top names who ran Sunday night programs at Tunis before the track quit its weekly races.

Knaack says there should be plenty of parking for the event. The Food for Less store in front of the track will be open Monday night and some of the lot will reserved for grocery shoppers.

STOCK CAR RACES
TUNIS SPEEDWAY
Waterloo, Iowa
Highway 218 Between Waterloo and Cedar Falls
DEERY BROTHERS
LABOR DAY SPECIAL
MONDAY, SEPT. 5
Racing Excitement Returns To Tunis Speedway For The First Time This Year!
IMCA Modifieds — Point Race
Demolition Derby — $250 To Win
Altered Street Stock
Figure 8 Races
Races Start at 6:00
LOW, LOW ADMISSION PRICES!
FOR INFORMATION CALL 319-472-3117
A CAR PAC PROMOTION

Permit sought to reopen Tunis Speedway for races

By NANCY RAFFENSPERGER
Courier Staff Writer

Two auto racers with 56 years of combined experience are proposing to reopen Tunis Speedway for weekly stock car racing.

Vic Frey and Bob Hilmer went before the city's Planning, Programming and Zoning Commission earlier this week seeking a special permit to reopen the speedway.

A public hearing was set for Nov. 18.

The speedway, located in the 3700 block of University Avenue, was the site of weekly stock car races for 31 years until 1979. Races were conducted periodically at the track through 1982 and then stopped altogether.

One of the problems has been citizen complaints about loud noise. In 1982, the City Council ordered that all stock cars be equipped with mufflers while racing at Tunis.

Frey said the plans to reopen the track are still in the preliminary stages and that several obstacles must be overcome before racing begins.

Plans call for Frey and Hilmer to be the promoters of the track. They plan to run Sunday shows, ending by 10 p.m., from May through Labor Day. The track would employ 15 to 20 part-time workers and the goal is to draw 2,000 spectators each week.

"We think we know what it takes to run a race track. The closest place anybody has to go around here for stock car racing is Independence. That's a lot of money leaving our area each week," Frey said.

He noted that the track could draw up to 75 racers each week, with each car bringing in a minimum of four people. In addition, many racers draw their owns fans.

"People from three to four counties will come in here and spend money. They all buy gas, eat and stay in motels. It's up to the people to make this work. This area has a bad economy, but we've got to keep the taxpayers in this town," Frey said.

He said he and Hilmer do not want to cause problems with residents, but they will not operate the track if the cars must be equipped with mufflers.

"Most racers don't run just one night a week. They will run several other tracks and no other track has to run mufflers in this area. If racers start placing makeshift mufflers on their cars for races here, you're going to have half of them laying all over the track. They won't get permanent mufflers because the cars don't run as well with mufflers and because they don't have to have them at other tracks," Frey said.

"In the end, it will mean that fewer drivers will want to race at Tunis."

A major obstacle in their plans is obtaining the track itself. The track is owned by Marie Tunis, widow of Judd Tunis, who sponsored numerous entertainment events at the track for many years.

Details on whether the track will be leased or sold are being worked out, Frey said.

October 18, 1985

HARNESS HORSE RACES
The King of Sports
SUNDAY, AUG. 28th 2 P.M.
5 EVENTS
10 RACES
Starting Gate Will Be Used
FREE ADMISSION!
TUNIS SPEEDWAY
Between Waterloo & Cedar Falls on University Avenue
ENTERTAINMENT
By Shrine Clowns with
Music By Bill Shepard

August 1983

Harness racing returns and draws 500 to Tunis

By MARK THALACKER
Courier Sports Writer

Harness racing returned to Tunis Speedway Sunday before a modest crowd of 500 spectators.

Some braved the broiling sun because they were dedicated fans. Many others had never seen a harness race and may have had their interest piqued by the thought of parimutuel betting at future racetracks. But there was no parimutual betting Sunday. In fact no money officially changed hands because the program was admission free on the track built by Jud Tunis for racing and training horses but made famous by some 30 years of stock car racing.

The season's first race card (a stock car event is scheduled for Labor Day night) called for five events, three for pacers and two for trotters, with two heats of each.

The 90-degree temperatures eventually took their toll, and the crowd melted away after the first hour.

By the start of the five second heats only 150 people remained in their seats. The final two races were viewed by less than 60.

THE NINTH race was the most exciting of the day. It was the second heat of the Free-for-All Pace, with a 10-horse field.

The reason for the excitement was the speed of Cash's Lad, owned by Royal and Roger Roland of Grinnell and driven by Duane Roland. Fourth in the first heat, Cash's Lad took control on the first turn and pulled away from the rest of the field to lead by three lengths.

Although Fire Skipper closed the gap on the final straightaway, Cash's Lad set a new track record of 2:07.3 for the one-mile course and won by more than a length. It was exactly five seconds faster than the fourth event's first heat, which was the fastest of the first five heats.

WATERLOO'S Kevin Nanke drove two horses Sunday.

In the first event he drove his father Bernie's pacer, Melrick, to a pair of second-place finishes, almost catching winner Paint Your Wagon in the second heat.

In the third race Nanke drove his own trotter, Match Mat. Match Mat edged Hickory Nut by a nose for third in the first heat, but finished fifth in the second heat.

The first heat of that race was won by Noble Tuffet, owned by W.D. Card of Cedar Falls and driven by Dave Sertz.

Three horses won both heats of their events.

Paint Your Wagon, owned by Pat Smith of Oskaloosa and driven by Don Smith, took both firsts in the 750 Pace. St. Patrick, owned by R.D. Lewis of Cowley, Wyo., and driven by Dick McDanel, turned the 1500 Pace into Irish property. And Jubilie John, owned and driven by Sac City's Roger Owens, swept the Free-for-All Trot.

NON-WINNERS 750 PACE
FIRST HEAT—1. Paint Your Wagon 2. Melrick 3. [illegible]
SECOND HEAT—1. Paint Your Wagon 2. Melrick 3. [illegible]
NON-WINNERS 1500 PACE
FIRST HEAT—1. St. Patrick 2. [illegible] 3. San Padre
SECOND HEAT—1. St. Patrick 2. San Padre 3. [illegible]
NON-WINNERS 1000 TROT
FIRST HEAT—1. Noble Tuffet 2. [illegible] 3. Match Mat
SECOND HEAT—1. [illegible]
FREE-FOR-ALL PACE
FIRST HEAT—1. [illegible] 3. Fire Skipper
SECOND HEAT—1. Cash's Lad 2. Fire Skipper 3. [illegible]
FREE-FOR-ALL TROT
FIRST HEAT—1. Jubilie John 2. [illegible]
SECOND HEAT—1. Jubilie John 2. [illegible]

The Deery Brothers
present
the
FIRECRACKER SPECIAL!
MONDAY, JULY 5th
Gates Open at 4 • Races at 6
TUNIS SPEEDWAY
Hwy. 218
Between Waterloo and C.F.
(Behind Food 4 Less, Open 24 Hours)
Stock Car Racing
NASCAR — Grand American
Altered Street Stock
IMCA Modified — Sportsmen
SPECTACULAR FIREWORKS DISPLAY
— PRICES —
Adults $5, Kids 6-12 $2
Under 6 — FREE
Buckaroo Side $3

Waterloo
T
Iowa
3/8-Mile Dirt
TUNIS SPEEDWAY
A Car Pac Promotion, Vinton, Iowa
Hwy. 218 Between Waterloo and Cedar Falls
JOHN DEERY MOTORS
MEMORIAL DAY SPECIAL
Monday, May 31st
Gates Open 5:00
Races 7:00
$5,000 Plus Purse
$600 To Win NASCAR Grand American
50-Lap Feature
• NASCAR Grand American • IMCA Modifieds • Altered Street Stock
Admission Prices: Adults $5, Kids 6-12 $2, Under 6 Free
Buckaroo Side $3 (East Bleachers)
Information: Phone 319-472-4713

Claus and Marlene Stricker

TUNIS SPEEDWAY
TUNIS STAFF

Front row (l to r) Dick Gerst (Ass't Flagman), Debbie Bohr (Pit Ass't), Claus Stricker, Sr. (Promoter), Dan Stricker, Marlene Stricker, Cy Bohr (Flagman).

Back row (l to r) Butch Stricker (Ass't Pit Stewart), David Stricker (Ass't Flagman), Richard Hinz (Race Director), Leroy Russell (Scorer). Not shown, Craig McGee (Chief Pit Stewart).

LAVERNE
75

Driver Laverne Lehman

Driver Scott Braun

Drivers D. Arthur Nesteby and Ed Sanger

14

Claus Stricker--The Driver

5

SAND'S
WATERLOO, IA.
8

5
JOHNNY'S SUPERIOR
'400'
Hiway 218 N. Cedar FaLLs
Ia.

14

HANSEN AUTO SALVAGE
Cedar Falls
Ia
5

8
LARRY
LANGE
FORD
CEDAR FALLS
24 HR.
SERVICE
WESTERN STATION
217 WASHINGTON
WATERLOO

RACING
ASS'N. INC.
EVERY SUNDAY NITE
TUNIS SPEEDWAY

Support Vehicles

Jeep

Ray Donovan in the KWWL
Summer Fun Machine

USED CARS
AUTO
MARKET

TUNIS
SPEEDWAY

The Water Truck

TUNIS SPEEDWAY

Tunis SPEEDWAY
PACE CAR
SUNDAY NIGHT

PACE CAR
Tunis SPEEDWAY
STOCK CAR RACES
SUNDAY NIGHT
DEERY Pontiac

TUNIS SPEEDWAY
STOCKCAR RACES

Welcome
RACE FANS
TUNIS SPEEDWAY
SPORTSMEN TAP 121
RED &
24

Kid's night

JULY 30

Kid's Night on Sunday July 30 this year will be noted as the biggest ever. Ten thousand pennies and an assortment of wrapped candy will be strewn over the track surface for the grand melee of young coin and candy conoisseurs.

In addition to the "coin and candy chase," two free bicycles will be given away.

The Drivers...

LLOYD DRAPER of Grundy Center

FLAG SIGNALS

Green Flag: Start — course is clear.
Yellow Flag: Indicated only to exercise caution and to follow directions of track supervisors in the danger area.
Red Flag: STOP — race is halted.
Crossed Flags: "Half Way" mark.
Blue Flag: Layover, being lapped.
Black Flag: Indicates an unsafe operating condition or unsportsmanlike conduct displayed.
White Flag: Entering last lap.
Checkered Flag: You are finished.

A PREVIEW OF UPCOMING EVENTS--10,000 pennies and a large assortment of wrapped candy will be strewn over the track surface on Kid's Night, Sun., July 30, plus other prizes to be given away.

Banner night

JULY 2

Race fans will be given an opportunity to show their artwork, imagination, and creativity as the famous Tunis Speedway presents Banner Night Sunday, July 2. Fan club banners are the type accepted and the Tunis Speedway staff representatives will judge the banners.

The best-looking banner in overall appearance will be awarded a fifteen dollar cash prize. The largest banner in square inches will be awarded a ten dollar cash prize, and five dollars will go to the creator of the most-original banner design.

Also on tap for the evening's entertainment is a full array of fireworks.

POINT LEADER--Ed Sanger of Waterloo.

CURT HANSEN, 27, of Dike started racing in an old $300 Ford at Nashua.

LARRY WASSER of Cedar Falls

WATERLOO T IOWA TUNIS SPEEDWAY

ERFORMANCE ENGINEERING 4

STAN STOVER of Reinbeck, a driver to watch out for.

SUBSCRI NOW HAWKEYE RACI BOX 53 VINTON, IOWA

Where Would All This Be Without...The FANS!

Racing is a sport that comes in many flavors and fans of racing many times can't quite explain what draws them to events to watch other people go around in circles.

But it's one sport that has tested time itself and today is one of the largest spectator sports in the entire world.

Welcome
RACE FANS
TUNIS SPEEDWAY

Judd Tunis knew he neede to please the fans, not only with good racing, but with an atmosphere of excitement, maybe some danger and a whole bunch of community. So he made every effort to make the fans happy. And every race promoter during the Tunis Speedway years knew just how important that was.

Here's just one story.

My Memories of Tunis Speedway

By Eugene Bentley

As a child, my first love was cars. It was anything about cars, sports cars, drag racing, NASCAR, Indy --as long as it had four wheels it was great. I watched them on TV, saw them in magazines and books-you name it. I could name makes and models of cars when I was five.

I loved cars so much that I would draw them – on anything including walls doors and the back of homework assignments.

It was not hard to figure out why. My Dad at one time was a Buick mechanic and retained his interest in fixing cars for most of his life (even though it was no longer his profession). He quit when automatic transmissions came into the picture.

He would frequent Ben & Dicks Garage or get a part from Bentley Chevrolet (no relation). Some Saturday mornings he used to take me on his junkyard trips to get a part for the 1937 Cadillac he was restoring.

I was thrilled one time when there was the shell of a 1955 Buick stock car sitting next to a car he was trying to get a tail light off of. That brings me to my favorite of all the things about cars -- Sunday nights at Tunis Speedway.

Sunday nights during the summer were something I always looked forward to. Our family of six kids loaded up in our yellow 1957 Desoto station wagon and trek on to Tunis Speedway.

Sometimes we'd make a stop at the Holiday Station on Highway 218. I'd look up in the clear blue sky and just hear the roar of the engines as if the cars were doing hot laps right in front of me.

Well, it could have been early heat races – it seemed like Dad was never in a hurry to get there (much to my chagrin). But the track was still just over the hill.

At tender age of 3 (that's what I figure my first memories were) I had no concept of what the classes were. I think at the time they had two. I just knew that there were cars that had no front fenders and hoods that were current vintage '55-'57 Chevrolets and quite a few coupes and sedans. Then there were the mass of these full bodied cars they ran at the end (which I later found out were the Road Runners). So I assigned them 'hoods off' (Late Model/Sportsmen) and 'hoods on' (the Road Runners). Well that's what I called them when I had my own races with my little Matchbox and Hot Wheels cars in the dirt.

At the tender age of 3 (that's what I figure my first memories were) I had no concept of what the classes were. I think at the time they had two. I just knew that there were cars that had no front fenders and hoods that were current vintage '55-'57 Chevrolets and quite a few coupes and sedans.

Then there were the mass of these full bodied cars they ran at the end (which I later found out were the Road Runners). So I assigned them 'hoods off' (Late Model/Sportsmen) and 'hoods on' (the Road Runners). Well that's what I called them when I had my own races with my little Matchbox and Hot Wheels cars in the dirt.

"It was the roar of the engines, the way the cars backfired as they downshifted to make the turns, the spurts of fire from the exhausts, the smell of the burning fuel (and oil) mixed in with cigarettes and cheap perfume..."

But lord help everyone if we had other plans other than Tunis Speedway on a Sunday. I would kick up such a fuss if we went by the track and we didn't stop. At first it was easy just to take a route that didn't pass by Tunis. One evening we were coming home from Charles City and my parents thought it would be ok to take me by the track since it rained hard and the races were likely rained out. I saw the stock cars being hauled off to go home. I still had a fit!

Well who could blame me for being such a brat? I was hooked on the whole experience of the dirt track. It was the roar of the engines, the way the cars backfired as they downshifted to make the turns, the spurts of fire from the exhausts, the smell of the burning fuel (and oil) mixed in with cigarettes and cheap perfume, the way the track's surface changed from wet and tacky to dry slick as the rubber was laid down on the dirt. And since they were held in the evening there was a beautifully dramatic sun setting over the track. And I got to stay up late. It was all very intoxicating for a child.

Ultimately it was the action with the cars broad sliding the turns, kicking up dirt that sometimes hit you in the face or someone dogging it out with a stiff competitor. And don't forget the wrecks.

In the Road Runner division I remember seeing a '58 Ford doing a cartwheel in the midst of 50 or so cars on the backstretch.

There was a '57 Chevrolet flip 3 times in turn 3 and 4 in the Sportsmen division. And then there was an incident where all I could see was a cloud of dust and smoke heading for the fence in turn 4 that sent the crowd (including me, my Dad and younger brother) scurrying for cover leaving a '66 or '67 Chevelle resting at the guard rail there when all the dust settled . I think his throttle stuck. That car sat there until that race was over.

Wheelbarrow races

And don't forget the cars themselves. There were a myriad of 1955-57 Chevrolets, a '55 or '56 Ford Crown Vick here or '57 Ford Fairlane there and some Buicks, Pontiacs, Oldsmobiles, Mercurys, Dodges sprinkled throughout.

I think that's why I like that vintage of cars to this day. And then there would be a die-hard running a Flathead V8 with a '49 or a '53 Ford among the Chevy Sixes.

To me, there was no other track that had that kind of racing. I would see racing on TV, but they were the big races at Daytona and Indianapolis. On TV in the 1960s and most of the 1970s, there wasn't much coverage of any kind of racing (the first flag to flag Daytona 500 broadcast was in 1979). TV was so stupid I thought. There was racing on Wide World of Sports but you only got a half hour of the entire race and the closest thing they showed of grass roots stock car racing was figure 8 races held in New York somewhere.

But in 1965 I visited my first track other than Tunis. That was Lake Hill Speedway near St Louis. It was built between two railroad tracks and we had to walk through a tunnel underneath them. It was incredible music hearing the roar of the engines echoing through that tunnel. I heard the same sounds, smelled the same smells and saw the same sights as Tunis.

At the time Lake Hill was a dirt track as Tunis was, but the pit area was the infield and not off to the side on the turns. We got to see all the behind the scenes action in front of us. It was fun seeing the hustle of pit crews changing tires or welding the barred bumpers back on the cars that knocked loose. The track was a little bigger but the cars were just like the ones at Tunis and the racing was too. We visited there a second time in 1970 but I was disappointed that it was paved. But I think we may have seen a young Ken Shrader and Russ Wallace (Rusty's Dad) racing and not even known it.

After our first visit to Lake Hill, we sometimes made a point to seek out a track when we went on our long vacations. We went to Lake Side Speedway in Denver Co. It was a clay track that ran a neat class of old coupes and sedans with GMC engines.

There was also a dirt track we went to in New Mexico (whose name escapes me). We also visited other tracks in Iowa. We made a visit to Knoxville in 1970 when they were running a Supermodified class.

We also visited Independence and Vinton speedways as well. But it was always nice to come home to Tunis.

In 1968 I saw trailers for a film when I was in 1st grade. It had the same type of stock cars as I saw at Tunis and figured it was filmed there. For years I didn't know what film that was. My sister insisted it was Red Line 7,000. I thought so too until I saw the film. But they were NASCAR type cars and not the dirt cars I was expecting. I then thought I dreamed the whole thing.

Some 30 years later I found out that it was Fever Heat and actually was filmed at Stuart Speedway and other tracks in Iowa (but not Tunis).

As I grew older I became more aware of the drivers. At first the only driver I paid attention to was Red Droste because he won a lot.

One night we took another neighbor friend Tim and his dad. I was rooting for number 99 because I liked the number (I didn't care who drove it). His dad mentioned that they used to be neighbors with Ed Sanger. When Tim was talking it somehow jumped from being Ed Sanger as neighbors to him being his uncle (or some close relation). So Tim was urging me to cheer for the 95.

When we got home my father told me that he'd better not hear me talk about Ed Sanger again. It was concerning the BS that Tim was telling me which was going in one ear and going out the other. I was taken aback and didn't get a chance to tell my dad that I really couldn't care a less if Sanger was Tim's uncle or not. I still cheered for the 99 --whoever he was.

Other drivers caught my attention like Red Dralle, Curt Hansen (whom we saw regularly at Independence) and Denny Osborne whom we saw at Midway Downs. And then in 1971 and 1972 I was extremely honored to have a stock car in my neighborhood. It was a blue 1957 Chevrolet Sportsmen number 40 of Roy Stephen.

We saw Roy Stephen race at Tunis and Independence and seemed to do quite well. I would consistently see him among the top four finishing the heats and features. My brother and I would be riding our bikes and had to stop and watch Roy and his crew load up the car every Saturday for Independence.

Of course I would rather I didn't have my younger brother tag along with me. And we managed to annoy Roy and his crew even though we kept our distance. You know how brotherly love works – squabbles and fights.

Around this time I opened up my first Stock Car Racing magazine and a whole new world of racing opened up to me. There was all the news about NASCAR and Grand National and the usual stuff you find in Motor Trend and other car magazines. But the part I was most interested in was the grass roots racing happening all over the country. Other states in the country were running '57 Chevrolets,' 64- '67 Chevelles on dirt.

I was also fascinated by the modified coupes and sedans running out of the Northeast and New England states. They reminded me of the early cars at Tunis (OK maybe if they were injected with steroids). I saw names like Ray Evernham, Buzzie Ruetimann (David's Father) and Geoff Bodine as well as articles by Dick Bergren.

I also was thrilled that the October 1972 issue had a picture of '55 Chevrolet hobby stock taken at Independence (close enough to Tunis). My friend's Uncle Vernon ran that track. The car was Judy Hickey's and the issue was all about women's lib and her spearheading a campaign to allow women to race. At many tracks they weren't even allowed in the pits at the time. Any racing they did were in what they called Powder Puff Derbys where they competed against other women and not competing against the boys.

The 1975 season at Tunis opened to a revamped track. It was no longer a ¼ mile, it was a 3/8 mile with steeper banks. There was some pretty exciting racing going on. They had trouble getting a Late Model feature going because of some heat between Doc Mayner and Schaefer. The Doc kept running into Schaefer in turn three after the green came down causing three restarts before the Doc got kicked off the track.

On a more somber note, a 1975 issue of Stock Car Racing had an interview with Keith Knaack. Among his discussion on how to get the advantage over the other guy off the turns and how Ed Sanger was beating everyone with a small block engine, there was a deep concern about the cost of racing and its effects on grass roots racing.

The advances in racing technology were strangling the sport with increasing the price tag. Yes, the cars were getting faster but the cars were relying more and more on racing parts and less on stock. The cars were being built for the driver and his crew at businesses instead of by them in the backyard.

I noticed the change as '55-'57 Chevrolets were bumped from Late Model to Sportsmen status. And then from Road Runner/Street Stock to off the charts completely by 1977.With a brief stint with Chevelles, the Camaros and Firebirds took over. They had better aerodynamics, lighter bodies and better engine displacement. Broader tires and bigger engines were being used along with the Quick Change rearends sent the price tag soaring for the drivers and their crew and the need for higher purses for the promoters.

At this time, I had moved from the middle of west Waterloo to just inside Cedar Falls city limits. Tunis was within walking distance. I went there a lot when I had the time and money. I noticed that the cars were looking all the same and the count was smaller. The stands were looking bare.

In the back of my mind Keith Knaack's words were ringing true for Tunis

One night in 1979 I went to an event that got rained out but I noticed what looked like an old silver 1930s sedan with no fenders. They were driving it to the pits and damned if it wasn't an old stock car with probably a Flathead V8 Ford engine. We were thus informed that there was going to be an old -timers stock car exhibition race next Sunday.

I had to go see that, but was disappointed that there were only 4 of those old coupes and sedans in the field. But it was a small beginning of the Midwest Vintage Stock Car Club. But a thought crossed my mind that Tunis is ending up where it started. Tunis was giving its bow to the past and with a hint of sadness that it was all going to end

It was 1979 and the sun had set on Tunis. The track stopped weekly programs but held special events until 1983. A couple of those events gave a bow to the future of racing. One was a hobby stock/ street stock event.

Due to the increasing expenses, some track owners and promoters were faced with dropping the top tier classes such as the Late Models. Before Street Stocks were viewed as something a little better than demolition derby, here they stepped up to fill the void as young drivers got their foot in the door.

Even more important, was a special Sportsman event and a brand new class of racecar called an IMCA Modified. Keith Knaack had a prototype he raced in the road runner and street stock divisions at Tunis and Independence in the late 70s.

Keith Knaack--January, 1980 Hawkeye Racing News

Lots of things have been happening in Midwest auto racing since the last issue of Hawkeye Racing News was printed in October. Some changes have been good — others, we will wait and see. Promoters have changed — tracks have closed — yes, 1979 has been a funny year for auto racing. I am not predicting gloom for the 1980s — far from it. I believe we have a great future to look forward to auto racing in the next decade. Auto racing was indeed — the Sport of the 70s

It was a shock when Judd Tunis informed that Tunis Speedway will not run regular races after 31 years of continuous Sunday night racing. Tunis, pictured below right with his race track in the background, cited several reasons for giving up the regular Sunday night grind. Just tired of every week hassle is one reason given by the 85-year-old track owner. "It's just not worth all the effort and work to fight everyone to put on races," Tunis added, "I might put on some special car races and also some horse races during the year. Who knows."

I did my best to talk Judd into holding regular races at his track but he has made up his mind and I couldn't change it. I really feel badly about Tunis Speedway closing down, but I certainly understand how Judd feels. I want to thank Judd Tunis for the 31 years he has given to auto racing. Everyone knows about Tunis Speedway and it used to be you were not a noted driver if you never drove a race car at Tunis Speedway. We will all miss the regular Sunday night races at Waterloo.

Jack Mitchell's IMCA modified won the race. The cars reminded me of the Northeast modifieds when they went from old coupes and sedans to Pintos, Gremlins and Vega for bodies.

IMCA started a virtual renaissance in grass roots auto racing. The sanction brought its own Stock Car, Hobby Stock, Sprint Car and Late Model divisions. There were increased car counts with stiffer competition at tracks. It all culminated in the IMCA Supernationals at Boone Speedway and as strange coincidence is a track that resembles Tunis in its shape and size.

Unfortunately it was all too late for Tunis. The combination of costs, urban sprawl and noise ordinances took its toll on Jud Tunis.

It was a reality that became more and more evident in the 80s for many tracks. The headaches weren't coming from the noise of the cars, but from the noise of politics, expenses and general upkeep.

But in the end, Tunis stock car racing left such an impression on us all. For me, it was a compulsion to draw stock cars in the back of homework assignments, on the walls in the house I grew up in and on the chalk boards in class.

And for others it was very fond memories of a fun and exciting family activity.

The writer of this story,--

Eugene Bentley, was born in Waterloo, graduated from Cedar Falls High, received his BFA from UNI, is an Air Force veteran and is currently employed in a printing business in Urbandale.

Midget Auto Races
Tunis Speed Bowl
Official Program 10c
West Hi-Way 218 - Waterloo, Iowa
1949
Entries for Sunday, August 14, 1949
EVENT NO. 1—TIME TRIALS
Next Race Here Sunday, August 21
Flag Signals
Raceway Officials
EVENT No. 2 — FIRST QUALIFYING HEAT FOR FINALS
BUNS, ROLLS & DONUTS
CHUMLEY'S Auto Market
Stock Car Races
TUNIS SPEEDWAY
Races Every Sunday Night
Official Program 10c
CASEY'S Cycle Center
Chicken-on-Wheels
Official Entry List
Shipp Bros.
Iowa Golden Dairies
Buy Goodyear
Dodger
OFFICIAL PROGRAM
Stock Car Races
TUNIS SPEEDWAY
RACES EVERY SUNDAY
OFFICIAL PROGRAM
STOCK CAR RACES
TUNIS SPEEDWAY
May 30 - Memorial Day
EVENT No. 3 — SECOND QUALIFYING HEAT FOR FINAL
Altstadt-Langlas Baking Company
KLEEN-MAID
Bread - Cakes - Rolls
EVENT No. 4 — THIRD QUALIFYING HEAT FOR FINAL
THE RATH PACKING CO.
EVENT No. 5 — HANDICAP RACE
SILVER INN
DINE and DANCE
EVENT No. 6 — SEMI-MAIN
J. L. TUNIS
College Hill Print Shop
Have a Coke
NAGLE & HEALD ELECTRIC COMPANY
LUCKY NUMBER
Nº 8840 B
OFFICIAL PROGRAM
Midget Auto Races
TUNIS SPEEDWAY
Sunday, July 29th

The very first program for a racing event held at Tunis Speedway, August 14, 1949.

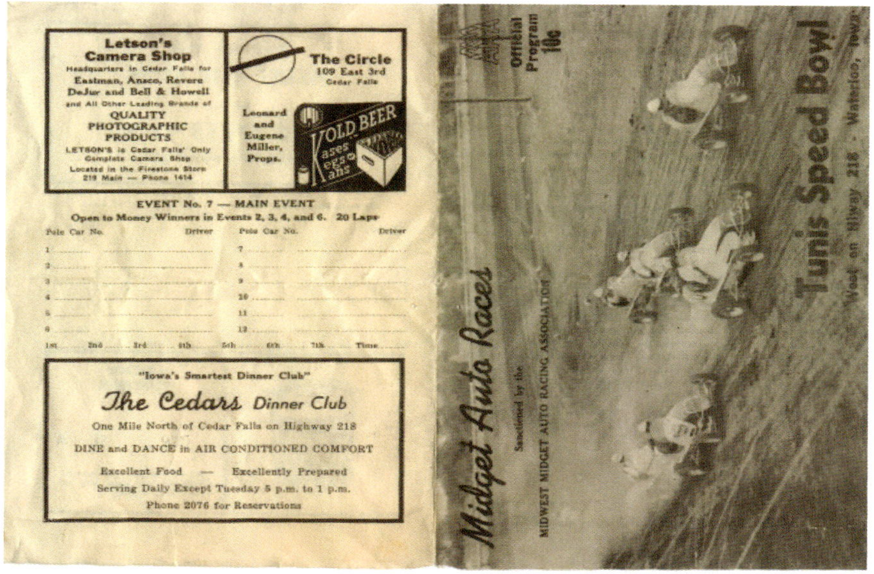

Letson's Camera Shop
Headquarters in Cedar Falls for
Eastman, Ansco, Revere
DeJur and Bell & Howell
and All Other Leading Brands of
QUALITY PHOTOGRAPHIC PRODUCTS
LETSON'S is Cedar Falls' Only Complete Camera Shop
Located in the Firestone Store
219 Main — Phone 1414

The Circle
109 East 3rd
Cedar Falls
Leonard and Eugene Miller, Props.
KOLD BEER
Kases Kegs Kans

EVENT No. 7 — MAIN EVENT
Open to Money Winners in Events 2, 3, 4, and 6. 20 Laps

Pole	Car No.	Driver	Pole	Car No.	Driver
1			7		
2			8		
3			9		
4			10		
5			11		
6			12		

1st ... 2nd ... 3rd ... 4th ... 5th ... 6th ... 7th ... Time ...

"Iowa's Smartest Dinner Club"
The Cedars Dinner Club
One Mile North of Cedar Falls on Highway 218
DINE and DANCE in AIR CONDITIONED COMFORT
Excellent Food — Excellently Prepared
Serving Daily Except Tuesday 5 p.m. to 1 p.m.
Phone 2076 for Reservations

Official Program 10c
Midget Auto Races
Sanctioned by the
MIDWEST MIDGET AUTO RACING ASSOCIATION
Tunis Speed Bowl
West on Hiway 218 - Waterloo, Iowa

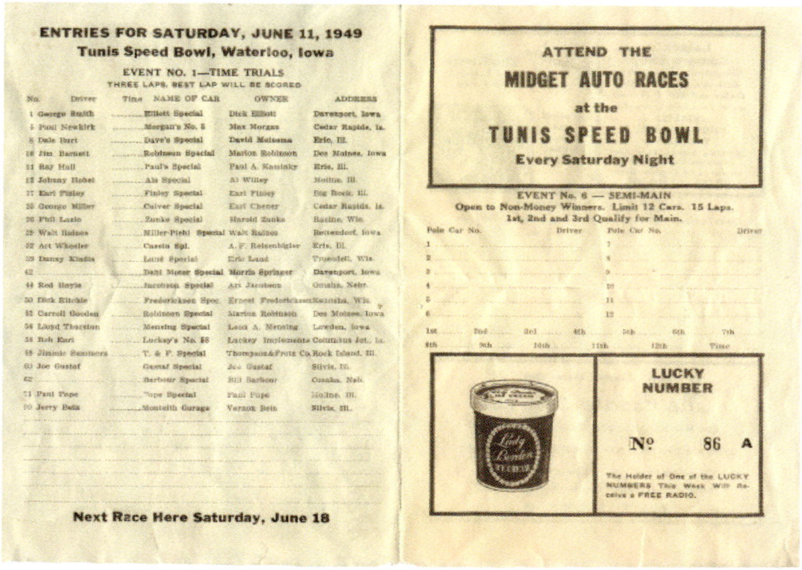

ENTRIES FOR SATURDAY, JUNE 11, 1949
Tunis Speed Bowl, Waterloo, Iowa

EVENT NO. 1—TIME TRIALS
THREE LAPS, BEST LAP WILL BE SCORED

No.	Driver	Time	NAME OF CAR	OWNER	ADDRESS
1	George Smith		Elliott Special	Dick Elliott	Davenport, Iowa
5	Paul Newkirk		Morgan's No. 5	Max Morgan	Cedar Rapids, Ia.
8	Dale Burt		Dave's Special	David Meinema	Erie, Ill.
10	Jim Barnett		Robinson Special	Marion Robinson	Des Moines, Iowa
11	Ray Hall		Paul's Special	Paul A. Kaminky	Erie, Ill.
12	Johnny Hobel		Als Special	Al Willey	Moline, Ill.
17	Earl Finley		Finley Special	Earl Finley	Big Rock, Ill.
25	George Miller		Culver Special	Earl Cheney	Cedar Rapids, Ia.
26	Phil Lazio		Zunke Special	Harold Zunke	Racine, Wis.
29	Walt Baines		Miller-Piehl Special	Walt Baines	Bettendorf, Iowa
32	Art Wheeler		Cassin Spl.	A. F. Reisenbigler	Erie, Ill.
39	Danny Kladis		Lund Special	Eric Lund	Truesdell, Wis.
42			Dahl Motor Special	Morris Springer	Davenport, Iowa
44	Red Hoyle		Jacobson Special	Art Jacobson	Omaha, Nebr.
50	Dick Ritchie		Fredericksen Spec.	Ernest Fredericksen	Kenosha, Wis.
52	Carroll Gooden		Robinson Special	Marion Robinson	Des Moines, Iowa
56	Lloyd Thurston		Mensing Special	Leon A. Mensing	Lowden, Iowa
58	Bob Kart		Luckey's No. 58	Luckey Implements	Columbus Jct., Ia.
59	Jimmie Sanders		T. & F. Special	Thompson&Frotz Co.	Rock Island, Ill.
60	Joe Gustaf		Gustaf Special	Joe Gustaf	Silvis, Ill.
62			Barbour Special	Bill Barbour	Omaha, Neb.
71	Paul Pope		Pope Special	Paul Pope	Moline, Ill.
90	Jerry Bein		Monteith Garage	Vernon Bein	Silvis, Ill.

Next Race Here Saturday, June 18

ATTEND THE
MIDGET AUTO RACES
at the
TUNIS SPEED BOWL
Every Saturday Night

EVENT No. 6 — SEMI-MAIN
Open to Non-Money Winners. Limit 12 Cars. 15 Laps.
1st, 2nd and 3rd Qualify for Main.

Pole	Car No.	Driver	Pole	Car No.	Driver
1			7		
2			8		
3			9		
4			10		
5			11		
6			12		

1st ... 2nd ... 3rd ... 4th ... 5th ... 6th ... 7th ...
8th ... 9th ... 10th ... 11th ... 12th ... Time ...

LUCKY NUMBER
№ 86 A
The Holder of One of the LUCKY NUMBERS This Week Will Receive a FREE RADIO.

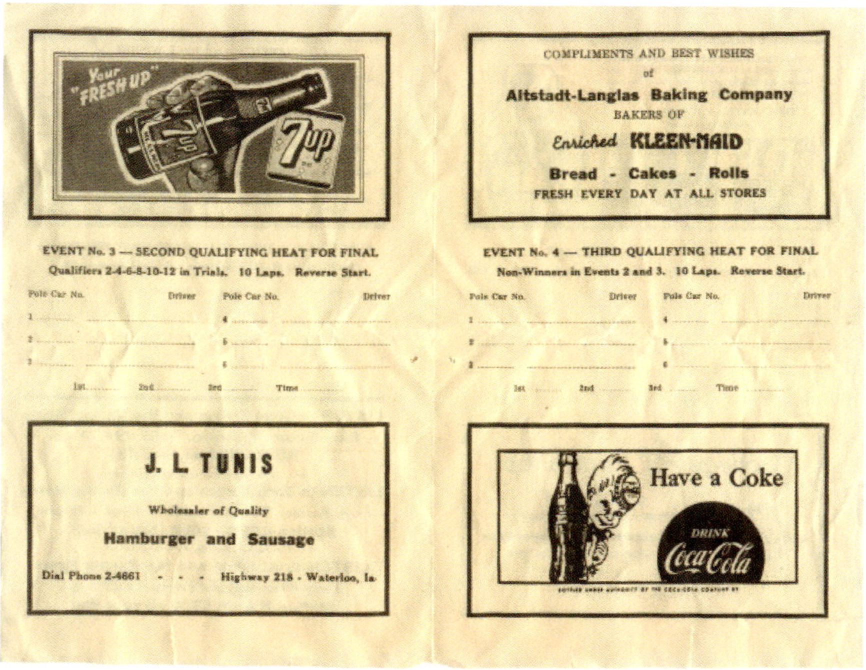

Your "FRESH UP"
7up

EVENT No. 3 — SECOND QUALIFYING HEAT FOR FINAL
Qualifiers 2-4-6-8-10-12 in Trials. 10 Laps. Reverse Start.

Pole	Car No.	Driver	Pole	Car No.	Driver
1			4		
2			5		
3			6		

1st ... 2nd ... 3rd ... Time ...

J. L. TUNIS
Wholesaler of Quality
Hamburger and Sausage
Dial Phone 2-4661 - - - Highway 218 - Waterloo, Ia.

COMPLIMENTS AND BEST WISHES
of
Altstadt-Langlas Baking Company
BAKERS OF
Enriched KLEEN-MAID
Bread - Cakes - Rolls
FRESH EVERY DAY AT ALL STORES

EVENT No. 4 — THIRD QUALIFYING HEAT FOR FINAL
Non-Winners in Events 2 and 3. 10 Laps. Reverse Start.

Pole	Car No.	Driver	Pole	Car No.	Driver
1			4		
2			5		
3			6		

1st ... 2nd ... 3rd ... Time ...

Have a Coke
DRINK Coca-Cola

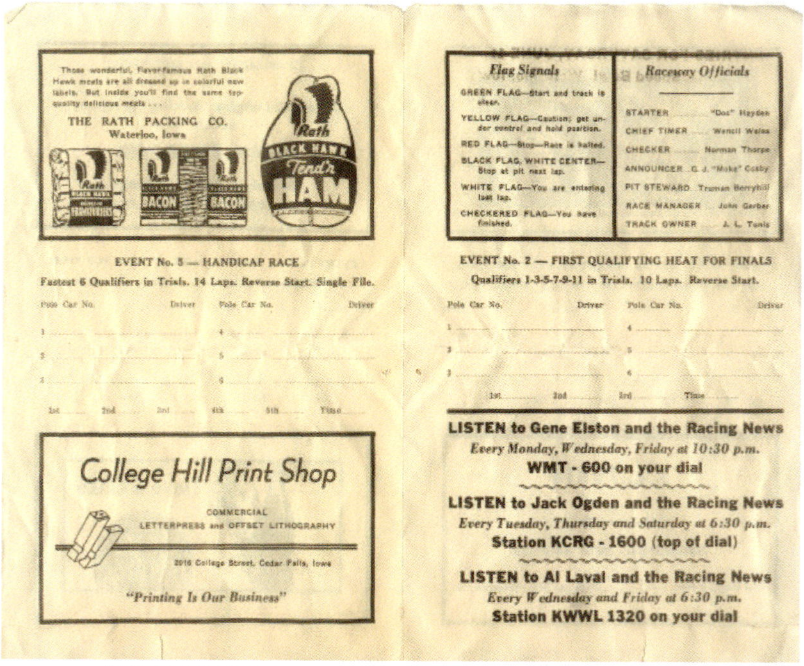

Those wonderful, flavor-famous Rath Black Hawk meats are all dressed up in colorful new labels. But inside you'll find the same top-quality delicious meats . . .
THE RATH PACKING CO.
Waterloo, Iowa
Rath Black Hawk Frankfurters — Bacon — Bacon
Rath BLACK HAWK Tend'r HAM

EVENT No. 5 — HANDICAP RACE
Fastest 6 Qualifiers in Trials. 14 Laps. Reverse Start. Single File.

Pole	Car No.	Driver	Pole	Car No.	Driver
1			4		
2			5		
3			6		

1st ... 2nd ... 3rd ... 4th ... 5th ... Time ...

College Hill Print Shop
COMMERCIAL
LETTERPRESS and OFFSET LITHOGRAPHY
2016 College Street, Cedar Falls, Iowa
"Printing Is Our Business"

Flag Signals
GREEN FLAG—Start and track is clear.
YELLOW FLAG—Caution; get under control and hold position.
RED FLAG—Stop—Race is halted.
BLACK FLAG, WHITE CENTER—Stop at pit next lap.
WHITE FLAG—You are entering last lap.
CHECKERED FLAG—You have finished.

Raceway Officials

STARTER	"Doc" Hayden
CHIEF TIMER	Wencil Weiss
CHECKER	Norman Thorpe
ANNOUNCER	G. J. "Moke" Cosby
PIT STEWARD	Truman Berryhill
RACE MANAGER	John Gerber
TRACK OWNER	J. L. Tunis

EVENT No. 2 — FIRST QUALIFYING HEAT FOR FINALS
Qualifiers 1-3-5-7-9-11 in Trials. 10 Laps. Reverse Start.

Pole	Car No.	Driver	Pole	Car No.	Driver
1			4		
2			5		
3			6		

1st ... 2nd ... 3rd ... Time ...

LISTEN to Gene Elston and the Racing News
Every Monday, Wednesday, Friday at 10:30 p.m.
WMT - 600 on your dial

LISTEN to Jack Ogden and the Racing News
Every Tuesday, Thursday and Saturday at 6:30 p.m.
Station KCRG - 1600 (top of dial)

LISTEN to Al Laval and the Racing News
Every Wednesday and Friday at 6:30 p.m.
Station KWWL 1320 on your dial

"Have a good day."
Coke
Every SUNDAY Night
WELCOME TO
TUNIS SPEEDWAY
Waterloo, Iowa
Home of Iowa's Best Late Model Drivers
1972
Official Program
25¢
TUNIS SPEEDWAY
"CONTEST OF RACING KNOW-HOW"
LARRY LANGE FORD
Largest Dealer in Eastern Iowa
268-0451

Seize the hop-portunity!
HOLDIMAN MOTOR
University Ave.
Cedar Falls 277—1210
TUNIS SPEEDWAY
Bicenntenial Souvenier Program
WATERLOO
Every Sunday Night
7:30 p.m.
1976
30¢
Between Waterloo and Cedar Falls on Highway 218
PROMOTER: CLAUS W. STRICKER
Best Drivers in the Midwest
Read all about it in the
Waterloo Courier

Seize the hop-portunity!
HOLDIMAN MOTORS
University Ave.
Cedar Falls 277—1210
TUNIS SPEEDWAY
Souvenir Program
WATERLOO
Every Sunday Night
7:30 p.m.
1977
30¢
Between Waterloo and Cedar Falls on Highway 218
PROMOTER: CLAUS W. STRICKER
"Best Drivers in the Midwest"
Read all about it in the
Waterloo Courier

SHRIVER PONTIAC WIDE TRACK TOWN
SHRIVER PONTIAC
"Where You Buy With Confidence"
Phone 266-1705
27th and Main — CEDAR FALLS, IOWA
OPEN EVENINGS TILL 9

Racing at its Best!
WATERLOO
Every Sunday Night
8:00 p.m.
Presented by
TUNIS SPEEDWAY, INC.
Between Waterloo and Cedar Falls on Highway 218
THIS IS YOUR LUCKY NUMBER
NO. 926
1969
Official Program
25¢

It's worth it…it's Budweiser
FAHR BEVERAGE INC.
WATERLOO, IOWA
"MAKE MINE BUD"
323 WEST 17th STREET, WATERLOO, IOWA

E S C O
The World's Largest And Most Complete Automotive Discount Store Since 1944 — The Car Owner's Dept. Store. We Guarantee To Meet Or Beat Any Mail Order Prices On Nationally Advertised Speed Equipment And Chrome Wheels!
- QUALITY MERCHANDISE AT DICOUNT PRICES FOR AUTO AND BOAT
- NATIONALLY ADVERTISED MERCHANDISE
- MIDWEST'S LARGEST STOCK OF SPEED PARTS AND WHEELS

200 Car Free Parking Lot
OPEN EVERY FRI. EVENING AND ON SUNDAY MORNINGS
ESCO DISCOUNT AUTO SUPPLY
"World's Largest Automotive Discount Store"
116 E. 11th — By the Bridge
WATERLOO

ENTRY LIST

00	Bill Zwanziger	65 Chevelle
0	Chub Leibe	67 Fairlane
1	Gale Card	65 Chevelle
2	Vince Wells	66 Chevelle
8	Claus Stricker	67 Mercury Cyclone
9	Curt Hansen	68 Ford Torino
10	Butz Jensen	64 Ford
13	Al Iben	
15	Willy Klingfus	66 Ford
16	Harold Odeen	
21	Bob Nesteby	
22	Bob Hilmer	
23	Red Droste	
25	Bob (Ty) Burger	
29	John Smith	67 Fairlane
30	Tom Hughes	
31	Red Droste	68 Chevelle
33	Pat Hamilton	62 Dodge
34	Jim Cusick	
35	Willy Richardson	
39	Lorton Grummitt	
43	Lynn Idler	67 Olds
44	Glen Martin	66 Chevelle
45	Bob Hesse	65 Chevelle
49	Stan Stover	65 Chevelle
52	Dave Plum	
63	Dave Bedard	66 Plymouth
67	Dave Erickson	67 Fairlane
69	Bill Barthelmes	68 Chevelle
71	Dr. A. E. Mayner, M.D.	65 Chevy
74	Richard Nesteby	
75	Dave Noble	65 Chevelle
77	John Webb	64 Chevy
80	Cal Swanson	69 Chevelle
81	Lynn Ricklefs	
84	Roger Kruse	65 Chevelle
86	Dave Manson	
89	Terry Messersmith	
90	Paul Fitzpatrick	66 Chevelle
92	Leo Schamhorst	61 Chevy
93	"Shorty" Hayward	65 Ford
94	Karl Sanger	62 Ford
95	Ed Sanger	69 Chevelle
96	Mert Williams	65 Chevelle
98	Dick Chapman	66 Chevelle

The Reunion

On October 5, 2013, just over 30 years after Tunis Speedway held it's very last race, a reunion was held that drew just over 700 people.

THE REUNION
of
TUNIS SPEEDWAY
Sponsored By
PERFORMANCE BODIES
Stock Car Bodies & Parts
1-800-RACING 1
EST. 1980
Oct. 5, 2013

Scott Braun, a former Tunis driver who learned not only the racing business but also developed a nationally successful company because of his Tunis experience, hosted the event at his facilities in Cedar Falls, Iowa.

The Performance Bodies building was the perfect backdrop for the people who came to see some of the images that had been gathered in the previous year that provided wonderful memories and they were able to see old friends, some of whom they had not seen since those racing days.

Barbara Higgins, granddaughter of Judd and Marie Tunis, brought Judd's entire collection of scrapbooks he had kept for posterity. They provided a fascinating look back at how the track changed over it's 35 year history.

Well over 100 former drivers came to remember the best of times, share personal stories and meet fans, many of whom came hoping to shake a hand, get a picture of a hero or just bask in the memories of the 35 years of Tunis Speedway history.

Judd Tunis's granddaughter, Barbara Higgins, was completely awed by the outpouring of gratitude people expressed about her grandfather's efforts to provide the very best racing experience, for both the fans and the drivers.

She brought the collection of scrapbooks Judd had kept of each year of the track's history, pasting both advertisements and newspaper articles in the large books that people could lovingly view.

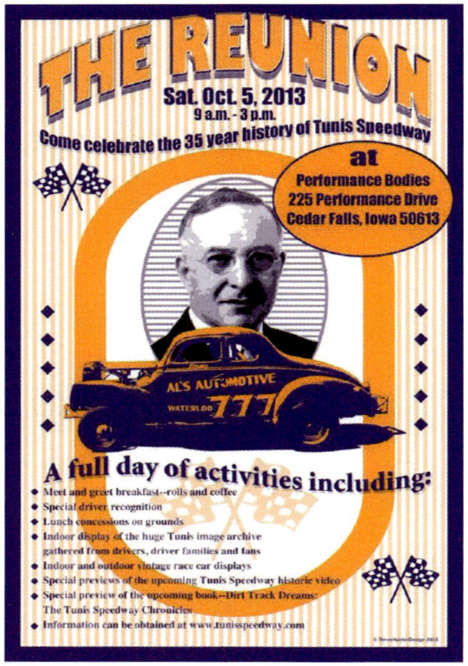

THE REUNION
Sat. Oct. 5, 2013
9 a.m. - 3 p.m.
Come celebrate the 35 year history of Tunis Speedway
at
Performance Bodies
225 Performance Drive
Cedar Falls, Iowa 50613
AL'S AUTOMOTIVE
WATERLOO 777
A full day of activities including:
Meet and greet breakfast--rolls and coffee
Special driver recognition
Lunch concessions on grounds
Indoor display of the huge Tunis image archive gathered from drivers, driver families and fans
Indoor and outdoor vintage race car displays
Special previews of the upcoming Tunis Speedway historic video
Special preview of the upcoming book--Dirt Track Dreams: The Tunis Speedway Chronicles
Information can be obtained at www.tunisspeedway.com

Judd could not have imagined that his scrapbooks would become so valuable, at least to those who just wanted to feel and smell the speedway atmosphere just one more time.

Curt Hansen brought his modified racer that celebrates the racing career of his Dad, Bob Hilmer. Bob was one of the well known drivers who began his career at Tunis Speedway and established himself as one of the best in the Midwest.

STOCK CAR RACES–3 BIG EVENTS
TUNIS SPEEDWAY
Zwanziger Wins Feature
TUNIS SPEEDWAY

Judd Tunis's scrapbooks were available for viewing.

The Drivers

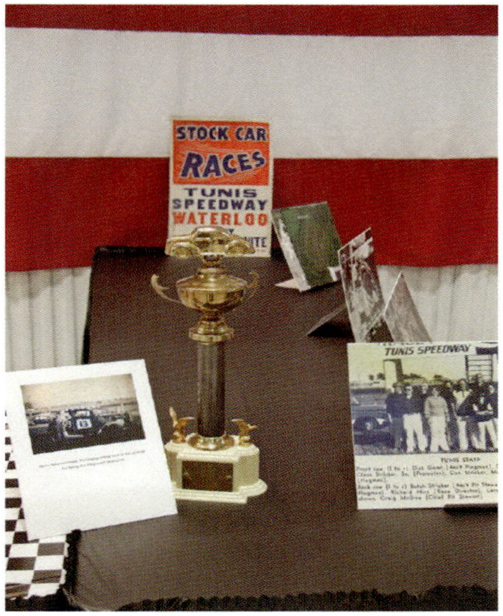
STOCK CAR
RACES
TUNIS
SPEEDWAY
WATERLOO
TUNIS SPEEDWAY

Harry Petersen's 1952 Championship trophy.

Merlin Benning brought his 1933 Ford coupe he built in 1959 to race at Tunis Speedway. He raced the car for nearly 4 years before retiring it, but it still runs and looks exactly as it did when he put it away. Talk about a time capsule!

Merlin Benning's helmet.

THE COURIER

SUNDAY | OCTOBER 6, 2013 WATERLOO www.wcfcourier.com CEDAR FALLS

A day at the races

Waterloo racing fans recall glory days of Tunis Speedway

TUNIS
SPEEDWAY
WATERLOO

OLYMPIA
BEER
"It's the Water"
Welcome...
TUNIS
RACE FANS!
thank You from "Oly"

50

Aerial Images of Tunis Speedway

1949

1950s

Aerial Images of Tunis Speedway

1960s

1970s

Aerial Images of Tunis Speedway

1978

Greenhill Rd
Tunis Circle
Hobby Lobby

2015

Rules, Rules, Rules

You'd think anyone willing to jump into a car, race around a track as fast as possible and maybe run into other cars or solid objects during the process might not care much about rules.

In the very earliest years of racing, there wasn't a lot of thought about safety. These race car drivers knew what they were getting into, right? Anyway, any mishaps were always going to happen to the "other guys".

Those early races, even at Tunis Speedway, were wide open affairs. It wasn't unusual for a wanna-be driver to head down to the local car lot, find a suitable steed for a few dollars and he was ready to go racing. Maybe he might strip off some trim and remove things like the headlights, but most of the time, the "race car" looked just like Aunt Tilly's and in some cases, it probably was.

Drivers realized, however, that there was danger lurking. After turning a car over 1-2 times during a race, a driver, after finding himself wandering aimlessly around the pit area, found good rasons to install at least a lap belt and maybe a rudimentary helmet for his head.

At Tunis Speedway the first driver associations were organized to do two things...provide a level playing field for everybody so you weren't racing against someone who had a more powerful car then you and provide some level of safety so those flips wouldn't turn drivers into vegetables well before they reached a ripe old age.

Early rules were pretty straightforward. You had to belong to the driver's association to race. Duess were usually just $5 for the entire racing season so it wasn't an outrageous sum and it could be used to help police the events for rules breakers.

Things like pit passes were required so not every Tom, Dick and Harry could prowl around the pit areas without permission. And that included the women and children! No women in the pits!

Anyone agitating or causing a ruckus was subject to being pointed toward the gate outside, though that didn't seem to stop an occassional disagreement where fisticuffs were the preferred method of settling a disagreement.

But as race cars became a bit more sophisticated (i.e. fast) it becamse necessary to begin restricting certain types of equipment and trying to decrease the chances for things like fires or anything that might injure not only the driver but anyone else, including spectators.

Pit stewards began patrolling the pit areas to watch for problems and the entire process began to be much bigger than what many driver associations could handle. That was when local sanctioning organizations came into existence so drivers could expect essentially the same safety requirements at every track.

Class rules came about from competition that pitted the same types of vehicles together with a specific range of modifications that everyone had to follow in order to race. Of course, those restrictions weren't always followed to the letter. After all, these were innovative people and going fast was the name of the game!

22 RULES PRESCRIBE SAFETY OF TUNIS RACERS

Racing Bits and Pieces

Fuel Restrictions Rigid

OFFICIAL
RULE BOOK
GREATER IOWA
RACING ASSOCIATION, INC.
Independence, Iowa 50644

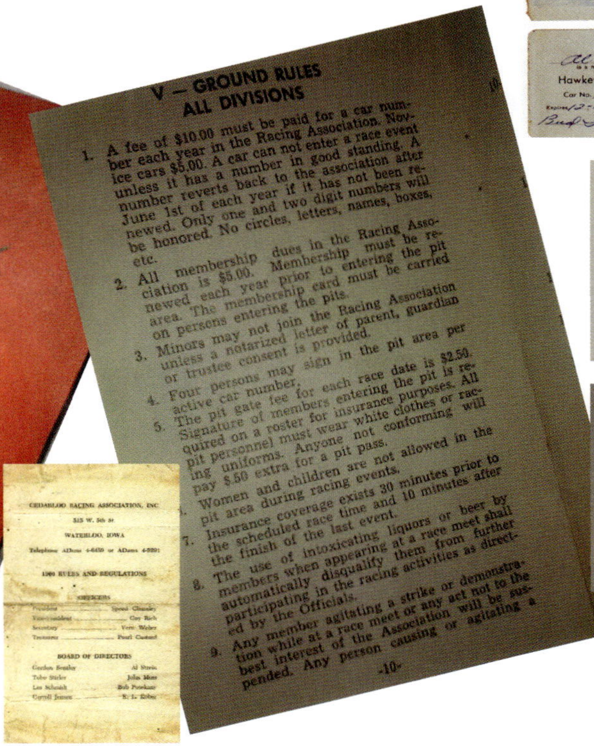

V — GROUND RULES
ALL DIVISIONS

1. A fee of $10.00 must be paid for a car number each year in the Racing Association. Novice cars $5.00. A car can not enter a race event unless it has a number in good standing. A number reverts back to the association after June 1st of each year if it has not been renewed. Only one and two digit numbers will be honored. No circles, letters, names, boxes, etc.
2. All membership dues in the Racing Association is $5.00. Membership must be renewed each year prior to entering the pit area. The membership card must be carried on persons entering the pits.
3. Minors may not join the Racing Association unless a notarized letter of parent, guardian or trustee consent is provided.
4. Four persons may sign in the pit area per active car number.
5. The pit gate fee for each race date is $2.50. Signature of members entering the pit is required on a roster for insurance purposes. All pit personnel must wear white clothes or racing uniforms. Anyone not conforming will pay $.50 extra for a pit pass.
Women and children are not allowed in the pit area during racing events.
7. Insurance coverage exists 30 minutes prior to the scheduled race time and 10 minutes after the finish of the last event.
8. The use of intoxicating liquors or beer by members when appearing at a race meet shall automatically disqualify them from further participating in the racing activities as directed by the Officials.
9. Any member agitating a strike or demonstration while at a race meet or any act not to the best interest of the Association will be suspended. Any person causing or agitating a

-10-

CEDARLOO RACING ASSOCIATION, INC

515 W. 5th St

WATERLOO, IOWA

RULES AND REGULATIONS

OFFICERS

BOARD OF DIRECTORS

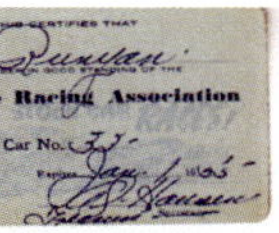
Hawkeye Racing Association
Car No.

This Certifies That
Hawkeye Racing Association
Car No. 121
Expires 12-31 1955
Secretary

PIT PASS
Cedarloo Racing Association, Inc.
A

PIT PASS
Nº 52162
Tunis June 24
Must Be Worn In Plain Sight

RULES-REGULATIONS
Hawkeye Racing Association, Inc

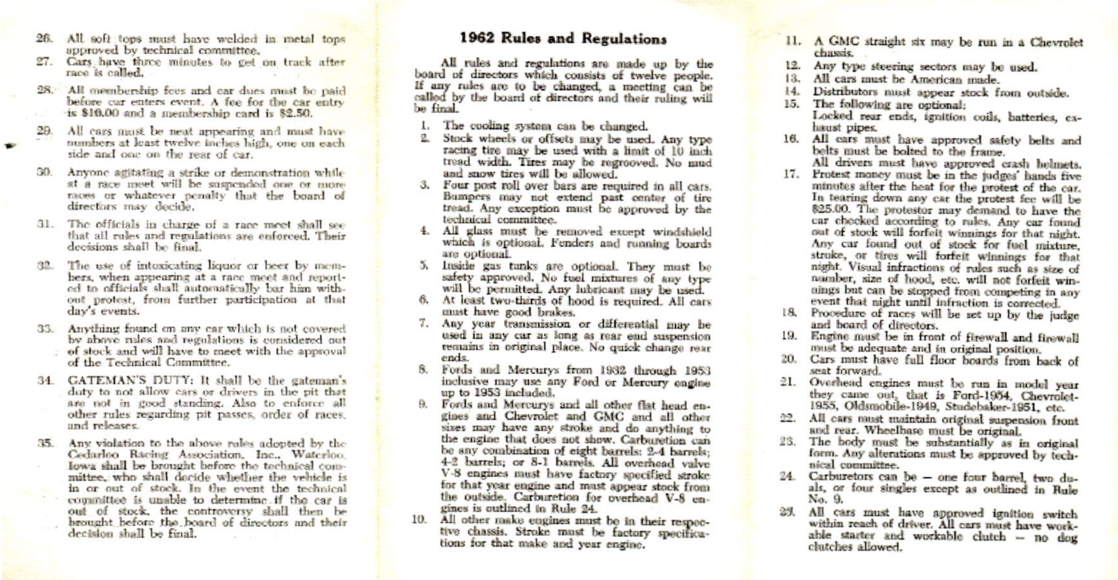

26. All soft tops must have welded in metal tops approved by technical committee.
27. Cars have three minutes to get on track after race is called.
28. All membership fees and car dues must be paid before car enters event. A fee for the car entry is $10.00 and a membership card is $2.50.
29. All cars must be neat appearing and must have numbers at least twelve inches high, one on each side and one on the rear of car.
30. Anyone agitating a strike or demonstration while at a race meet will be suspended one or more races or whatever penalty that the board of directors may decide.
31. The officials in charge of a race meet shall see that all rules and regulations are enforced. Their decisions shall be final.
32. The use of intoxicating liquor or beer by members, when appearing at a race meet and reported to officials shall automatically bar him without protest, from further participation at that day's events.
33. Anything found on any car which is not covered by above rules and regulations is considered out of stock and will have to meet with the approval of the Technical Committee.
34. GATEMAN'S DUTY: It shall be the gateman's duty to not allow cars or drivers in the pit that are not in good standing. Also to enforce all other rules regarding pit passes, order of races, and releases.
35. Any violation to the above rules adopted by the Cedarloo Racing Association, Inc., Waterloo, Iowa shall be brought before the technical committee, who shall decide whether the vehicle is in or out of stock. In the event the technical committee is unable to determine if the car is out of stock, the controversy shall then be brought before the board of directors and their decision shall be final.

1962 Rules and Regulations

All rules and regulations are made up by the board of directors which consists of twelve people. If any rules are to be changed, a meeting can be called by the board of directors and their ruling will be final.

1. The cooling system can be changed.
2. Stock wheels or offsets may be used. Any type racing tire may be used with a limit of 10 inch tread width. Tires may be regrooved. No mud and snow tires will be allowed.
3. Four post roll over bars are required in all cars. Bumpers may not extend past center of tire tread. Any exception must be approved by the technical committee.
4. All glass must be removed except windshield which is optional. Fenders and running boards are optional.
5. Inside gas tanks are optional. They must be safety approved. No fuel mixtures of any type will be permitted. Any lubricant may be used.
6. At least two-thirds of hood is required. All cars must have good brakes.
7. Any year transmission or differential may be used in any car as long as rear end suspension remains in original place. No quick change rear ends.
8. Fords and Mercurys from 1932 through 1953 inclusive may use any Ford or Mercury engine up to 1953 included.
9. Fords and Mercurys and all other flat head engines and Chevrolet and GMC and all other sixes may have any stroke and do anything to the engine that does not show. Carburetion can be any combination of eight barrels: 2-4 barrels; 4-2 barrels; or 8-1 barrels. All overhead valve V-8 engines must have factory specified stroke for that year engine and must appear stock from the outside. Carburetion for overhead V-8 engines is outlined in Rule 24.
10. All other make engines must be in their respective chassis. Stroke must be factory specifications for that make and year engine.
11. A GMC straight six may be run in a Chevrolet chassis.
12. Any type steering sectors may be used.
13. All cars must be American made.
14. Distributors must appear stock from outside.
15. The following are optional: Locked rear ends, ignition coils, batteries, exhaust pipes.
16. All cars must have approved safety belts and belts must be bolted to the frame. All drivers must have approved crash helmets.
17. Protest money must be in the judges' hands five minutes after the heat for the protest of the car. In tearing down any car the protest fee will be $25.00. The protestor may demand to have the car checked according to rules. Any car found out of stock will forfeit winnings for that night. Any car found out of stock for fuel mixture, stroke, or tires will forfeit winnings for that night. Visual infractions of rules such as size of number, size of hood, etc. will not forfeit winnings but can be stopped from competing in any event that night until infraction is corrected.
18. Procedure of races will be set up by the judge and board of directors.
19. Engine must be in front of firewall and firewall must be adequate and in original position.
20. Cars must have full floor boards from back of seat forward.
21. Overhead engines must be run in model year they came out, that is Ford-1954, Chevrolet-1955, Oldsmobile-1949, Studebaker-1951, etc.
22. All cars must maintain original suspension front and rear. Wheelbase must be original.
23. The body must be substantially as in original form. Any alterations must be approved by technical committee.
24. Carburetors can be — one four barrel, two duals, or four singles except as outlined in Rule No. 9.
25. All cars must have approved ignition switch within reach of driver. All cars must have workable starter and workable clutch — no dog clutches allowed.

1948

In the News

To Open Golf Driving Range About Apr. 15

Louis Frost, 616 Elm street, Waterloo, said yesterday he will open a golf driving range across from the Starlight drive-in theater on highway 218 "when weather permits, probably about Apr 15" The driving range will be located on property owned by Jud Tunis, Frost said

Frost

He plans to install what he described as "regular driving range lights" for night operation off 12

Though planning had begun for an auto racing track, Judd Tunis was still intent on getting horses on his 1/2 mile oval, tending his acreage and...adding a driving range?

According to family, the discussions concerning auto racing started when Judd's son-in-law, Bill Higgins, suggested they talk with John Gerber in Davenport about racing midget cars on the track, but it would require building a smaller 1/4 mile circuit inside the horse track.

Starting Horses as Racing Returns to Waterloo

Here's the start of the free for all trot at the opening of horse racing on the Tunis track here Sunday. Buzz Dusenberry of Mt. Pleasant, Ia., is operating his starting gate. Seconds later the horses were closer to the gate, and the arms of the gate folded as the car sped away from the horses at the starting line. (Photo by Courier Sportographer Clyde Artus.)

Judd Tunis

1949

In the News

Waterloo Driver to Seek Birthday Win Here Saturday

56

Lloyd Thurston, who lives at 33 Lafayette street here, hopes to celebrate his 34th birthday anniversary Saturday with a victory in the midget auto races at the Tunis Speed bowl between Waterloo and Cedar Falls. Thurston is one of approximately 30 drivers entered in the third Saturday night of midget racing here. His big victory this season was a sweep of the feature, handicap and first heat Memorial day at Davenport before 11,000 fans. Thurston drives the Mensing Brothers entry from Lowden, Ia. He currently stands sixth in the Midget association point standings. When Thurston isn't driving the midgets, he works as a bartender in Cedar Falls. Time trials Saturday night start at 7 o'clock, with the races at 8:15.

Midgets Jockey for Position

5
26

Lloyd Thurston, driving No. 56, and Phil Lezio, driving No. 26, jockey for position on a curve during the midget auto racing card at the Tunis Speed Bowl here last night. Thurston, a Waterloo driver, failed in a bid for a win on his 34th birthday anniversary. (Photo by Courier Sportographer Clyde Artus.)

* * *

Death Dodgers Wreck 'Em and Live

LYNCH
DEATH DODGERS

This is a Gross(ly) foolhardy trick which would land the ordinary driver in hospital or jail but only earns Al Gross, driver for Jimmy Lynch's Death Dodgers, his weekly salary. Gross is not attempting to stand the car on its nose. He is just one-half way through a deliberate complete roll. The Lynch show will appear at the Tunis Speed bowl at 8 p. m. Wednesday.

1950
In the News

Waterloo Driver Wins Main Event Stock Car Races

Jerry Arnold of Waterloo won the feature event of the stock car racing program at the Tunis speedway Tuesday.

The attendance was listed at 3,060. There were no injuries to drivers despite several spins, roll-overs and collisions.

Curly Richter of Waterloo was the hard luck driver. He rolled his car early in the afternoon's events and then at the start of the feature was involved with Don Dennis of Cedar Falls in an accident. Both cars were damaged, with a door torn off Richter's car and the frame twisted.

The Championship Stock Car Racing association will sponsor stock car races again next Tuesday night at the Tunis speedway.

Tuesday's results:

First heat 1, Harold Schroeder, Bettendorf, Ia.; 2, Bob Munsell, Cedar Rapids; 3, George Bass.

Second heat—1, Skip Blaser, Milan, Ill.; 2, Mike Moody, Cedar Rapids; 3, Richter.

Third heat 1, Arnold; 2, Howard Carpenter, Waterloo; 3, Keith Maust, Waterloo.

Novelty 1, Elmer Carter, Cedar Rapids; 2, Bob McIlrath, Denver, Colo.; 3, Dennis.

Semi-main 1, McIlrath; 2, Dennis; 3, Darrell Dake, Cedar Rapids.

Feature 1, Arnold; 2, McIlrath; 3, Schroeder; 4, Dake.

Rock Island Driver Wins Tunis Feature

Big car drivers met with the stock car drivers Tuesday night at the Tunis Speedway as Tommy Vardeman of Tulsa, Okla., battled all evening with the Benner brothers of Rock Island, Ill. To climax his evening of wins, Gene Benner eased through the traffic in the 20 lap feature to first place after starting outside in the sixth row.

Close on his heels was 24-year-old Vardeman, who will be driving one of the big racing cars which will appear next Sunday afternoon at Tunis Speedway. Vardeman had two wins to his credit Tuesday night, with a first in the consolation and second in the feature.

Bud Benner crossed the line in third place after bumping Vardeman repeatedly. Throughout the entire evening, aside from spins or cars being forced off the track, no one rolled. In time trials, Cotton Hodges of Hollywood, Fla., continued his sweep of time trial records. Hodges turned in fastest time trial of the evening with 21.17. Cash customers totaled 2,164.

Next race card for Tunis Speedway is Sunday afternoon, with big cars scheduled for the one-half mile oval. Among the dirt track stars competing will be Emory Collins, Rabbit Musick and Vardeman. Time trials are set for 1:30 with the first race at 2:30 p. m.

Tuesday stock car results.

Time trials: Hodges, 21.17.

First heat—1, Dick Hengl, Ogden, Utah; 2, Mike Moody, Cedar Rapids; 3, Bill Chumley, Waterloo.

Second heat—1, Lester Dykes, Cedar Rapids; 2, Gene Benner, Rock Island; 3, Keith Maust, Waterloo.

Third heat — 1, Wally Urban, Rock Island; 2, Howard Carpenter, Waterloo; 3, Jack Fleming, Davenport.

Consolation — 1, Tommy Vardeman, Tulsa, Okla.; 2, Jerry Arnold, Waterloo; 3, Don Dennis, Cedar Falls.

Semimain—1, Wally Urban; 2, Gene Kaskadden, Davenport.

Feature—1, Gene Benner; 2, Vardemann; 3, Bud Benner; 4, Moody; 5, Hodges; 6, Hengl.

Not Healthy—but a Living

Rolling a car is not exactly the most healthful way of making a living, but the Jimmie Lynch Death Dodgers think nothing of it. Here one of them is shown rolling a car in an attempt to bring it back on its four wheels after a complete roll. The stuntman is Walter Ruth. The Death Dodgers will be at the Tunis Speedway Thursday night in a single performance.

* * *

Lynch Death Dodgers Here Thursday

Thursday night will again be auto smash-up time at Tunis Speedway when the Jimmie Lynch Death Dodgers make their second appearance in Waterloo. They are using open cars this season.

The Death Dodgers have added several new stunts to their long list of acts. Highlighting the program this year, and shown for the first time in Waterloo, will be a game of auto polo played in stripped down Model T Fords, the crashing of an auto against a solid mass of five tons of ice, and the dive bomber in a new and different form.

Frank Collord, Waterloo automobile dealer, will sponsor the ice act.

The roll over will be repeated, as will several other of the stunts which thrilled several thousand persons in the Tunis bowl last year.

A Wrecker

Most people find it hard to believe that a lovely young lady like the one pictured above is the type that would be out nights seeing how many cars she could smash up, or how easy it is to roll her new sedan. But Linda Lombardo is that kind of a girl and is expected to prove it Thursday night at the Tunis Speedway where she will appear for the first time in public in

Millard Cops Feature Race at Tunis'

Jim Millard of Hollywood, Fla., won the feature race of Tuesday night's stock car events at the Tunis Speedway here. He began on the pole in the sixth row and moved up through heavy traffic to ease Jack Kasparian of Davenport out of the lead. Cotton Hodges, also of Hollywood, Fla., and driving the same make and model of car as Millard, edged Kasparian for second place.

Hodges turned in the fastest trial at 20:58 before the crowd of 2,897. The flips were numerous, with a three car pileup in the first heat involving K...

first turn. Neither driver was injured and Bass continued in the consolation after the event was restarted. The feature was marred by a spectacular flip by Mike Moody of Cedar Rapids, Ia., whose car tangled with Marvin Sams of Montezuma, Ia.

Neither was hurt.

Next stock car races at the Tunis speedway will be next Tuesday night. One event will be a trophy dash, with a trophy going to the winner. The event will be open to the first three cars in the three heats.

Tuesday's results:

Time trials—Hodges.

First heat—Vardeman, Millard, Moody.

Second heat—Blinstrup, Sams, B. Benner.

Third heat—Barta, Carpenter, Arnold.

Consolation—Kasparian, Chumley, Hannah.

Semi—Benner, Kaskadden, Barta.

Feature—Millard, Hodges, Kasparian, Blinstrup, Sams, Vardeman.

BEARS GET FARM CLUB.

1950 Driver on Waterloo Track in 1903

A. L. Bradley, who will drive two horses in today's races at Tunis speedway, here is up behind Grand Baroness, a trotter, before the grandstands of the old Home Park track. The picture was taken in 1903 at Waterloo's last horse racing site before the Tunis speedway was equipped for horse racing. The Baroness set a track record of 2:22¼ later that summer.

* * * * * *

Horse Racing at 2 O'Clock Today

A new sport makes its debut in Waterloo at 2 p. m. today — new, that is, to anyone born since World war I, and then some.

Hurried plans to accommodate an unexpectedly large entry of from 75 to 100 horses—both runners and standard breds—were completed yesterday at the Tunis speedway, highway 218, where the horses will race on the one-half mile track this afternoon.

A total of at least eight races—six harness and two running—is on the card, first of two successive Sundays that the horses will run on the Tunis track. They are to return for a second program next Sunday.

Not since the early part of the 20th century — few of the fans in the stands today will recall—has there been horse racing in Waterloo. The track then— Home park it was called—was located on the flats near the end of Home Park boulevard.

Jud Tunis, proprietor of the new track, was keeping his fingers crossed yesterday as workmen continued grading the track and working it into shape. It will be soft at best, but barring further rains should be in good shape for the horses today.

Most of the early arrivals managed to get in workouts Friday afternoon and yesterday, and activity was brisk around two permanent barns built to house 16 horses each and three temporary tents for the overflow.

Races today will be run in this order:

Heat one, 2:26 pace; heat one, 2:20 trot; heat one, free for all pace; heat two, 2:26 pace; heat two, 2:20 trot; heat two, free for all pace; four and one-half furlong race, five furlong running race.

Each harness heat is for one mile. The latter running race is five-eighths of mile or slightly over one lap. In it, the horses will go by the stands twice.

Twelve horses are entered in the 2:26 pace, seven in the 2:20 trot and 19 in the free for all pace.

The Dusingberry starting gate will be used for the harness races. Officials are: J. H. Nutter, Rockwell City, Ia., presiding judge; W. J. Campbell, Jesup, Ia., clerk of course, and W. Barske, Independence, Ia., superintendent of speed.

The size of the entry list may cause some of the races to be split into two sections, Tunis said.

This is the first major racing event in northeast Iowa this year and owners and trainers from Iowa, South Dakota, Minnesota and Wisconsin are bringing their animals here for an early test.

The harness horses are racing for $300 added purses which would mean at least $150 for a horse that could win both heats in his race. The size of the entry list will swell the prize because the $5 entry fee per horse is thrown into the prize pool.

The runners are competing for $75 purses in each race.

Among the large stables here are seven horses owned by K. B. Collar, Elkpoint, S. D. Several running horses from the Tripoli, Ia., vicinity are here including Bee Hill, a 7-year-old, who Dale Schmidt rode to second in the six furlong event at the Iowa State fair last fall.

Among the Waterloo owned horses entered is Charlie Miller, popular pacer owned by A. L. Bradley.

4,620 Fans See 10 Cars Spin Out of Single Heat of Stock Car Race Card

Thirteen still is an unlucky number—at least so far as stock car racing is concerned.

Thirteen cars started the third heat of the Fourth of July racing program at Tunis speedway here, and when the race finally ended two laps early only three cars still were running.

As 4,620 screaming fans looked on, the third heat produced all of the night's pileups and flipovers. Four cars went out in a wreck on the first turn, and the race was restarted with nine cars. Those

* * *

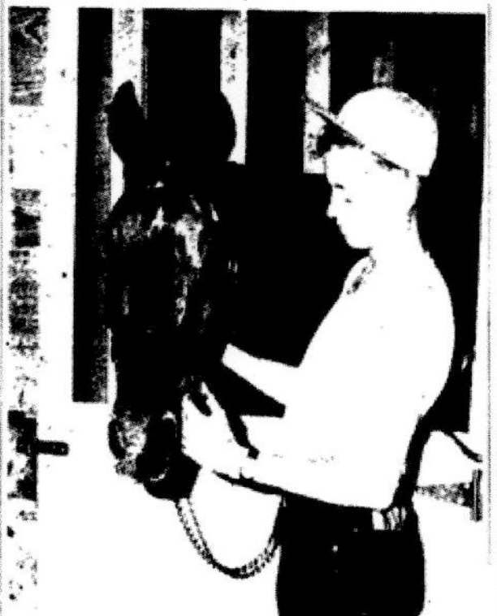

YOUNGEST DRIVER—Possibly the youngest driver in today's horse races at Tunis speedway will be 15-year-old Clayton Collar, above, posing in one of the Tunis barns with the horse he's going to drive, Bobby Welch. Clayton is the son of K. B. Collar, Elkpoint, S. D., and Bobby is one of the seven head of horses Collar has entered in the harness events today.

ON THE BEE—Working an easy half mile is Bee Hill, above, ridden by Jockey Dale Schmidt who piloted the 7-year-old runner to second in a state fair race last fall. Bee Hill, with Schmidt up, is entered in one of the running race events in the season's first horse racing card at the Tunis speedway this afternoon. Schmidt is from Tripoli, Ia.

Indians Defeat Athletics When

Women to Drive Stock Cars at Tunis Speedway Tuesday

Women drivers will be behind the wheel for the first time at Tunis Speedway this Tuesday when they'll take over for one event in the holiday stock car races.

Mrs. George Bare and Mrs. Bill St. Clair of Waterloo are expected to drive against women from Cedar Rapids and Davenport, and track officials hope to line up a field of more than 10 women and cars.

Dottie Harris, who won the women's race at Cedar Rapids two weeks ago, is scheduled to be on hand. Any other women over 21 years of age interested in driving may contact the Tunis Speedway so that cars for them to drive can be obtained.

Time trials are set for 7 p. m. Tuesday night, with the first race at 8:15, and rivalry is expected between stock car drivers of Waterloo and Cedar Falls and those from Cedar Rapids and Davenport.

1951
In the News

Just Before the Go-Round

10

No one got hurt, but car No. 205, driven by Darrel Dake, Cedar Rapids, spun into the infield and was out of the race split seconds after this jam up on the first turn of the consolation race at the Tunis speedway Tuesday night. Car No. 10, driven by Melvin De Vilder, Moline, Ill., which skidded into the rear of Dake's car, managed to stay on the track, but finished far back in the field at the end of the race.

Dickinson Wins Final Tunis Race

The climax to the final stock car race meeting of the season at Tunis speedway came in Thursday's feature. Roy Dickinson, 26-year-old driver from Bettendorf, Ia., started back in the seventh row and after battling most of the 15 laps with Hal Schroeder and Benny Lybarger, Davenport, Ia., drivers, roared into the lead and took the checkered flag.

At one time five cars were bunched tightly fighting for the led. The feature had one flip involving Al Runyan, Waterloo, after his car tangled with one driven by Bill Sanders, Palo, Ia. Runyan was unhurt.

Another outstanding race came in the second heat when Lybarger and Schroeder battled back and forth for seven laps of the 10 lap heat before the Bettendorf pilot was able to beat out Schroeder for the win.

Bill Zwanziger, Waterloo, was a close third, and almost on the finish line when his car was struck by one driven by Elmer Carter with both cars badly damaged.

The most spectacular flip occurred in the first heat when George Bass and Bob O'Brien, both of Waterloo, tangled, with Bass rolling and O'Brien swerving wildly and shooting off the high bank of the track, his car jumping about 18 feet into the air. Neither driver was injured.

Other drivers involved in rolls included Flip Tucker, Cedar Rapids, and Dick Barta, Waterloo. Russ Murray, Waterloo, crashed his car through the rail and fence in front of the bleachers, stopping about 10 feet short of the front row seats.

Attendance Thursday was 1,793.

Summaries:

Time trials—R. Dickinson; :19.75.

First heat—Arnold Spore, Bill Sanders, Gene Phillips.

Second heat—Benny Lybarger, Hal Schroeder, Bill Zwanziger; 3:50.5.

Third heat—Bob Hilmer, George Bass, Russ Murray; 3:32.62.

Novelty—Bill Sallow, Gene Phillips; 3:28.99.

Semimain—Bob Hilmer, George Bass, Jay Sharp; 4:50.4.

Feature—Roy Dickinson, Hal Schroeder, Bob Piper, Benny Lyberger, Bill Swallow, Gene Phillips.

Al Ney's Column
The Sports Alley

Auto Racing:

The half mile track at the Tunis speedway here — the one not used by either the midget cars or the stock cars —will have to be used Sunday when big car races make their debut.

The big car simply need more room to get up speed.

This show Sunday is the only big car card scheduled for the Tunis track but if enough rac-

Schroeder Wins Stock Feature

Hal Schroeder of Bettendorf, Ia., continued his string Tuesday by winning the stock car races feature at the Tunis speedway here. He edged out Roy Blinstrup of Rock Island, Ill.

The feature included a flip by John Thede of Gladbrook, Ia., but he was not injured and the race continued after a restart. John Friedley of Waterloo escaped injury in a spectacular flip on the last lap of the semimain. His car was badly damaged and he was put out of action for the evening.

Jim Millard of Hollywood Fla., turned in a fast time trial at :20.73 before 1,861 spectators

The next stock car race card at Tunis' is scheduled for Tuesday night of next week.

Time trials: J. Millard; 20:75.

First heat: 1. J. Redier; 2. M. DeVilder 3. H. Schroeder; 3:32:77.

Second heat: 1. R. Blinstrup; 2. B. Carr 3. A. Spore; 3:37:92.

Third heat: 1. B. Zwanziger; 2. H Pries; 3. D. Angel; 3:45:04.

Novelty (12 laps): 1. M. Moody; 2. C Hodges; 3. J. Thede; 3:33:30.

Semi-main: 1. B. Zwanziger; 2. J Barta; 3. H. Pries; 4:06:74.

Feature (15 laps): 1. H. Schroeder; 2 R. Blinstrup; 3. M. DeVilder; 4. Millard; 5. M. Moody; ... A. Spore; 5:31:32.

Rain, Sun Help Track, Tunis Says

"That rain was just what we needed," Jud Tunis, owner of the Tunis speedway here, said Monday. "Yesterday's rain, combined with today's sun, will make the track fast for Tuesday night."

The regular weekly stock car races are scheduled at Tunis' Tuesday, starting with time trials at 7 p. m. and races at 8.

Tunis said that Arnold Spore of Waterloo, who was in a car that flipped and rolled five times here last week, will be driving again this week. George Bass of Waterloo, who went to the hospital for a checkup last Tuesday after a flip, also will be driving this week.

1952
In the News

Peterson Wins 100 Lap Race

Harry Peterson Jr. of Waterloo won the feature 100-lap season championship stock car race at Tunis Speedway Sunday before 2,054 fans. He drove the 25 miles in 35.32 minutes.

Second place in the feature event went to Bob Ledtje of Gladbrook with Red Droste of Waterloo and Jim Krogh of Cedar Falls third and fourth, respectively.

Bill Zwanziger and Bob Hilmer battled for the lead in the early laps of the 100-lap race but both were forced into the pits with engine trouble and lost valuable time in doing so.

Cal Swanson of Cedar Falls set a new Hawkeye Racing Association record in the time trials with a 19.32 performance. Swanson was a leading contender in the main event but tangled with two other cars and rolled on the 16th lap.

Drivers from all stock car tracks in Iowa have been invited to take part in the Iowa Open championship race at Tunis Sunday as the next scheduled racing program.

Sunday's results:

Time trials, 1. Cal Swanson (Cedar Falls), 19.32.

First heat (10 laps)—Arnold Spore, Waterloo; George Bass, Waterloo; Red Droste, Waterloo; 3:41.

Second heat (10 laps)—Bob Hilmer, Dysart; Gene Peterson, Waterloo; Gene [redacted] **dar Falls; Bill Zwanziger, Fairbank; Hal Schroeder, Bettendorf; 3:51.**

Main event (100 laps)—Harry Peterson,

4,827 See Schroeder Win 50 Lap Feature at Tunis'

Hal Schroeder of Bettendorf, Ia., fought a see saw battle with [redacted] championship of the Hawkeye Racing association at Tunis speedway here Sunday night.

The lead changed hands half a dozen times during the event and seldom was there more than a car length between the two leaders. No one else even had a chance as Swanson and Schroeder fought it out right down to the finish before a season's record of 4,827.

Bill Zwanziger of Fairbank, pre race favorite and leading point winner of the association, spun out early in the race and did not

Hawkeye association's official [redacted]

Mr. and Mrs. Bashford were presented with a wedding gift from members of the association.

In the time trials Zwanziger showed his heels to the pack by posting a neat :19.69 in fast competition.

Only mishap of the evening

badly damaged. Winner of the first heat was Red Droste.

In the second heat it was all Swanson, edging Jim Krogh and Schroeder in the 10 laps. The third heat, for the slower qualifiers, went to Benny Lybarger of Bettendorf.

Time Trials: Bill Zwanziger, Fairbank, :19.69.

First Heat (10 laps): Red Droste, Waterloo; Zwanziger, Ray Barkhart, Waterloo, 3:12.9

Second Heat (10 laps): Cal Swanson

Memorial Day STOCK CAR RACES

FRIDAY 8 P. M. TIME TRIALS 7 P. M.

[redacted] . . $1.00 (Inc. Tax)
Kids 10 to 12 . . . 50c
Children Under 10 FREE
When Accompanied by Parents!

Busses leave Interurban Station 45 minutes after the hour.
EXTRA Bus Service on the grounds immediately after the races!

TUNIS SPEEDWAY
On Highway 218 Between Waterloo and Cedar Falls

FREE PARKING!

Zwanziger Wins Three Firsts in Races at Tunis'

Bill Zwanziger of Fairbank, Ia., drove off with all the major firsts in the stock car races at the Tunis speedway here Sunday night.

He won the time trials, the first heat and the main event in the Hawkeye Racing association card.

A crowd of 3,417 saw the races.

One of the association's most popular cars, No. 245, was a complete loss when it rolled in the backstretch and was rammed by a car driven by Arnold Spore in the main event.

John Proctor was driving 245 Sunday in place of Bob Hilmer, who was out because of burns suffered when a radiator hose blew out during tests Friday. Spore's car may be beyond repair.

Other rollover victims Sunday were Ray Moritz of Waterloo, who went over in the second lap of the consolation, and Cal Swanson of Cedar Falls, whose car did a double sommersault in the north turn on the eighth lap of the 20 lap main event.

The results:

Time trials—Zwanziger; :20.70.

First heat (10 laps)—Zwanziger; Jim Krogh, Waterloo; ...

Consolation (10 laps) — John Reiter,

4,952 See First Stock Car Races of Season Here

That stock [redacted] racing is one of northeast Iowa's favorite [redacted] was shown again Sunday night when 4,952 persons turned out to see the Hawkeye Racing association ... Tunis speedway here.

The big opening crowd watch... dorf, Ia., win the 15 lap main even... Lybarger also posted the low tim... and won the first heat.

Lybarger's only defeat came in a special two car race, billed as a grudge match against Cal Swanson of Cedar Falls. Swanson got the checkered flag in the five lap unscheduled event.

Al Warneke went into a roll coming out of the last turn in the final lap of the third heat and suffered a face cut.

TWO BIG DAYS STOCK CAR RACES
TONIGHT AND SUNDAY AT 8 P. M. Time Trials at 7
ADDED ATTRACTION SUNDAY EVE — GIANT FIREWORKS DISPLAY!

TUNIS SPEEDWAY
On Hwy. 218 Between W'loo and Cedar Falls
BUS SERVICE ON GROUNDS

Hilmer Wins 3rd Straight in Memorial Day Race, But Flip Sends One Driver to Hospital

Hawkeye Racing association drivers still haven't stopped Bob Hilmer of Waterloo and his Red Droste-built stock car.

Hilmer won the feature again Friday evening in the races at the Tunis Speedway here for his third straight. He had won the previous feature at Tunis' and repeated last Sunday in Mason City.

The Memorial day card that drew 3,428 fans was marred by a double flip that sent Cleo Rice to the hospital with possible head injuries. He was released from the hospital yesterday after Xrays showed no serious injuries.

more laps Wayne Fox went into a double flip. His car was damaged, but he escaped injury. The other flip came when Mike Rogers turned during the first qualifying heat.

Fast times were clocked in the time trials with Bill Zwanziger of Fairbank turning in :19.9 to lead the 30 cars.

Hilmer won the second qualifying heat and then the feature.

[redacted]

Time trials—Zwanziger, :19.9.

First heat, 10 laps—Cal Swanson, Cedar Falls; Ray Barnhart, Waterloo; Don Isley, Waterloo; no time, due to interruption of race.

Second heat, 10 laps—Hilmer; Jim Krogh, Waterloo; Al Runyan, Waterloo; 3:47.

Third heat, 10 laps—Vic Paylon, Waterloo; Frank Lagle; John Proctor, Waterloo, 3:03.

Semimain, 15 laps—John Thede, Gladbrook; Proctor; Swanson; Harry Peterson, Jr., Waterloo; Howard Carpenter, Waterloo; no time, due to interruption of race.

Feature, 20 laps—Hilmer; Isley; Zwanziger; Krogh, Runyan; 8:54.

1953
In the News

Wedding on Wheels

Bob Rowe, center, driver of car No. 127 in Hawkeye Racing Association stock car races, and Betty May Colburt are married at Tunis Speedway here Sunday night by C. S. Thorsrud, justice of the peace. They were married before the feature race.

* * *

Peterson Wins Feature at Tunis'

A wedding, a spectacular crash and a three-way neck and neck battle in the main event were highlights of Sunday's stock car card at Tunis Speedway before 3,032 fans.

Just before the main event Bob Rowe, of Waterloo, driver of car 127, made a quick change into a gray business suit and took as his bride Betty May Culbert of Waterloo. A wheel-mounted platform decorated in white with a bridal arch and flowers was the scene of the ceremony. C. S. Thorsrud, justice of the peace, officiated at the double ring ceremony.

Immediately following the ceremony the couple drove around the track in 127 and then received gifts from Waterloo merchants, members of the Hawkeye Racing Association, track owner Jud Tunis and others.

Once again the elusive traveling trophy for the feature continued its travels as Cal Swanson, Arnold Spore and Gene Peterson battled it out on almost even terms for 16 laps. Gene Peterson finally took the lead and won. Swanson dropped out in the 17th lap, leaving Spore in second spot.

The most spectacular crash of the season took Bob Ledtje and Bud Slater out of the race. Although Gene Hultman also rolled over he

Dogs Race at Tunis' Friday:

HOBBY TURNS INTO GREYHOUND RACING CLUB

A hobby of raising dogs has flourished into a parttime business for Ernest Prindle of Independence and Melvin Canfield of Hazleton. They operate the E and M Dog Racing Association, which Friday night will sponsor greyhound races at Tunis Speedway here.

Prindle and Canfield began raising greyhound dogs three years ago. They now own several racing dogs and occasionally enter them as fill-ins at races sponsored by the association, whose members mostly are owners of greyhound racing dogs.

The association's members supply 25 to 30 dogs for the races.

Greyhounds have been racing for hundreds of years. Object of the chase at about 45 miles an hour is a fox hide pulled ahead of the dogs at a speed of from 50 to 60 miles an hour for the 40 rod distance. The fox hide is tied to a strong cord attached to a windlass powered by a motor.

Hide Disappears.

Canfield explains that greyhounds have an intense hatred of the fox. At the finish line the fox hide disappears into a box covered with burlap sacking so that the dogs won't tear the hide to pieces.

In addition to making the apparatus to draw the hide over the track at a rapid speed, Canfield and Prindle spent several hours constructing a starting box. It is made of wood and has four stalls for the dogs. At a signal from the starter, a trap-like door is opened after the fox hide has been waved in front of the dogs housed in the starting box.

The door springs up and the dogs are off. The association awards prize money at each race.

The race card at Tunis' will be the 13th one of the season. Other race sites have included Independence and Central City.

Northeast Iowa Owners.

Several dogs owned by Northeast Iowa residents are entered in the races Friday. Mel Adams of Waterloo owns Ralph J. and Peggy, two consistent winners. Art Grandon of Cedar Falls owns Rocket and Randa. They have been battling Ralph J. and Peggy for first places recently. Rocket recently won the Eastern Iowa championship card at Independence.

John Maas of Cedar Falls owns Spike, a good racer. Albert Thoren of Grundy Center is a trainer of greyhounds. His Red and Black Beauty placed first and third earlier this season at Oelwein and two weeks later were sent to the major tracks where dog racing is a business, not a hobby. Thoren probably will enter two young dogs here.

Earl Simpson of Cedar Falls is a breeder of registered greyhounds. Other owners from the Northeast Iowa area who will have dogs racing Friday include Karl Weltzin of Jesup, Everett Hebel of Jesup, Dallas Sterling of Shell Rock, Harvey Haurum of Cedar Falls, Derald Minikus of Cedar Falls and Roy Canfield of Aurora.

Friday's races start with the time trials at 7:30 p. m., followed by the parade of champions at 8 p. m. and then the actual races.

* * * * * * *

THEY'RE OFF—Melvin Canfield of Hazleton starts four greyhounds from the starting box for a E and M Dog Racing Association race. Dogs are scheduled to race at Tunis Speedway here Friday night.

Rams Win 2nd Straight Football Exhibition 27-0

Wedding, 3-Way Battle to Retire Trophy Feature of Stock Car Card at Tunis

Wedding bells will mingle with the roar of motors at the regular stock car racing program at Tunis speedway at 8 p. m. Sunday night.

Bob Rowe, driver of car No. 127, will take Betty Mae Colburt as his bride in a track side ceremony just before the start of the feature race.

The racing card, itself, will feature a battle among Bob Ledtje, winner of the main last Sunday, Cal Swanson, winner of a special polio benefit program at Tunis Wednesday and Bob Hilmer. Each has two legs on the feature traveling trophy which is retired upon the third victory.

Swanson Comes From Last to First to Win Stock Race

Cal Swanson, in last place at the start, battled past the entire field to win the stock car 20-lap main in a thrilling battle with Red Droste at Tunis Speedway Sunday night.

A crowd of 3,104 saw Swanson sweep to victory in the time

Zwanziger Wins Final Tunis Race; Raise $686 for Fund for Injured Starter Bashford

Bill Zwanziger of Fairbank, on leave from the armed forces, piloted No. 35 to victory in the invitational feature event Sunday afternoon to wind up the stock car racing season at Tunis Speedway.

Zwanziger was trailed to the finish line by Arnold Spore of Waterloo, winner of the semimain.

The crowd of 1,425 at the final card contributed $111 toward the

Bob Hilmer Wins Feature Before 2,547

Bob Hilmer gained on the point leaders as he won the stock car main in the fast time of 6.67 over a rough Tunis Speedway track that contributed to six rollovers during the program Sunday night.

Hilmer's brother, Carrol, made it a family night for the two drivers from Dysart by winning the time trials.

Cal Swanson and Red Droste clung to their 1-2 ratings in the point standings by winning an event each. Swanson copped his race while Droste won the African pursuit novelty, an added attraction

Free Wheeling in Stock Car Races Here

Red Droste, right, driving circle 245, has to dodge to his left to miss the wheel from Cal Swanson's No. 5-9 in the main event of the stock car races at Tunis Speedway Sunday afternoon. It slowed down Droste and he finished third. Swanson plowed a furrow for 50 yards before coming to rest on the back stretch. (Photo by Courier Sports Photographer Ken Payton).

1954
In the News

Spore Wins Again in Stock Car Races at Tunis Track

Arnold Spore still is the only driver to win a feature stock car racing event at Tunis Speedway here.

Sunday he won his second straight feature in as many Sundays of racing as 1,214 fans looked on.

Bob Hilmer and Gene Peterson finished second and third. Spore had finished third behind Peterson and Carroll Jensen in the time trials.

Bob, Carroll Hilmer Finish 1-2 in Tunis Races Again

The leading driver in the Hawkeye Stock Car Racing Assn., Bob Hilmer, won his seventh feature race of the season Sunday at Tunis Speedway as his brother Carroll finished second for the same finish as last week.

Bob finished first in the 20-lap main in a time of 6:48.79. The Hilmers dominated the evening as Bob and Carroll finished one-two in the time trials and Carroll came in first in the second heat race.

Cal Swanson Cops Feature on Tunis Speedway Track

Cal Swanson pushed his car 5-9 across the line Sunday at the Tunic Speedway to cop the stock car feature event before 1,710 fans. No time was recorded for the race because Bob Roe in car 127 rolled in the third lap when he smashed into cars 63 and 115. No one was hurt.

Al Runyon in First Feature Win at Tunis

A crowd of 2,415 stockcar fans watched Al Runyon win his first Tunis Speedway feature stock car event of the season Sunday night. Runyon nosed out Bob Hilmer, leading point maker in the Hawkeye Stock Car Racing Association, this summer, who finished second. Runyon won last Sunday on a Hawkeye card at Vinton, but this was his first victory here this year.

No time was recorded on the novelty race Sunday because Jack Nelson, in car No 9, rolled six times in the fifth lap. Nelson escaped unhurt.

The Hilmer brothers dominated the time trials. Bob finished first while younger brother Carroll placed second. Al Heideman won the junior novice race.

Time trials—Bob Hilmer (35), Carroll Hilmer (35A), Red Droste (Circle 245), Arnold Sport (64), Cal Swanson (245), Al Runyon (121), Chub Liebe (17), Harry Petersen (113), Jerry Galligar (18).

Bob Hilmer Wins Tunis Feature

Bob Hilmer nosed out brother, Carroll Hilmer, to win the feature for the sixth time this season before 1,195 stock car racing fans at Tunis Speedway Sunday night.

Only one mishap occurred in the snappy program that was concluded at 9:45 p. m. Wayne Liebe rolled in the sixth lap of the ...

Droste Feature Winner; to Run Again Monday

Red Droste was the feature event Sunday night in the first card of a two-day stock car racing program at Tunis Speedway here.

Droste posted a time of [illegible] in the 20-lap feature. Bob Hilmer, who won the features in two previous weeks did not place.

The Hawkeye Stock Car Racing Assn., is conducting another racing card at the speedway Monday night. Time trials are at 7 p. m. with the first race at 8. Monday's program includes a women's race.

Bob Hilmer drove the fastest time trial lap in [illegible] and his brother, Carroll, who was married Saturday night, took a first in the second heat race.

The novice event went to Junior Gellner in [illegible].

Bud Slater rolled his No. 3 car in the first lap of the feature when four cars piled up on a curve. Don Graham rolled on ...

Play Finals in Wapsi Golf Meet

Courier Special Service

INDEPENDENCE — Brook Burkart met Alan Fisher and Bob Titsworth met Hank Anderson Monday morning in the semi-finals of the Wapsipinicon Golf Club championships.

The winners of the matches were to meet each other in the finals in the afternoon.

Golfers qualified and played two 18 hole matches Sunday ...

Red Droste Wins Championship Race; Then Blacks Out

Red Droste, so tired and overheated at the end of 100 laps that he blacked out for 10 minutes, Sunday won the 1954 Hawkeye Stock Car Racing Assn. 100-lap season championship in a time of 14.82 minutes.

Droste and Gene Petersen, who finished second, battled back and forth for the last five laps, but on the final lap it was Droste who came in for the checkered flag.

He pointed his car for the infield and blacked out for about 10 minutes, the time it took to revive him.

Bob Hilmer, who had the pole position and during the season became the association's leading driver, dropped five laps behind on a pit stop which he had to make to cool his over-heated motor.

Hilmer had engine trouble before the feature. It took five minutes to pull the old engine and about 15 minutes to go to Hudson for a second. The second engine was new and its cooling system did not work well. Hilmer lost his five laps on his pit stop and never was able to make them up.

Droste and Petersen, along with the other three top drivers, did not make pit stops in the 100 laps.

Bud Slater won the 30-lap junior championship race to register his first victory in three years of racing. He led second place Kenny Crook across the finish line.

A paid attendance of 1,696 watched the season championships. Next Sunday the association is sponsoring an open invitational card. Any kind of motor can be used by any driver in the state of Iowa.

The Sports Alley — Ney's Column

Darnado & Friends:

Darnado has a fine collection of friends at his home on highway 218 between Waterloo and Cedar Falls.

They all live in a couple of barns and for a good reason. They're horses.

Darnado is a 3-year-old trotter owned by Jud Tunis, the Tunis speedway proprietor. Instead of having just an old buggy mare and a pony for company, Darnado now has 22 other stablemates with excellent reputation or breeding in various classes of the horsey set.

They room with Darnado, and their owners work them regularly around the barns or on the Tunis track. Some are being trained for harness racing, some for horse shows and others for pleasure.

One of the 1954 Iowa harness race meets will be on the Tunis track in June. A show horse program also is being planned there for the summer.

Mr. and Mrs. George Dewey of Waterloo have three American saddle horses at Tunis'. One is a 3-year-old fine harness horse. Another is a 2-year-old being broken to saddle, and the other is a yearling being readied for showing.. They were bought in Missouri last summer.

Paul Porter of Waterloo has two hackney mares, both about 5 years old, one for the harness class and one to ride. He also has two palomino stud ponies and a 4-year-old parade horse.

Frank Nanke of Waterloo has an American saddle yearling colt and an older black mare riding horse.

Bud Adams of Waterloo works with his young hackney and a 7-year-old western pleasure horse. The hackney will be used either to drive or to ride, depending upon its aptitude.

Rodney Rice of Oxford, Wis., set up headquarters at Tunis' last fall with two trotters and two pacers of good breeding. Rice's trainer, David James, also works with the horses. They are being readied for the summer racing season.

Tony Amfahr of Waterloo bought a 4-year-old pacing mare a couple of weeks ago and moved her in the Tunis barns.

Dr. D. L. Ball of Cedar Falls has an Arabian yearling at Tunis', and Jud thinks it may be the highest price horse in the barns. Dr. Ball also has a black and white western pleasure mare.

John Scharwat of Waterloo and Jack Hubanks, also of Waterloo, have western pleasure mares. Dr. Ike Hayes has a 4-year-old gelding that is due to join Darnado and his friends. The gelding will be trained as a pacer.

The 11-year-old black gelding pictured above, Uncle Rob, is entered in the running horse races Friday at 6 p. m. at Tunis Speedway here. The pictures were taken as Uncle Rob won a race last July at Thistledowns in Ohio. Last fall Walter Sommer of Tripoli bought the horse and now is racing it on the Iowa Thoroughbred Racing Assn. circuit. Uncle Rob will run in the six-furlong event at Tunis'. Pictured at the left is R. J. House of Waterloo who trained the horse at the time it won the Ohio race. Sommer, who now trains the horse, will have Uncle Rob and two other runners entered here Friday.

1955
In the News

African Pursuit Sunday, Demolition Race Monday Feature Tunis Programs

A demolition race, an African Pursuit and two racing programs in two days will keep members of the Hawkeye Racing Assn. busy at Tunis Speedway.

The African Pursuit will highlight Sunday's program at Tunis' with time trials at 7 p. m. and the racing schedule starting at 8 p. m. The demolition race will be included on the program Monday night.

An African Pursuit is a race in which cars must weave between truck tires laid flat on the stretches of the track. Because of the straightaway obstacles, passing cars can be done only on the turns or by weaving opposite ways around the tires.

With six racing programs remaining this season including the Labor Day weekend double-header, Gene Peterson leads in driver point standings with 304 and Carroll Hilmer is second with 293.

The leaders:

1.	Gene Petersen	304
2.	Carroll Hilmer	293
3.	Bill Zwanziger	260
4.	Chub Liebe	217
5.	Red Droste	195
6.	Cal Swanson	170
7.	Harry Petersen	159
8.	Bob Earl	147
9.	Al Runyon	123
10.	John Hill	95

STOCK CAR RACES!

MID-SEASON CHAMPIONSHIP!

SUNDAY – 8 P. M.

. . . TIME TRIALS 7 P. M. . . .

333

Trophy to be presented to the winner!

TROPHY Sponsored by GENE DuBOIS

BUS SERVICE
Busses leave Interurban Station 45 minutes after the hour.
EXTRA Bus Service on the grounds immediately after the races!

ADMISSION
Adults . . . $1.00 (Incl. Tax)
Kids 10 to 12 . . . 50c
Children Under 10 FREE
When Accompanied by Parents!

★ ★ FREE PARKING ★ ★

TUNIS SPEEDWAY
On Highway 218
Between Waterloo and Cedar Falls

Swanson Wins Tunis Feature for 3rd Time

Cal Swanson, who ended a brief "retirement" from stock car racing in July, Monday became the first driver to win three Hawkeye Racing Assn. features this season.

He retired the Thorsrud traveling trophy by copping the 20-lap main during the Labor Day meeting of the Hawkeye Association at Tunis Speedway. The traveling trophy went to the winner of each feature until one driver won three times. Paul Kemp had it after winning Sunday's race.

Swanson, a favorite here in past seasons, bowed out of racing at the conclusion of last season. but succumbed to the hard to catch in Gene Petersen's No. 100.

A crowd of 1,905 saw the program which featured a special demolition race won by Leonard Carlson.

Howdy Hutchins rolled No. 333 in the first lap of the second heat and was uninjured.

Time trials (29 cars)—1. Red Droste, Circle 35; 2. Carroll Hilmer, 18; 3. Cal Swanson, 100; 4. Don Isley, 21; 5. Bill Zwanziger, 35; 6. Harry Petersen, Circle 113; 7. Carroll Jensen, 777; 8. Bud Slater, 2; 9. Bob Ledtje, 22; 10. Bob Posekany, 555. :20.46.

First heat (10 laps)—1. Gene Petersen, 99; 2. Vic Payton, 113; 3. Bill Kemp, Circle 2, 3:52.

Second heat (10 laps)—1. Chub Liebe, 17; 2. Al Runyon, 121; 3. John Hill, 89. 3:38.

Third heat (10 laps)—1. Don Isley, 21;

Pinkie George Show
TV STARS
Here in Person to
WRESTLE
TUNIS SPEEDWAY
THURS., JULY 16
8:30 P. M.
SPECIAL BUS SERVICE
at Ticket Office After Matches
TEAM BOUT
The Two Mad Russians
RASPUTIN and KALMIKOFF
Team vs. Team

REGGIE LISOWSKI
AND
GENTLEMAN
JIM DOBIE

ANDRE DRAPP
VS.
ART BULL

Adm. $1.00 - Child 50c
Special Ringside $1.50
TICKET HEADQUARTERS
PRESIDENT HOTEL
Phone 2-7994
SALE: Monday thru Thursday
10 A. M. to 6 P. M.

USE EXTREME CAUTION AT ALL TIMES!

DRIVE TO STAY ALIVE!

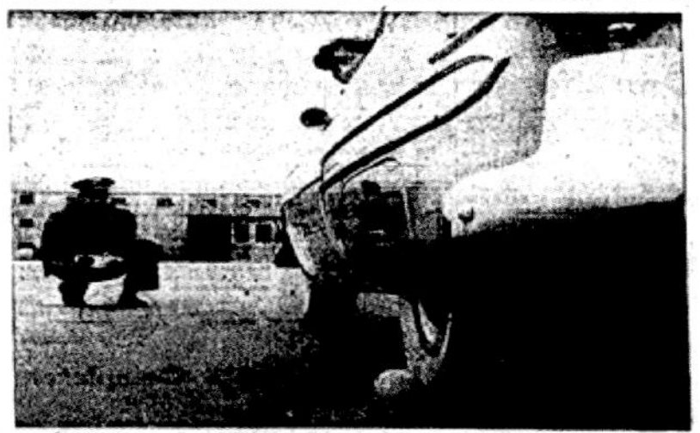

May

Each School in City May Enter Five

Traffic Violators Can't Compete in Safety Contest

The Waterloo Junior Chamber of Commerce will sponsor a Teen-age Driving Road-e-o on May 21.

According to the Jaycees entries will be limited to five contestants from each high school in Waterloo and Cedar Falls.

To be eligible, contestants must not reach their 20th birthday anniversary on or before July 22. Also contestants must not have previously competed in national Road-e-o finals. Teenagers guilty of a moving traffic violation within six months prior to May 21, are also ineligible.

State Meet in July.

The winner of the Waterloo contest will represent the area in a state Road-e-o in July.

State winners compete for $3,000 in scholarships in the national contest July 25-29 in Washington, D. C. Jaycee officials pointed out that winner of local or state Road-e-os, who are guilty of a moving traffic violation previous to the state or national contest, will be declared ineligible.

Byron Hawn, Waterloo Jaycee safety chairmen, announced Saturday that Jack Grose will serve as chairman of the Road-e-o.

Police to Judge.

Judging and scoring will be done by the Waterloo and Cedar Falls police departments and Iowa State Highway patrolmen, under the direction of Jaycee Bob Poulsen, Waterloo Police Chief Harry Krieg, Cedar Falls Police Chief Al Riebe and Lt. James Machholz of the highway patrol.

Lt. Machholz and Larry Sullivan will lay out the test courses at Tunis Speedway.

Eligibility and certification of entrants will be handled by Jim Fox and Donald Nutting, adviser to the Cedar Falls High School Teen-age Driving Club. Industrial arts classes of the Cedar Falls High School will make the necessary markers and course equipment from materials furnished by the American Lumber Co. and the Young Lumber Co.

Competition by Schools.

First, second and third place winner plaques will be donated by the Waterloo Automobile Dealers Association. Bob Jessup, president of the group, will present the awards.

Grose pointed out that competition will be on a school basis, with the five-person team from each school carrying the high school colors.

Driver instructors or advisers in teen-age driving clubs at the schools will receive lists of rules and eligibility requirements in the near future, Grose said.

Schools which do not have driver courses or clubs will be able to enter five person teams, but the competitors' eligibility must be certified by the school principals.

The Waterloo Jaycees announced that other prizes, in addition to the plaques, will be awarded.

Further information can be received by calling Grose at Adams 3-4326.

's Fishing to B

(Reprint from May 1 Courier)

WATERLOO and CEDAR FALLS

TEENAGERS!

Boost Your High School by Attending the FREE!

TEENAGER ROAD-E-O

SATURDAY, MAY 21

12 NOON AT TUNIS SPEEDWAY

. . . Sponsored by the Waterloo Junior Chamber of Commerce in the interests of encouraging safe, sane responsible driving habits in the minds of Waterloo and Cedar Falls teenagers!

"Teenage Road-E-O" Prizes Are on Display in Black's 4th St. Windows!

JUDGING AND SCORING

Will Be Done by the Waterloo and Cedar Falls Police Departments, and Iowa State Highway Patrolmen, Under the Direction of the Gentlemen Pictured Here:

Waterloo Police Chief
HARRY KRIEG

Cedar Falls Police Chief
AL RIEBE

Iowa Highway Patrol
LT. JAMES MACHHOLZ

and remember TEENAGERS --

DRIVE CAREFULLY AT ALL TIMES!

★ ★ This Traffic Safety Message Sponsored and Paid For by a Group of Safety-Minded Business and Industrial Firms. ★ ★

Zwanziger Wins Semi-Main, Main

Bill Zwanziger and Carroll Hilmer placed one-two in the semi-main and main at the Tunis Speedway stock car races, Sunday night and in the process Hilmer won the pole position for next Sunday afternoon's season championship race.

The two completely dominated the final regular Sunday night racing card of the season, with Zwanziger winning the third heat and Hilmer the second before they tangled in the two final races.

The point totals Hilmer won pushed him into first place in the season point standings ahead of Gene Petersen, the mid-season champion and nearly season long point leader. Petersen went to second place and Zwanziger held third.

Cars are started in the 50-lap season championship race according to the order of their point standings.

Next Sunday's program will open with time trials at 1 p. m.

An open race in which stock car drivers from other tracks around Iowa will be invited to participate will wind up the season at Tunis Speedway Sunday afternoon, Sept. 25.

A crowd of 1,305 saw the races Sunday night—

Time trials (25 cars)—1.—Harry Petersen, circle 113; 2. Red Droste, circle 35; 3. Chub Liebe, 17; 4. Bud Slater, 2; 5. Bob Posekany, 555; 6. Don Isley, 21; 7. Bill Zwanziger, 35; 8. Cal Swanson, 100; 9. Gene Petersen, 99; 10. Carroll Hilmer, 18; :19.72.

First heat (10 laps, 8 cars)—1. Jack Hickman, 63; 2. Arnold Spore, 81; 3. Don Graham, 245; 3:42.

Second heat (10 laps, 8 cars)—1. C. Hilmer, 18; 2. Harry O'Dean, 16; 3. John Hill, 89; 3:33.

Third heat (10 laps, 9 cars)—1. Zwanziger, 35; 2. G. Petersen, 99; 3. Swanson, 100; no time.

Novelty (12 laps, 10 cars)—1. Vic Payton, 113; 2. Bill Kemp, circle 2; 3. Carroll Jensen, circle 18; 3:55.

Novice (10 laps, 13 cars)—1. Dick Morgan, 121; 2. Leo Halligan, 9A; 3. Bob Schmidt, 4; 4. Walt Lang, 45; 5. Bill Smith, 243; no time.

Semi-main (15 laps, 10 cars)—1. Zwanziger, 35; 2. C. Hilmer, 18; 3. Kemp, circle 2; 4. Petersen, 99; 4:55.

Feature (20 laps, 18 cars)—1. Zwan-

Local Sports Calendar

TUESDAY.

Sports of Sorts Club meeting at Amvets Home, 5:15 p. m. social hours, 6:15 p. m., dinner, 7 p. m., sports panel featuring football.

High school football, 7 p. m., O. R. Latham Field, Cedar Falls, Teachers High vs. Eldora, Reinbeck vs. Traer, La-Porte City vs. Ackley, Grundy Center vs. Jesup in North Iowa Cedar League jamboree.

THURSDAY.

High school football, 7:30 p. m., O. R. Latham Field, Cedar Falls, Teachers High. vs. Eldora.

FRIDAY.

High school football, 7:45 p. m., Sloane Wallace Field, East High vs. Cedar Rapids (Wilson); 7:30 p. m., Waterloo Stadium, St. Mary's vs. Rockford; 8 p. m., Cedar Falls High, Cedar Falls vs. Charles City.

SATURDAY.

College football, 8 p. m., O. R. Latham Field, Cedar Falls, Iowa Teachers vs. Hastings (Neb.) Teachers.

SUNDAY.

Stock car racing, Tunis Speedway, time trials 1 p. m., first race 2 p. m.

Skeet shoot, 9:30 a. m., Izaak Walton grounds.

Stocks Open With Tune-up Race Sunday

Drivers of the Hawkeye Racing Assn. will tune up their cars Sunday in a full scale racing program at Tunis Speedway with admission free.

The first official racing program is scheduled for Sunday, May 1.

Howard Boslough, publicity director for the stock car racing group, said the public is invited to watch free of charge this Sunday.

Al Warnke, president of the association, has said that several new cars and new drivers will be among those on hand Sunday along with Jim Krogh and Bill Zwanziger, former drivers here now returned after service in the armed forces.

Carroll Hilmer Wins Season Championship at Tunis' in 27:52

Carroll Hilmer of Vinton, the season point champion of the Hawkeye Racing Assn., led from green flag to checkered flag Sunday night to win the 100-lap season championship stock car race at Tunis Speedway.

Hilmer's time for the 25 miles was 27 minutes, 52 seconds, a record in a the four-year-old Hawkeye Racing Assn. It was the first major race — other than a weekly 20-lap feature— won by Hilmer.

He was dogged for the first 35 laps or so by Bill Zwanziger in car No. 35 but his machine overheated and he was forced to withdraw.

From then on it was mainly a race for second place as Hilmer finished first by a half lap over Arnold Spore. Spore, of Waterloo, went ahead of Chub Liebe of Oelwein on the 95th lap when Liebe's car spun. Liebe hung on to finish third.

Nine Finish.

Vic Payton of Waterloo, Bob Posekany of Dike and Harry Petersen of Waterloo were the next three finishers. The next three, Bill Kemp, Bob Earl and Harry O'Dean, all are from Ce-

1956
In the News

Tunis Speedway Opens 8th Season Sunday

Tunis Speedway will open its eighth season of stock car racing under the lights Sunday night with a seven-event program. The speedway has scheduled races for every Sunday night with special programs slated for Memorial Day, July 4th and Labor Day.

Several rule changes have been made by the Hawkeye Racing Assn. The new rules allow drivers from all over northeast Iowa to compete on the Waterloo track and also allow cars even though their engines are not completely stock.

again will be a battle between the racing Hilmer brothers, Carol and Bob, as Carol defeated Bob in the first heat race and again in the feature.

Both have e competition other drivers ins, Bud Slat Vic Payton, Jack Hickma Gene Welch, Petersen and

THE HA ASSN. and t are offering novice and ers. These

SEASON CHAMP BOB HILMER

Hilmer Brothers Share Tunis Speedway Honors

The Hawkeye Racing Assn. staged its annual "Free Day" for the racing fans of Waterloo at Tunis Speedway Sunday afternoon. Free Day was the annual final tuneup for the stock cars and their pilots before next Sunday's grand opening of the speedway which is starting its eighth season.

The racing brothers, Carol and Bob Hilmer, headlined the program which provided some excellent races and times despite a wet and rough track. Bob had the fastest time trial when he toured the quarter-mile oval in :20.27 seconds. Brother Carol was second with :20.65.

CAROL, HOWEVER, had the best of the dueling with brother Bob in the races as he won first in the first heat and the feature event. Bob chased him home in the first heat with Jack Hickman finishing third.

The second heat race, also a ten lap affair, was won by Al Runyan, with Bob Posekany of Dike second and Cal Swanson finishing third. Runyan's winning time for the ten laps was 3.77 minutes.

The third heat race was won by Harry Odean of Cedar Rapids driving a Hudson, with Vic Payton finishing second, Howdy Hutchins third and Bud Slater of Cedar Falls fourth.

THE FEATURE RACE WAS also captured by Carol Hilmer as he turned in the outstanding time of 4.75 minutes for 12 laps. The race was only open to the first two finishers in each heat race and featured quite a duel between Hilmer and Harry Odean. Odean led for 7 laps but spun out in the seventh and then went on to finish second. Bob Posekany was third with Al Runyan fourth and Bob Hilmer taking fifth.

The weekly racing programs under the sanction of the Hawkeye Racing Assn. will begin next Sunday night at the Tunis speedway.

Time trials—Bob Hilmer; Caroll Hilmer, Jack Hickman, Harry Petersen, Bob Posekany, Cal Swanson, Al Runyan, Harry O'Dean, Bud Slater, Howdy Hutchins, Vic Payton, Bill Zwanziger, Gene Welch, :20.27.

First heat—Caoll Hilmer, Bob Hilmer, Jack Hickman.

Second heat—Al Runyan, Bob Posekany, Cal Swanson.

Third heat—Harry O'Dean, Vic Payton, Howdy Hutchins.

Main event—Caroll Hilmer, Harry O'Dean, Bob Posekany, Al Runyan, Bob Hilmer

Bob Hilmer Nips Carroll for Tunis Championship

Dysart's Bob Hilmer took the lead on the 33rd lap Sunday night and retained it to win the 75-lap season's championship stock car care at the Tunis Speedway.

Bill Zwanziger led the field the first 25 laps but was then forced out with mechanical difficulties and Carroll Hilmer, the Hawkeye Racing Assn. point leader, took over. waged a battle the rest of the way with Bob taking over on the 33rd lap. The two were never more than a car's length apart. Carroll won the season championship last year and had captured the mid-season race this year.

Bob, in winning the main event was the only double winner of the night as he earlier had paced the field in the third tured the 25-lap season consolation race for cars which didn't qualify for the championship race. Johnston led all the way even though the race was stopped and restarted when Chuck Perron rolled over.

OTHER WINNERS during the evening were Bod Ledge in the first heat and Vic Pay-

3.26.

Second heat race (10 laps)—Payton; 2. Jerrey Sherbon; Slater; 4. Jack Hickman; 5. O'Dean; 3:33.

Third heat race (10 laps)—Hilmer; 2. John Mullink; 3. Hilmer; 4. Bill Zwanziger; Droste; 3.24

Consolation championship laps)—1. Less Johnston; 2. V ton; 3. Dick Kauek; 4. Galey 5. Ron Hutchinson; 6. Larry no time due to rollover.

Season championship race (75 1. Bob Hilmer; 2. Carroll Hil Gene Petersen; 4. Carroll Jen

3,083 See Zwanziger Win

Bill Zwanziger won his second feature event of the season at Tunis Speedway Sunday night before the largest crowd of the season, 3,083. Zwanziger also won the first heat race and the class A semi-main event.

The crowd witnessed two oth- the second. The second heat was highlighted by Diana Hickman rolling her car over three times. The first four finishers in each heat will race Sunday night to determine the winner.

he was involved in a three-car crackup.

The next racing date is Sunday. The card will feature a novice event and the runoff between the heat winners in the powder puff derby along with

Third heat race (10 laps)—1. Les Johnston; 2. Dick Hoyt; 3. Bill Mark; 4. Al Heldeman; 5. John Hill; 3.50.

Novice race (10 laps)—1. Bill Smith; 2. Chuck Halligan; 3. Ernie Summefelt; 4. Don Heldeman; 5. Red Morgan; 3.83.

Class A semi-main (12 laps)—1. Bill Zwanziger; 2. Carroll Hilmer; 3. Gene

laps)—1. Norma Lynes; 2. Betty Halligan; 3. Jean Rust; 4. Esther Grandon.

Consolation (12 laps)—1. Cal Swanson; 2. Al Runyan; 3. Al Heldeman; 4. Wayne Rosler; 5. Bill Mark; 4.04.

Feature event (20 laps) — 1. Bill Zwanziger; 2. Gene Petersen; 3. Carroll Hilmer; 4. Cal Swanson; 5. Harry Petersen; 6.48.

Two in Hospital After Stock Car Crashes Into Pit Area; Hilmer Wins

Two of the five men taken to Schoitz Memorial Hospital here after a Tunis Speedway stock car race accident Sunday night still were hospitalized Monday morning.

Listed in fairly good condition with multiple bruises and cuts was Larry Orser, 24, 927 W. 12th St., Cedar Falls. Reported in good condition was David Custard, 50, 417 Allen St., Waterloo. He has a broken left ankle.

They were among those hurt when one of the two cars involved in the accident crashed through a barricade in front of the pits at the first turn.

THE CARS WERE driven by Jack Campbell (car No. 39) and Harry O'Dean (car number circle 2). As they came down the straightaway, the front wheels of the two cars locked.

Campbell's car, on the outside, couldn't make the first turn and it crashed into the barricade at the head of the pit area. O'Dean's car couldn't make the turn either, but his car missed the barricaded area.

Campbell, 26, 616 Dundee Ave., Waterloo, was treated at Schoitz for a chin gash. He was required six stitches. He was released along with Claude Black, 32, 417 Allen St., who suffered a foot injury, and Howard Hutchin, 31, 1121 Ansborough Ave., who suffered a bruised leg. Track owner Jud Tunis said three of the four hurt in addition to driver Campbell were pit crew members. He, however, could not identify which of the injured persons was a spectator.

The accident occurred during the third lap of the class A semi-main.

OTHERS AMONG SOME 20 persons in the area suffered some minor injuries that were treated on the scene.

Track officials said spectators are not permitted in the area, but that some spectators were among those hurt. Some were sitting on the barricade. Track officials also said spectators had been warned away from the barricaded area three times prior to the accident.

O'Dean escaped from the accident without serious injury.

A CROWD OF 2,735 saw the races and watched Bob Hilmer win the feature for the second time in three cards this season.

Carl O'Dean, brother of one of the drivers involved in the accident, took first place in the first heat.

Harry Peterson nosed out Red Droste in the second heat and won the class B semi-main in one-hundredth of a second short of record time.

Hilmer won the third heat. Dick Krafka took the class A semi-main as Jerry Sherbon, who was close behind, rolled his car in the final turn of the 15th and final lap. Bill Zwanziger came from the tail position to win the class C semi-main.

Walt Lang took first in the novice event after a re-start because of a rollover by Jerry Clark during the second lap.

Racing is scheduled each Sunday night at the Tunis track.

FIRST HEAT, 10 laps—1. Gene Peterson (99), 2. Dick Krafka (24), 3. Jerry Sherbon (8); 3:36.

SECOND HEAT, 10 laps—1. Harry Peterson (113), 2. Red Droste (77), 3. Jack Hickman (64); 3:31.

THIRD HEAT, 10 laps—1. Bob Hilmer (22B), 2. B. Zwanziger (35), 3. C. Hilmer (18); 3:27.

A SEMI-MAIN, 15 laps—1. Dick Krafka (24), 2. Gene Peterson (99), 3. Red Droste (77), 4. Harry O'Dean (2), 5. Carl O'Dean (18), 6. Ron Hutchins (50); no time.

B SEMI-MAIN, 15 laps—1. Harry Peterson (113), 2. John Mullink (27), 3. Bob Hilmer (22B), 4. Bob Ledje (68), 5. Carrol Hilmer (18), 6. Carrol Jensen (11); 4:83.

C SEMI-MAIN, 8 laps—1. B. Zwanziger (35), 2. Jack Hickman (84), 3. Vic Payton (63), 4. Dick Krenic (111), 5. Chuck Halligan (7-0), 6. Gene Welch (62); no time.

NOVICE, 10 laps—1. Walter Lang (46), 2. Ernie Sommerfelt 44), 3. Kenny Olsen (4), 4. Jerry Hogan (5), 5. Irv Ventor (71), 6. Don Heideman (66); no time.

FEATURE, 20 laps—1. Bob Hilmer (22B), 2. Harry Peterson (113), 3. John Mullink (27), 4. Carrol Jensen (11), 5. Red Droste (77), 6. Bill Zwanziger (35); 6:42.

Courier Sports

WATERLOO, IOWA, MONDAY, JUNE 3, 1957 PAGE ELEVEN

STOCK CAR RACING

Car Club From Hudson Entering a Project in Novice Races at Tunis

By ROGER MATZ
Courier Sports Writer

The novice car with the large golden hawk painted on its side belongs to the Golden Hawks, a car club of almost two years' standing in Hudson. The club, numbering about 18 members, bought the car, a 1941 Ford that formerly raced at Vinton, as a club project. Because of the novice rule requiring fenders, another 1941 Ford had to be purchased to obtain fenders and other parts. The car is painted in club colors, gold and black. Paul Smith, oldest member of the Golden Hawks, drives the car. Club president is Doug Sloan of Hudson.

A stock car formerly owned by another car club, the Ramblers of Waterloo, is now owned by Irvin Venter and Carrol Jensen and driven by Jensen.

* * *

Elmer Bradley, driver of uncontrollable No. 51, didn't show up at Tunis Speedway last Sunday night for the stock car races. After two or three tries on the track, perhaps Elmer has decided that old No. 51 just isn't a good stock car. Track rumors say that Bradley is soon to show up with another car, possibly a 1948 Ford powered by the Mercury engine from his old car.

* * *

Vern Weber, who flipped and rolled Chumley's No. 10 on the first turn two weeks ago, had considerable trouble negotiating the same turn this past Sunday. Weber spun out twice there in the second heat and once in the class B semi.

* * *

Bill Zwanziger, scratched from the second heat Sunday with steering difficulties, lowered the outside tie rod and went out in the third heat in his new car's first test against its chief rival, 22b, driven by Bob Hilmer. John Mullink outraced them both and took first in the heat. Hilmer was third and Zwanziger didn't place. Zwanziger wrecked his front-end assembly when he ran into the side of Dale Hickman's car as Hickman spun out early in the main event. Zwanziger said Monday afternoon that the trouble was limited to broken spring shackles and that the 35 would be ready for Thursday night's holiday races at Tunis.

* * *

Oelwein's Chub Liebe won the 300 lap feature race at Hutchinson, Kan., Sunday afternoon by four laps. He also finished third in the 100-mile race at Bellville, Kan., Saturday night. Liebe ranked fifth in IMCA point standings at last report but the victory and the third place finish could shove him up to fourth. Liebe raced last season at Tunis Speedway.

* * *

For the second time in two weeks, the novice race had to be split in two heats when about 27 cars showed up for Sunday's race.

* * *

The owners of No. 20, winner of the first novice heat, obviously do not believe in conformities. The car, pulled to the track on a trailer bearing Fayette county plates, is a 1949 Ford station wagon and one of the pit crew was observed unloading the car while clad in Bermuda shorts and knee-length argyles.

* * *

The Cedar Valley Stock Car Racing Assn. says that the 350-horsepower Studebaker from the Hawkeye Racing Assn. (Waterloo) will compete in the Fourth of July racing program at the Benton County Fairgrounds in Vinton at 2 p. m. Thursday. Red Droste has been driving the car at Tunis Speedway. The driver in Vinton is due to be Luce Small. The car is driven from the backseat area to give the driver a better feel of the rear wheels.

The car driven by Small will race another modified auto out of the Waterloo circuit—the latter to be driven by Les Johnson of Vinton.

In addition to the special modified racing event and the regular stock car program, there will be a "kiddie kar" derby and a couple of motorcycle races on the holiday card.

STOCK CAR RACING -- By Roger Matz

Spore Was Driving Sunday-- Between Here and New York

Arnie Spore, who drove stock car No. 555 to a main event win at Tunis Speedway two weeks ago, doesn't get to drive too often — in races, that is. Spore is a ~~truck driver~~ and wasn't entered in last Sunday's races because he was driving somewhere between here and New York. Bob Posekany took the wheel of 555 Sunday and drove the little coupe to first in the second heat and the class A semi and to third in the feature.

* * *

The point system employed there by the Hawkeye Racing Assn. Points are awarded for places won in the races and the cars with the most points are started to the rear of the flying starts.

* * *

AT LEAST TWO of the novice cars entered at Tunis Sunday were driven to the track, license plates and all. One, 210, has been driven in several races and the other was a newcomer Sunday. The newcomer, a 1949 black four door sedan, the money.

* * *

A $10 MEMBERSHIP fee in the Hawkeye Racing Assn. includes the member's choice of ~~a number for his car~~, so long as no one else is using it. Once a number is chosen, it is safe from duplication. If a member then decides to enter two cars, the number for the second car costs an additional $10. A driver can change his number for nothing provided he forfeits his old number to leave it open for someone else. Num-

1958
In the News

Mullink Seeks Second Victory in Row

John Mullink and Charlie Moffet pushed their modified Ford coupes past Bill Zwanziger on the last lap of the 20 lap stock car feature at Tunis Speedway here Sunday night and edged the Cedarloo Racing point standings leader into third place after he had led the feature for 12 laps.

The three drivers, who carried on a nip-and-tuck battle throughout the feature, will have another chance at each other when the stocks run again here Monday night at 7:45 in a special Labor Day program.

Zwanziger grabbed off the lead in the eighth lap from Les Schmitz, who had led since starting on the pole, and moved out to a slight lead before Moffet and Mullink were able to break loose from a fast moving pack.

Mullink again took the inside on Zwanziger, who was driving much higher on the track than he usually does, and shot out into first. Moffet fell in behind Mullink on the turn and he also went by Zwanziger. Zwanziger gained a bit on the pair on the backstretch and both Mullink and Moffet handled their cars through the turn well enough to keep a slight edge. Both Moffet and Zwanziger finished on Mullink's rear while the fourth and fifth place finishers, Les Johnson and Gene Peterson, were right behind Zwanziger and Moffet.

JOHNSON, WHO won both the second heat and the class A semi, had moved up steadily on Peterson in the feature and edged him for fourth by inches. Johnson, running with a newly-

out during the fi[...] landed in the middl[...] about 15 feet from car. Albertson esc[...] injury.

THREE DRIVER[...] solation race also [...] jury in a three car [...] the first turn at [...] the race. Gale Ca[...] sideways slide in t[...] the turn and was h[...] by Rip Kirby. Car turned on its side a[...] over the top of it a[...] ligan slammed into [...] was knocked off th[...] roll Jensen won th[...] it was restarted.

Norma Lynes wo[...] heat of the Powder[...] before a crowd of 3[...] night the top six [...] Sunday's derby will

Gene Petersen Captures Feature Race, 2 Others

By ROGER MATZ
Courier Sports Writer

Gene Petersen, after a so-so season last year, started off the 1958 stock car racing season at Tunis Speedway by winning the first heat, the class A semi and the feature here Sunday night. Petersen [...] O'Dean, John Mullink and Bill Zwanziger.

ZWANZIGER, battled up during most of the race behind O'Dean, finally slipped past O'Dean's 16 Jr. and began to edge up on Petersen. Zwanziger's bid came too late [...]

Dick Krafka, who won the season championship last year, was second in the trials with an 18:69 timing but he had to scratch from the feature with front end trouble.

GENE WELCH turned in what was probably the best [...] end of the 10 laps.

Bill Kemp won the second heat, Dick Storch the class B semi and Cal Swanson the consolation.

The stocks will race again next Sunday night at 7:30 with no time trials.

[illegible]

McPhergus Sets Tunis Track Mark

The Tunis Speedway harness track record was broken Thursday night by McPhergus with a 2:09.4 in the first heat of the 2:20 pace. McPher-

First Stock Car Race Here May 4

The Hawkeye Racing Assn., whose members drive the stock cars that race at Tunis Speedway here, set Apr. 27 as test run date and May 4 as the first racing date for 1958 at a meeting here Tuesday night.

Harry Peterson, Bob Ledjee and Bob Wright were selected as a technical committee in a special conference of the board of directors. The committee supervises and officiates at teardowns during the racing season.

Mullink Wins Second Feature Race of Season

John Mullink, who won the stock car feature at Tunis Speedway here last week but lost out to Red Droste in the Independence Day races, won again Sunday night before 3,925 fans.

Mullink had to work hard for the victory and wasn't sure of the win until starter Vinton Jones gave him the checkered flag on the 20th lap with Carroll Jensen and Ben Hoefer hot on his tail. Mullink took the lead from Bill Starr, who had led most of the race, when Starr spun out and into last place on the first turn of the 15th lap.

JENSEN AND HOEFER then went hard after Mullink and nearly caught him on several turns. At the white flag that signalled just one lap to go, Jensen was right on Mullink's bumper and Hoefer on Jensen's bumper. As all three drivers cocked for the last turn, Jensen's inside wheel flew off and Hoefer sped past into second, inches behind first-place Mullink. Mullink's win Sunday made him the only driver besides Bill Zwanziger to win two features at Tunis so far this season.

The feature had to be stopped on the 12th lap when Les Johnston, driving Kenny Jensen's new No. 11, rolled on the far turn. Bob Dautremont, who won the third heat, smashed into Johnston during the accident and had to be taken to a hospital for a checkup when he collapsed after leaving his car. Dautremont, from Iowa City, was released from the hospital late Sunday night after an examination by a doctor.

Dick Krafka, who won Friday's consolation race, duplicated that feat again Sunday night but had a much tougher time of it. Bob Posekany first led the race with Gene Petersen and Krafka in pursuit. Petersen then passed Posekany and was followed by Krafka. Krafka, however, couldn't get around Petersen until Petersen slid in a soft spot coming into the 12th lap. Petersen finished second while [...]

three novice victories a driver is banned from novice driving and put into the regular events.

Arnie Spore won the special rollover contest after four other drivers failed to roll their cars. Vern, LeRoy and Leon Parker and Merle Smith all attempted to roll junk cars picked up for the event by running them off a ramp. After several near misses, Spore took a novice car and made a few runs over the ramp but this didn't work so he rolled the stock down a high bank on the first turn.

The annual 50-lap midseason championship race is on next Sunday's card which will start at 7:45 p. m. with no

STOCK CAR RACING—

Holmlund Heads Novice Drivers Into 40 Lap Final Race Sunday

Somewhere between 20 and 30 novice drivers will compete this Sunday night in a 40-lap season novice championship but the winner will probably be one of the 10 or 11 drivers who have consistently finished in the top five places in each novice event since the midseason championship.

Dale Osborn, who went 30 laps for the midseason championship win earlier this season, is not eligible for the season race since, shortly after his midseason victory, he moved up into competition in the modified division.

Bob Holmlund, who won his third novice race this season on Labor Day, will be one of the top favorites. Holmlund probably has one of the heaviest and most powerful cars in a field—a 1941 Buick with stock dual carburetors.

HOLMLUND'S car has been through nearly two seasons of novice racing at Tunis and about the only things that

The other 10 drivers who have consistently placed in almost every novice race since the midseason championship include Jerry Holback, Vern Schoonover, Jim Hoerman, Lloyd Hesse, Walt Lang, Red Morgan, Bill Halupnik, Tom Osborn, Dick Dugan and Bill White. Lang has won two events while most of the others have won at least once.

HOLBACK, WHOSE car was ordered torn down after his second victory here several weeks ago, finished second in the midseason race. Holback failed to appear for the teardown and he was forced to forfeit his win to Lang.

The third place finisher in the midseason race, Gale Card, has since moved up to modified competition with Osborn. Ernie Sommerfelt, fourth place finisher, has retired from racing. Morgan finished fifth, Hesse sixth and Halupnik eighth.

Regular season novice rules

usual card at Tunis which starts at 7:45 p. m. with no time trials.

• • •

MARION'S BILL Kemp, the Tunis Speedway veteran who was injured seriously last month when his late model stock crashed through a fence at Donnellson, Iowa, showed up at Tunis last Sunday as a spectator. Bill's eye injury and concussion are clearing up now and he says he'll try to make it to the last race of the season here this year. If he doesn't make it by then, he'll be back here next season.

• • •

Arnie Spore, whose late model went out of control Sunday night because of a broken tie rod and then crashed into the gate and fence near the judges' stand, must have seen how close he came to starter Vinton Jones. The first thing Arnie said when he regained consciousness was "Where's Jones?" Only after Jones assured Spore that h[...]

Hilmer Cops 3rd Feature Despite Leaky Radiator

Bob Hilmer won his third 20-lap stock car race in as many tries at Tunis Speedway here Monday night, but overheating caused by a bad radiator almost cost him the win.

Hilmer, who started off with a win in the first heat, developed radiator trouble while

judges' stand four-abreast with the front of Krafka's coupe inches ahead of his competitors. However, Hilmer broke through on the next turn for a car length lead. Moffet then lost control momentarily and fell back as did Krafka and Hickman.

That left only Johnson, who

out of the turn abreast of Hilmer, but he was fishtailing slightly and Hilmer regained enough of an edge to last through the next two turns to victory.

HILMER AND John Mullink, who won the main event Sun-

third as the three leaders came down the back stretch of the last lap.

Flagman Vinton Jones narrowly escaped injury when a stock car driven by Arnie Spore went out of control at the start of the class A semi and smashed into a woven wire gate and a

Kemp's Late Model Stock at Tunis

Bill Kemp stands beside the late model stock that he will drive this summer at Tunis Speedway as Cedarloo Racing, Inc. drivers begin a conversion to late-model racing. The car formerly owned by Russ (Peppy) Gross of Quincy, Ill., is a 1953 model powered by a '53 engine boasting two carburetors. The stock has a 1949 front end and coil springs. Kemp and owner, Roy Lansing, were pleased with the car's performance during its test run at Tunis Sunday afternoon.

Hickman Wins Feature; Novice Title to Holmlund

Jack Hickman won his first stock car feature in several seasons at Tunis Speedway here Sunday night while Bob Holmlund closed out his novice career by winning the season novice championship.

Hickman pitted six six-cylinder GMC-powered coupe against Bill Zwanziger's Corvette-powered late model for the last 19 laps of the stock car feature for the victory that was just .05 of a minute off the track record of 6.28. Hickman started on the outside of the second row and moved into first place ahead of Jerry Sherbon on the second lap. Zwanziger pulled in behind Hickman and began a frustrating chase that saw Hickman counter every attempt Zwanziger made to pass him.

HICKMAN HAS had handling trouble all season but his 70 handled and ran perfectly in the feature. Every time the Cedarloo point leader tried to move around inside or outside in the curves, Hickman was able to out-maneuver him and stay just enough in front on the straight stretches to keep his edge through the turns.

The novice championship race was stopped on the 37th lap by two separate accidents and Holmlund, who has won three times previously this season, was declared the winner. Walt Lang and Frank Roe locked wheel coming out of the last turn of the 36th lap and smashed through the fence in front of the grandstand just as Bill Padget, who was going into the first turn of the 37th lap, rolled his car. None of the three drivers was injured.

Lloyd Hesse started on the outside pole in the championship race and led the early laps until Holmlund and Padget came up to pass him and begin a two-lap duel for first. Holmlund won out and went on to build up a sizable lead until the race was stopped on the 37th lap. Placings were decided reverting the race to the last completed lap, which was the 36th.

HARRY PETERSON picked up two wins before the crowd of 2,376 to become the night's only double winner. Peterson won the second heat after it had been stopped on the fifth lap by a rollover. Bob Hilmer had been leading while Peterson and Vern Weber were battling for second and third. On the fifth lap, Hilmer's car hit a bad bump in the turn and swung into the side of Arnie Spore's late model. Spore's car flipped into the air and turned over several times before landing on its nose in the center of the track. Spore was not injured. Hilmer then broke an axle on the restart of the race and Peterson burst into first and stayed there for the remaining five laps. Peterson then went on to win the class B semi.

Gale Card won the first heat after it had to be restarted on the fifth lap when Larry Harsch, a newcomer to the speedway, rolled on the fifth lap.

HICKMAN LOST a chance for a victory in the calss A semi when Don Donovan and Les Schmitz collided and Donovan rolled. Donovan had come up to take the lead from Gale Card early in the race while Schmitz moved into second behind him. Hickman finally broke loose from the pack on the 12th lap to pass both Schmitz and Donovan but Schmitz hit Donovan broadside coming into the 13th lap

A crowd gathers around Bob Holmlund Sunday night after he won the 1958 novice season championship in an accident-shortened 37-lap race. Holmlund was presented the trophy by Irene Hill, sister of stock car driver, John Hill, from her wheel chair after the race.

Cedarloo Racing, Inc. Replaces Hawkeye Group

A new stock car racing association, Cedarloo Racing, Inc., has been formed to promote late model auto racing at Tunis Speedway here.

The new group has a contract with J. L. Tunis, owner of the speedway, to sponsor the weekly stock car races there this summer. Since 1952, the Hawkeye Racing Assn. had sponsored the races at Tunis. The new association's officers are about the same as those for Hawkeye Racing Assn.

Speed Chumley, president of Cedarloo Racing, Inc., says he hopes that the group can convert over to late models (1949 and newer) by midseason. He said that a few members are building late models now and more will appear throughout the season so that by next year all the cars will be late models.

Chumley was Hawkeye Racing Assn. president, too.

The same drivers are expected to drive under Cedarloo Racing, Inc., sponsorship as drove at Tunis' in previous seasons.

tion of July 27 suspende[...]

Hawkeye Racing Assn. Elects

Ira (Speed) Chumley, president of the Hawkeye Racing Assn., was one of two officers reelected at the association's monthly meeting Tuesday night. The association sponsors weekly stock car races at Tunis Speedway during the summer months.

1959
In the News

Again Elect Chumley Cedarloo Racing Head

Three of four officers of the Cedarloo Racing Assn., were elected to another term at the club's monthly meeting Tuesday night. Eight members were named to a board of directors.

President Ira (Speed) Chumley, vice president Guy Rich and treasurer Pearl Custard retained their offices. Vern Weber was elected secretary.

Retiring secretary Carroll Jensen was one of the eight named to the board of directors. Others included Gordon Bentley, Ed Hedges, Lester Schmitz, Al Strein, Tobe Stirler, Bob Posekany and attorney Kay Kober.

The board of directors scheduled a meeting for Friday night to discuss plans for the 1959 racing season. Cedarloo sponsors the weekly stock car races at Tunis Speedway.

Karla Prummitt, 17-year-old Fredericksburg girl, makes the mid-season championship trophy presentation to Bill Zwanziger. Zwanziger drove a late model stock car owned by Gordon Bentley of Fairbank to a new 50-lap record at Tunis Speedway Sunday night.

Courier Sports
WATERLOO, IOWA, MONDAY, AUGUST 24, 1959 PAGE THIRTEEN

Zwanziger Gets Fourth Feature Win of Season

Bill Zwanziger won his fourth modified stock car feature of the season at Tunis Speedway here Sunday night on a partially darkened track.

The lights around the southeast turn went out just as the consolation race ended, three minutes before the feature was scheduled to begin. Attempts to find the cause of the light failure failed, and the drivers decided to run the race even though one-fourth of the quarter mile track was in complete darkness.

Dick Sturch took an early lead in the main event as Zwanziger and Charley Moffett worked themselves free of traffic. By the third lap Sturch had a sizable lead, but the race had to be halted when Dale Osborn rolled his car on the backstretch. The restart put Zwanziger and Moffett third and fourth behind Sturch and Bill Hap.

MOFFETT AND Zwanziger stayed close together until they passed Hap and Sturch. Then Zwanziger moved out away from Moffett and ran the remaining eight laps without any serious competition.

Zwanziger was one of two double winners. His first win Sunday was in the class B semi. Marion's Harry O'Dean took both the first heat and the class A semi. In the semi. O'Dean took over from Sturch on the seventh lap and kept his lead after the race had to be restarted when Tuffy Meyer rolled his car.

Arnie Spore spoiled Zwanziger's chances for a sweep early in the night. In the third heat, Spore moved out to a wide lead that was too much for Zwanziger to overcome. However, Zwanziger finished a close second.

Harry Petersen won the consolation after a last minute delay allowed him to enter the race. Petersen switched carburetors in the pits after failing to place in any of his first two events. The job took Petersen a little longer than expected and he wasn't ready when the consolation started. A minor accident on the first lap caused the race to be restarted and Petersen asked officials to be allowed to join the race. He received permission to start on the rear of the 15-car field and

Courier Sports
WATERLOO, IOWA, MONDAY, SEPTEMBER 14, 1959 PAGE ELEVEN

Zwanziger Wins After Moss Victory Protested

Bill Zwanziger won the annual 75-lap modified stock car season championship race at Tunis Speedway here Sunday night after an upheld protest eliminated John Moss, who had finished first in the race.

Moss

Zwanziger

Moss won the race, moving from third to first on the 21st lap, passing second-place Charley Moffett and front-running Zwanziger.

Before the race was over a Waterloo driver, Boots Ellery, put up $25 protest money with Cedarloo Racing Assn. officials. At a teardown late Sunday night, the Cedarloo technical committee found an electric fuel pump—a violation of the modification rules — on Moss' flathead coupe.

THE TECHNICAL committee turned the matter over to the board of directors. The board awarded the winning driver's trophy to Moss, but the cash and the title went to Zwanziger, who had finished second before the crowd of 4,016.

Moss, from Iowa City, would have been the first out-of-town driver in two years to take home a modified championship.

The Iowa City driver's greatest opposition during the race came from Gene Petersen who trailed him for some 40 laps. At times it appeared Petersen would take the lead as Moss bogged behind slower cars. Each time, however, Moss broke away just in time.

A spinout ended the Petersen threat on the 65th lap, but a display of driving skill kept him in the money. Coming out of the last turn of the 65th lap, Petersen hit a bump and bounced into a skid. The car turned completely around and was slammed into from the side by another racer. Petersen kept the accelerator at full throttle, careened off the other car, skittered across the front stretch and had his car righted around and running full speed by the time he hit the next turn. Even after all this, he only lost one place as Zwanziger went by into second. As it turned out, however, it appears that Petersen lost the title right there, for Zwanziger won the race after the protest.

DICK KRAFKA of Dysart took an early lead in the 25-lap consolation and kept it for the win. Bill Kemp of Marion, who won the second heat, followed him closely but couldn't quite catch him.

Clarence McCombs of Waterloo was taken to a Waterloo hospital for observation after an accident at the start of the consolation. McCombs rammed Gale Card's car on the bounce as Card rolled on the backstretch. Card was uninjured. McCombs was released from the hospital later Sunday night.

Bob Shephard of Fairbank

See STOCKS
Continued on page 12, col. 9

5,520 SEE MARK LOWERED TO 15.75--

Zwanziger Sets Record in 50-Lap Mid-Season Race

Bill Zwanziger of Waterloo drove his late model to a record time in winning the annual mid season modified stock car championship at Tunis Speed- the way in a tight parade. Fifth was Carroll Jensen who started from back in the field.

Zwanziger started on the in-

Gale Card and Don Feckers, fell a lap behind before the race was half over. Sherbon was handicapped considerably when the hood on his late model flew

Dick Krafka won the second heat. Arnie Spore won the third heat but stalled during the championship race when his

Zwanziger Wins Fifth Feature; Nears Record

Bill Zwanziger won his fifth modified stock car feature of the season at Tunis Speedway here Sunday night with a time just four-hundredths off his own track record.

It was the second main event win in a row for the 1959 midseason champion and ties him in total features won this summer with point standings leader Charley Moffett.

A crowd of 2,483 sat through

features this year, won the consolation. Another Iowa City driver, John Mullink, won the second heat.

Dick Francis won the junior novice race after a sideswiping collision with Larry Sommerfelt, who was leading at the time. Two drivers were slightly shaken up and a third uninjured in three novice rollovers. Jim Cunningham, leading on the first lap, came into the first turn a bit high and

Horses Race Thursday, Friday Now

Rain forced postponement of Wednesday night's scheduled harness racing card at Tunis Speedway to Friday night.

Thursday night's program will go on as scheduled at 7:45 p. m. with a 2:20 trot, 2:20 pace and the meet's featured free-for-all pace in addition to three pony races.

Because of the unexpectedly heavy entry list, the 2:25 pace on Friday's card has been split into two sections making Friday's program a total of eight one mile heats of horse racing plus the three Shetland pony races.

A maximum of 12 horses will be permitted to start in each heat.

Track proprietor Jud Tunis said that, although Wednesday afternoon's heavy rain left the track too wet for racing Wednesday night, the track's overall condition is excellent.

Harness Racing At 7:45

Harness racing makes its annual stand in Black Hawk county Wednesday and Thursday night when some 170 standardbred horses and Shetland ponies take over the Tunis Speedway track where the stock cars race on weekends throughout the summer.

There will be nine heats of racing each night starting at 7:45 p. m. with the trotters running under United States Trotting Assn. rules and the ponies under the Iowa Shetland Pony Racing Assn. rules.

Wednesday's card will include two 1-mile heats each of the 2:25 trot, 2:25 pace and free-for-all trots as well as three half mile heats of pony races.

Thursday's card will be the same except that the rated trot and pace will be 2:20.

In case of rain postponements either night, the card will be set back one day. Purses in the horse races will be $200 added money for each event.

The horses will race over the half mile track and the ponies over one-fourth mile.

16 Women Will Vie in Powder Puff Derby

1960
In the News

Gene Petersen Wins Feature As Stock Car Season Opens

Gene Petersen of Waterloo won the 25-lap feature in the opening stock car racing program of the season at Tunis Speedway here Sunday night.

Petersen drove the biggest engine in the pack to victory over runnerup Bill Zwanziger of Waterloo. Charlie Moffett of Stanwood was third.

Track owner Jud Tunis said the opening attendance of 3,-256 was a thousand more than for the 1959 first card.

Heat winners were Moffett, Petersen and Zwanziger. Ca

Spore Wins at Tunis After Two Are Disqualified

The feature event at Tunis Speedway was marred for the second week in a row Sunday night by dispute.

Apparently feature winner, Bill Zwanziger, and runnerup Ernie Speth were disqualified after a protest for cutting corners on the quarter-mile dirt oval. First place then went to the man who came in third, Arnold Spore.

Last week Gene Petersen was disqualified in the feature because a pit man allegedly worked on his car during an accident delay. Hard-luck man Sunday night before the 3,150 fans was Jack Hickman of Waterloo who lost his right-rear wheel in two separate races. The third time his wheel stayed on and he placed fourth in the consolation event.

In the novice run, winner Bob Hess of Waterloo almost didn't get in the race because one fender was barely hanging on. Fenders are required, at least to start the race. In winning, the fender did come off and he picked it up along with the checkered flag from starter Vinton Jones.

Another novice driver, Ronnie Sells placed third and spilled his car on the corner after finishing the race.

Stock Car Racing to Start Here May 8

The 1960 stock car racing season at Tunis Speedway will open May 8 with a warmup session.

Drivers of the Cedarloo Racing Assn., Inc., which sponsors the weekly races, will spend that afternoon at the quarter mile track testing their cars. The warmup session will be free to the public.

First formal racing of the year will be the following Sunday night.

THE ONLY time trials of the year will be run that night to establish a basis for the point system on which drivers will start each race for the remainder of the year.

Also on the first card there will be three heats, one semi main, a consolation and a feature.

After the first race, Cedarloo will return to its regular program of three heats, two semis, a consolation and a main event, with novice racing scheduled to start later in the year.

AT A MEETING of the Cedarloo Board of Directors Friday night it was decided to keep about the same rules as last year.

Speed Chumley is president of Cedarloo, with Vern Weber as secretary and Pearl Custard treasurer.

Stock Car Drivers Try For Points

The point-rating system for drivers and cars is now in its fourth year at Tunis Speedway. Unlike the state system for highway drivers, the more points the modified stock drivers get the happier they are.

After four cards this season, bunched near the top, pointwise, are three veteran race drivers, Charlie Moffett of Stanwood, Gene Petersen and Bill Zwanziger of Waterloo. Mid-season champ last year was Zwanziger, with Moffett copping the championship. The final standings last year showed Moffett had 600 points, Zwanziger 537 and John Moss

Racing

STOCK CARS and Tunis Speedway had one of their best years, while micro-midget racing got its start during 1959.

Bill Zwanziger of Waterloo and Charley Moffett of Stanwood topped the stocks at Tunis.

Zwanziger

Carroll Jensen, was the micro leader winning the point standings and the Midwest championship.

Moffett, with an early rush, won the point standings title, while Zwanziger was the mid-season and season championship races. It took a disqualification of John Moss to give Bill the season title, however. At that he didn't get the trophy. Moss had carried that back to Iowa City before his car was found not in stock.

Bill Hoerman of Clarksville won the mid-season novice title. Bob Sheppard won the season novice feature.

Jack Persson of Waterloo won the Iowa Tourist motorcycle title.

Moffett Nips Zwanziger in 50-Lapper Before Over 7,000

By ROGER MAYE
Courier Staff Writer

Charlie Moffett replaced Bill Zwanziger as the Tunis Speedway mid-season champion here Sunday night and broke Zwanziger's time record in the process.

Moffett, from Stanwood, raced to a record 13.50 with Zwanziger, last year's mid-season and season champ, rubbing bumpers with him all the way. Zwanziger's time last year was 13.73.

Track owner Jud Tunis said the paid attendance was 5,164, in addition to some 2,000 children admitted free.

ONE OF THE men who was considered among the favored contenders wasn't in the line-up. Gene Petersen, who has won several features this year, broke a connecting rod in his 400-cubic inch engine while warming up the motor in the Tunis pits before the first heat and never got the [illegible] behind.

After traffic thinned out, Moffett stretched his lead to about a car length for a few laps, until Zwanziger, one of the top Waterloo drivers competing at Tunis, again closed in within inches.

One mistake on Moffett's part would have put Zwanziger into the lead and a similar mistake on Zwanziger's part would have put Moffett out of reach for certain.

NEITHER DRIVER overstepped a corner. They seemed to be attached to each other by an invisible cable.

On at least two occasions, Zwanziger was able to pull up alongside, but Moffett always slid ahead again.

Other top finishers in the race were Jim Hoerman of Clarksville third, Bob Deutremont of Iowa City fourth, Bob Hilmer of Dysart fifth, and Tuffy Meyers of Davenport sixth.

[illegible] in the first 30-lap event, John Mullink, of Iowa City, in the second, and Moffett in the third.

Bob Poeskany of Cedar Falls was knocked unconscious and suffered an ear injury when the car he was driving rolled seven times in the third heat.

Poeskany was leading the race when Moffett, in second, tried to go by on the inside of a seventh lap-turn. The two cars bumped slightly and Poeskany began his roll along the turn.

MOFFETT, who said "I had my brakes on and was sliding all the way" at the time of the accident, went inside the wrecked car to retrieve Poeskany after track attendants had difficulty freeing the injured driver because of jammed doors.

Poeskany, eligible to drive the 50-lapper but left without a car because of the accident, borrowed a novice car for the midseason race but had a flat tire.

Willie Kleinfort, of Waverly, won the novice race and Bill Fiskle, of Cedar Falls, won the consolation.

Highlight of next Sunday's race at the speedway will be the 35-lap mid-season novice championship race.

Busy Schedule at Tunis Next Week; Petersen Feature Victor

The eight days beginning July 3, next Sunday, will see five days of racing at Tunis Speedway, proprietor Jud Tunis announced Monday.

Modified stock cars will compete both next Sunday and Monday on the quarter-mile oval and Monday's Fourth of July card will be followed by a fireworks display.

Standardbred horses will make their annual appearance at the Speedway Friday and Saturday, July 8 and 9, with a pair of harness race programs on the half-mile track. Then the stocks will return Sunday, July 10.

Gene Petersen outdueled Bill Zwanziger to win the stock car feature Sunday night before 3,-[illegible] fans after an eighth-lap flip knocked Bob Hilmer of Dysart out of the feature event running.

Earlier a five-car pileup in the semi-main took two drivers out of the running. Gerald Halbach of Waterloo tried a turn sideways and piled up four others [illegible] behind him.

Courier Sports

WATERLOO, IOWA, MONDAY, JULY [illegible], 1960 — PAGE THIRTEEN

Sells Wins Novice Title, Bill Zwanziger Feature

Ronnie Sells of New Hartford outlasted Vern Spaneman of Waterloo to win the 35-lap mid-season novice feature stock car race at Tunis Speedway here Sunday night.

Spaneman, who battled Sells for over 25 laps, finished second.

The trophy was awarded Sells by Nan Harlen, 11, whose father, Jacob, owns the second place car.

The regular feature was won by Bill Zwanziger of Waterloo.

The novice race was marred by one major accident. Gilbert Marsh of Waterloo flipped his No. 12 but was uninjured.

Paid attendance was 3,428.

Last week's modified stock 50-lap champ, Charlie Moffett of Stanwood, was second behind Zwanziger. John Moss of Iowa City was third in the feature.

Volkswagen Dealer to Build on Falls Ave.

This is an architect sketch of the building which will house Forest Hill Motors, Inc., Waterloo's first factory-authorized Volkswagen dealer for nearly two years. The face brick and cement block building will have some 7,000 square feet of floor space, of which about 3,000 will be devoted to a service area with a capacity of 21 cars daily. Construction on the site, 3623 Falls Ave., should begin by June. The location is on the Waterloo side of Tunis Speedway. Forest Hill is currently located at 418 W. 10th St. Grow and DeYoe, Cedar Falls, were the architects.

Moffett Nips Zwanziger in 50-Lapper Before Over 7,000

By ROGER MAYE
Courier Staff Writer

1961

In the News

Zwanziger Wins Season Opening Feature Before 2,716 at Tunis

Hilmer Wins Feature Before 3,178 at Tunis

Bob Hilmer of Dysart, the current record-holder for a 20-lap race at Tunis Speedway, returned to top form Sunday night at Tunis before 3,178 fans and won the feature race of the evening along with the first heat.

He also finished third in the 15-lap "A" semi-main.

Hilmer set the track record in 1958 with a time of 6.23 for 20 turns around the track.

Bob Posekany of Cedar Falls also was a double winner Sunday. He won the 10-lap second heat and "A" semi-main.

Bill Zwanziger of Waterloo, the current Cedarloo Racing Assn. point leader, finished second in the feature race. He won the third heat and finished fourth in the "B" semi-main.

The stock cars resume action Tuesday night with another full racing card at Tunis Speedway. The races start at 7:30 p. m. There will be no time trials.

First heat (10 laps)—1. Bob Hilmer, Dysart; 2. Jerry Holbach, Waterloo; 3. Al Runyan, Waterloo [illegible]

Second heat (10 laps)—1. Bob [illegible]kany, Cedar Falls; 2. Jerry [illegible] Iowa City; 3. Larry Sommerfelt, [illegible]terloo; 3.28.

Third heat (10 laps)—1. Bill Zwanziger, Waterloo; 2. Charlie M[illegible] Stanwood; 3. Arnie Spore, Wa[illegible] 3.39.

A Semi-main (15 laps)—1. [illegible]kany; 2. Sommerfelt; 3. Hilmer; [illegible] Dale Osborne, Cedar Falls; [illegible] van; 6. Jim Hoerman, Clarks[illegible] 4.06.

B Semi-main (15 laps)—1. [illegible] Meyers, Big Rock; 2. Spore; [illegible]fett; 4. Zwanziger; 5. Moss; 6. [illegible] Petersen, Waterloo; 4.93.

Consolation (12 laps)—1. Cal Swanson, Waterloo; 2. Gale Card, W[illegible]loo; 3. Larry Candee, Stout; 4.5[illegible]

Feature (20 laps)—1. Hilmer; [illegible] Zwanziger; 3. Osborne; 4. Moss; [illegible] Spore; 6. Meyers; 6.3[illegible]

Petersen Wins 75-Lap Race in Record Time

By JIM AYERS
Courier Sports Writer

Gene Petersen of Waterloo broke his string of runnerup finishes and a Tunis Speedway track record at the same time while winning the 75-lap season championship here Sunday night before 2,883 thoroughly chilled racing fans.

Petersen toured the quarter-mile oval 75 times in 23 and 58 hundredth minutes to erase the old mark of 23.82 set by [illegible]

[illegible] to retire on the 51st lap. Transmission trouble forced Bob Hilmer of Dysart out on the seventh lap. Cal Swanson of Waterloo, winner in four of the last five feature races, lost a wheel and quit on the 22nd lap.

ZWANZIGER, who won the point trophy with a record 706 points, missed nine laps due to an ignition wire that fell off. He was running in [illegible]

[illegible] of Waterloo (234); Harry O'Deen of Marion (186); Hoerman (183); Carroll Jensen of Waterloo (177); Tuffy Meyers of Big Rock (168); John Mullink of West Liberty (166); Harry Petersen of Waterloo (163); Larry Sommerfelt of Waterloo (151); John Connolly of Delhi (148); Gale Card of Evansdale (146); Bill Hopp of Muscatine (142); Bob Posekany of Waterloo (140); Keith Knaack of Vinton (136); Mer[illegible]

Hilmer Increases Lead, But All Eyes on Finkle This Sunday at Tunis

Bob Hilmer of Dysart stretched his lead over Iowa City's Johnny Moss in Cedarloo Racing Assn. point-standings this week.

Hilmer led Moss by only seven points going into last Sunday's program. This week, with the new standings computed, Hilmer leads over Moss 230-200.

BILL ZWANZIGER of Waterloo moved up on second-place Moss with a total of 193 points. Zwanziger is followed by Arnie Spore and Gene Petersen, both of Waterloo, with [illegible]

[illegible] depths of the standings last Sunday night to cop the 20-lap feature. Finkle also won the two other events in which he appeared.

ALTHOUGH several drivers and mechanics eyed Finkle's car suspiciously after last Sunday's feature—some on hands and knees with flashlights — talk of a teardown was postponed pending Finkle's accomplishments this Sunday night.

Under Cedarloo rules, a teardown may be requested to check on a car conforming to [illegible]

4,226 See Finkle Win 3 Tunis Firsts

Zwanziger Goes Into Lead on 40th Lap, Wins Before 5,860

Mullink Wins Feature in Best Time Of the Season Before 4,333 Fans

Hilmer Wins 3rd Feature Of Year Before 4,258

Moss Wins Feature Before 3,022 Fans

Johnny Moss of Iowa City outdueled Gene Petersen of Waterloo to capture narrow victories in the 20-lap feature and the "B" semi-main at the stock car races at Tunis Speedway Tuesday night.

Tuffy Meyers of Big Rock finished third behind Moss and Petersen in the feature and the "B" semi-main and [illegible] fans braved threatening skies to view the races Tuesday night.

Bob Shepard was the only Waterloo racer to win a first place. He won the 15-lap "A" semi-main.

The next racing program is next Sunday at Tunis. Novice races are on tap along with the regular events next Sun-[illegible]

Hughes, Monticello; 6. Harry Petersen, Waterloo; 5:29.

"B" Semi-Main (15 laps)—1. Johnny Moss, Iowa City; 2. Gene Petersen, Waterloo; 3. Tuffy Meyers, Big Rock; 4. Arnie Spore, Waterloo; 5. Bill Zwanziger, Waterloo; 6. Charlie Moffett, Stanwood; 5:07.

Consolation (12 laps)—1. Gale Card, Evansdale; 2. Bob Hilmer, Dysart; 3. Dale Osborne, Cedar Falls; 4:16.

Feature (20 laps)—1. Johnny Moss, Iowa City; 2. Gene Petersen, Waterloo; 3. Meyers, Big Rock; 4. Arnie Spore, Waterloo; 4. Charlie Moffett, Stanwood; 5. John Connolly, Delhi.

1962
In the News

WMAK

This "dive bomber" stunt is is one of the daredevil numbers which will be featured at the Tunis Speedway by the Trans World Auto Daredevils at 8:30 p. m. Tuesday. In this exhibition, Bumps Willert of Tipton, Ia., drives a junker up a ramp and down into two other parked cars at about 50 miles an hour. Willert has numerous scars to show as the result of this stunt, but has never been seriously injured. Willert, before joining the Daredevils had his preparation by driving huge cattle trucks from points in Iowa to the Chicago Stockyards, battling traffic and all kinds of weather.

Red Droste Top Driver At Tunis

Waterloo's Red Droste swept the honors in Wednesday night's Memorial Day races at Tunis Speedway before the largest Memorial Day crowd on record.

A crowd of 4,860 fans watched Droste take a special 10-lap trophy dash among the top four drivers and win three other events. Droste and his chief rival, Bill Zwanziger of Waterloo drove the first seven laps of the dash hub-to-hub before Zwanziger threw a crank shafte balances — taking him out of action for the night.

Droste then picked up first in the third heat, the B semi-main and the feature to become the season's first triple winner. The wins added 74 points to Droste's total, leaving him way out in front in the Cedarloo Racing Assn. point standings with 177. Gene Peterson of Waterloo, like most of the top drivers, was plagued with mechanical troubles Wednesday night and picked up no points.

Red Droste Returns With Bang

Waterloo's Red Droste returned to the racing wars at Tunis Speedway and had himself a night before a record opening night crowd of 3,920 Sunday night.

Droste tooled his high-powered rig to a new track record for a time-trial lap with a mark of 18.32 seconds, eclipsing the old record of 18.43 set back in 1956 by Waterloo's Bill Zwanziger. Zwansiger, himself, was only .01 off his 1956 mark with an 18.44 lap.

Petersen Edging Closer to Droste in Point Standings

Gene Petersen has taken over second place in the Cedarloo Racing Association point standings and is giving leader Red Droste his closest challenge of the season.

Petersen's total of 496 points is within easy shooting distance of Droste's 521.

Bill Zwanziger, in third, is well within range of both Droste and Petersen with a total of 483 points. Zwanziger was last season's point champion. All three drivers are from Waterloo.

Aside from the point scramble, the Waterloo drivers will be out to show their stuff to the Minnesota drivers who walked off with seven money finishes at Tunis Speedway last Sunday in this week's card.

A full card of eight events will be staged at Tunis Sunday starting at 7:30 p. m.

Tunis Feature Boosted To 25 Laps for Sunday

Cedarloo Racing Assn. President Speed Chumley announced Friday that beginning Sunday the feature races at Tunis Speedway will be 25 laps instead of 20.

He added that this is just in the experimental stage and may last only a few weeks.

Droste picked up 74 points Wednesday and now leads the drivers with 177. Second is Gene Peterson of Waterloo with 96. Next drivers are Tuffy Meyers of Big Rock with 78, Bill Zwanziger of Waterloo with 68 and Jim Hoerman of Clarksville and Charlie Moffett of Iowa City tied with 64.

Auto Daredevils At Tunis Tuesda

A two-hour program of chills and spills will be prese by the Trans World Auto Daredevils on the Tunis Speed Tuesday evening beginning at 8:30.

There will be crashes through fiery board walls, iberate rolls and headlong dives into parked cars. T vill also be a 10-lap race topped off by a demolition contest.

This premier group of stuntmen are due to arrive in Waterloo tonight for their annual appearance Tuesday in Waterloo on their way to some of the biggest fairs in the Middle West.

AMONG THE contestants will be Iowans, Jimmy Canton of Cedar Rapids, Bumps Willert of Tipton and numerous others who will relegate about a dozen autos to the scrap heap in the course of the smashing performances.

Other events will be precision driving by Al Gross, Willert, Canton and Whitey Wichert in twos and fours; a 75 foot ramp jump by ton in a compact and als a motorcycle and the s tional two-wheel drive Gross.

LEO OVERLAND new of the show has annou that he has signed Wimpy British clown for the ba of the season. Wimpy played his many talen Shrine circuses all over country last winter and s He has signed a $1,000 a contract with George F for the next indoor seas was reported that next to mett Kelly he is the h salaried clown.

Wimpy is the proud of a $6,000 sedan, whi won in a contest.

BILL ZWANZIGER
. . . repeats mid-season win

New 50-Lap Record

Bill Zwanziger of Waterloo set a new track record for 50 laps and won his second consecutive mid-season championship at Tunis Speedway Sunday night.

A crowd of 5,563 paid customers saw Zwanziger win the trophy in a record time of 15.63 erasing the old mark of 15.70 set by Charlie Moffett of Stanwood in 1960.

Chilled temperatures and overcast skies failed to dampen the enthusiasm of the fans who had watched Bob Hilmer of Dysart take the lead from Zwanziger on the fourth lap. Hilmer then led for 32 laps until his engine blew a piston on the 37th go-round.

ZWANZIGER had maintained second within a half lap of Hilmer before making his move in the 35th lap. Point-leader Red Droste once again suffered from a mechanical jinx and dropped out after one lap because of car trouble.

Zwanziger credited his win to good luck and to Gordon Bentley of Fairbank, owner of the No. 31 entry. Prior to the big race, Bentley had the winning car's big engine completely re-balanced and tuned to a fine edge.

Gene Petersen of Waterloo finished second — just making the finish with a broken gas line.

Novice Championship Sunday Night at Tunis

The 35-lap season's championship race for novice drivers will highlight Sunday's modified stock car racing action at Tunis speedway in Waterloo.

The event will be packed with 25 novice drivers expected to be entered in the run for the trophy, signifying the champion of the 1962 season. Entries will be based on point standings of the Cedarloo Racing Association, with the point-winner "on the pole" in the finale.

Red Droste this week continues to hold a strong lead in points with 620. Bill Zwanziger has re-captured the second spot with 549. Gene Petersen is third with 496 points.

Droste 287, Zwanziger 163 in Tunis Standings

Red Droste of Waterloo, winner of three consecutive features in stock car racing at Tunis Speedway, continues to so far, has 287 points.

Bill Zwanziger of Waterloo, who set two track records in wins last Sunday night has

1963
In the News

16 in Powder Puff Derby

Sixteen women drivers have signed, so far, for the powder puff derby Sunday night, an annual feature of the Tunis Speedway stock car race meeting.

The powder puff derby will be one of nine events on Sunday's card which will start, as usual, at 7:30 p. m.

The regular men drivers are in pursuit of point leader Bill Zwanziger of Waterloo who has 420, so far. Others in the top 10 are Red Droste, Waterloo, 381; Charlie Moffett, Stanwood, 357; Gene Petersen, Waterloo, 341; Bob Hilmer, Dysart, 265; John Moss, Iowa City, 169; Dave Noble, Blooming Prairie, Minn., 169; Bob Posekany, Cedar Falls, 160; Tom Hughes, Monticello, 152, and Verlin Eakers, Austin, Minn., 145.

Wagner Is Winner At Tunis

Pleasantville's Earl Wagner, driving a "hoo-doo" — super-modified miniature dragster—sped to victory in the 35-lap feature in the final stock car racing program of the year at Tunis Speedway here Sunday night.

A total of 3,602 fans turned out for Sunday's action, bringing the total paid attendance for the 1963 season to 108,959 for 22 racing sessions.

First heat (10 laps)—1. Norm Sceley, Marengo; 2. Stan Stover, Reinbeck; 3. Russ Zook, Iowa City; 3:24.

Second heat (10 laps)—1. Chub Liebe, Oelwein; 2. Tom Hughes, Monticello; 3. Dick Warbertone.

Third heat (10 laps)—1. Moose Johnson, Sussbury, Wis.; 2. Merl Williams, Rochester; 3. Johnny Moss, Iowa City.

Fourth heat (10 laps)—1. Earl Wagner, Pleasantville; 2. Joe Jones, Madison, Wis., Charlie Moffet, Stanwood.

Consolation (15 laps)—1. Joe Wunst, Rochester; 2. Jerry Sherbon, Cedar Falls; 3. Bill Barghahn, Waterloo.

Semi-main (15 laps)—1. Lee Kunzman, Guttenberg; 2. John Connely, Delhi; 3. Bob Posekany, Cedar Falls.

Feature (35 laps) — 1. Earl Wagner, Pleasantville; 2. Stacy Rodman, Des Moines; 3. Cal Swanson, Waterloo; 4. Joe Rassmussen; 5. Chub Liebe, Oelwein.

Zwanziger Wins Before 6,192

Bill Zwanziger of Waterloo captured the feature event of Thursday night's stock car racing card before a Memorial Day record crowd of 6,192 fans.

Red Droste of Waterloo, the current point leader in the Cedarloo Racing Assn. standings, won the trophy dash for the 10 top point winners.

Droste leads the drivers with 88 points, one more than runnerup Charlie Moffett of Stanwood. Others in the top 10 are Bob Hilmer of Dysart with 84 points; Zwanziger with 77; Gene Petersen of Waterloo with 75; Tom Hughes of Monticello with 46; John Moss of Iowa City with 45; John Connolly of Delhi with 38; Cal Swanson of Cedar Falls with 32 and Mert Williams of Albert Lea, Minn., with 31.

The only double winner of the evening was Bob Poseckany of Cedar Falls with first place in the second heat and the A semi-main.

Another racing program is scheduled for Sunday evening starting at 7:30. It will include the first novice event of the seven events.

First heat (10 laps)—1. Lee Kunzman (Guttenberg), 2. Keith Knoack (Vinton), 3. Ralph Hinzman (Guttenberg), 3:24.

Second heat (10 laps)—1. Bob Posekany (Cedar Falls), 2. Bumps Willard (Tipton), 3. Mert Williams (Rochester, Minn.) 3:34.

Third heat (10 laps)—1. Red Droste (Waterloo), 2. Gene Petersen (Waterloo), 3. Charlie Moffett (Stanwood); 3:15.

A semi-main (15 laps)—1. Posekany, 2. Willard, 3. Knoack; no time.

B semi-main (15 laps)—1. Petersen, 2. Moffett, 3. Bill Zwanziger (Waterloo);

Moffett Cops Tunis Feature

Stanwood's Charlie Moffett sped to a victory in the 20-lap feature race at Tunis Speedway Sunday night before 5,921 stock car racing fans.

Sunday's attendance brought the season total to over the 50,000 mark for 10 racing dates.

Red Droste of Waterloo, current point-standings leader in the Cedarloo Racing Assn., placed third in the consolation race Sunday for his best effort of the night. Bill Zwanziger of Waterloo, who is right behind Droste, placed second in that event.

Next Sunday the mid-season ... program also will include three heat races and the consolation event.

First heat (10 laps)—1. Bill Barnett, Austin, Minn.; 2. Jim Herman, Clarksville; 3. Tony Conrad, Waterloo; 3:42.

Second heat (10 laps)—1. Skip Kennedy, Davenport; 2. Dave Noble, Blooming Prairie, Minn.; 3. Ralph Hinzman, Guttenberg.

Third heat (10 laps)—1. Tom Hughes, Monticello; 2. Charlie Moffett, Stanwood; 3. Bob Hilmer, Dysart.

"A" semi-main (15 laps)—1. Bill Barnett, Austin, Minn.; 2. Lee Kunzman, Guttenberg; 3. Jim Herman, Clarksville.

"B" semi-main (15 laps)—1. Dave Bjore, Austin, Minn.; 2. Dave Noble, Blooming Prairie, Minn.; 3. Gene Petersen, Waterloo.

Consolation (12 laps)—1. Cal Swanson, Cedar Falls; 2. Bill Zwanziger, Waterloo; 3. Red Droste, Waterloo.

Feature (20 laps)—1. Charlie Moffett, Stanwood; 2. Gene Petersen, Waterloo; 3. Dave Bjorge, Austin, Minn.; 6:55.

Junior novice (20 laps)—1. Mike Plum, Waterloo; 2. Virg Carlson, Waterloo; 3. Buzz Jensen, Waterloo; 7:48.

Droste Sets New Record at Tunis

Waterloo's Red Droste broke ...e 75-lap record at Tunis ...peedway Sunday night and in ...oing so captured the season ...hampionship stock car race ...ere.

Droste raced over the 75 laps ...n 23 minutes, 20 seconds, to ...hip Tom Hughes of Monticello ...nd Charlie Moffett of Stanwood.

A total of 5,234 fans were on hand Sunday night to bring the ...eason gate past the 100,000 mark.

Hughes, who was second in the feature, won the 10-lap third heat earlier in the evening.

First heat (10 laps)—1. Jay Livermore, Vinton; 2. Willie Klingluss, 3. Dale Osborne, Cedar Falls.

Second heat (10 laps)—1. Jerry Sherbon, Cedar Falls; 2. Bob Posekany, Cedar Falls; 3. Harry Peterson, Waterloo; 3:85.

Third heat (10 laps)—1. Tom Hughes, Monticello; 2. Dave Noble, Blooming Prairie, Minn.; 3. John Connally, Delhi; 3:50.

Consolation (35 laps)—1. Russ Zook, Iowa City; 2. Keith Knoack, Vinton, 3. Tony Conrad, Greene; 11:95.

Feature (75 laps)—1. Red Droste, Waterloo; 2. Tom Hughes, Monticello; 3. Charlie Moffett, Stanwood; 23:20 (track record).

'Hoo-Doos' Entered At Tunis Sunday

The final stock car racing program of the season is slated to start at 7 p. m. Sunday at Tunis Speedway here.

This week's program calls for open competition with anything going. Entries from throughout the state as well as from adjoining states are expected.

Entered thus far, in addition to the regular Cedarloo Racing Assn. members, are Earl Wagner of Pleasantville, Chub Liebe of Oelwein, three "hoo-doos" from Madison, Wis., and racers from Estherville and Knoxville.

Time trials are slated to begin at 7 p. m. with the regular 7-race card starting at 7:30 p. m.

1,000 Bleachers Added at Tunis

Jud Tunis, owner and operator of Tunis Speedways here, has added 1,000 more bleachers to the stands at the Speedway that will be ready for Sunday night's stock car racing program, slated to start at 7:30 p. m.

The main reason for the addition is the increased crowds the races have drawn thus far this season. A new Sunday night attendance mark of 6,252 was established just last Sunday.

Bill Zwanziger is currently leading the Cedarloo Racing Association point standings with a total of 239. Charlie Moffett of Stanwood is second with 200 and Gene Petersen of Waterloo is third with 197. Last year's champion, Red Droste of Waterloo, is fourth with 193

Droste Edges Zwanziger For Victory in Feature

Waterloo's Red Droste grabbed the lead after the fifth lap and held on the rest of the way to capture the 20-lap feature race at Tunis Speedway Sunday night.

Droste was hard-pressed by Waterloo's Bill Zwanziger throughout, and ended up winning by half a car length.

Third place went to Tuffy Meyer of Big Rock and Charlie Moffett of Stanwood was fourth.

In the special car owners' race Irvin Bohlken of Monticello, driving Tom Hughes car, won the 10-lap event. Don Graham in Droste's auto was second and Joe Johnes of Cascade, driving John Connally's vehicle, placed third.

First heat (10 laps)—1. Bill Barghahn, Waterloo; 2. tie between Bob Shepard, Waterloo, and Russ Zook, Iowa City; 3:53.

Second heat (10 laps)—1. John Hill, Cedar Falls; 2. Gale Card, Waterloo; 3. Tom Hughes, Monticello; 3:41.

Third heat (10 laps)—1. John Connally, Delhi; 2. Cal Swanson, Cedar Falls; 3. Red Droste, Waterloo; 3:16.

"A" semi (15 laps)—1. Glen Martin, Waterloo; 2. Bill Barnett, Waterloo; 3. Dick Heiden, Cedar Rapids; 4:93.

"B" semi (15 laps)—1. Tuffy Meyer, Big Rock; 2. Bob Hilmer, Dysart; 3. Dave Noble, Blooming Prairie, Minn.; 4:73.

Consolation (12 laps)—1. Charlie Moffett, Stanwood; 2. Harry Peterson, Waterloo; 3. Rick Brock, Waterloo; 3:78.

Feature (20 laps)—1. Red Droste, Waterloo; 2. Bill Zwanziger, Waterloo; 3. Tuffy Meyer, Big Rock; 4. Charlie Moffett, Stanwood; 5. Cal Swanson, Cedar Falls; 6. Tom Hughes, Monticello; 6:27.

Junior novice (20 laps)—1. Mike Plum, Waterloo.

Owners' race (10 laps)—1. Irvin Bohlken, Monticello; 2. Don Graham, Waterloo; 3. Joe Johnes, Cascade.

TUNIS OPENS SUNDAY

The 1963 stock car season at Tunis Speedway opens here Sunday night at 7:30 p. m. ... the Tunis Speedway policy.

Returning this season are such veterans as Red Droste, the defending Cedarloo Racing Association point champion.

1964
In the News

Williams Captures Third Straight Tunis Feature

Mert Williams of Rochester, Minn., won his third straight feature and Bob Posekany of Cedar Falls came in for a share of glory at the Tunis Speedway stock car races Sunday night.

A crowd of 4,693 saw Williams win the feature for the fourth time this year as Red Droste of Waterloo, the point standings leader and a seven-time winner, could do no better than sixth.

Posekany finished second in the feature after copping the second heat and the A semi-main. Williams won the B semi-main that was marred by a rollover that sent Charlie Moffett to Schoitz Hospital where he was treated and released.

It was also a good night for

Rochester Driver Is Tunis Pick

(COURIER NEWS SERVICE)

Quiet-spoken Mert Williams who does all his own mechanic work and unloads his car without help, will again be the crowd favorite as the Rochester, Minn. driver endeavors to make it two features in a row at Tunis Speedway Sunday evening.

Williams broke Red Droste's four feature winning streak Sunday night by taking the lead on the 18th lap to edge Droste by a car length.

The Owner's Race will be the ninth event on this Sunday's racing card. Only the owner may drive the modified in the event, although if the regular driver owns his own car, a member of the pit crew is required to take the wheel.

The first heat takes the track at 7:30 p. m.

(Courier Photo)

To the Victor Belongs the Spoils

Mert Williams has a big smile as he accepts a large trophy and the checkered flag in his car after winning the 75-lap season championship race at Tunis Speedway Sunday night. Williams, from Rochester, Minn., set a new track record in winning the championship.

Two Nights Of Racing At Tunis

Red Droste of Waterloo will try to protect his newly-earned Cedarloo Racing Assn. point standings leadership in a doubleheader Memorial Day weekend program at Tunis Speedway Saturday and Sunday.

A nine-race card, including the first two novice races of the season, is scheduled for both Saturday and Sunday nights beginning at 7:30 p. m.

After two second-place finishes to John Connolly of Delhi, Droste won his first feature of the season last Sunday and took a 130-111 point leadership over Connolly in the current standings.

Following, in order, are Bill Zwanziger 82, John Moss 79, Charlie Moffett 74, Mert Williams 66, Lee Kunzman 58, John Hill 58, Dave Bjorge 55 and Tuffy Meyers 52.

Cedar Rapids also will have two days of racing this weekend. The Mid-Continent Racing Assn. has upped its purse from the usual $250 for the feature to $350 and is extending its feature from 25 to 30 laps Saturday where Dick Krafka of Dysart won last week.

The Hawkeye Twin 50s are scheduled for 2 p. m. Sunday at Hawkeye Downs with three heat races preceding the two 50-lap features.

Williams Feature Winner, Brustkern Novice Champ

Mert Williams of Rochester, Minn., won the final regular season feature Monday at Tunis Speedway and John Brustkern of Waterloo won the 1964 season championship junior novice race.

Next week's feature will be the 75-lap season championship race for the top 20 drivers in the Cedarloo Racing Assn. point standings. Two more races are planned later with all modifying restrictions lifted from the autos.

The junior novice championship was a 35-lap event.

A crowd of 2,994 saw the Labor Day night program.

First heat—1. Jerry Sherbon, Cedar Falls; 2. Don Berg, Waterloo; 3. Bud Slater, Cedar Falls; 3:78.

Second heat—1. Keith Knaack, Waterloo; 2. Roger Klingfus, Waterloo; 3. Rich Krafka, Dysart; 3:50.

Third heat—1. Lee Kunzman, Guttenberg; 2. John Connolly, Delhi; 3. Verlin Eakers, Blooming Prairie, Minn.; 3:21.

A semi-main—1. Klingfus; 2. Ralph Ainzman, Guttenberg; 3. Glenn Martin, Waterloo; 4:89.

B semi-main—1. Tom Hughes, Monticello; 2. Bill Zwanziger, Waterloo; 3. Eakers; 4:61.

Consolation—1. Dick Hagen, Cedar Falls; 2. Bill Borghahn, Waterloo; 3. Joe Wurst, Blooming Prairie; 3:88.

Junior novice 1964 championship—1. John Brustkern, Waterloo; 2. Dan Pettit, Waterloo; 3. Dick Calvin, Waterloo; no time.

Feature—1. Mert Williams, Rochester,

Tunis Tops 100,000 in Year's Finale

Only 1,687 fans turned out Sunday night as the Tunis Speedway stock car racing reason came to a close.

But the crowd put the season total past the 100,000 mark by about 400.

Modification rules were thrown off for the competition open only to Cedarloo Assn. drivers and Bill Zwanziger of Waterloo was a double winner. He copped the feature and the A semi-main after finishing third in the third heat.

First heat—1. Bob Hilmer, Dysart; 2. Don Brown, Morrison; 3. Robert Hesse, Waterloo; 3:89.

Second heat—1. Stan Stover, Reinbeck; 2. Mert Williams, Rochester, Minn.; 3. Bob Posekany, Cedar Falls; 3:38.

Third heat — 1. Cal Swanson, Cedar Falls; 2. Verlin Eakers, Blooming Prairie, Minn.; 3. Bill Zwanziger, Waterloo; 3:17.

A semi-main—1. Zwanziger; 2. Hilmer; 3. Dick Hagen, Cedar Falls; no time.

B semi-main — 1. Williams; 2. Red Droste, Waterloo; 3. Dave Bjorge; 4:54.

Consolation—1. Rich Krafka; 2. Glenn Martin; 3. Rick Brock; 3:85.

Feature—1. Zwanziger; 2. Droste; 3. Hilmer; 4. Swanson; 5. Bjorge; 5. Stan Stover; 6:05.

Rich New Cedarloo Racing President

Guy Rich was elected president of the Cedarloo Racing Association at the annual meeting

Minnesota Driver Tunis Upset King

Mert Williams played the hero role at Tunis Speedway Sunday evening. The Rochester, Minn. speedster caught Red Droste on the 18th lap of the feature and hung on for a car-length victory over the Waterloo redhead.

Droste, winner of four consecutive features on the quarter-mile oval going into Sunday's semi and second in the third heat Sunday.

Hilmer showed up with a completely new car and copped second in the A semi and third

1965
In the News

CHUB LIEBE OF Oelwein accepts the season championship racing trophy at Tunis Speedway Sunday afternoon from Rae Lynne Findley of Waterloo. Liebe won the 75-lap final race and the $500 check that goes with it. (Courier Photo)

Liebe Wins Season Championship Race

Chub Liebe of Oelwein, taking over when Verlin Eaker of Blooming Prairie, Minn., had o drop out because of engine rouble after the 36th lap, won he 75-lap season championship race at Tunis Speedway Sunday afternoon.

Charles Moffitt of Stanwood came in second in the thrice postponed event that formally closed the Tunis season.

The crowd was officially listed

Card of Waterloo on the final lap of the 10-lap race to win the powder puff championship derby.

Championship (75 laps)—1. Chub Liebe, Oelwein; 2. Charlie Moffitt, Stanwood;

Three Title Races On Weekend Card

Red Droste, with a two-point edge over John Connolly of Delhi 388-386, will start in the pole position for the 75-lap season championship stock car race at Tunis Speedway Sunday night in Waterloo. Connolly had motor trouble and failed to score any points here last Sunday.

The veteran Waterloo driver who trails Connolly in average points per appearance over the Cedarloo Racing Assn. season also will start on the outside of the first row in the 75-lap Mid-Continent Racing Assn. season championship event at Hawkeye Downs in Cedar Rapids Saturday night.

Darrel Dake of Cedar Rapids drew the No. 1 position for the 8 o'clock card there.

Independence Racing Assn. is also having its season championship race, a 50-lapper, Saturday night and Dave Noble of Blooming Prairie, Minn., and Chub Liebe of Oelwein are in the one-two positions.

Twenty cars will start the feature there with the program starting at 8 p.m. and including three heat races and a 30 lap consolation race along with a novice race and a powder puff derby.

The Tunis program will also consist of a 35-lap consolation race for drivers who didn't qualify for the feature and 35-lap novice season championship race in addition to a demolition derby. The first race will start at 7:30 p.m.

Title Race On Tap For Tunis

Tunis Speedway will feature the 75-lap season championship stock car race tonight with veteran Waterloo driver Red Droste in the pole position.

Droste holds a two point lead over John Connolly of Delhi, but trails the latter in average points per appearance.

There will also be a 35-lap consolation race for drivers who failed to qualify for the feature, and a 35-lap novice season championship race. A demolition derby will be an added attraction.

The first race will start at 7:30 p.m.

Droste Winner in Short Feature Before 4,917

Point leader Red Droste of Waterloo won his first feature victory of the season at Tunis Speedway Sunday and after five weeks there still hasn't been a repeat victor.

Sunday's feature was halted after 23 of the scheduled 25 laps because of an accident. Glen Martin of Waterloo, who earlier had won the first heat and the A semi-main, was having car trouble and was being lapped by cars driven by Bill Zwanziger of Waterloo and John Connolly of Delhi. Martin's car spun and was hit by the other two and then burst into flames.

Martin escaped from the wreck without injury.

The Sunday card, witnessed by 4,917, marked the return to the Tunis track for the first time this season of Mert Williams of Rochester, Minn., who won the 75-lap season championship here last season. He won the consolation and placed fifth in the feature Sunday.

The track was slippery early during Sunday's card and times in the heat races, especially, were unspectacular.

First heat (10 laps)—1. Glen Martin, Waterloo; 2. Errol Olsen, Waterloo; 3. Henry Hesse, Waterloo; 4:19.

Second heat (10 laps)—1. Bob Posekany, Cedar Falls; 2. Charlie Moffitt, Stanwood; 3. Ed Sanger, Waterloo; 3:27.

Third heat (10 laps)—1. Dave Noble, Blooming Prairie, Minn.; 2. John Connolly, Delhi; 3. Verlin Eaker, Blooming Prairie; 3:05.

A semi-main (15 laps)—1. Martin; 2. Buzz Jensen, Hudson; 3. Robert Hesse, Waterloo; 4. Bill Barghahn, Waterloo; 5. Harry O'Deen, Marion; 6. Harold Wilcox, Waterloo; 4:98.

B semi-main (15 laps)—1. David Bjorge, Austin, Minn.; 2. Connolly; 3. Dick Krafka, Dysart; 4. Lee Kunzman, Guttenberg; 5. Red Droste, Waterloo; 6. Eaker; no time.

Consolation (12 laps)—1. Mert Williams Rochester, Minn.; 2. Chub Liebe, Oelwein; 3. Bill Zwanziger, Waterloo; no time.

Novice (15 laps)—1. John Brustkern, Waterloo; no time.

Feature (23 laps)—1. Droste; 2. Zwanziger; 3. Connolly; 4. Kunzman; 5. Williams; 6. Liebe; no time.

Tunis Property Deed

Meanwhile, a deed was filed Friday in the county recorder's office involving the site for a proposed department store on Hwy. 218 North.

The deed conveys 12.43 acres from Mr. and Mrs. J. L. Tunis to Raceway Plaza, Inc., for an indicated price of about $51,000.

That parcel of land, on the southwest corner of property formerly owned by Tunis, has been announced as the site of Welles Department store, a Miller-Wohl subsidiary.

It was announced in June that construction on the department store is scheduled to begin early in 1966. Plans were to construct a store of more than 80,000 square feet with parking facilities for more than 1,000 cars.

Bob Posekany Heads Cedarloo Race Assn.

Bob Posekany was elected president of the Cedarloo Racing Assn. at its annual meeting here this weekend. The group conducts weekly stock car races at Tunis Speedway here during the summer.

Other officers for the 1966 season will be Guy Rich, vice president; John Hill, secretary; Cal Swanson, treasurer; Jerry Sherbon, sergeant-at-arms, and Gale Card, Glenn Martin and Ed Sanger, trustees.

Other members of the board of directors are Dick Krafka, Stan Stover, Vern Weber and K. L. Kober, legal counsel.

Verlin Eaker Wins First Feature of Year at Tunis

Verlin Eaker of Blooming Prairie, Minn., captured the first feature race of the season at Tunis Speedway here Sunday

(Oelwein), 2. David Noble (Blooming Prairie, Minn.), 3. Joe Wurst (Blooming Prairie, Minn.).

Second heat (10 laps)—1. Red Droste (Waterloo), 2. John Connolly (Delhi), 3 Dick Krafka (Dysart).

1966
In the News

Hilmer Wins Championship Race

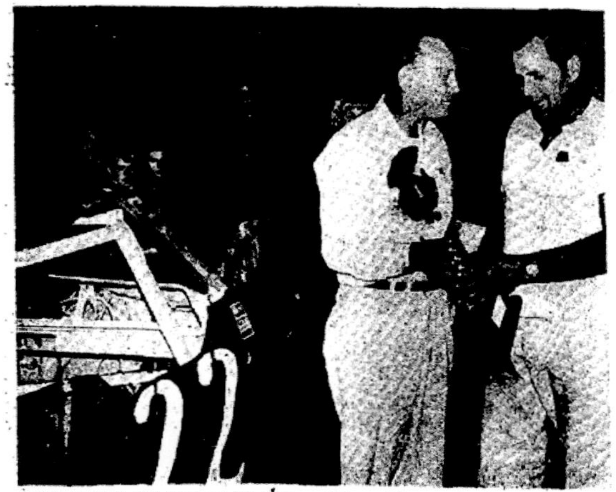

AFTER FAST 50—Bob Posekany, left, president of Cedarloo Racing Assn., presents the season's championship trophy to Bob Hilmer of Dysart after he won the 50 lap stock car feature race at Cordes Speedway Sunday night in his car No. 22.

Droste Loses After Spin-Out

Bob Hilmer of Dysart won the 50-lap season championship race at Cordes Speedway here Sunday night before 3,800 fans, defeating Waterloo's Bill Zwanziger and Rochester's Mert Williams, the No. 2 and 3 finishers.

Red Droste of Waterloo had led for 38 laps, but spun out on the No. 4 turn with his engine catching fire, taking him out of the race.

Claus Strickler of Waterloo won the consolation championship, holding the lead all the way.

In the 35 lap novice championship race, Gary Bass of Waterloo repeated his mid-season championship win, lapping the field in the process.

At Independence S a t u r d a y night Chub Liebe of Oelwein took home his fifth season feature win, with Waterloo's Ed Sanger close behind.

Cal Wins Finale

Cal Swanson, of Reinbeck driving a Chevy-powered, super-modified stock car, swept all three events in which he entered in the season's finale at Cordes Speedway Sunday night.

Swanson defeated Waterloo's Bill Zwanziger and Mert Williams of Rochester in the 20-lap feature race. He won over Chub Liebe of Oelwein in the A Semi-Main, and took the first heat race of the night before 2,500 racing fans.

Mert Williams, of Rochester, a consistent winner at Cordes all season long, also took his share of firsts, copping the B semi-main by edging out Red Droste of Waterloo, and winning the third heat race.

In other events in the night of Open Competition racing, Ed Sanger of Waterloo took the second heat race and Reinbeck's Stan Stover won the consolation.

Saturday night Chub Liebe of Oelwein won the 50-lap modified season championship race at Independence, edging Bob Hilmer of Dysart.

Prior to the race the rookie of the year award was presented to Ty Burger of Waterloo.

Waterloo's J a c k Beckman copped the Cadette season championship race.

The final night of stock car racing at Independence this year will be next Sunday. It will be an open invitational with time trials starting at 6 p. m.

STOCKS' MOST FAITHFUL FANS: LAGES OF LINCOLN

ONE THING that's almost as sure as death and taxes is that the Norman Lages of Lincoln, Iowa, will be at Cordes Speedway, seated in the stands across the track from the judges' stand, next Sunday night.

Ross SMITH'S COLUMN

They've seen every stock car race ever run on the quarter mile Waterloo oval, until this year known as Tunis Speedway — except one. And that adds up to 18 years and a lot of races.

They missed the one in order to serve as attendants at friends' wedding. Lage apologized for that miss: "We'd have been at the races then, but we couldn't get our friends to schedule their wedding on a Saturday instead of a Sunday.

Some 13 or 14 years ago Lage, who has worked 27 years as a farm equipment mechanic in Lincoln, helped Kenny Kroeger of Lincoln build a stock car to drive at Tunis. But most of the time the Lages have been coming to the races they've been coming just as fans.

"I'd be driving, myself," Norman said, "but my age is against me."

"That's right," agreed his wife, Esther. "Sixty-four is a little too old for stock car racing."

Driving the 20 miles or so weekly — or oftener in the case of holiday races here — is just a lark for the Lages. They've driven half-way across the country twice to see the Daytona, Fla., stock car 500.

But the Indianapolis Memorial Day 500? "I don't care for that kind of racing," Norman says of the speedway type car.

His attendance record wouldn't attest to any dissatisfaction with the Cordes operation, but, "I'd like to see them open up the half mile track," Lage offered when asked for suggestions.

LLOYD RYAN, one of the city's fine bowlers, may be forced to watch from the sidelines as the result of a foot injury he suffered recently in an accident with a power saw . . . Charles Sawyer, once a member of the Waterloo Daily Courier sports staff and later sports editor of the Marshalltown Times-Republican, and his family have been visiting here recently. Chuck has been with the San Diego Union sports staff for the past 10 years.

THERE IT IS — In their 18 years of regular attendance (one miss) at stock car races in Waterloo Norman Lage and his wife, Esther, of Lincoln have become acquainted with most of the regular drivers. They join Waterloo's Red Droste (left) for a look under the hood of his racer.

1st Feature Win For Zwanziger

Bill Zwanziger of Waterloo edged out Mert Williams of Rochester, Minn., by half a car length to win the 20 lap feature race before 4,000 fans at Cordes Speedway here Sunday night. It was Zwanziger's first feature win of the season at Cordes.

In the A semi Keith Knaack of Vinton, topped Willie Klingfus of Waterloo after two restarts. Ed Sanger of Waterloo took the B semi while Don Kayser of Independence won the novice.

Another night of stock car racing was scheduled at Cordes Monday night. A women's demolition derby will highlight the evening with the gates opening at 5:30 p. m. and the first race at 7:30.

ding anniversary.

The Independence night of championship races will be Sept. 17th with a $2,000 guaranteed purse.

Races at Monticello were rained out Friday night, but the season championship will be run this Friday for a $1,500 purse.

SUNDAY AT CORDES

1st heat—1. Joe Wurst, Bing. Pr., Minn.; 2. Dave Bjerge, Austin; 3 Claus Strickler, Waterloo.

2nd heat—1. Dick Sturch, Waterloo; 2. Ed Sanger, Waterloo; 3. Don Brown, Waterloo.

3rd heat—1. Rich Krafka, Dysart; 2. Bob Hilmer, Dysart; 3. Bill Zwanziger, Waterloo.

A semi—1. Keith Knaack, Vinton; 2. Willie Klingfus, Waterloo; 3. Ty Berger, Waterloo; 4. Bjerge; 5. Ken McCombs, Cedar Falls; 6. Strickler.

B semi—1. Sanger; 2. Hilmer; 3. Zwanziger; 4. Krafka; 5. Red Droste, Waterloo; 6. Mert Williams, Rochester, Minn.

Consolation—1. Gale Card, Waterloo; 2. Daryl DeVries, Charles City; 3. Glen Martin, Waterloo.

Feature—1. Zwanziger; 2. Williams; 3.

(Courier Photo)

New Proprietor Takes Over From Old

New proprietors, left to right, Roger Beck of Hudson, Bill Zwanziger and Jim Cordes, and retiring Jud Tunis gather around the car Zwanziger will drive when the newly refurbished Cordes Speedway opens its stock car racing season Sunday night. Several changes in the layout, including a new entrance about two blocks nearer downtown Waterloo, new parking facilities and bleachers on both sides of the track instead of just the west side, have been made. Cordes leased the track this year from Tunis who has operated auto racing there the past 18 years. Racing programs will start at 7:30 p.m. both Sunday and Monday, Memorial ...

Williams, Droste Duel Tonight

Red Droste's earlier commanding lead in point standings among the Cedarloo Racing Assn. drivers at Cordes Speedway in Waterloo this season has been whittled down to just 34. Droste has rung up 1,546 to second place Mert Williams' total of 1,512. Charlie Moffett is in third with 1,435.

Others in the top ten are: Bob Hilmer, 1,345; Bill Zwanziger, 1,285; Chub Liebe, 1,234; Lee Kunzman, 840; Stan Stover, 631; Verlin Eaker, 555; Ed Sanger, 446.

Both Droste and Williams will be out to break their tie of three feature wins apiece tonight at Cordes Speedway. The duel was postponed from last week as both drivers were out of the racing picture with blown engines.

Gates to the track will open at 5:30 p.m. with the first race starting at 7:30 p.m.

First Time Entry Wins Three Races at Cordes

Gerhard Wollenburg of Austin swept three events in his first appearance at Cordes Speedway here Sunday night.

Curt Hansen of Dike won the trophy dash, after the race was delayed when Dysart's Rich Krafka and Paul Fitzpatrick of ...

terloo.

Feature—1. Wollenburg, 2. Cord, 3 Williams, 4. Moffett, 5. Liebe, 6. Droste 7. W. Klingfus, 8. Donovan.

SATURDAY AT INDEPENDENCE

First heat—1. LeRoy Scharkey, Roch

Liebe in First Feature Win of '66; Stocks Run Again Monday

A full race program is set for Cordes Speedway Monday night at 7:30 with a fireworks display to follow.

Chub Liebe of Oelwein won his first feature race of the season at Cordes Sunday night, edging ...

Krafka of Dysart won the Powder Puff derby after a spectacular roll by Sharon Bass of Waterloo.

Monticello's Friday night feature race was won by Kunzman who also won the B semi-main.

Ed Sanger of Waterloo won the A semi - main with Dick Heiden of Cedar Rapids on his bumper for almost the entire race. Sanger led the feature un-...

Consolation—1. George Peasen, Marble; 2. Jon Wurst, Austin, Minn.; 3. Keith Knaack, Vinton.

Feature—1. Droste; 2. Kunzman; 3. Hilmer.

Cadette—1. Alan Nagel.

Powder Puff—1. Carol Krafka, Dysart.

FRIDAY AT MONTICELLO

First Heat—1. Dick Heiden, Cedar Rapids; 2. Bill Birodorn, Monticello; 3.

1967

In the News

Droste Leads for 36

Swanson Cops Title

Cal Swanson of Reinbeck won the 50-lap Mid-Season championship race at Tunis Speedway Sunday night before 5,000 fans.

3 Winners for Hilmer at Tunis

Bob Hilmer of Dysart drove three winners to take top honors at the Tunis Speedway stock car track here Sunday night, before an estimated 4,000 fans.

Hilmer won the third heat, the B semimain and then the feature, taking the feature lead the seventh lap to go all the way.

races Saturday night. The accident ocurred about three and one-half miles south of Independence.

Traux, 28, was building a new car to race this summer, after competing other years in his car No. 112, a white Pontiac.

First heat—1. John Hills (Ced. Falls), 2. Stan Stover (Reinbeck), 3. Darrel DeVries (Charles City).

Stocks Race Two Nights At Tunis

The Independence Racing Association is sponsoring a five-night stock car racing program over the Memorial Day weekend.

Tonight will be the third race at Tunis Speedway.

A Monza Special will be staged at Independence tomorrow and a 100-lap Holiday Special will be held at Tunis Speedway Tuesday.

A $2,630 purse will be offered at Tunis Tuesday and $2,350 will be offered at Independence tomorrow. The fastest time trial at both tracks will win $100 and the second fastest will receive $50.

The first two days of the program are already over with as a result of races Friday night at Monticello and last night at Independence.

AT INDEPENDENCE

1st Heat—1. Shornhorst (Waterloo) 2. Jenson (Hudson), 3. Bliss (Cedar Rapids)

2nd Heat—1. Jensen (Charles City, 2. Fitzpatrick (Rochester, Minn.), 3. Webb (Independence)

3rd Heat—1. Zwanziger (Waterloo), 2. Liebe (Oelwein), 3. Nestby (Dubuque)

A Semi-main—1. Shornhorst, 2. Kruse (Independence), 3. Webb, 4 Stover (Reinbeck), 5. Hansen (Dike)

B Semi-main—1. Hilmer (Dysart) 2. Liebe, 3 Sanger (Waterloo), 4. Fitzpatrick, 5. Freitheim (Ridgeway), 6. Nestby (Dubuque)

Consolation—1. Krafka (Dysart, 2. B. Nestby (Dubuque), 3. Burger (Waterloo), 4 Stricker (Waterloo), 5. O'Deen (Marion)

Feature—1. Hilmer, 2. Liebe, 3. Stover,

(Courier Photo by Chuck Anderson)

FRUITS OF VICTORY — Waterloo's Red Droste stands beside his car, while on the hood is the first place trophy he won Sunday night by copping the 50-lap season championship stock car race at Tunis Speedway. Droste is the leading point getter at Tunis this season, earning him the pole position for Sunday's race.

Droste Earns $600 for Winning 50-Lap Championship Event

Red Droste of Waterloo, running off the pole position at the start of the race, won the seasonal championship Sunday night at Tunis Speedway.

Droste, veteran driver, won $600 for winning the 50-lap championship. He qualified for the pole position by scoring the most points during the regular season of racing.

Coming in second to Droste was Bob Hilmer of Dysart while Myrt Williams of Rochester, Minn., was the third place finisher.

Curt Hansen of Dike won the 25-lap consolation race. The consolation was for the bottom half of finishers in point totals during the season. Top point finishers ran in the main event.

Richard Wilcox of Waterloo won the cadette title and Gary Bass of Waterloo won the cadette consolation title.

Most of the drivers will be competing at Independence Saturday night in the seasonal championship race at that track.

Independence.

Consolation—1. Curt Hansen, Dike; 2. Dave Bedard, La Porte City; 3. Claus Stricker, Waterloo; 4. Bob Nesleby, Dubuque; 5. Harold Odeen, Cedar Rapids.

Cadette championship—1. Richard Wilcox, Waterloo; 2. Shorty Hayward, Independence.

Cadette consolation—1. Gary Bass, Waterloo; 2. Robert Johnson, Waterloo.

SATURDAY AT INDEPENDENCE

First Heat—1. Gale Card (Waterloo); 2. Claus Stricker (Waterloo); 3. Leo Schornhorst (Waterloo).

Second Heat—1. Roger Klingfus (Waterloo); 2. Glenn Martin (Waterloo); 3. Curt Hansen (Dike).

Third Heat—1. Red Droste (Waterloo); 2. Bill Zwanziger (Waterloo); 3. Rich Krafka (Dysart).

A-Semi—1. Joe Wurst (Blooming Prairie, Minn.); 2. Harold Odeen (Cedar Rapids); 3. Leo Schornhorst (Waterloo).

B-Semi—1. Chub Liebe (Oelwein); 2. Red Droste (Waterloo); 3. Curt Hansen (Dike).

RED BANKS $3,697.50

Droste Leads at Two Tracks, Second at Indy

With over 1,000 points at each track, Red Droste of Waterloo is currently the leader in total points at the Waterloo and Monticello race tracks and is in second position at Independence.

Chub Liebe of Oelwein is the leader at Independence, holding a 115-point lead over Droste. Drivers receive a point for every dollar won at the three tracks of the Independence Racing Assn.

Droste's earnings add up to $3,697.50 at the three tracks so far. There have been seven racing cards at Independence and six each at Waterloo and Monticello plus a special

day at Monticello. Saturday and Monday the stocks will race at Indeepndence and Sunday and Tuesday will compete at Tunis Speedway in

who started out slowly this season, has already begun his move and currently holds the fourth position at Independence and the sixth spot at Monticello. Last week Zwanziger jumped from 11th to fifth at Waterloo.

This season 50 different cars have run at Independence, which averages 28-30 cars per race night. Monticello has had 37 different cars and a 22-24 average, and Waterloo 47 and a 26-28 average.

Listed below are the point leaders at the three tracks:

At Waterloo—1. Red Droste 1,427½, 2. Cal Swanson 1,042½, 3. Bob Hilmer 972½, 4. Chub Liebe 672, 5. Bill Zwanziger 630, 6. Ed Sanger 554, 7. Stan Stover 475, 8. Tom Hughes 440, 9. Glen Martin 385, 10. John Connally 375.

RED DROSTE
Ahead at Waterloo, Monty

Droste Through Driving

REGARDING a fellow who's made a decision that may INCREASE his life expectancy, Red Droste says he's through with stock car racing and will devote his energy, exclusively, to managing (not driving on) the NEITA drag strip north of Cedar Falls this summer.

Waterloo's quarter mile stock car track this year, incidentally, will be under the proprietorship of Lyle Shriver who takes over after one year's operation by Jim Cordes. The place, for many years known as Tunis Speedway in deference to owner Jud Tunis, was called Cordes Speedway last year.

Shriver still is pondering a name for his operation this summer.

Droste's first drag action of the season is currently scheduled for Sunday, April 16.

1968
In the News

Fitzpatrick Wins Tunis Feature

Paul Fitzpatrick came back from a second-place finish in the third heat to win both the B-semi and feature races at Tunis Speedway Monday night.

Fitzpatrick of Rochester, Minn., placed second behind Bob Hilmer of Dysart in the third heat but finished ahead of the pack in his next two races.

Cal Swanson of Reinbeck was a double winner, taking both the consolation and trophy dash events.

Driver Jim Parkhouse of Evansdale, who rolled his car, was treated at Sartori Hospital for a lacerated right hand and released.

First heat — 1. Leo Scharnhorst (Waterloo), 2. Bill Barthelmes (Troy Mills), 3. Ty Burger (Waterloo).

Second heat — 1. Curt Hansen (Dike), 2. Dave Bedard (La Porte City), 3. Claus Stricker (Waterloo).

Third heat — 1. Bob Hilmer (Dysart), 2. Paul Fitzpatrick (Rochester, Minn.), 3. Red Droste (Waterloo).

A-semi — 1. John Webb (Independence), 2. Karl Sanger (Waterloo), 3. Scharnhorst, 4. Barthelmes, 5. Doc Mayner (Winthrop), 6. Buzz Hansen (Waterloo).

B-semi — 1. Fitzpatrick, 2. Curt Hansen, 3. Bedard, 4. Droste, 5. Ed Sanger (Waterloo), 6. Hilmer.

Consolation — 1. Cal Swanson (Reinbeck), 2. Glen Martin (Waterloo), 3. Stan Stover (Reinbeck), 4. Bob Nesteb (Dubuque), 5. Red Drolle (Evansdale), 6. Bill Zwanziger (Waterloo).

Feature — 1. Fitzpatrick, 2. Ed Sanger, 3. Droste, 4. Karl Sanger, 5. Scharnhorst, 6. Curt Hansen.

Trophy dash — 1. Swanson.

Droste in Weekend Race Sweep

Red Droste finished a perfect weekend Sunday by winning the season opening feature before a crowd of 3,400 at Tunis Speedway here.

The veteran Waterloo driver won every race he entered including a sweep of the features at Cedar Rapids Friday and Independence Saturday in the 1966 Chevelle he's driving this season.

His victory in the feature at Tunis was a squeaker over Chub Liebe of Oelwein.

First heat—1. Stan Stover, 2. Curt Hansen, 3. Terry Messersmith

Second heat—1. Red Droste, 2. Glenn Martin, 3. John Webb

Third heat—1. Paul Fitzpatrick, 2. Leo Scharnhorst, 3. Harold Odeen

A semi—1. Droste, 2. Claus Stricker, 3. Stover, 4. Chub Liebe, 5. Messersmith, 6. Martin

B semi—1. Roger Klingfus, 2. Karl Sanger, 3. Fitzpatrick, 4. Odeen, 5. Dave Bedard, 6. Ty Burger

Consolation—1. Lynn Idler, 2. Ed Sanger, 3. Buzz Jensen, 4. Doc Mayner, 5. Bob Horlimer

Feature—1. Droste, 2. Liebe, 3. Stricker, 4. Fitzpatrick, 5. Stover, 6. Burger, 7. Odeen, 8. Martin, 9. K. Sanger, 10. [illegible]

Hilmer Persists To Win at Tunis

Bob Hilmer of Dysart took the lead in the feature race with five laps to go in the 25-lap stock car race, then held on for his first feature win of the season at Tunis Speedway here Thursday night.

An Independence Day crowd of 4,500 allowed promoters to pay off a $2,300 purse, with the first 10 finishers in the feature collecting a share.

Three spinouts in the feature helped Hilmer to the win. Bob Hesse of Waterloo had led more than half the race, but spun out, eventually finishing ninth. After Hesse spun out, Cal Swanson of Reinbeck took a temporary lead before suffering the same fate.

Mert Williams of Rochester, Minn., moved into first place, only to spin out too, allowing Hilmer to take over.

Williams finished second in the feature and Swanson seventh. Tunis Speedway point leader Red Droste of Waterloo was third. Williams had earlier won both the third heat and B Semimain.

Cars will gather next at Independence Speedway Saturday night and return to Tunis Sunday for the weekend's regular cards at both.

First heat—1. Dave Maxson (Cedar Falls), 2. Roger Kruse (Independence), 3. Curt Hansen (Dike)

Second heat—1. Bill Zwanziger (Waterloo), 2. Dave Bedard (LaPorte City), 3. Glen Martin (Waterloo)

Third heat—1. Mert Williams (Rochester, Minn.), 2. Stan Stover (Reinbeck), 3. Paul Fitzpatrick (Rochester, Minn.)

A Semi—1. Karl Sangre (Waterloo), 2. Bob Hesse (Waterloo), 3. Gale Card (Evansdale), 4. Kruse, 5. Hansen, 6. Leo Scharnhorst (Waterloo)

B Semi—1. Mert Williams, 2. Bedard, 3. Bob Hilmer (Dysart), 4. Red Droste (Waterloo), 5. Stover, 6. Ed Sanger (Waterloo)

Consolation—1. Cal Swanson (Waterloo), 2. John Webb (Independence), 3. Harold O'Deen (Marion), 4. Don Donovan (Brandon), 5. Tom Hamilton (Jesup), 6. Delyle Russell

Feature—1. Hilmer, 2. Williams, 3. Droste, 4. Ed Sanger, 5. Zwanziger, 6. Fitzpatrick, 7. Swanson, 8. Stover, 9. Hesse, 10. Karl Sanger

Novice—1. Chuck Larson (Waterloo), 2. George Banehy (Independence)

Over 6,000 See Droste Triumph

(COURIER NEWS SERVICE)

Red Droste recovered from an early collision to win the Mid-Season Championship race at Tunis Speedway Sunday night as more than 6,000 people, the largest crowd in five years, looked on.

[D]roste of Waterloo and Mert [Wi]lliams of Rochester, Minn., bumped cars on the second lap of the Speed Chumley Memorial Race, causing the race to be temporarily halted.

Droste, who as mid-season total points leader started at the pole position, was placed at the back of the pack because he had been involved in stopping the race.

But he rallied and won the 50-lap race by one-half lap over Doc Mayner of Winthrop.

Both of the night's two other events were stopped two laps early because of the red light.

In the mid-season consolation race a collision between Vince Wells of Cedar Falls and Joe Bagsby of Independence on the 28th lap caused the race to be halted with Roger Klingfus of Waterloo in the lead.

Don Berg spun out on the 18th lap of the novice race blocking the track with Roger Johnson of Independence in the lead, after a collision on the second lap had stopped the race temporarily.

RED DROSTE
. . . comeback victory

Total prize money was nearly $3,000, the largest pot in the track's history.

Mid-Season Consolation (30 laps)—1. Roger Klingfus (Waterloo), 2. Doc Mayner (Winthrop), 3. Dave Pium (Waterloo), 4. Rich Krafka (Dysart).

Novice (20 laps)—1. Roger Johnson

Droste, Sanger Out, Dave Noble Wins Feature

Red Droste and Ed Sanger, both from Waterloo, were forced out of the race due to a flat tire and auto difficulties, respectively, and Dave Noble of Blooming Prairie, Minn., took advantage to win the feature race of the stock car racing program at Tunis Speedway

4. Doc Mayner (Winthrop).

B-Semi — 1. Idler, 2. Red Droste (Waterloo), 3. Stover, 4. Ed Sanger (Waterloo), 5. C. Sanger, 6. Cal Swanson (Reinbeck).

Consolation — 1. Swanson, 2. Glenn Martin (Waterloo), 3. Buzz Jensen (Dike), 4. Dave Noble (Blooming Prairie, Minn.), 5. Dave Maxson (Cedar Falls), 6. Mert Williams (Rochester, Minn.).

Feature — 1. Noble, 2. Swanson, 3. Stover, 4. Martin, 5. C. Sanger, 6. O'Deen.

Liebe, Williams Win Weekend Stock Features

Chub Liebe copped three races for the second week in a row at Independence Saturday night, then could do no better than a second place finish in the consolation on the Independence Racing Assn. card at Tunis Speedway in Waterloo Sunday.

The feature Sunday went to Mert Williams of Rochester, Minn., who finished second to Liebe in Saturday's feature at Independence.

Ty Burger of Waterloo won three races between the two cards Saturday and Sunday.

Waterloo's Red Droste, who copped the consolation Sunday at Tunis after being shut out Saturday, was running second to Williams in the feature Sunday when the rear-end locked on his car and he was forced out of the race.

AT INDEPENDENCE

First heat—1. Ty Burger (Waterloo), 2. Roger Kruse (Independence), 3. Dave Pium (Waterloo).

Second heat—1. Curt Hansen (Dike), 2. [illegible] (La Porte City).

Third heat—1. Chub Liebe (Oelwein), 2. Red Droste (Waterloo), 3. Terry Messersmith (New Hampton).

A semi—1. Larry Kebell (Oxford Junction), 2. Hesse, 3. Kruse, 4. [illegible]

Spectator Hurt By Flying Part Of Racing Car

Gary L. Halleck, 30, of 3[illegible] Gilbertville Rd., was taken b[y] police car to Allen Memori[al] Hospital Sunday night after h[e] was injured by a flying piec[e] of metal during stock car race at Tunis Speedway, 3715 Fall Ave.

Halleck, a spectator, wa[s] watching a race from th[e] stands when a part flew fro[m] a passing stock car and struc[k] his hand.

Police said Halleck wa[s]

Rainout Last Sunday, Mid-Season Race Set for Tonight at Tunis

(COURIER NEWS SERVICE)

The Annual Speed Chumley Memorial race at Tunis Speedway, which was rained out last Sunday, will be tonight and will determine the Tunis Mid-Season champion.

Added emphasis will be given to the championship race by the tight total point race among the leaders. Red Droste of Waterloo, leader in total points with 1,565, will defend his lead against contenders Ed Sanger of Waterloo who is second in total points with 1,515 and Mert Williams of Rochester, Minn., who is third with 1,245. Droste, Sanger and Williams each have two features to their credit at Tunis this year.

Droste will attempt to repeat as mid-season champion in a field that includes seven previous season and mid-season champions. They are Ed Sanger, Williams, Paul Fitzpatrick, Bill Zwanziger, Bob Hilmer, Chub Liebe, and Cal Swanson.

The evening will begin at 8 p.m. with a 20-lap novice race followed by a 30-lap consolation race for drivers not in the top point standings. The 50-lap championship race will end the evening.

1969
In the News

Racing Fan Disappointed

WATERLOO—To the Editor: I know I am not the only person disappointed about hearing that there will probably be no races at Tunis Speedway this summer because of the lease being up, bleachers needing repair and track probably needing work.

But I'm sure with a little work it could all be fixed, just as in the last 20 years there have been races there. I believe a new stock car track is being built at Dubuque, but that's too far for most of us to go and so the only close place to go is Independence on Saturday night and maybe that's too far for some of us, or just not so handy as the Waterloo track always was. It's not only Waterloo - Cedar Falls people who came to Tunis but people from all directions and smaller towns.

Waterloo needs a stock car track. Of course, the people around the track have complained of the noise, and dust, but they've got to remember the stock car track was there for 20 years at least and most houses in that area have been built since then.

NAME WITHHELD

Tunis: Waterloo Stock Car Races Planned

WATERLOO — To the Editor: Two letters have appeared in your column regarding the stock car races for the coming season at Tunis Speedway. The information that they had was incorrect.

We are having races this year which will be our twenty-first consecutive year. Weather permitting, we will open about the middle of May.

The Racing Association will run modified cars. There will be a large number of cars and drivers from last year, plus some new ones.

The track has been leased for the last three years. This year it will be operated by J. L. Tunis who opened and operated the track for the first seventeen years.

We are looking forward to a season of good racing with entertainment for all.

J. L. TUNIS
President of Tunis
Speedway, Inc.

Tunis Purse Not Unusual

JUD TUNIS, proprietor of Tunis Speedway, says no agreement, verbal or otherwise, was involved when he decided to promote a July 4 race at his Waterloo stock car track.

"We had only run four races and here we were in July when we should be getting ready for the mid-season championship," Tunis said.

Tunis indicated his decision was firmented by rumors that promoters of weekly Friday night stock car races at Hawkeye Downs in Cedar Rapids were planning a Sunday card as a final day program for the all-Iowa fair that ended last Sunday in Cedar Rapids. Sunday is the traditional day for racing at Tunis Speedway although he has conducted races on the Fourth of July in the past.

Tunis said his $3,250 guarantee for the Friday races wasn't, necessarily, far off from other holiday purses. The last Fourth of July race Tunis sponsored before he began leasing the track the past few seasons was in 1965 and the drivers split $3,050.51. On July 5 that same year he paid $2,687.28 in prizes. His July 4, 1964, purse was $3,031.89 and in 1963 it was $3,081.15.

Drivers Guaranteed $1,200

THE DRIVERS in the Independence Racing Assn. that race here Sunday and in Independence every Saturday night are guaranteed $1,200. Tunis also gives them an option of 50 per cent of the gross, minus taxes, if that is greater, and it generally is, he points out. The driver's share this year was $1,215.16 on May 18, $1,655.30, May 25, $1,596.86, June 8, and $1,559.52, June 15.

"I am not aware that the Cedar Rapids track has a standard guarantee for their drivers although I know that some of the top names are paid appearance money whether they win or not. I do not pay appearance money," Tunis said.

Tunis' races last Friday attracted 22 cars and Ed Sanger won the main and the $500 prize that went with it. Sunday's card, which also was to have been worth $3,250, was rained out.

COMPETITION FOR DRIVERS

A STOCK CAR war? Perhaps it was bound to happen with the mushrooming growth of the sport.

Russ SMITH'S
COLUMN

Tunis Speedway in Waterloo appears to have gone into a bidding war with the Hawkeye Downs in Cedar Rapids for drivers and cars for its Fourth of July program here Friday —at least that's the way they see it in Cedar Rapids, according to Cedar Rapids Gazette racing writer Al Miller.

There are races every Friday at the Downs but, because it is a holiday, Tunis has scheduled a race card for that night, as well as its usual Sunday night, and is offering purses of $3,250 for both nights, compared to the $1,200 purses that are normal at Tunis.

Many drivers who hit the Friday (Cedar Rapids), Saturday (Independence) and Sunday (Tunis) circuit will have to choose between Cedar Rapids and Waterloo Friday and the deciding factor may be the prize differential. Cedar Rapids is guaranteeing its usual $2,400.

The drivers who belong to the Independence Racing Assn., which encompasses Waterloo and Independence, may also risk losing their membership by passing up the Waterloo card.

Miller says: C. R. had been racing on Saturday nights, but (the late Frank) Winkley moved the program to Friday so as not to conflict with Indee (on Saturday) and thus make more cars available to C. R. The marriage was a good one—that is, until Tunis pulled the latest funny.

"Even Ed Sanger of Waterloo, who is the secretary of the IRA, was apologetic last week.

" 'It's none of my doing,' said Sanger, who is the Downs point leader. 'You may still see me back here on Friday, although I may not be secretary up there any longer.'

"(Hawkeye Downs promoter Nick) Nachicas said he already had '24 signed entries for the Fourth of July. They are expected to be honored and if they race somewhere else they will be penalized. I'm not sure yet what the penalty will be.' "

Liebe Wins Crown At Tunis

(COURIER NEWS SERVICE)

Chub Liebe won the season championship at Tunis Speedway Sunday night. Leibe edged out Lynn Idler for the title in the 50 lap championship event.

Larry Defiance, who took third in the title race, won the first heat.

HANSEN 4-WAY WINNER AT TUNIS

Dike's Curt Hansen stole the show here at Tunis Speedway Sunday night, winning four events.

Hansen took top honors in the 3rd heat, B Semi, the Trophy Dash and the feature races before a crowd of 1,479.

from the rear of the pack to the front in four laps to win the event.

SUNDAY AT TUNIS

Hansen Double Winner Of Stock Car Features

Curt Hansen of Dike won a sweep of the feature victories in stock car races at Independence and Waterloo this

Porte City; 2. Curlon Grumm; 3. Ty Burger.
Third Heat — 1. Chub Liebe, Oelwein; 2. Glen Martin; 3. Curt Hansen.
A-Semi — 1. Chub Liebe; 2. Red Droste, Waterloo; 3. Cal Swanson, Waterloo;

Ed Sanger Wins First Feature

Waterloo's Ed Sanger became the first big winner of the year Sunday night at Tunis Speedway when he captured the A feature 20 lap stock car race. A crowd of 1,800 saw the season opener.

Sanger outran La Porte City Dave Bedard for first place in the A main.

In the B feature, also a 20 lap race, Bob Hesse of Waterloo came in front of Chub Liebe

car races at the Independence speedway were washed out.

That sets up a double feature program for this Saturday, with last year's Indy track champ, Red Droste, slated to run along with Liebe, Cal Swanson, Bill Zwanziger, Ed Sanger, Curt Hansen, Glen Marti and Paul Fitzpatrick.

Droste, last year's champ at Waterloo also, won one heat, the first, Sunday at Tunis, then

LeCroy Wins 2nd Feature In a Row

Jerry LeCroy of Des Moines, fresh from a feature win in his first appearance at Tunis Speedway Aug. 10, won his second straight feature event in a row Sunday night at Tunis.

LeCroy, who finished second in the third heat to Waterloo's Glen Martin, beat out track veteran Karl Sanger in the feature as over 1,700 fans watched Sunday's events.

At Independence Saturday, a new track surface produced some fast times, some so fast

Hansen Stretches Point Lead With Third Feature Victory at Tunis

Curt Hansen, who holds a commanding point lead in the seasonal standings at

points to 395 for Ed Sanger.

Then, in the 20-lap feature, Hansen won with Ed Sanger

Karl Sanger, fourth in points,

See RACES

Tunis Newcomer, LeCroy, Edges Hansen in Feature

A newcomer — Jerry LeCroy of Des Moines — made his raceway debut in grand style as he captured the feature and the third and B-semi heats in

AT INDEPENDENCE SATURDAY
First Heat — 1. Bob Hesse; 2. Joe Schoeller; 3. Jim Welsh.
Second Heat — 1. Roger Klingius; 2. Roger Kruse; 3. Dave Bedard.
Third Heat — 1. Glen Martin; 2. Ed Sanger; 3. Karl Sanger.
A-Semis — 1. Joe Schoeller; 2. Doc

1970
In the News

Courier Inaugurates Racing Column

Season Starting Notes

Must Coordinate With Car

New Management, Bigger Purses

Larry D. Spears
Sports Department
Waterloo Courier
Park and Commercial
Waterloo, Iowa 50701

Sanger New Car, Old Car 1-2

By LARRY D. SPEARS
Courier Sports Writer

Mid-Year Championship To Be Decided At Tunis

WATERLOO SUNDAY COURIER, WATERLOO, IO

By LARRY D. SPEARS
Courier Sports Writer

Half a summer of racing efforts culminate tonight as 22 drivers pilot their late model stock cars onto Tunis Speedway's newly refurbished quarter-mile dirt oval for a try at the rich Mid-Season Championship.

The 50-lap late model feature is the last area mid-year championship to be decided with both Cedar Rapids and Independence tracks having hosted their races earlier, and will conclude an action packed night of racing that will also feature 25-lap junior and mini stock championships, a special "Hot Scoop Classic" for members of the news media and a motorcycle jumping exhibition by 17-year-old Steve Droste of Waterloo.

In preparation for the 8 p.m. racing card, Tunis managers have completely rebuilt the south end of the D-shaped oval track, moving the No. 1 and No. 2 turns approximately 15 feet farther out to bypass a bad hole and washboard area ... truck tires ... ried upright ... ur turns to ... into the infield and to reduce the dust problem which has been plaguing spectators.

Four hundred dollars will go to the winner of the 50-lap late model chase, $100 more than the regular Tunis winner's purse, and increased purses will also be offered to entice the junior and mini stock drivers.

The "Hot Scoop Classic" will feature nearly 20 area radio, television and newspaper personalities racing in the mini-stockers and a $300 prize fund has been set up for the 12-lap journalist feature.

Droste, who displayed his two-wheel jumping talents for the first time earlier this year at Tunis, will add an additional touch to the five car jump.

The 17-year-old bike whizz will ride his specially prepared motorcycle up a 30-inch wide ramp traveling at nearly 70 miles per hour in order to clear the five cars, which will be parked side by side at the end of the ramp. The new twist will be the addition of two people playing cards at a table placed just beyond the last car.

Unlike other performers who have done similar stunts, Droste will land on the ground ramp.

Top contenders for the late model championship will probably be current Tunis point front-runners Ed Sanger, Glen Martin and Bill Zwanziger.

ED SANGER — GLEN MARTIN — BILL ZWANZIGER

Sanger, a Waterloo native who works as a mechanic at Shriver Pontiac in Cedar Falls, is a five year racing veteran and has been a consistent winner at Tunis this season in his new yellow Monte Carlo.

The No. 95 car has carried Sanger to the current Tunis point lead as well as to respectable positions at Cedar Rapids, Marshalltown. The car is sponsored by Performance Engineering of Waterloo.

Sanger, who won championships last season at Cedar Rapids, Marshalltown and Dubuque, will have to expect his keenest competition from Chevelle and Zwanziger's green No. 80 car.

Martin, driving out of Independence, has been one of the hottest Tunis runners all season and though he hasn't cracked the leading spot in the point standings, has kept Sanger on his toes.

His car sports an L88-427 ... by the C&M Racing Team consisting of Martin, Ray Call of Waterloo and Dale Hackwell. Call is the chief mechanic for the car, which he built.

Martin, a plumber by trade, is a four year veteran.

Zwanziger, the early points leader at Tunis and on the Greater Iowa Racing Assn. three-track circuit, has had some mechanical problems of late but seems to have them worked out and should also pose a threat for the Tunis gold.

Other top drivers in contention are Dike's Curt Hansen, Jerry LeCroy of Des Moines, Dan Nesteby of Waterloo, Dr. Al Mayner of Winthrop, Karl Sanger of Waterloo and Ty Burger of Cedar Falls.

The championship racing will be co-sponsored by Bartine Chrysler-Plymouth of Cedar Falls and the CF auto dealer will give away a 1962 Ford 4-door sedan at intermission.

Entries in the "Hot Scoop Classic" include "Speedy Roger" Thurston and "Wild" Bill Johnston of KCRG-TV in Cedar Rapids, Jim "Parnelli" Martin, Warner "Ernie" Bantz and Dick "Petty" Peck of KOUR radio in Independence, J. D. "McCluskey" Ball and By "Yarbrough" Gosdin of KXEL radio in Waterloo, Larry "Ramo" Spears of the Waterloo Courier, "A. J." Dick Hogan of the Cedar Valley Times in Vinton, Quin "Allison" Jones of KOEL radio in Oelwein, Bob "Bomber" Lana of the Marion Sentinel Lee "Bullitt" Bonorden of the Oelwein Daily Register and Don "Scoop" Timmerman and four mystery drivers from KWWL radio in

McDonough Wins Final Tunis Feature Before Mid-Season

By LARRY D. SPEARS
Courier Sports Writer

Two late model stock mid-season championships were decided in racing action this week and preparations finalized for a third.

Waterloo's Ed Sanger took the middle-of-the-year crown at Independence Raceway Saturday night and Waterloo's Red Droste ran away with the 50-lap All-Iowa championship feature at Cedar Rapids' Hawkeye Downs Friday.

Bill McDonough of Cedar Rapids captured the 25-lap feature at Tunis Sunday, the last regular racing event before the Waterloo mid-year title chase next Sunday, in one of the season's most exciting chases.

Eight cars finished the grueling battle for the $300 first-place money and seven of the ran were within a half-lap of McDonough back at the checkered flag.

The race started with 18 cars but a miscalculation on turn one of the opening lap by Waterloo's Bill Zwanziger forced a restart and brought a protest from Independence's Glen Martin.

Zwanziger jumped to the inside at the green flag and found himself trapped as the field jammed into the first turn. Trying to work back into the pack, Zwanziger smashed Martin spinning the Indee driver, then sailed over the track rim and out of the race.

Protest Refused

Martin's car blocked the track and a restart was called, sending Martin to the rear. Following the race, in which Martin worked his way back up to the fourth spot, a protest was lodged ... of Waterloo.

Garwin's Paul Uhlenberg moved from the third starting position to capture the first heat event and Karl Sanger ran away for a seven-car-length victory in the second after Dave Bedard of La Porte City caused a restart with a first lap spin-out.

Martin took third heat honors, taking over the lead on the first lap and fighting off consistent challenges by LeCroy.

Young Junior Winner

The semi wins went to Roger Kruse of Independence who led the 15-lap event from the beginning and to Martin. Martin barely edged Ed Sanger for his semi win, crossing the line just less than a car length ahead of the Tunis point leader. Waterloo's ... shalltown finished second but never seriously challenged Young.

Bob Newmire of Cedar Rapids captured the mini-stock feature as 12 small car drivers worked the final bugs out of their cars before turning them over to members of the press next Sunday for the first annual "Hot Scoop Classic."

The Classic, a special race in the mini-stockers for members of the newspaper, television and radio media members, will highlight the mid-season championship festivities which will also include a repeat of Steve Droste's daring five-car motorcycle jump.

The quarter-mile oval at Tunis will receive major alterations prior to the championship ...

Sanger Comes From 8th To Win Second Feature

By LARRY D. SPEARS
Courier Sports Writer

Waterloo's Ed Sanger pushed his way from a No. 8 starting slot into first place in five laps, then fought his way through three race stopping wrecks to capture his second consecutive 25-lap feature win at Tunis Speedway Sunday.

The victory netted Sanger the regular $300 first-place money, plus a $100 bonus for the repeat win.

... in turn one.

Idler got the A semi crown after battling his way from a fifth place spot to the lead on the 16th lap. Farrell was second and Hesse got third.

Heat winners were Bedard, Stover and Zwanziger.

Saves Junior Class

Nine cars turned out to fill a usually sparse junior stock field and their action-filled race which included two multiple roll-overs, gave rise to speculation that the class might be continued.

Tunis promoter Kieth Knaack, who had contemplated dropping the junior stockers and replacing them with a special

See RACES
Continued on Page 20, Col. 2

Waterloo Daily Courier — Sports Section
MONDAY, JUNE 29, 1970 PAGE 13

Kids' Night Successful, Hilmer Wins Initial Feature at Tunis

By LARRY D. SPEARS
Courier Sports Writer

Waterloo's Tunis Speedway unveiled its version of "Kids' Night" Sunday night and by the time the three-hour festivities reached a conclusion nothing but happy faces could be found in the crowd exceeding 4,000.

About 800 youngsters under 10 were among the happiest of the group as a result of the "Gold Rush" following the feature race, which was won by Dysart's Bob Hilmer.

Seven thousand - five hundred shiny new pennies plus countless pieces of assorted candy and gum were scattered along the front straightaway of the Tunis quarter - mile oval and, on command from WMT "Kartoon King" Dr. Max, the kids were released from the track infield in a mad dash for the gold.

The entire spectacle lasted about seven minutes and when the swarm of youngsters cleared, a quick survey of the racing surface disclosed not a single left - over coin.

Two Bicycles Given

Two bicycles were also given away by lucky drawing, the first bike going to Nancy Elliott of Wellsburg and the second to 10 - year - old Lynette Siebel of Orange, a fourth - grader at Waterloo's Orange school.

The night was also "Jim Denning Chevrolet Night" and Denning's Rebbeck sales agency gave away a 1959 4 - door Chevrolet hardtop. Marilyn Johnson of 237 Auburn in Waterloo was the lucky winner in the adult half of the Tunis give - away program.

Probably two of the happiest faces anywhere around the track belonged to Hilmer and Cedar Falls' Roger Klingfus. Hilmer broke into the Tunis winners circle for the first time this season on the "A" Semi, then won the 25 - lap feature after a grueling bumper to bumper duel with Glen Martin of Independence.

Hilmer moved his newly painted No. 122 car from the fifth starting spot into second place on the first lap, and after chasing Garwin's Paul Uhlenberg for five laps, took over the lead on the sixth circuit.

Martin came from the number 12 starting position and moved steadily through the pack until he too passed Uhlenberg on the ninth lap to begin the chase.

Martin Pressed

Trailing by over 10 car lengths, Martin continued to press and by the 15th lap was right on Hilmer's tail, but he could never get around and the two cars crossed the line one-two within inches of each other ... tested feature with Uhlenberg hanging on for fourth and Ed Sanger working his way from 13th at the start to fifth.

Klingfus managed only a seventh place feature finish, but that in itself was a milestone for the hardluck driver, who has finished only two races previously this season.

Klingfus also picked up his second win of the year, a first in the first heat, and finished fourth in the "A" Semi in his purple No. 6 Dodge Charger, for three complete races in one night.

Martin won the third heat and Waterloo's Karl Sanger took the second in one of the evening's best racing displays.

Sanger took over the second spot on lap one of the 10 lap heat race and played bumper tag with Burger for nine tours ... just a half - car length in front.

Other winners included Dr. Al Maynor of Winthrop in the "B" Semi, Larry Padden of Waterloo in the Mini - Stock feature, and Richard Wilcox of Evansdale in the Junior Stock Feature. The mini-stock event ran for its first purse of the season, Padden picking up the lion's share of the $100 Tunis offering.

New NEITA Winner

A new face broke into the winner's circle in Sunday drag action at NEITA Raceway, while the other eliminator spot went to one of the season's top performers.

Ron Jenison of Clarksville was the repeat winner, picking up his second straight Street and Competition eliminator titles in two weeks of combined

Midgets Memorial Day Tunis Feature

RAIN ROBBED MOST AREA stock car fans of their weekly outing to the track last weekend, but the special Memorial Day holiday will give them a chance to double up and catch up.

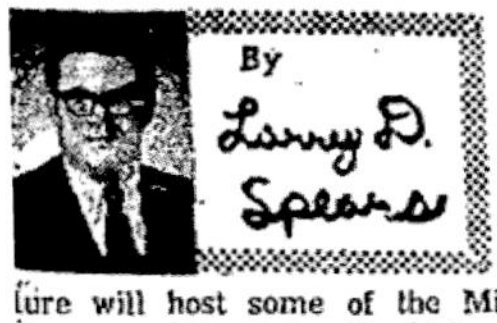

Numerous area tracks, including Hawkeye Downs in Cedar Rapids and Waterloo's Tunis Speedway, will feature bonus racing programs Saturday evening in addition to their regular weekend stock cards.

Tunis' Memorial Day feature will host some of the Midwest's finest full midget performers while Cedar Rapids' spectators get to view the chase for Hawkeye Downs' two-year-old IMCA sprint car records.

Heading the list at Tunis will be 1969 champ Joe Demko of Minneapolis. Demko will be piloting a Chevy II powered midget bearing the No. 1.

Another top victory lane prospect, also driving a Chevy II equipped car, is 1969 IMCA Rookie of the Year Joe Bell of Cedar Rapids.

CHUCK SNYDER, ALSO OF MINNEAPOLIS, was another early entry on the Tunis program with his new machine based

TUNIS MID-SEASON CHAMPION — Waterloo's Ed Sanger shows nothing but smiles Sunday night as he receives the Tunis Speedway Mid-Season Championship Trophy after virtually running away from the field to win the 50-lap feature. Presenting him with the trophy is Tunis Queen Miss Kathy Kavanaugh of Cedar Falls while official Tunis flag man Bob Posekany waves the traditional checkered flag overhead. (Courier Photo by Steve Willard)

Martin Leads for 21 Laps

Sanger Cops Mid 50

By LARRY D. SPEARS
Courier Sports Writer

Waterloo's Ed Sanger played fender tag with Glen Martin of Independence for 21 laps Sunday night, then stormed away from the rest of the Tunis Speedway Mid-Season championship pack when Martin dropped out and collected the $400 mid-year gold.

... two car lengths at the checkered flag.

Waterloo's Bill Zwanziger, who fought off Sanger's lapping effort until the 48th circuit, finished third with La Porte City's Dave Bedard crossing the line fourth.

Karl Sanger of Waterloo and Bill McDonnough of Cedar Rapids put on the best show in the No. 777 Waterloo Wagon Pit VW captured the Tunis gold.

Tony Dunlap of Cedar Rapids got second, just two car lengths back, while Cedar Rapids' Tim McDonnough finished third. Chuck Demuth and Jerry Holbach, both of Waterloo, completed the top five.

The junior-stockers also ran an accident-free 25-lap feature rate for cars in the mini-stock feature, the special "Hot Scoop Classic" for members of the radio, television and newspaper media had to be run in two heats.

Tom McCoy of KHAK radio in Cedar Rapids walked away with the first press heat and Jim Martin of KOUR radio in Independence captured the se-

MONDAY, AUGUST 3, 1970 Page Fifteen

Ed Sanger Slips by Brother, Karl, on 15th Lap for Tunis Win

By LARRY D. SPEAR
Courier Sports Writer

Waterloo's Karl Sanger made only one mistake in Tunis Speedway's 25-lap feature event Sunday, but that was enough to cost him victory.

Sanger started in the No. 6 slot at the green flag and needed only two laps to move into the lead when Dr. Al Mayner spun going into the No. 1 curve.

Stretching out ato a comfortable four-car length lead over Waterloo's Bill Zwanziger, Sanger held onto the advantage ... recovered from a street accident on the way to Tunis to take the junior stock feature, edging Rodney Brandt, also of Waterloo, and Bob Newmire of Hiawatha bypassed Waterloo's Kenny McCombs in the fifth lap to capture the mini-stock feature.

Mayner Wins Two

Mayner was the big winner in the preliminary action, capturing the third heat in a bumper to bumper battle with Martin and holding off ...

... Assn. record holder Ron Jenison put his A-HR-1 "Stump Puller" Camaro with the program again Sunday and took home the combined Street & Competition Eliminator gold while Waterloo's Fowlkes Brothers, also AHRA record-holders, took the Stock Eliminator bracket.

Tracer's Roy Fuller won the new class, Horsepower Stock, which is based on the National Hot Rod Assn. standard of horsepower to weight ratio rather than the AHRA's cubic inch to weight standard.

Cedar Rapids Sandi Price powered Dan Kennedy's 0-3 Camaro to a 14.44, 94.43 effort in the upper division and Jean Hartley of Waterloo took the slower bracket in a Maverick with a 19.31-70.53 run.

TUNIS SPEEDWAY
First Heat—1. Larry Wasserfort (Waterloo); 2. Roger Kruse (Independence); 3. Jim Burger (Cedar Falls).
Second Heat—1. Joe Shaefer (Waterloo); 2. Bill Zwanziger (Waterloo); 3. Ed Sanger (Waterloo).
Third Heat—1. Al Mayner (Winthrop); 2. Glenn Martin (Independence); 3. Karl Sanger (Waterloo).
"A" Semi—Mayner; 2. Wasserfort; 3. Kruse; 4. Burger; 5. Red Droste (Evansdale); 6. Dave Plum (Waterloo).

Payoff Changes Set at Tunis

TUNIS SPEEDWAY PROMOTER Keith Knaack has announced the adoption of a new purse arrangement beginning this Sunday at the Waterloo track with the new payoff schedule giving Tunis the highest paying feature race in the state of Iowa.

The change represents a possible overall purse increase of $465 over the previous payoff schedule, depending on the number of cars in the field.

Regardless of the number of participants each night the winner of the 25-lap feature

1971
In the News

Evansdale Driver Injured In Mini-Stock Roll-Over

By LARRY D. SPEARS
Courier Sports Writer

A roll - over injuring an Evansdale mini-stock driver marred Sunday's races, but the largest Tunis Speedway crowd of the year still got plenty of legitimate racing thrills as the largest field of the season battled for shares of Tunis' new $3,000 purse.

Russell Tucker of 750 Colleen in Evansdale was listed in good condition at Allen Hospital following the accident in the first lap of the mini-stock feature. Doctors reported he suffered a fractured back and would be hospitalized for at least three weeks.

The wreck occurred just seconds after the green flag as Tucker's car, near the end of the 14-car pack, was involved in a collision with Roger Zeaman. Tucker's car spun sideways out of the number one turn, rolled once, went airbourne for about 30 feet, then loaded and rolled twice more.

Tucker was thrown from the car as it rolled the third time, landing in the middle of the track, but he fell clear of the traffic.

for second, pocketed $400 from the final race.

Glen Martin of Independence, the only other driver to win a Tunis feature this season, came across the line third, a position he had taken and held from the seventh circuit.

Curt Hansen of Dike finished fourth, winning a close battle over Karl Sanger and Dan Nesteby, both of Waterloo. Those six were the only cars still on the same lap as Sanger at the flag.

Finishing seventh but a lap back was Phil Reese of Des Moines. Waterloo's Larry Wasserfort got eighth ahead of Marlyn Cornelius of Cedar Falls and Willy Klingfus of Waterloo.

$600 Total Winnings

Sanger ran his winnings for the night to $600 with additional victories in the heat race and trophy dash.

Starting in the back row again, Sanger worked his way through the pack and took the heat lead from Hansen on the ninth lap, finishing just two car lengths in front of the Dike driver. Karl Sanger was third and Martin grabbed fourth

that race.

Nesteby got his semi lead on the second lap and was never seriously challenged as he topped Ron Schafenbeul of New Hampton and Arlo Becker for the win.

Fifteen of the new Road Runner class cars made the scene for their first night of competition at Tunis and Waterloo's Gary Kaune took the checkered flag. The women's title went to Lois Johnson of Waterloo. She finished just ahead of Betty Sanger as both girls capitalized on a two-car spin involving the early leaders.

Don Thompson of Waterloo and Jim Schmuecker of Vinton got all the "B" Modified glory finishing one-two in both the heat and feature race.

Roy Stefan, who finished fourth in the feature, took third in the heat, while C. J. Skinner of Cedar Falls earned the show spot in the feature.

LATE MODELS

First heat—1. Marlyn Cornelius (Cedar Falls); 2. Red Dralle (Evansdale); 3. Willy Klingfus (Cedar Falls); 4. Phil Reese (Des Moines); 5. Larry Wasserfort (Waterloo).

Second heat — 1. Ed Sanger (Waterloo); 2. Curt Hanson (Dike); 3. Karl Sanger (Waterloo); 4. Glen Martin (Independence); 5. Dan Nesteby (Waterloo)

Semi — 1. Nesteby; 2. Ron Schafenbeul (New Hampton); 3. Arlo Becker.

Fireworks, Cash Spice 4th Celebration at Speedway

By LARRY D. SPEARS
Courier Sports Writer

Things at Tunis Speedway Sunday night will be popping — and banging, shooting, exploding and sparkling — and, most important, paying.

A huge fireworks show will spice the top late model racing

area tracks, and was scheduled to run the full six weeks if no one bested Sanger.

Originally, the reward was $100 and it was stipulated that Sanger had to finish the race for the pay-off to be in effect. Sanger met the challenge by winning the first two features

the third week.

Recognizing the unusual nature of that race, which had to be restarted seven times, CarPac, Inc., the Tunis promoter, put up $50 the next week on a "bet you can't do it again" basis — and, nobody has.

Sanger won each of the past

must enter through the south gate off Sager Street.

There will be no drag racing at NEITA Raceway Saturday night, but NEITA will have grudge racing Wednesday, gates opening at 6 p.m., and the regular racing program will resume next Saturday with a

4,200 Watch Stan Stover Top Sanger to Earn $700 at Tunis

By LARRY D. SPEARS
Courier Sports Writer

Shades of Batman and Robin — Tunis Speedway is developing its own dynamic duo.

They don't wear long capes and they don't drive a winged, jet-powered car — but, like

driver with a Tunis 25-lapper to his credit, sandwiched between him and Stover.

The circumstances of this Stover victory were almost identical to his earlier win, which featured a slower pace due to seven restarts. Monday's

disintegrated on that same lap, paving Stover's way to the final flag.

Martin, who got by Sanger for second on the 19th tour of the quarter-mile dirt oval, had a good shot at Stover but was handicapped by vision pro-

of more than a quarter-lap.

Arlo Becker of Atkins won the other "B" heat and was making a shot at the feature before losing his steering. Jim Stodola of Shellsburg was second in the feature and in the heat won by Becker, while C.

Tunis Starts 24th Season Here Sunday

By LARRY D. SPEARS
Courier Sports Writer

Straight line racing fans in the Waterloo metropolitan area have had three weeks head start, but the "roundy-round" speed enthusiasts get their first chance to catch up on the thrills Sunday as Tunis Speedway opens for its 24th consecutive year of late model stock car action.

Race time for the season-opening program is 8 p.m. with time trials starting at 7:15 p.m.

Many new attractions prevail this year at Tunis, located on Highway 218 between Waterloo and Cedar Falls, including various track improvements, a new bargain admission section and an entirely new racing class featuring the fairer sex.

Headlining the program will be the ever-popular late model stockers.

25-Lap Feature

The late model program will feature three heats, a semi-main and a 25-lap feature race with a guaranteed $300 winner's payoff. In addition, the tracks promoters, CarPac, Inc., will present feature races for "B" Modifieds, the extremely quick and exciting mini-stockers and the newly formed women's street racing class.

Total guaranteed purse for the evening of racing will be $2,000.

Many of the Midwest's best late model drivers will be on hand for the Tunis season including Waterloo's Ed Sanger, who has terrorized other area tracks which have already opened.

Sanger, the defending season points champ at both Tunis and Independence, has piloted his 1971 Chevrolet Monte Carlo to five straight feature wins this season including two each at Dubuque and Marshalltown and one in last Saturday's Independence season opener.

Zwanziger Here

Other top drivers familiar to local fans include Glen Martin of Independence, Bill Zwanziger of Waterloo and Curt Hansen of Dike.

More than 15 women have announced that they have prepared cars for racing in the new women's street class and Waterloo-Cedar Falls fans will be the first to see the new powder-puff action, though the ladies will later begin running at both Independence and Cedar Rapids.

For the budget-minded racing fan, the new admission policy will probably hold great interest.

CarPac plans a special $1 section on the east side of the quarter-mile dirt oval, with entry to the special economy section from the south gate on Sager Street. Regular admission of $2 per adult will prevail at the other track gates with kids six through 11 admitted for 50 cents and children five and under free.

Concessions will be available in all spectators areas.

Ed Leads 49 of 50 Laps for Tunis Win

By LARRY D. SPEARS
Courier Sports Writer

Everyone has heard of the Everly Brothers and the Righteous Brothers, but it was the Sanger Brothers who headlined the action at Tunis Speedway's grand finale for the 1971 season Sunday night.

Ed Sanger, in the now famous No. 95 Monte Carlo, proved his overall Tunis points lead was no fluke as he led all but one of the 50 trips around the quarter-mile oval in capturing

light pole and two retaining posts with him.

The mishap forced a restart and Stover was unable to come back out, having caught a rock in his radiator sometime during the melee.

Karl moved into second after the new start and the order stayed that way until the checkered flag.

Dr. A. E. Mayner of Winthrop and La Porte City's Dave Bedard finished third and fourth, the only other drivers

ahead of Independence's John Webb and two in front of Waterloo's Bill Bartholomew. Plum recovered from the encounter with the poles to take ninth and Waterloo's Dave Trower, driving his sportsman car, held on for 10th.

Close Women's Finish

In earlier late model action, Red Dralle of Evansdale went from pole to flag in the trophy dash and Webb fought off Trower for the semi title.

ED SANGER DOMINATES '71 STOCK CAR RACING SCENE

Talk about auto racing in Black Hawk County in 1971 and almost every sentence has to include the words "Ed Sanger."

Sanger was the dominating force for the entire circle track season at Waterloo's Tunis Speedway and also garnered considerable honors elsewhere.

"roadrunner" class and a women's class. Ginny Stout of Cedar Rapids wound up as the women's season champ and the roadrunners — little more than safety-improved street stocks — provided countless thrills for Tunis fans.

Straight-line racing fans also

as NEITA Raceway north of Cedar Falls inaugurated night racing.

Early probelms with in-

Racing

adequate lighting marred some

those troubles were worked out with ample success before chilling weather forced a return to daytime racing in September.

Among the highlights of the season were several special funny car shows and appearances by the turbine-powered "Odyssey" dragster

The jet set a pair of new NEITA track records, blasing through the quarter mile in 6.90 seconds, the first time a car has ever gone under seven seconds at NEITA. The fire-breathing machine, driven by Bob Motz of Akron, Ohio, also set a new speed record of 241.93

Martin Takes First Tunis Win

By LARRY D. SPEARS
Courier Sports Writer

Mechanical failures, slow-finishing car builders and previous commitments reduced the racing field, but 1,563 "roundy-round" fans still got quite a show as Tunis Speedway opened for its 24th consecutive season of late model stock car racing Sunday.

Ed Sanger, the defending Tunis points champ, failed to appear because of a previous commitment at Dubuque, but last year's runner-up, Glen

car field for the first heat win.

Martin, who also started on the pole of that heat, found the early going a little rougher and fell to third before rallying for second in the heat. Bob Hesse was third in the opening race and the Waterloo driver finished fifth in the main.

Red Dralle of Evansdale pulled another pole-to-flag showing in the second heat, topping Doc Mayner of Winthrop and Reese, but Mayner came back to win the six car trophy dash featuring the top

dependence Saturday night left only three cars running for Tunis' premier of the women's street stock class and Waterloo's Lois Johnson edged Lisbon's Lois Ricklefs for the flag.

The "B" cars ran a single heat and a feature but the results didn't change any as Don Thompson and Roy Stefan, both of Waterloo, finished one-two in each race. Lloyd Draper was third in the semi, but Joe Benhoff of Evansdale got the show position in the feature.

2. Roy Stefan (Waterloo); 3. Lloyd Draper (Grundy Center); 4. Joe Benhoff (Evansdale); 5. Gary Kaune (Waterloo); 6. Vern Weber (Independence).

Feature — 1. Thompson; 2. Stefan; 3. Benhoff; 4. Jim Stodola (Shellsburg); 5. Kaune; 6. Draper.

SUPER STOCK

First heat — 1. Curt Hansen (Dike); 2. Glen Martin (Independence); 3. Bob Hesse (Waterloo); 4. Dave Trower (Waterloo).

Second heat — 1. Red Dralle (Evansdale); 2. Doc Mayner (Winthrop); 3. Phil Reese (Des Moines); 4. Larry Wasserfort (Waterloo).

Semi — 1. Trower; 2. Karl Sanger (Waterloo); 3. Wasserfort; 4. Tom Bartholomew (Waterloo); 5. Marlyn Cornelius (Cedar Falls); 6. Richard Scott (Fredericksburg).

Trophy Dash — 1. Mayner; 2. Reese; 3. Hesse; 4. Martin.

Feature — 1. Martin; 2. Sanger; 3. Hanson; 4. Reese; 5. Hesse; 6. Wasserfort; 7. Dralle; 8. Batholomew; 9. Cornelius; 10. Scott.

Dralle, Sanger Win in Twinbill

By LARRY D. SPEARS
Courier Sports Writer

Red Dralle of Evansdale and Ed Sanger of Waterloo copped respective ends of Tunis Speedway's big double feature program Sunday night — but the comparison of the two wins ended at the green flag.

Dralle started in the No. 4 position in the first feature, postponed from last week when rain interrupted the program, blasted into the lead on the first turn and paced the field for the full 25 laps to take the opening victory.

Jim Burger of Cedar Falls worked his way from the No. starting spot to take second, but never seriously challenged Dralle, who's margin of victory was almost one-quarter lap. Joe Schaefer of Waterloo bested Sanger in a battle for third.

Started in Tenth

Sanger didn't have quite as easy a time in the second feature. He started in the No. spot and didn't manage to get ahead of the pack until the 11th circuit when he slipped by both Bob Hesse of Waterloo and

together in time to win the Australian Pursuit race, while Ed Sanger and Hesse captured heat events.

Harlan Sergeant of Hudson was the winner in the roadrunner feature.

Tunis' new Total Contest produced its second winner of the season as Jack Majewski of Greene correctly predicted the finish of the final late model feature and pocketed $300. The prize will be $100 next week and if there is no winner, the money will be added on to each succeeding week's prize fund.

MAKEUP FEATURE — 1. Red Dralle (Evansville); 2. Jim Burger (Cedar Falls); 3. Joe Schaeffer (Waterloo); 4. Ed Sanger (Waterloo); 5. Gary Crawford (Independence); 6. Tom Bartholomew (Waterloo); 7. Karl Sanger (Waterloo); 8. Bob Hesse (Waterloo); 9. Don DeFrance (Marshalltown); 10. Glen Martin (Independence).

FIRST HEAT — 1. Hesse; 2. Len Wasserfort (Waterloo); 3. Bartholomew.

SECOND HEAT — 1. E. Sanger; 2. Dralle; 3. Burger.

AUSTRALIAN PURSUIT — 1. Curt Hansen (Dike); 2. Crawford; 3. Schaeffer; 4. Tom Moore (Waterloo); 5. Lloyd Draper (Grundy Center).

FEATURE — 1. E. Sanger; 2. Hansen; 3. Hesse; 4. Dralle; 5. Wasserfort; 6. Bartholomew; 7. Schaeffer; 8. Burger; 9. Crawford; 10. Draper.

ROADRUNNER FEATURE — 1. Harlan Sergeant (Hudson); 2. Bob Kaiser (Cedar Falls); 3. Gary Allen (Waterloo); 4. Rick Swarts (Cedar Falls); 5. Len Sommerfelt (Waterloo).

Tunis Purse Boosted to $3,000

LOAD THOSE LATE MODELS on the trailers and head for Waterloo boys—somebody cut the purse strings at Tunis Speedway and the money's pouring out.

In an effort to offer the finest quality racing show in the Midwest, Tunis promoter CarPac, Inc., has announced that it is upping the weekly booty to more than $3,000. That figure compares with a total four-class purse of slightly more than $2,000 which has been offered in the early weeks of the season.

By
Larry D. Spears

The late model feature race, always the top crowd-pleaser the night, will be the recipient of most of the added cash as an extra $730 will be pumped into the feature pay-off.

In past events, top money in the 25-lap event has been ..00, but the new distribution schedule will guarantee the taker of the checkered flag an even $500.

Second-place will be worth $400, third will equal the old first-place total of $300 and the remainder of the top 10 will earn checks to the tune of $200, $100, $90, $80, $70, $60 and ..0.

Still in effect at Tunis is the special $50 added bounty to any driver who can best Waterloo's Ed Sanger in a feature. Sanger, last year's Tunis season champion, has captured at least 10 feature races at various Iowa tracks including last week's Tunis finale.

The way Sanger has been piloting his 1970 Monte Carlo, earning the extra $50 might seem like a difficult task, but Jackie Lyons of Cascade proved it could be done last Friday at Hawkeye Downs in Cedar Rapids.

Lyons led all the way in his 1970 Camaro to win that 25-lapper, ending Sanger's reign on the Downs' oval, which he has dominated since the season opener. Eager drivers are reminded, however, that the $50 bounty is in effect only if Sanger

1972
In the News

No Clear-Cut Favorite In 50 Lap Mid-Season

Larry D. Spears' Column

It will take 50 laps to do it, but some of the confusion concerning who's top dog at Waterloo's Tunis Speedway should be cleared up Sunday night.

Tunis, which has provided some of Northeast Iowa's most thrilling and unpredictable racing through the first half of the 1972 season, will host its annual Mid-Season Championship races Sunday, the first contest getting the green flag at 7:45 p.m.

Unlike last season when Waterloo's "Fast Eddie" Sanger was dominating stock circuits throughout the area, there has been no consistent front-runner this year. In eight races, the Tunis victory circle has been visited by a total of six different drivers.

Waterloo's Karl Sanger has been the only repeat winner this year, winning a pair of 25-lappers early in the year then cashing in again last Sunday at Tunis' Banner Night program.

Ed Still Points Leader

DESPITE TAKING the checkered flag three times, Karl has not run consistently at Tunis and, as a result, will not own the pole for the big 50-lap Mid-Season feature. The No. 1 spot will instead feature Ed Sanger's familiar No. 95 Monte Carlo, sponsored by Waterloo's Performance Engineering.

Ed, while a collecting first-place money in just one regular race this season (he also crossed the line first in a special Tunis 100-lap race which did not count in the point standings), has been one of the quarter-mile dirt track's most consistent runners and thus earned the top spot in both the point standings and the Mid-Season field.

In addition to Karl Sanger and Ed, other past feature winners expected to challenge for top money are Larry Wasserfort of Cedar Falls, Red Dralle of Evansdale, Dave Bedard of La Porte City and Stan Stover of Reinbeck.

Wasserfort has been a contender in almost every race this year but misfortune has dogged the heels of the other Tunis winners.

Dralle, Bedard EngineTrouble

DRALLE WAS involved in a serious roll-over at Independence several weeks ago and was running well until a blown engine sidelined him last Sunday night. Bedard was one of the most competitive racers earlier in the season but also blew an engine three weeks ago and didn't get back on the track until last week. In contrast, Stover missed most of the early races while recovering from a broken arm suffered in the off-season and has just begun to get back into the groove.

Other top drivers who have to be considered as contenders for the Mid-Season crown despite failing to win yet include Glen Martin of Independence, Curt Hansen of Dike, Jim Burger of Cedar Falls and Joe Schaefer and Bob Hesse, both of Waterloo.

In addition to the 50-lap feature, the late models will also run two shorter heat races.

The "Roadrunner" class will also have its Mid-Season championship Sunday with the street stockers slam-banging their way around the track for 30 gruelling laps. The Roadrunners are also lacking a strong favorite on the basis of previous wins.

Hudson Triple Winner

AS WITH THE late models, a total of six drivers have scored victories with only one multiple winner, Harlan Sergeant of Hudson, who has copped three checkered flags.

Other winners include Rick Claassen of Grundy Center, Chuck Larson of Cedar Falls, Bob Baumgartner of Waterloo, Dennis Heath of Denver and Earl Pruitt.

To top off the Mid-Season card Tunis will also host the "Women on Wheels" program, sponsored by the Women's Auto Racing Club of Cedar Rapids. All WARC members will be participating in the race, plus any area resident women who wish to race and can arrange for a car.

Tunis' Total contest will have a $100 prize this week for any fan or fans who can correctly predict the top five finishers in the late model feature in order. The jackpot had risen to $800, but a pair of the record 4,500 fans on hand last week correctly guessed the finish and took home $150 each.

Drags Resume Sunday

ALSO ON TAP for racing fans Sunday is a regular program of drags at NEITA Raceway north of Cedar Falls. NEITA, which took last weekend off after a successful Midwest Pro Dragster meet July 4, will have racing in competition, street and stock eliminator classes plus the usual large contingent of trophy cars.

Gates at NEITA open at 8:30 a.m. with time trials at 9:30 a.m. and final eliminations at 1:30 p.m. Admission is $2 for spectators with an additional $1 fee for pit passes.

Sanger Not As Dominant In '72 Races

Ed Sanger, who completely dominated Northeast Iowa stock car racing in 1971, didn't enjoy as much success in the "big" race in 1972 as he won just one

Racing

of the three top attractions on this past season's Tunis Speedway card.

The race Sanger won was the special 100-lap Memorial Day event. Curt Hansen of Dike provided the chief competition for Sanger as the two fought it out bumper-to-bumper before a flat tire forced Hansen out of the race on the 93rd lap.

Hansen went on to later win the 50-lap season's championship at Tunis as he grabbed the lead from Sanger on the first turn and never gave it up. Sanger's brother, Karl, won the mid-season championship in a similar manner as he moved from the No. 2 starting spot into first place on the first lap and held that position until the checkered flag 49 laps later.

Ed Sanger was successful throughout the regular Tunis season, however, as he was once again point leader.

NEITA Raceway didn't hold

Knaack to Stage Two Programs

By LARRY D. SPEARS
Courier Sports Writer

Last Sunday's season championship race, won by Dike's Curt Hansen, marked the end of the regular season at Waterloo's Tunis Speedway — but, it didn't mean the end of top-flight late model action at the track.

Tunis promoter Keith Knaack will host two big holiday programs tonight and tomorrow night at the quarter-mile oval, both events getting underway at 8 p.m.

Tonight's program will feature open competition for late models of 1965-72 vintage with three heats, a "B" feature and an "A" feature.

Time trials for the late models get under way at 6:30 p.m. with the 20 fastest qualifiers earning spots in the 30-lap "A" feature. The "A" event will be started straight up in order of qualifying time and first place will be worth $300. The total purse for the "A" feature will be $1,200 and all 20 cars will be paid.

Qualifiers above 21 will go into the "B" feature, 20-laps with a reverse start (fastest qualifier at the rear). The race will pay 10 places with the winner collecting $75.

Each of the heats will be 10 laps with a reverse start according to qualifying times. Each heat will pay five places with $30 to the winner and cars must run in the heats in order to qualify for the feature.

Tomorrow's program will feature open competition for roadrunner cars only and the evening will be highlighted by a post-race demolition derby.

The roadrunners will run three heats, a semi and a 20-lap feature and the cars will draw for positions.

A $300 claim will be in effect for all cars entered.

The heat races will pay four places with the winner earning $20. The winner of the semi will pick up $35 and will earn a starting spot at the rear of the feature, which is worth $100 to the winner and pays 18 places.

The demolition derby will also pay $100 to win with seven other places also earning money.

There is no entry fee for cars in either tonight's or tomorrow's race, but demo entries

K. Sanger Takes Mixed-Up Feature

By LARRY D. SPEARS
Courier Sports Writer

Hansen Nips Sanger in One-Two Daytona Finish

(COURIER NEWS SERVICE)

DAYTONA BEACH, Fla.—A pair of Waterloo area drivers proved here Thursday night that Northeast Iowa features some of the country's finest stock car racing.

Curt Hansen of Dike and Ed Sanger of Waterloo, both in Florida for the Daytona Speed Weeks program, opened the dirt track portion of the activities with a one-two finish in a 50-mile event, besting 22 drivers from throughout the United

by anyone but Sanger, the pair taking the checkered flag less than a car length apart and almost a full lap ahead of the rest of the field.

Two more dirt track events are on the Daytona schedule and the Iowa duo will rank as favorites for both races, scheduled for Friday and Saturday night.

The Daytona 500 will conclude speed weeks activities Sunday.

Bedard Starts Last, Finishes 1st

By LARRY D. SPEARS
Courier Sports Writer

Dralle Nips Ed By Half Length

By LARRY D. SPEARS
Courier Sports Writer

Tempers among the late model drivers at Waterloo's Tunis Speedway were considerably more subdued Sunday night than they were two weeks ago, but action was just as furious as Evansdale's Red Dralle scored one of the narrowest victories of the year.

Dralle, who powered his red No. 24 Chevelle into the front spot on the 12th lap of the 25-lap feature, had Tunis points leader Ed Sanger, center of the track's controversy two weeks ago, on his heels the entire distance, but refused to give any ground.

Sanger made his strongest bid on the white flag lap, powering his No. 95 Monte Carlo full-bore out of the No. 4 turn, but Dralle kept the inside groove and edged Sanger at the finish by half the length of his car.

The remainder of the feature

who edged Waterloo's Joe Schaefer for the second heat victory, edged him again for the No. 6 spot in the feature. Larry Wasserfort of Waterloo was eighth and Dave Bedard of La Porte City finished ninth after being involved in a pair of accidents that caused the only restarts in the race.

Eighteen-year-old Mike Osborn, subbing for his dad, Dale, in the No. 72 '57 Chevy, started on the pole and out-maneuvered the field for 11 laps before losing the top spot to Dralle. He finally finished 12th. Dr. A. E. Maynor of Winthrop, winner of the first heat, dropped out of the feature due to mechanical problems.

Bob Bennett of Waterloo captured the Roadrunner feature, Gary Freeland of Waterloo won the barrel race and hare Kenny McCombs took the Hare 'n' Hound title after the hounds were disqualified for rules in-

3,500 Bikini Night Fans

Stover Takes Feature

By LARRY D. SPEARS
Courier Sports Writer

Spurred on by a whole bevy of bikinied beauties, a newly-crowned Tunis "Bikini Queen," and the largest crowd of the 1972 season, Tunis Speedway's stock car drivers put on one of the finest racing shows in Iowa history Sunday night.

Whether the 44 drivers present were inspired by the crowd of approximately 3,500 or merely fired up after their duties as judges in Tunis' first Bikini Contest isn't known, but they recovered from a pair of lackluster late model heat races to put fans on their feet numerous times with outstanding high-speed, bumper-to-bumper and fender-to-fender racing action.

Both the 20-lap roadrunner feature, finally captured by Marshalltown's Earl Pruitt, and the 25-lap late model main, taken by Reinbeck's Stan Stover, were the most hotly contested of the year.

Stover, who's first feature win of the season completed a sweep of races for the evening, was constantly in jeopardy during the 25 circuits of the quarter-mile dirt oval. Six other cars, all running flat out, were within easy striking distance, ready to take advantage of any mistake by the leaders.

Drive Train Goes

And, Stover didn't have a free ride into the top spot. Jim Burger of Cedar Falls started in the No. 3 spot in the feature and blasted out of the pack and by Joe Schaefer on the third lap. Burger, his No. 25 Camaro running harder than it has all year, quickly opened up a wide lead over the rest of the cars, still tangled in the pack, but disaster struck on the eighth circuit.

With the engine still screaming, his drive train let go down the front staight and he was forced to pull off the track letting Schaefer, from Waterloo, regain the lead.

By that time, Stover had moved up from his No. 5 starting position and was right on top of Schaefer with Tunis points leader Ed Sanger close behind.

These three cars, along with Red Dralle of Evansdale, already back after a serious roll-over Saturday night at Independence, jockeyed for position without a change in order until the 19th lap, often barreling through the turns as many as three abreast.

Goes Low

Then, on the 20th circuit, Schaefer slipped too high and Stover got by on the underside. Taking advantage of Schaefer's loss of control, both Sanger and Dralle passed as well, going on to a one-two-three finish five laps later.

Schaefer got passed one more time, winding up in fifth behind Karl Sanger of Waterloo, but still stayed within four lengths of the winner.

Larry Wasserfort of Waterloo, Curt Hansen of Dike and Bob Hesse of Waterloo were tightly packed about three lengths further back, while Arnie Braland of Boone, Roger Klingfus of Cedar Falls and Dave Plum of Waterloo all finished on the same lap as the leaders.

Plum was also involved in one of the year's most thrilling finishes in the consi. Starting in the No. 2 spot in the six-lapper, Plum had built up a lead of almost eight lengths coming into the final turn of the race.

But, he got a little too high and Independence's Gary Crawford highballed through the No. 4 turn in a desperate catch-up bid. The maneuver worked as the two cars streaked down the final straight side-by-side, sparks flying high into the air from the scraping metal and Crawford taking the checkered flag by two feet.

Klingfus Takes First

In earlier action, Klingfus edged Schaefer by less than a length for the first heat win; Stover ran away with the second heat; and Hansen fought off Hesse for the semi victory.

Pruitt survived three early field-reducing restarts in the roadrunner event, then outdueled Chuck Larson of Cedar Falls for the victory, his first of the year.

New Image for Fast Eddie

By LARRY D. SPEARS
Courier Sports Writer

Pre-race advertising didn't bill it that way, but Waterloo's Tunis Speedway held a "demolition derby" Sunday night — and, may have gotten a new track "villain" in the process.

What emerged as the demolition derby was actually the 25-lap late model stock car feature — and the new villain, at least in the eyes of many observers, is Waterloo's Fast Eddie Sanger, current Tunis points leader and winner of Sunday's temper-filled main event.

Sanger, once the darling of Tunis crowds, received an angry greeting of jeers instead of cheers from the more than 3,000 fans when he took the final checkered flag after literally battering his way to victory.

The cat calls erupted after Sanger, generally one of the track's mild-tempered drivers, lost his cool over an apparent injustice and took raging retaliation against Jim Burger, spinning the Cedar Falls driver into a chain-reaction accident that involved most of the cars in the late model field and eventually sent Burger's car to the pits, dangling from the boom of a Tunis wrecker.

Sanger's ire seemed to stem from what he thought was Burger's deliberate forcing of Sanger's No. 95 Monte Carlo off the track three laps earlier as Sanger tried to gain the lead — but many fans saw the incident in a different light and several drivers condemned Sanger's fender-smashing method of gaining revenge.

Burger, who left the track immediately after the feature and could not be reached for comment, apparently made the original move against Sanger under pressure, having had two wide margins erased earlier by restarts.

Starting in the No. 4 position, Burger moved to the front on the second circuit when first-lap leader John Webb of Independence went out with engine trouble. Burger quickly built up a commanding lead, heading the pack by almost one-quarter lap, but had the distance erased on the 14th lap when Dave Bedard of La Porte City spun, forcing a restart.

Burger survived that restart, fighting off Waterloo's Joe Schaefer, and stretched his lead out to three car lengths, only to have a spin by Karl Sanger of Waterloo, running third, bring out the red flag again.

This time, Burger found Ed Sanger right behind him on the restart. He outran Sanger through the first three turns, but on the fourth Ed made his move to the outside.

Trying desperately to avoid being passed, Burger rode high out of the groove and laid iron on Sanger, forcing him over the rim. The maneuver successfully thwarted Sanger, but still proved costly as Schaefer took advantage of Burger's exit from the groove and went by on the low side.

Burger's move was even costlier for Sanger.

The brief detour over the rim dropped Ed from second to eighth, and the Sanger that stormed back into the pack bore no resemblance to the Sanger that had been pushed out of it.

Driving as if possessed, Sanger charged full-throttle around the track, riding the fenders of other cars through the curves and muscling his way back toward the front.

In just two laps, Sanger moved back behind Burger, now running third behind Schaefer and Dike's Curt Hansen. Then, on the fourth turn of the 23rd lap, Schaefer got sideways and tangled with Hansen.

Burger slowed behind the mishap, but Sanger barrelled right into his rear end. Burger slide sideways and Sanger bumped him again, sending him spinning into the straightaway where he was hit by several other cars and finally broadsided by Bedard.

The rest is history. Burger was hauled to the pits and Sanger passed both Schaefer and Hansen on the restart to take the $350 top money. Burger was credited with a 12th place finish.

"Too many people have begun to think you don't have any right to pass on the outside," Sanger said after the race. "I got tired of being pushed around when I try to pass on the outside. When Burger hit me, I decided I was going to get back in there and get the race, even if I had to do some

See TUNIS
Continued on page 14, col. 7

Bedard's Car Survives Crash To Win Feature

By LARRY D. SPEARS
Courier Sports Writer

La Porte City's Dave Bedard ran into another car, but Larry Wasserfort of Cedar Falls ran into rear end problems and Bedard still managed to take home the $350 winner's share in Tunis Speedway's inaugural late model feature Sunday night.

Bedard, who had streaked to a two-car-length win over Wasserfort in the first heat race of the night, got into trouble in a special Australian pursuit race held just before the feature.

$107,500 Asked In Speedway Suit

A Polk County man claims that a broken lease concerning use of Tunis Speedway will cost him over $57,000, according to a damage suit filed Friday in district court.

The charge is made in a $107,500 suit filed by William J. Moyner against J. L. Tunis of Tunis Speedway in Waterloo.

Earlier this year, the petition states, Moyer and Tunis negotiated for purchase by Moyer of the speedway, but "because of misrepresentations on the part of (Tunis,) the sale was not consummated."

Lease Arrangement

Instead, a lease agreement was entered into under which Moyer operated the speedway for a rental fee of $500 per racing program.

However, after two nights of racing, Tunis "wrongfully terminated the lease agreement," the petition alleges.

Moyer states he realized profit of $3,000 on each of the first two nights of racing.

With 18 potential nights remaining on the summer program, Moyer claims losses of $54,000, according to the petition, because of the alleged premature lease termination.

The suit also seeks $50,000 for damages to Moyer's business and personal reputation, and reimbursement for $3,500 expended to publicize the racing programs.

1973
In the News

Jim Fickess' Column

Tunis Changes Schedule Format for Sunday Card

TUNIS SPEEDWAY PROMOTERS have changed both the schedule and format for Sunday night's stock car racing program.

Due to the interest shown in the powder-puff derby last week, another women's race will be run Sunday to accomodate the surplus of aspirant female stockers from last Sunday.

"We had 26 girls sign up for last Sunday and we just ran out of cars," said powder-puff organizer, Mrs. Marlene Stricker, wife of Tunis co-promoter . Claus.

"This week we'll have a car for everyone who signed up last week." The gals will be driving roadrunner machines again this week.

Stricker has cancelled the Hare 'N Hounds event for this week due to additional powder-puff derby as well as some scheduling difficulties.

"LAST WEEK WE tried to get the races in on time," said Stricker, referring to a court order of last year which said Tunis races should be over by 10 p.m. "We would have made it if it hadn't been for so many restarts late in the program. We're sure going to try to make the deadline this weekend!"

Stricker also said he had been having problems lining up cars for a possible Hare 'N' Hounds race Sunday, but indicated he planned to schedule the event for future programs.

Sportsmen Eliminated

The track management has also changed the class division of the cars, putting the sportsman machines in with the late-models.

"We're dropping the sportsmen because of lack of cars competing in that class," Stricker said.

"I've changed the pay-off for the late-model events. , so the sportsmen can pick up some money even though they don't finish too high. Also I've added a third heat to accomodate the extra cars. It met with the approval of the sportsman drivers I talked to,"Stricker asserted. "Both they (the sportsman drivers) and I agree that they can be competitive with some of the late-models," he added.

KEITH BRAUN, ONE of the top sportsman point-getters, decided to pull out of Tunis in favor of the Dubuque Speedway before Stricker made his decision to run the sportsman with the late-models. The Cedar Falls circle-burner cited an incident during last Sunday's powder-puff event which caused him to leave Tunis.

Braun's wife, Becky, and his sister, Janie, allegedly were the third and fourth women to sign up for the powder-puff, but were not provided roadrunner cars to drive. The two .who were originally under the impression they could compete in sportsman cars, took Braun's and Ron Plum's machines on the track and were black-flagged.

Stricker and Braun both admitted the incident was one in a series of misunderstandings between themselves. Plum, who is Mrs. Braun's brother, indicated that he too is also considering competing at Dubuque on Sundays.

Judd Tunis Returns to Racing

Judd Tunis will return to active stock car race promoting for the first time since 1969 when he assumes management of the quarter mile track that bears his name here Sunday.

Tunis announced Tuesday that he is forming a partnership with Claus Stricker of Waterloo to replace the Des Moines-based corporation, International Raceway, Inc., which promoted the first two racing cards of the season here last Sunday and two weeks ago.

Stricker, associated with stock car racing for the past 12 years, served as track maintenance and pit maintenance director for Keith Knaack of Vinton who managed the track here the past three years. Illness has forced Knaack out of racing and his interest in the Tunis track here was assumed by International Raceway, Inc., earlier this spring.

Tunis said his track will operate without a racing circuit connection, but will adhere to the general rules and format that have been observed here in the past.

He said that, starting Sunday, the purses will be increased from $2,000 to $2,600 for a program with a victory in the main worth $500 to the winner.

Mayner Cops Tunis Late-Model Feature

By JIM FICKESS
Courier Sports Writer

Dr. Al Mayner batted 1.000 at Tunis Speedway Sunday night as he won both late-model stock car races in which he competed.

The Winthrop physician claimed the 25-lap late-model

on the 166th lap of a Sunday afternoon race at the Iowa State Fair. The Reinbeck circle-burner competed in a pair of borrowed cars, using Jim Mauer's machine in the semi-main before getting a ride from Denny Osborn in the feature, but failed to place high in either event.

as he took the lead for good from Raymond's Dan Etringer on the sixth circuit.

Tunis co-promoter Claus Stricker, a former stock car driver, was able to elude the two hound cars drven driven by Larry Johnson and Greg Heath, both of Cedar Falls to win the Hare 'N' Hound mini-

Mechanics' Race on Tunis Card

Tunis Speedway is scheduled to run its final regular program of stock car racing this year tonight before next Sunday's season championship card.

Tonight's action will feature a mechanics' race where pit crew members will get a chance for some glory by driving the cars they usually work on.

Reinbeck's Stan Stover enjoys a sizable late-model point lead going into tonight's competition but Karl Sanger of Waterloo could overtake him and earn the pole spot for next Sunday's 50-lap championship with an extremely successful performance this evening.

Races are scheduled to get under way at 8 p.m. at the Tunis quarter-mile oval located behind the old Welles Department Store off Highway 218.

Knaack Steps Down at Tunis

Tunis Speedway, site of weekly Sunday night modified stock car racing sponsored by Carpac, Inc., will be under new management this year. Health has forced Keith Knaack of Vinton to step down.

Knaack, also editor of the Hawkeye Racing News, suffered a heart attack last winter and his recovery has been slower than originally anticipated.

Dralle Stays in Front

By JIM FICKESS
Courier Sports Writer

Evansdale's Red Dralle led all through the race to capture the second 25-lap late model feature of the Tunis Speedway season Sunday night.

In the sportsmen's feature, Keith Braun of Cedar Falls grabbed the lead from Jack Mitchell, whose car began to falter on the tenth lap, and coasted to the 15-lap victory.

feature victory as Mitchell, also of Cedar Falls, captured the other two Sportsmen races — the six-lap trophy dash and the first heat by large margins.

The opening event of the card, the trophy dash, will feature a different classification of car from week to week.

Usually a late-model event, Iowa International Raceways, Inc. plans to alternate the

at it during the first program of the season.

Grundy Center's Duane Van Deest won the 15-lap roadrunner feature which concluded the evening's races.

The program got started a little late due to an extremely wet and muddy track which had to be dried out by the cars taking slow warm-up laps.

LATE MODEL

FIRST HEAT — 1. Joe Schoeller (Waterloo); 2. Red Dralle (Evansdale); 3.

Martin (Independence); 4. Karl Sanger (Waterloo).

FEATURE — 1. Dralle; 2. Curt Hansen (Dike); 3. Stover; 4. Sanger; 5. Tom Bartholomew (Waterloo); 6. Mayner; 7. Martin.

SPORTSMEN

TROPHY DASH — 1. Jack Mitchell (Cedar Falls); 2. Denny Osborn (Cedar Falls); 3. John Weers (Waterloo).

FIRST HEAT — 1. Mitchell; 2. Osborn; 3. Roger Buchholz (Cedar Falls); 4. Ron Plum (Waterloo).

SECOND HEAT — 1. Keith Braun (Cedar Falls); 2. Tom Moore (Waterloo); 3. Bill Pierce (Waterloo); 4. Gene Earley (Ackley).

FEATURE — 1. Braun; 2. Osborn; 3. Weers; 4. Plum; 5. Buchholz; 6. Greg Konli (Waterloo).

1974
In the News

Dennis Peters 'critical' after surgery

Mid-season race ends on 38th lap after crash

By JIM FICKESS
Courier Sports Writer

An accident which injured five persons, one critically, cut short Sunday night's mid-season championship stock car racing program at Tunis Speedway.

The accelerator on Roger Klingfus' car apparently stuck on the 38th lap of the 50-circuit Ira (Speed) Chumley Memorial late model mid-season title race causing his car to go off the first turn of the quarter-mile track, through a fence and straight into the roadrunner pits.

Klingfus' car collided with Dennis Peters' roadrunner machine which was parked 100 feet beyond the retaining fence, critically injuring the 20-year-old Peters who was pinned between the two cars.

THE RACE was called at that point and Tom Bartholomew was declared the winner.

Peters remained in critical condition at Waterloo's Allen Memorial Hospital Monday morning after being in surgery for almost nine hours. The Denver resident sustained multiple fractures of both legs and severe injuries to the lower body.

Three other people were taken to the hospital.

David Cobb, 26, of Cedar Falls is currently in Sartori Memorial Hospital in good condition with possible back injuries.

A roadrunner driver, Steve Hatcher, 21, also of Cedar Falls, sustained a foot injury and was treated and released at Sartori.

KLINGFUS, himself, was treated for shock at Schoitz Memorial Hospital and released.

A fifth person who was injured, Dwayne Wright of Waterloo, was not taken to the hospital. He was hit by a piece of the fence.

After he and other track officials were able to clear out a throng of curious on-lookers from the roadrunner pits and get the crash victims on ambulances, promoter Claus Stricker met with the 18 drivers still left in the Chumley Memorial, who agreed to call it a race after 38 laps instead of continuing it next Sunday.

The roadrunner feature, which was to be run after the 50-lapper, was postponed until next Sunday.

Eyewitnesses agree the accident was caused by a mechanical malfunction.

Denny Pencil, 17 of Denver, who was sitting next to Peters on the hood of the car.

"I SAW the car crash

See TUNIS
Continued on page 12, Col. 1

MONTY PENCIL of Denver looks over the wreckage of a roadrunner car he was sitting on during Sunday's stock car racing program at Tunis Speedway. Roger Klingfus' car went through the fence dividing the roadrunner pits from the track during the Ira (Speed) Chumley Memorial Mid-Season Championship and struck the parked car. Dennis Peters, who was unable to jump out of the way of Klingfus' oncoming car, was pinned between the two autos. He was listed in critical condition at Allen Memorial Hospital Monday morning. Pencil was able to get out of the way in time and was uninjured. (Courier photo by Jim Wigdahl)

Nesteby takes point lead in final regular season race at Tunis

By SCOTT SERGEANT
Courier Sports Writer

D. Arthur Nesteby of Waterloo accomplished three things in winning the late model feature at Tunis Speedway Sunday night.

The victory was the third feature win at Tunis this season for him; it was his second feature win of the weekend; and with the win, he moves into first place on the point standings board at Tunis for late models this season.

The third accomplishment could not come at a better time for Nesteby. Sunday was the last regular season program for Tunis as next week is the season championship at the Waterloo quarter-mile oval.

Nesteby captured his sixth consecutive late model feature at Boone.

The veteran Waterloo driver took over the lead in Sunday's feature on the third lap following one of just two restarts during the relatively accident-free race. He received stiff competition from four other drivers for the next 17 laps but was beginning to pull away from them at the end.

Roger Klingfus stayed right on Nesteby's tail the minute the winner took to the front. Jack Mitchell joined the chase as did Bartholomew of Waterloo and Red Dralle of Evansdale. But one by one, the four began to slip back until the 22nd lap when Nesteby put it out of reach when he opened up about a coming in the opening race and Mitchell's the very next one.

Burger took over the lead from Jim Buhlman of Waterloo on the seventh lap and won easily. Mitchell had a more difficult time handling Nesteby, Klingfus and Karl Sanger of Waterloo in the second heat.

Larry Sommerfelt won the roadrunner feature after he came from almost nowhere from the middle of the pack on the ninth lap to bolt into the lead for good in the 15-lap event. O that lap, a made scramble for position resulted in leader Dave Frost of Waterloo dropping to fifth, fifth place Ivan Chip of Waterloo moving to third and Sommerfelt taking the lead from his fourth-place position.

LATE MODELS

FIRST HEAT—1. Jim Burger (Cedar Falls), 2. Don Etringer (Raymond), 3. Jim Buhlman (Waterloo), 4. Roger Bucholz (Cedar Falls)

SECOND HEAT—1. Jack Mitchell (Cedar Falls), 2. Roger Klingfus (Cedar Falls), 3. D. Arthur Nesteby (Waterloo), 4. Karl Songer (Waterloo)

SEMI—1. Red Dralle (Evansdale), 2. Tom Bartholomew (Waterloo), 3. Greg Kostli (Waterloo), 4. Chuck Smith (Waterloo), 5. Tom Moore (Waterloo)

CONSOLATION—1. Bedard, 2. Denny Osborne (Cedar Falls), 3. Bob Hilmer (Dysart), 4. Hesse

FEATURE—1. Nesteby, 2. Klingfus, 3. Mitchell, 4. Osborne, 5. Songer, 6. Dralle, 7. Etringer, 8. Smith, 9. Kostli, 10. Bucholz

TROPHY DASH—1. Bartholomew, 2. Songer, 3. Dralle, 4. Osborne

ROADRUNNERS

FIRST HEAT—1. Dave Frost (Waterloo), 2. Mike Moslek (Cedar Falls), 3. Steve Hatcher (Waterloo)

SECOND HEAT—1. Duane Von Deest (Waterloo), 2. Roger Persson (Cedar Falls), 3. Larry Sommerfelt (Waterloo), 4. Ron Kent (Waterloo)

FEATURE—1. Sommerfelt, 2. Von Deest, 3. Kent, 4. Frost.

Tunis banquet to be Oct. 26

Tunis Speedway's season-ending banquet is scheduled for Oct. 26 at the UAW Security Hall.

Any interested persons should contact Klaus Stricker, 232-0673, to make reservations for the Saturday night social hour, dinner and program.

Wet track prevents Tunis start

Tunis Speedway's planned season-opening program Sunday night was not run since the quarter-mile dirt track was too wet.

Tunis promoter Claus Stricker plans tto open the season next weekend with races both Sunday night and on the following evening, Memorial Day.

Race time is 7:30 p.m.

Jim Fickess' column

Stricker to operate Tunis; Races will start May 19

THE LEGAL WORK has been completed. Mr. and Mrs. Claus Stricker's Cedarloo Raceways Inc. will lease Tunis Speedway from that quarter-mile oval's owner, Judd Tunis, for the upcoming stock car season.

Stricker, a long-time driver and track manager at Tunis, co-promoted the races with Tunis last season. This year, however, Tunis will not be active in the promotion end of racing as Stricker has an independent leasing contract similar to that of Keith Knaack's CarPac, Inc., when that group managed the track a couple of years back.

No drastic changes in the Tunis format are planned. Races will be run every Sunday night again and will start a half-hour earlier than in the past, 7:30 instead of 8 p.m.

Stricker hopes the move will accomplish several goals. First of all, it will save energy since the track lights will have to be used less. The earlier finish will make going to the races more attractive to people who have to work early on Monday mornings and help end complaints from near-by residents about the noise late Sunday evening.

The field will be divided into two brackets, late-models and roadrunners, as it was during the final half of last season. The individual races themselves will be the same length.

Stricker is optimistic that many new faces will be in the starting lineup when Tunis Speedway plans to open on May 19.

Muffler experiment

Vern Weber's Greater Iowa Racing Assn. will once again promote stock car races in Independence and Dubuque. Weber is planning for a Saturday night, May 4, start at the Buchanan County Fairgrounds while he anticipates the Dubuque County Fairgrounds will probably open up for action on Sunday night, May 12.

Weber has started his Independence programs sooner in the past, but has decided to cut out a few of the earlier programs this year due to the gasoline shortage.

A progressive move will be undertaken at Independence—the mandatory use of mufflers on the racing machines.

"It's really an experimental thing, that's for sure,' Weber said in reference to his decision. "We used to always say we needed noise to have an attractive racing program and we were probably right. But since then the size of engines have doubled and so has the amount of noise they make," Weber pointed out.

"I think it will provide a much more pleasant atmosphere and draw more people out to the races if we use mufflers, especially at Independence. The closed grandstand there intensifies the sound," he went on.

Weber has strong evidence to back his contention. "I was lucky enough to be a part of the Promoters' Prime Panel at Daytona. I really was exposed to some good ideas down there," said Weber.

"A lot of promoters have been forced to do it, and they all think it was really great," Weber revealed. "It increased everybody's attendance."

WEBER WILL GIVE the drivers until June 1 to have the mufflers on their cars. "The kind of mufflers they'll need to run at Independence are inexpensive, as cheap as $8. With them on, the cars will sound similar to street cars that have Hollywood or glass-pack mufflers," Weber asserted. "There will still be the noise, which is necessary, but it will be a more pleasing sound."

Stricker, at the present time, doesn't intend to make mufflers mandatory. However, he expects most of his cars will be equipped with them if they are required at very many area tracks.

Both Cedarloo and Greater Iowa Racing also plan to have their cars go from rain tires, used last year, to super sport tires. This will cut down racing expenses since the super sports are not only less expensive than the rain tires, but are much more durable.

Weber will once again offer packages of season tickets for a 20 per cent reduction of the regular prices, which are the same as last year's.

Hilmer fifth Tunis winner in five nights

By JIM FICKESS
Courier Sports Writer

Bob Hilmer drove unscathed through 25 laps of wreck-marred stock car racing to win Sunday night's late model feature at Tunis Speedway.

The Dysart veteran, making his second Tunis appearance of the season, became the fifth different late model driver to take home first place feature money in as many nights of racing action at the quarter-mile dirt oval.

In all, five wrecks necessitated restarts during Sunday's main event.

THE MOST controversial ... ning Dr. Al Mayner of Winthrop from Tunis for a week.

Mayner was accused of deliberately forcing Waterloo's Joe Schaefer off the track coming into the No. 4 turn after their cars allegedly crashed into each other down the back straight.

Mayner went head-long off the track and was immediately black-flagged and punished by Stricker.

The popular Schaefer was able to keep his car running only to be involved in a pile-up on the 19th lap which knocked his out for the night.

Still, he managed to finish 10th as only nine of the starting 16 cars were running ... defending track champion Stan Stover who tangled with Tom Bartholomew, last week's feature winner, down the back chute on the fifth lap.

LATE MODELS

FIRST HEAT—1. Jim Burger (Cedar Falls); 2. D. Arthur Nesteby (Waterloo); 3. Chuck Smith (Waterloo); 4. Willy Klingfus (Cedar Falls).

SECOND HEAT—1. Dr. Al Mayner (Winthrop); 2. Jack Mitchell (Cedar Falls); 3. Joe Schaefer (Waterloo); 4. Bob Hilmer (Dysart).

TROPHY DASH—1. Stan Stover (Reinbeck); 2. Karl Songer (Waterloo); 3. Red Drosle (Waterloo).

SEMI—1. Stover; 2. Red Dralle (Evansdale); 3. Songer; 4. Roger Klingfus (Waterloo); 5. Denny Osborne (Cedar Falls); 6. Droste.

CONSOLATION—Roger Buchholz (Cedar Falls).

FEATURE—1. Hilmer; 2. Dralle; 3. Nesteby; 4. Droste; 5. Tom Bartholomew (Waterloo); 6. Songer; 7. Smith; 8. Jack Mitchell (Cedar Falls); 9. Burger; 10. Schaefer.

ROADRUNNERS

HEAT—1. Dave Frost (Waterloo); 2 ...

THE REINBECK circle-burner was running exceptionally well, having won the trophy dash and semi-main earlier in the evening before moving all the way up to fifth from his 14th spot on the starting grid before being knocked out.

Mayner, who claimed the second heat's checkered flag, inadvertently put another driver out of a few races before the program even started. The Flying Physician headed straight for the pits after hot-laps, not seeing Waterloo's Mike Maurer, who was to his right. Mayner hit Mauer sending him to a car sitting of the track. Mauer was unable to get his car ready by the heat races but did compete in the semi-main.

Cedar Falls' Jim Burger, a comfortable winner in the first late model heat, started the feature on the outside of the first row and built up a relatively large margin before the first red flag on the third lap. He clung to the lead for two more laps before Hilmer took over first for good after the second restart of the event.

HILMER, WHO started on

See TUNIS WINNER
Continued on page 17, col. 3

Stover wins in new car

By JIM FICKESS
Courier Sports Writer

It was just like last year for Stan Stover, with one important exception—a new car—as the Reinbeck stock car driver won the late model feature at Tunis Speedway's season-opening program Sunday night.

Stover, who won big (the 1973 season championship race)du during his last appearance at the quarter-mile dirt oval last fall, took a while to regain his winning form Sunday night.

He finished second in his ... though Waterloo's Joe Schaefer might continue his hot streak from the night before.

Schaefer, who won the feature at Independence Saturday night, captured both the third heat and trophy dash at Tunis. He started far back in the pack in the feature and could manage only a fourth place finish although his car was running exceptionally well on the fast track.

The close late model heats

See STOCKS
Continued on page 14, col. 1

1975
In the News

Nesteby wins 50-lapper; breakdown foils Dralle

By RUSS L. SMITH
Courier Sports Editor

A breakdown on the 26th lap ended Red Dralle's bid for a fourth straight late model stock car victory Sunday night and point-leader D. Arthur Nesteby went from a first-place start to first-place finish to cop the 50-lap Tunis Speedway feature.

Nesteby of Waterloo, the defending champion and current point leader, started on the pole and gradually pulled away from the No. 2 starter, Glen Martin of Independence, to pick up the $500 prize and the mid-season championship after the rear end gave out on Dralle's car as it bounced through a soft spot on the first turn.

Nesteby zipped by Dralle on the inside and maintained a steady pace for the remaining 24 laps of a race that took its toll in machinery but was devoid of accident and moved swiftly from start to finish

52 Waterloo Courier Sun., Aug. 3, 1975

who won here last Sunday and also won at Dubuque Friday and Independence Saturday. "I'd have won in the usual 20-lap feature."

While Dralle has been hot, Nesteby has had his problems lately. "I hope this changes my luck," he said. "You know, I completely gave up tonight after the first lap. I don't know what happened. Something just snapped the wheel right out of my hands and I was way back."

He was in fifth place after starting in front, but soon he was back up in third trailing Bob Hesse and Dralle. Hesse dropped out with his radiator smoking after 18 laps and then it was a two-man race between similar cars.

"I sold Red that car earlier this year," said Nesteby. "We were both driving exactly the same gears and the same engine so it figures we'd be running right together."

Nesteby's car is a 1964 Chevelle and Dralle's a '70 Chevelle.

While the late model feature went off without flaw not so most of the other seven races on the program that lasted about three hours and a half.

John Weers of Readlyn, No. 2 in the point standings, survived restart-after-restart to win both the sportsman's heat and 25-lap mid-season feature.

Early leader Ray Abernathy of Brandon went out of the heat race after throwing a wheel.

In another race marred by frequent minor accidents causing restarts, Kenneth Kent won the 20-lap roadrunner mid-season race.

The program was interrupted once by efforts to repair the bump on the No. 1 turn. Over 3,000 paid to see the second race card on Tunis' new three-eighths mile track.

Jim Fickess' column

Finishing touches in progress at Tunis

ALTHOUGH FOUR NIGHTS of stock car racing have already been run on Tunis Speedway's three-eighths of a mile track, finishing touches are still being put on the new oval.

Among the improvements which will have been completed at the Waterloo track by Sunday's scheduled program, or will be made in the near future, are the widening of the front straightaway, retiling the track and a revamping of the lighting systems to better fit the longer, wider track.

The tiling project was completed this past week. Hopefully, it will help alleviate the problem of water under the area of the No. One turn.

A pump was used this past weekend to take some of the water out of that problem spot. Despite the recent dry weather, the pump ran all day Saturday and there was still some water left come Sunday night.

However, the holes caused by the underground water weren't as bad as usual this past Sunday. More progress should come with the retiling.

The track widening will start out of the No. 4 turn. In essence, the front straightaway will be regraded, blending it in with the old oval. Tunis promoter Claus Stricker estimates the new front straight will give the drivers 15 to 20 feet more feet to work with.

Wheel barrow race

Tunis Speedway will offer an added attraction Sunday night—a wheel barrow race. Six of the track's leading late model stock car drivers and their pit crews will compete for the keg of beer.

The race consists of the pit crews pushing their drivers around the quarter-mile oval in a wheel barrow. Drivers and their crews participating will be: Glen Martin, D. Arthur Nesteby, Joe Schaefer, Tom Bartholomew and Denny Osborn.

Sunday's program will also include two roadrunner heats. Last Sunday's roadrunner event wasn't run because of a hole in the fence in front of the main grandstand area caused by Rick Swartz' spectacular wreck. No one was seriously injured although Swartz' car went over the guard rail, through the fence and

In The Spring . . .

. . . a young man's fancy may very likely turn to thoughts of racing cars. And for those of you who'd like a closer look at some of the cars, stop by College Square anytime from May 16-23. We'll be displaying quarter midgets and the nicer looking stock cars, compliments of Tunis Speedway. You may just decide to take up racing yourself.

* * *

Tunis banquet next Saturday

Tunis Speedway will hold its annual post-season next Saturday night, Nov. 8, at the United Auto Workers' Local 838 Security House.

The evening will include a dinner, dance and awards presentation.

Tunis promoter Claus Stricker invites any interested stock car racing fans to attend. For further information and to make reservations, contact Stricker, 922 Franklin, Cedar Falls, 277-2216.

Takes career-high $7,000 purse

Sanger wins World 100

Successful Waterloo stock car driver Ed Sanger enjoyed the biggest win of his career in 1974 when he captured the lucrative World 100 race at Rosburg, Ohio's Eldora Speedway.

Sanger took home $7,000 for his victory in the 100-lap race on a half mile track. A total of 126 cars tried to qualify for the 22-car final field.

Other Waterloo racers made their mark in national contests.

Jim Sanborn finished fourth in the Sports Car Club of American's national championship at the Road Atlanta course. Sanborn was driving a B-Production Corvette. He also won the B-Production championship at Brainerd International Speedway.

Another Waterloo sports car racer, Tim Lind, piloted the Lind Brothers D-Production Jensen-Healey in the June Sprints at the Road American course.

Racing at home was good in

second portion of the season.

Nesteby claimed the 50-lap late model championship after winning four regular-season wins at Tunis. The Waterloo circle-burner also dominated the second portion of the Independence season as well as winning the final eight features at the Boone Speedway, from the mid-season race through the season championship.

The first part of the Tunis season was extremely well-balanced. Seven different drivers won the first seven Tunis features of the season.

The mid-season title event at Tunis was marred by an accident which injured five persons, one critically.

The accelerator on Roger Klingfus' car apparently struck on the 38th lap of the 50-lap mid-year title race and went off the first turn, through a fence and into the roadrunner pits. Denny

dragstrip located four miles north of Cedar Falls on Highway 218, went from a quarter-mile in racing length to an eighth-mile in 1974.

Two meets highlighted the 1974 NEITA season—the American Hot Rod Assn. Record Run and the Third Annual Street and Stock Bash.

The NEITA racers improved the quality of competition at the strip by setting 57 new AHRA records. That pretty well ended the problem of breaking-out, or disqualification for going faster than a national record, which plagued the early portion of the NEITA season.

Tom Akin promoted the Street and Stock Bash and brought in a pair of nationally-known fuel-burning funny cars for the event.

The largest NEITA crowd in several years watched Tom Hoover of Minneapolis better Charlie Proite's Pabst Blue Ribbon Dodge Charger in the best-out-of-three match race.

Auto racing

Jim Fickess' column

Changes in store for racing season

THE 1975 IOWA racing season, scheduled to get underway this weekend, promises several new features.

Changes made over the winter include: new promoters at two racing establishments, different racing nights for a pair of stock car tracks, two improved dirt ovals, a three-class setup at Waterloo's Tunis Speedway and a surprising number of new stock cars in action.

The Mid-Continent Racing Assn., under the leadership of Homer Melton, submitted the best bid in the off-season and will take over operations of Cedar Rapids' Hawkeye Downs. Since Melton's other two tracks—Davenport and Des Moines—run on Friday and Saturday, respectively, Hawkeye Downs switched its weekly night of competition to Sunday night.

That Cedar Rapids half-mile track is scheduled to begin its season 7:30 p.m. Sunday night.

With Hawkeye Downs changing days, it appeared for a while three tracks—Tunis Speedway, the Dubuque County Fairgrounds and Hawkeye Downs—would all be running Sunday night.

'Fun night' for Dralle

By DON KRUSE
Courier Sports Writer

When Red Dralle of Evansdale arrived at the pits Sunday night at Tunis Speedway, he announced that he was there for the fun.

Fun and all, Dralle certainly got more than he bargained for as he copped the top prize in the late model 50-lap championship race.

The big race, the late model 50-lapper, was pushed up on the program by Tunis promoter Claus Stricker when dark clouds started moving in early in the evening.

Stricker turned out the winner on that one when high winds and rain finally halted the races during the final event—the late model consolation 15-lapper.

The consolation event had officially clipped off only two laps when the rains came. Several red flags and restarts took place in that event when the drivers put a heavy foot on their gas pedals for what appeared would be a hot finale.

THE LARGE turnout which came to see D. Arthur Nesteby, the seasonal point-leader, and Karl Sanger duel it out in the 50-lap feature had to settle in their seats early when the race, slated last on the program, was moved up.

Oddly, though, Nesteby was the first to go as only nine of the 15 cars finished the race, and Sanger ended in third when it was all over.

Nesteby, exercising his option to take the outside start just as he did last year when he won this race, was in the lead after eight laps when his car came too strongly into the third turn and went over the bank, flipping over once before coming to a stop on its side. His gas pedal apparantly stuck after bolting the backstretch.

The popular Nesteby waved to the crowd's applause as he rode on the rear of his towed car, out of the race with front end damage.

With Nesteby gone, Bob Hilmer of Dysart took over and led for all but three laps until the gears went out of the quick-change.

But on the ensuing lap following Nesteby's mishap, Tom Hamilton of Jesup went off the back-side and the race had to be started for the third time.

SANGER LED briefly, on lap Nos. 9,

See STOCKS
Continued page 15, col. 4

RED DRALLE holds the trophy he received for winning Sunday night's late model stock car season championship race at Tunis Speedway. The Evansdale driver captured the 50-lap race with Denny Osborn of Cedar Falls finishing second.

Councilman Roehr reported receiving a letter as to noise at Tunis Speedway and asked the penalty for operating after hours. City Attorney Kennedy said this would come under the sound pollution ordinance.

Moved Getty, seconded Wilharm request of Carter's Sound Service, Cedar Rapids, Iowa, for permission to install and operate a Public Address System at Tunis Speedway on Highway #218, with events to be held each Sunday P.M. and various Holidays throughout the summer season, received, filed, permission granted and Police Department instructed to check area with sound meter this summer.

City council meeting minutes

TUNIS SPEEDWAY
OPENING NIGHT
LATE MODEL
STOCK CAR RACES

TONITE!!
MAY 18th . . .7:30 P.M.
This Sunday and Every Sunday
This Season . . . Races at 7:30 P.M.
NEW! . . . This Season
Sportsmen Class . . . and
Roadrunners
"THRILLS . . . EXCITEMENT
. . . and FUN"
HIWAY 218 (University Ave.)
Between W'loo and Cedar Falls (Across from Kmart)
FOOD and BEER AVAILABLE
On The Grounds
ADMISSION . . . ADULTS . . .$2.50
Children Under 12 FREE (With Parent)
BUCKAROO GATE . . .$1.50

44 Waterloo Courier Sun., May 25, 1975

Jim Fickess' column

Sells both drags and races stocks Sundays

INSTEAD OF BEING a time of leisure, Sunday is usually a busy day for auto racers.

It is a doubly hectic one this year for Waverly's Darrell Sells, who is the only driver to compete regularly at both NEITA Raceway and Tunis Speedway.

Sells had been away from stock car racing about five years before he bought a late model from Gene Sheetz in the off-season. The car was driven by Red Dralle, Red Droste and Larry Wasserfort last season.

He opened the Tunis campaign in the No. 31 Chevelle last Sunday night, winning a well-driven third heat and placing ninth in the feature. He also has run at Independence, Des Moines and Cedar Rapids stock car tracks this year.

SELLS HAS been competing at NEITA for three years, driving his red Malibu in the super stock class this season.

The 37-year-old owner-manager of a Cedar Falls service station hedges on picking his favorite sport.

"I really like them both, but I'd say I lean to stocks a little more," Sells says.

Naturally, Sells keeps a tight schedule on Sunday.

"It's kind of a trick," explains Sells with a laugh. "I just get done at NEITA in time to go home and eat supper real quick, then I go to Tunis. I couldn't do it if I didn't have someone else working on my stock car, that's for sure."

Duane Tjabring of Allison performs the mechanical preparations on the stock car while Sells does his own work on the drag car.

THIS WILL also be a doubly busy weekend for Sells' NEITA and Tunis colleagues.

Sunday is record day at NEITA as that eighth-mile strip is the site of the nation's first eighth-mile American Hot Rod Assn. Record Meet.

NEITA competitors will not only be trying to make the eliminator fields during morning time trials, but will also be out to set new AHRA class standards. No records can be set during the afternoon's eliminations. Time trials are scheduled to commence at 9:30 a.m. and eliminations 1:30 p.m.

Cedarloo Raceway promoter Claus Stricker scheduled an extra night of racing Monday to go along with Sunday's weekly program. Both races will be for the regular Tunis purse. Stock car races begin at 7:30 p.m. both nights.

1976
In the News

Hansen runs to early lead, wins stock finale

By JIM FICKESS
Courier Sports Writer

The first few laps Monday night provided the crucial ingredient in Curt Hansen's season-finale late model stock car feature win at Tunis Speedway.

Hansen, who got the top starting spot—the inside pole—by winning the first heat, bolted off to an astoundingly large lead by the end of the first five of the race's 35 laps.

Hansen, however, couldn't afford to let up as he in winning a Tunis feature the previous evening.

One big difference was the performance of Ed Sanger.

Sanger, who started 10th, soon worked his way out of the pack and was gaining on Hansen. Hansen encountered some difficulty lapping slower cars while Ed was turning the best times of the race. But, Sanger ran out of laps.

HANSEN LED by over a straight-away early. That margin had slipped to two lapped cars at the end. The Coca-Cola Night triumph was worth $600.

Bill Zwanziger finished six lapped vehicles behind Sanger in third. Gary Crawford and Roger Dolan rounded out the top five.

Hansen took the lead from Jack Mitchell on the eighth lap of the first 10-lap preliminary.

Joe Schaefer, a Waterloo driver who competes at Dubuque on Sundays (Tunis' normal race night), captured the second heat.

Bob Hilmer held on to nose out a charging Zwanziger in the third heat. Karl Sanger claimed the fourth 10-lapper.

Other late model events went to Glen Martin (the semi-main) and Bob Hesse (the consolation).

John Weers appeared to have the sportsman feature wrapped up, only to lose a wheel on the 12th lap.

Second-heat winner Steve Auringer went on to claim that race for his second double win in as many nights.

Weers had comfortably won the first heat.

ED SANGER appears to be heading for a national-best number of stock car feature wins. Ed elected to pull to Wisconsin for two races Sunday instead of racing at Tunis. He finished third and first in features for a total of 41 main event victories, the best of his career.

Sanger says the closest competitor he has read about is a California driver who had 35 features to his credit before this past week.

Patient Hansen wins Tunis

By JIM FICKESS
Courier Sports Writer

"I don't see why they (other late model drivers) try to win the feature on the first lap," said Curt Hansen after Sunday's stock car racing action at Tunis Speedway. "I just lay back awhile and try to keep the car straight when the track is like it was tonight."

That patient strategy paid off for Hansen, who breezed to victory in the 30-lap feature run on a treacherously dry, slick dirt track.

Hansen, however, had his difficult moments. Starting on the inside of the fifth row, he had to avoid four first-lap spinouts, caused by over-anxious drivers trying to get a jump at the start.

"I had to go off the track once and down into the infield another time," recalled Hansen. "And, I sprained a finger when I got it caught in the steering wheel one of those times."

THE POPULAR Dike driver had the lead by the third lap and maintained a straightaway long margin throughout the rest of the race on the three-eighth mile track.

Hansen admitted he "cooled it" most of the race.

"I had a big lead most of the race and won, but this isn't the kind of race I enjoy," continued Hansen.

"It's easier without Ed here, though," he admitted. Hansen was referring to Ed Sanger, who's enjoying his best winning season this year.

Sanger, who had won the previous two Tunis features, elected to run two races in Wisconsin Sunday.

However, he has indicated he'll be back in Waterloo for Monday's season-finale Coca-Cola Night races.

Sanger and Hansen are two of the favorites to win the $800 ... ceive a $500 bonus.

ALSO MISSING from Sunday's feature was Bill Zwanziger, who, along with Sanger and Hansen, has dominated the Tunis season.

Zwanziger ran impressively while winning the third heat but blew up the rear end of his car during hot lap warm-ups before the feature.

Jack Mitchell, who started on the outside pole, held off D. Arthur Nesteby for second place in the feature.

Karl Sanger was fourth and Red Dralle nipped Stan Stover for fifth.

The closest one-two finish of the evening came in the second late model semi-main.

Bob Hesse led most the race, driving with his hood raised in front of the windshield. But, Stover, managed to inch by him at the wire.

Bob Hilmer claimed the first semi.

Late model heat winners included Dave Trower, Mitchell, Zwanziger and Tom Fitzpatrick.

Steve Auringer enjoyed comfortable wins in both the first heat and feature of the sportsman class.

That main event was also marred by time-consuming restarts. Four red flags caused the 15-lapper to run for over 45 minutes.

There was no roadrunner class Sunday night although some thought there should have been. Promoter Claus Stricker had told that class that the previous Sunday was its last night for the season. He added they could run up in a better class, the sportsman, if their cars met safety standards.

Several roadrunners protested before Sunday's program but were not allowed to run since Stricker stuck to his previously-announced decision and none of the cars could ...

Just for the Fun of it. . . . .

Wheelbarrow Racing at Tunis Speedway

8,000 see Zwanziger win at Tunis

By JIM FICKESS
Courier Sports Writer

Bill Zwanziger won his second straight Tunis Speedway late model feature Sunday night in front of the largest crowd in the recent history of the Waterloo stock car track.

Tunis officials estimated a turnout of 8,000 including 4,500 paid admissions, 1,500 rain checks from last Sunday's cancelled program and 2,000 children under 12 years old who are admitted free with an adult.

The July 4 card with its fireworks is traditionally one of the top Tunis drawers.

The second half of Tunis' Fourth of July doubleheader is scheduled for 7:30 p.m. Monday. That features an open competition field vying for a $5,000 total purse.

ZWANZIGER overtook leader Tom Bartholomew on lap after a 17th-circuit restart in the feature. The Waterloo veteran held on for a football field-length victory.

He wasn't sure he could have won without that restart which bunched the field back together after a red flag.

"It's hard to say in a situation like this if my lead at the end was bigger than the lead Tom had when the red flag came out," said Zwanziger. "I could tell my car was running faster, though, when I did get around him and lengthen out a lead."

Zwanziger is on two win streaks. He claimed the last Tunis feature two weeks ago and won his second main event in as many nights Saturday, he captured the mid-season championship at Eldon.

HIS $600 feature earnings also vaulted him ahead of Ed Sanger in point standings at Tunis. Both had won $1,685 (a dollar equals a point) going into Sunday's action.

Sanger, meanwhile, finished third after starting in the back of the 21-car feature field. Ed failed to qualify in any of the preliminary events but gained a spot at the end of the feature starting grid because he's one of the top six point-getters.

Zwanziger began in the sixth two-car row under the inverted top 12 format where the front of the field lines up in ascending point order from 12th through 1st.

D. Arthur Nesteby led the early going of the feature before Bartholomew passed him on lap No. 8. Bartholomew ran first until being passed by Zwanziger.

Jack Mitchell finished fourth behind Sanger with Karl Sanger fifth and Curt Hansen second late model semi-main while Ken Hoeppner earned his first Tunis checkered flag in the first semi.

Jack White, Dick Schultz and Bartholomew were heat winners.

STEVE Auringer won the sportmen class' feature, taking the lead to stay on the third lap of the 15-lapper.

Curt Wellin took the first sportsman heat while Ben Schaefer survived a first lap pile-up for a win in the second heat. Only three cars were running after four cars were knocked out of commission by that accident.

Clarence Tucker and Fuzzy Liddell were roadrunner race victors.

John Straube had apparently defeated Tucker in the first event, but was disqualified when he failed to accept a $250 purchase claim on his car. The $250 claim is designed to keep roadrunner competitors from ...

LATE MODELS
FIRST HEAT—1. Jack White ...

Sanger 2 shy of season mark

By JIM FICKESS
Courier Sports Writer

Ed Sanger is fast approaching a season record in his brilliant stock car racing career.

Sanger won his fourth late model feature in three days Sunday night at Tunis Speedway to up his 1976 total to 38, just two short of the record 40 features he won in 1973.

This may be Ed's best year for total earnings, but it won't be his most profitable. Ever-increasing operating costs are taking bigger cuts of the purses.

"Expenses now are twice what they were in 1973 and almost three times what they were in 1971 when I won 37 features. That was my best year," said Sanger Sunday night.

"The purses haven't hardly gone up since then," he continued. "But I can see the promoters' point. They've got to make money, too. And, when they do pay more, they should pay more to the third through 10th places.

"Promoters like Claus (Tunis promoter, Stricker) have the right idea with that. Those guys have got as much money in their operations as we do. Things are alright with us so far. It's going to start hurting them before it does us."

Jack Mitchell in the first heat. Karl wound up sixth in the feature.

Zwanziger held off Ed throughout most of the second preliminary before going too high on the fourth turn of the ninth lap. Sanger went below him for the win.

Bjorge, who stepped by at Tunis after the Iowa State Fair race, edged Hansen in the third.

Bob Hilmer and Duane Van Deest won the late model semi-mains.

John Weers captured the sportsman feature after winning the first heat. Second heat winner Steve Auringer was second.

Fuzzy Liddell capped off the roadrunners' Tunis season finale with his 10th victory in that class.

Tunis plans a Labor Day doubleheader for next weekend. Sunday, a $1,500 purse will be offered. Fireworks will follow the racing show.

A $8,000 purse is up for Monday's race. Also, Stricker is offering a $500 bonus for any driver who has not raced at Tunis this year to win Monday's late model feature.

LATE MODELS
FIRST HEAT—1. Karl Sanger (Waterloo); 2. Jack Mitchell (Cedar Falls); 3. D. Arthur Nesteby (Waterloo); 4. Jim Summers (Waterloo).
SECOND HEAT—1. Ed Sanger (Waterloo); 2. Bill Zwanziger (Waterloo); 3. Stan Stover (Waterloo); 4. Red Dralle (Evansdale).

Sanger wins Mid-Season Tunis title

By JIM FICKESS
Courier Sports Writer

Ed Sanger bolted out ahead of Bill Zwanziger on the first lap and went on to win Sunday night's Mid-Season late-model stock car championship at Tunis Speedway.

"That early lead is what won it for me," said Sanger, who had just captured his fifth feature in a week and also his fifth Tunis main event triumph of the season.

Sanger, the second-leading Tunis late model point-getter going into the evening, started on the outside front row with top point driver Bill Zwanziger on the inside.

"Bill and I were neck-and-neck out of the second turn (of the first laps)," recalled Sanger. "It was the better traction on the high side that let me pull away.

"With a light car with a heavy engine, you can really tell when you are getting good traction, the car really takes off on you."

SANGER came out with about a three-car-length lead ... Bartholomew in a hard-fought battle for fourth position.

Red Dralle, driving Denny Osborn's car, placed fifth. Osborn has an injured hand.

Sunday's win climaxed a $4,000-plus week, Sanger indicated. He started it off last Monday night with an $800 feature win at Tunis and followed with victories at Oskaloosa Wednesday, Lake Superior Thursday, Cedar Rapids Friday and a second to Hansen Saturday at Eldon.

John Weers scored a relatively easy sportsmen mid-season title win while Gary Ekuall was declared the roadrunner champion in an accident-shortened race.

THE SPORTSMEN feature reflected the point standings as the top four placers finished in the same order.

Weers enjoyed a considerable distance over runner-up Steve Auringer in the 25-lapper while Roger Buchholz and Ben Schaefer were third and fourth, respectively.

Ekuall was running third when an accident started by ...

Hansen wins Tunis opener

By JIM FICKESS
Courier Sports Writer

Curt Hansen has a two-feature winning streak going at Waterloo's Tunis Speedway.

The Dike late model stock car driver set a blistering pace Sunday night to capture the season-opening main event on the three-eighths mile dirt track.

Hansen won the last feature of 1975. That open competition finale was the only time Curt ran at Tunis last season.

He's indicated he'll compete regularly here this year.

The second and third finishers in Sunday's feature were a couple of veteran Waterloo drivers who haven't competed at Tunis regularly—Ed Sanger and Bill Zwanziger.

Hansen started the 25-lapper on the pole while Ed was on the ...

Sanger wins Tunis feature on late move

By JIM FICKESS
Courier Sports Writer

Ed Sanger took full advantage of his one chance for the lead Sunday night and won the 25-lap late model stock car feature at Tunis Speedway.

That opportunity came on the next-to-last lap when Sanger was able to pass leader Bill Zwanziger on the backstretch.

"That's the first crack I had at getting past him," said Sanger. "I pulled up next to ... third in the feature while Dralle wound up fourth.

A fourth lap accident ended Curt Hansen's chances for a repeat late model feature victory.

Hansen, who won the season opener two weeks ago, hit Tom Bartholomew of Washburn broadside after Bartholomew had spun out between the No. 3 and 4 turns. Both cars were done for the evening.

A bad break also ended all chances for a title repeat in the ...

Sanger cruises to stock car crown

By JIM FICKESS
Courier Sports Writer

Ed Sanger doesn't believe in driving conservatively, no matter how big his lead.

"Once I get a pace going, I stick with it," said Sanger of his runaway victory in Sunday night's 50-lap season championship late model stock car race at Tunis Speedway.

"If the second or third place driver starts to gain on you, he thinks he can pass you and gets more confidence. You're in trouble then.

"Once you are in the lead, you can't drive too wildly because you could make a mistake and throw the race away," Sanger continued. "But, when you're in second, you think you have nothing to lose and you can give it hell."

RUNNERUP Tom Bartholomew, who changed his car's transmission in the Tunis pits, ran as hard as he could but couldn't mount a bid against Sanger.

"I really didn't know how much of a lead I had," said Sanger. "But I couldn't see anyone in my rearview mirror so I knew I was leading by a straightaway.

"I let up slightly the last 10 laps so I wouldn't risk blowing an engine or running over something on the track."

Sanger, the season's point leader, started the 50-lapper on the pole and led all the way.

The sportsman and roadrunner top point-getters, John Weers and Fuzzy Liddell, also scored decisive season title race victories to lock up total point championships.

Bill Zwanziger, who was outside of Sanger at the start of the late model feature, wound up third with Jack Mitchell fourth and Stan Stover, who won Sunday's races at the Iowa State Fair, was fifth.

Curt Hansen, winner of the last two regular season features at Tunis, dropped out on the first lap with a broken drive shaft.

CHUCK MOORE finished second to Readlyn's Weers in the 25-lap sportsman event. Moore was the only driver within striking distance of Weers most the race, but couldn't challenge him.

Only eight of the original 18 cars ran the final 10 laps of the 15-circuit roadrunner race, ...

Brother ends Sanger streak

By JIM FICKESS
Courier Sports Writer

It took a Sanger to break a Sanger winning streak Sunday night at Tunis Speedway.

Karl Sanger, whose brother, Ed, had won the last three late model features at the three-eighths mile stock car track, put on a late burst in Sunday night's 25-lapper to become the fourth driver to win a Tunis feature this season.

Karl turned in an impressively easy win in the third heat and started the feature on the outside of the fourth row.

He stayed among the short spurts," he said. "Sometimes you really get a good start then don't run so well at the end.

"I decided to save it for the end. I knew my car was running good enough that I could make a challenge if I got a chance. Sometimes you don't in such a short race."

Karl, who's four years older than Ed, runs a separate late model racing operation from his brother.

Ed, meanwhile, drove Gary Crawford's former car Sunday instead of his usual yellow and black Camaro. Crawford quit driving for Ed's four-car stable recently and purchased his own late model.

"I drove Gary's old car to get it working," said Ed. "It was running well but I made a couple of mistakes."

Ed finished fourth to third-place Em Fretheim in the

See TUNIS
Continued page 14, col. 3

LATE MODELS
FIRST HEAT—1. Curt Hansen (Dike); 2. Jim Summers (Waterloo); 3. Ken Hoeppner (Waterloo); 4. Tom Moore (Waterloo).
SECOND HEAT—1. Bob Hilmer (Dysart); 2. Em Fretheim (Decorah); 3. Dave Trower (New Hampton); 4. Jim Patterson (Cedar Falls).
THIRD HEAT—1. Karl Sanger (Waterloo); 2. Tom Bartholomew (Waterloo); 3. Ed Sanger (Waterloo); 4. Darrell Sells (Waverly).
FIRST SEMI-MAIN—1. Bill Zwanziger (Waterloo); 2. Tom Fitzpatrick (Gilbertville); 3. Duane Van Deest (Grundy Center); 4. Keith Pittmon (Waterloo).
SECOND SEMI-MAIN—1. Jack Mitchell (Cedar Falls); 2. Stan Stover (Waterloo); 3. Dick Schiltz (Waterloo); 4. D. Arthur Nesteby (Waterloo).
CONSOLATION—Red Dralle (Evansdale).
FEATURE—1. K. Sanger; 2. Bartholomew; 3. Fretheim; 4. E. Sanger; 5. Mitchell; 6. Nesteby; 7. Hansen; 8. Stover; 9. Sells; 10. Hilmer.
SPORTSMEN
FIRST HEAT—1. Steve Auringer (Waterloo); 2. Roger Buchholz (Cedar Falls); 3. Curt Wellin (Cedar Falls).
SECOND HEAT—1. John Weers (Readlyn); 2. Dave Rice (Waterloo); 3. Chuck Moore (Waterloo).
FEATURE—1. Weers; 2. Auringer; 3. Roger Buchholz (Cedar Falls).
ROADRUNNERS—1. Fuzzy Liddell (Cedar Falls); 2. Roger Patterson (Cedar Falls); 3. Don Cotton.

Stricker using new rules at Tunis for rest of year

Jim Fickess

TUNIS SPEEDWAY promoter Claus Stricker will be running his late model stock car races under a different set of rules starting Sunday night.

"I've thrown the old rule book out the window," reports Stricker.

In essence, Stricker has abandoned the point total system of structuring regular season races in favor of the open competition format, which until now has been used only for holiday specials on the three-eighths mile Waterloo oval.

Under open competition, a late model driver will draw for his position in the heats as he pulls into the Tunis pits each Sunday night. Then, his starting spot in the feature will be determined by his finish in the qualifying races with the heat winners starting up front of the main event pack.

The starting order was determined in the past by money winnings (or total points) with the highest earners going to the rear of the pack under the inverted starting setup.

CLAUS HAS also dropped the ban against late model cars with tube frames and has upped the purse to over $4,000 per night. First place in the late model feature will now pay $525, up $100, plus there will be a $100 bonus to win for anyone who does not have a Tunis feature victory to his credit this season.

All these changes should attract more drivers to Tunis, thinks Stricker. "A lot of drivers we've had up here for specials have indicated they'd like to race at Tunis regularly," says Stricker. "But, they're hesitant to come here and have to start out in the back of the pack right away (under the point system) and the ones with tube frames can't compete here at all."

Most Iowa tracks allow cars with tube frames, which are, of course, lighter than a solid frame car.

"Upping the purse and the $100 bonus is also a challenge to some of those guys who keep saying they could win a lot competing here regularly," Stricker adds. "We feel we have the state's best drivers here right now. But we sure are inviting other top drivers. We'll see how they'd do against our old regulars."

THE NEW open competition format will remain in effect until the season championship night, which is just five scheduled races away. Point standings will continue to be kept and the August 28 championship late model race will be based on them.

Stricker plans a Labor Day doubleheader special for the following weekend.

Plans for a Labor Day doubleheader the following weekend are in the works.

Stricker emphasizes the sportsmen and roadrunner classes will still use the point system. Also, the allowing of tube frames is the only technical rule that has changed.

Stover outruns Zwanziger

By DON KRUSE
Courier Sports Writer

Stan Stover of Reinbeck added his name to the list of late model feature winners at Tunis Speedway Sunday night, conquering a fast field.

Stover took the lead on the fifth lap after the first of two restarts and stayed ahead of Bill Zwanziger the rest of the way.

Zwanziger, the two-time feature winner at Tunis this season, chased Stover for 20 laps and finished second.

Klingfus ends Hansen Tunis string

By JIM FICKESS
Courier Sports Writer

Roger Klingfus benefited from Dave Plum's mechanical misfortunes Sunday night to win the 25-lap late model stock car feature at Tunis Speedway.

Klingfus' victory ended Curt Hansen's Tunis feature win string at five.

Klingfus, a veteran driver from Waterloo, ran second to Plum for the first 22 laps of the race.

Plum, whose Ford Mustang was the only non-Chevrolet product in the main event, appeared to have the race about put away after starting on the pole and leading all the way.

But, a spring fell off the coil of his engine, pulling the coil wire loose with it. That has the same effect as turning a car's key off—it kills the ignition.

KLINGFUS then inherited the lead. Dan Nesteby was running a close second but desperately attempted to overtake Klingfus on the low side on the final turn of the 25th lap. That unsuccessful maneuver cost Nesteby seven places and $225 in price money.

Klingfus garnered the $425 first place prize while Tom Bartholomew earned $325 for second. Nesteby's ninth place finish was good for $100.

None of the top point drivers, including Hansen, who start at the back of the pack under the inverted point order, were able to challenge for the lead.

As Nesteby proved on the last lap, drivers couldn't pass on the low groove of the Tunis three-eighths mile dirt oval Sunday night.

Jack Mitchell, who began in the front

Mon., June 27, 1977 Waterloo Courier 15

Curt Hansen ends drought at Tunis with late model victory

By JIM FICKESS
Courier Sports Writer

Curt Hansen, second-leading money-winner going into Sunday night's stock car races at Tunis Speedway, finally won his first late model feature of the year at that track.

Hansen earned the victory by getting by Ed Sanger on the low side during the 23rd of 25 laps. Sanger, the top Tunis cash earner, also is the owner of Hansen's race car.

Sanger wound up second, an exceptionally good finish considering a couple of problems he had in the feature. Ed hit the retaining barrier on the back straightaway during a fourth-lap accident but was able to keep his car going.

Later Sanger lost the lead to Dan Nesteby when he nearly spun out on the fourth lap.

Dysart veteran Bob Hilmer led the first four laps but dropped out at the first restart.

Jack Mitchell then assumed the lead and held it until Sanger passed him on lap No. 12.

Sanger held it for two circuits before Nesteby took advantage of the near spinout.

Ed went back into first place on the 18th lap only to lose it to Hansen.

Hansen has placed both second and third twice in previous Tunis main events. He's the sixth feature winner in eight nights of racing.

Greg Kastli, driving Tim Swope's car, captured the 15-lap sportsman feature, which was marred by five restarts. Swope is out with of action with a broken hand. Kastli also easily won the second sportsman heat.

Roger Patterson's five race roadrunner winning streak came to an end Sunday. Scott Braun won that class' feature. Patterson lost a wheel early and couldn't recover the ground he lost while fixing it.

Tunis promoter Claus Stricker banned late model driver Red Dralle from the track for the rest of the season after Dralle tried to dump a bucket of water on pit steward Dick Hinz. Dralle thought Hinz was going to disqualify Dick Schiltz, who was driving Dralle's car, for taking on water to cool his car during a feature restart.

Tunis is planning a Fourth of July open competition doubleheader for Sunday and Monday nights.

LATE MODELS

FIRST HEAT—1. Ed Sanger (Waterloo); 2. Bob Hesse (Waterloo); 3. Bill Zwanziger (Waterloo); 4. Stan Stover (Reinbeck).

SECOND HEAT—1. Bob Hilmer (Dysart); 2. Curt Hansen (Dike); 3. Denny Osborn (Cedar Falls); 4. Dan Nesteby (Waterloo).

SEMI-MAIN—1. Roger Klingfus (Waterloo); 2. George Brasil (Albuquerque, N.M.); 3. Jim Patterson (Cedar Falls); 4. Jim Brown (Ottumwa); 5. Mike Geltz (Evansdale); 6. Jack Mitchell (Cedar Falls).

CONSOLATION—Dave Plum (Waterloo).

FEATURE—1. Hansen; 2. Sanger; 3. Nesteby; 4. Klingfus; 5. Stover; 6. Mitchell; 7. Osborn; 8. Brown; 9. Hesse; 10. Schiltz.

SPORTSMEN

FIRST HEAT—1. Gary Schmidt (New Hampton); 2. Tom Moore (Waterloo); 3. Willy Klinglus (Cedar Falls).

SECOND HEAT—1. Greg Kastli (Waterloo); 2. Gene Ehlers (Independence); 3. Dave Venenga (Grundy Center).

SEMI-MAIN—1. Mike Krall (Waterloo); 2. Doug Frohm; 3. Bob Brenner (Jesup).

FEATURE—1. Kastli; 2. Venenga; 3. Brenner; 4. Ehlers; 5. Moore.

ROADRUNNERS

FIRST HEAT—Greg Seltz (Waterloo).

SECOND HEAT—Gary Kaune (Waterloo).

FEATURE—1. Scott Braun (Cedar Falls); 2. Dave Swarts (Cedar Falls); 3. Clarence Tucker.

Late Saturday

AT INDEPENDENCE

LATE MODEL

FIRST HEAT—1. Mike Geltz (Waterloo); 2. Dick Chapman (Dubuque); 3. Jack Mitchell (Cedar Falls); 4. Roger Bruggeman (Dubuque).

SECOND HEAT—1. Tom Fitzpatrick (Gilbertville); 2. Jim Burbridge (Delhi); 3. Bob Schulte (Delhi); 4. Joe Schaefer (Waterloo).

SEMI—1. Bill Barthelmes (Troy Mills); 2. Gary Crawford (Independence); 3. Larry Wasserfort (Waterloo); 4. George Brasil (Albuquerque, N.M.); 5. Dave Bentley (Fairbank); 6. Jim Patterson (Cedar Falls).

CONSOLATION—1. Bob Kinsello (Dubuque); 2. Jim Decker (Winthrop); 3. Harold O'Deen (Marion); 4. Steve Auringer (Waterloo).

FEATURE—1. Gary Crawford; 2. Tom Fitzpatrick; 3. Bill Barthelmes; 4. Dave Bentley; 5. Bob Schulte; 6. Jack Mitchell.

SPORTSMAN

FIRST HEAT—1. Rick Forbes (Evansdale); 2. Larry Doherty (Marion); 3. Jim Hirsch.

SECOND HEAT—1. Joe Churchill (Peosta); 2. Gary Henderson (Independence); 3. Duane Bentley (Fairbank).

SEMI—1. John Weers (Rodlyn); 2. Denny Ansel (Dubuque); 3. Carl Severson (Dubuque).

FEATURE—1. John Weers; 2. Denny Ansel; 3. Joe Churchill; 4. Duane Bentley; 5. Carl Severson; 6. Jim Methany (Shellsburg).

ROADRUNNERS

FIRST HEAT—1. Bob Rider.

SECOND HEAT—1. Bob Fisher.

CONSOLATION—1. Scott Braun (Cedar Falls).

FEATURE—1. Bob Fisher; 2. Daryl Slact (Vinton).

Courier photo by Tom Cochran

Stock car track championships are getting to be old hat for Dike's Curt Hansen this season. Here, Hansen stands behind his car with the Tunis Speedway championship trophy on the roof after he easily won the 50-lap championship late model feature. Hansen also has won the titles at Hawkeye Downs in Cedar Rapids and Des Moines.

Zwanziger wins feature

By JIM FICKESS
Courier Sports Writer

A near spinout on the 15th lap enabled Bill Zwanziger to take the lead in Sunday night's late model stock car feature at Tunis Speedway and the Waterloo veteran went on to win his third Tunis main event of the season.

Dan Nesteby, who started the race on the outside of the first row, beat pole sitter Ed Sanger into the race's first turn and led until his car started to drifted slightly sideways in the third turn of the 15th lap.

Zwanziger got by Nesteby there and went on to win by several car lengths over Sanger. Sanger passed Nesteby on lap No. 23. Dick Schiltz placed fourth.

A veteran of over 20 years of stock car racing, Zwanziger hadn't won at Tunis since the Memorial Day Special.

GREG KASTLI used a restart to help win the sportsman feature while two season champions were crowned inthe roadrunner class.

Marshalltown's Gary Eckvall apparently won the race, topping regular season point champion Roger Patterson of Cedar Falls.

But, a technical check after the race showed Eckvall had added weight to his car. He was originally disqualified for this, but because of a discrepancy in the rules, promoter Claus Stricker gave both drivers first place money.

PATTERSON LED the first three circuits of the 20-lap championship race before Scott Braun enjoyed a short-lived lead on the fourth lap. He rolled his car and Laverne Lehman was sent to the back of the pack for causing the accident. Braun was uninjured but his car was knocked out of commission.

Patterson led until the 15th lap before Eckvall, who started the race in the 15th point spot, caught him.

Tom Moore lost a big lead when the pack was rebunched on an eighth lap restart of the sportsman feature. He stayed ontop for three more laps before Kastli got by him for his second feature win in three nights at Tunis.

Moore wound up second with Mike Krall third.

ZWANZIGER FINISHED finished second to Sanger in the first late model heat. Zwanziger pulled even to Ed midway through the race but couldn't get by him.

Nesteby won the second head while Ron Plum breezed to victory in the late model semi-main.

Kastli also won the first sportsman heat while Moore took the second preliminary.

Dan Lake's car rolled over eight times after a second lap collision in the sportsman semi. He, too, was injured.

Betty Sanger, wife of late model driver Karl, easily won the special powder puff race for women.

Sunday's roadrunner season championship was the last action for that class at Tunis this season. Next Sunday is season championship night for both the late models and sportsmen.

The Tunis season concludes with a Labor Day doubleheader Sept. 4 and 5.

LATE MODELS

FIRST HEAT—1. Ed Sanger (Waterloo); 2. Bill Zwanziger (Waterloo); 3. Jack Mitchell (Cedar Falls); 4. Stan Stover (Reinbeck); 5. Dave Bedard (LaPorte City).

SECOND HEAT—1. Dan Nesteby (Waterloo); 2. Denny Osborn (Cedar Falls); 3. Dick Schiltz (Waterloo); 4. Tom Bartholomew (Waterloo); 5. Curt Hansen (Dike).

SEMI-MAIN—1. Dave Plum (Waterloo); 2. Em Frethem (Decorah); 3. Tim McDonough (Cedar Rapids); 4. Bob Hesse (Waterloo); 5. Jack Mitchell (Cedar Falls).

FEATURE—1. Zwanziger; 2. E. Sanger; 3. Nesteby; 4. Schiltz; 5. tie between Osborn and Stover; 7. Bartholomew; 8. Karl Sanger (Waterloo); 9. Plum; 10. Mitchell.

SPORTSMEN

FIRST HEAT—1. Greg Kastli (Waterloo); 2. Duane Von Deest (Grundy Center); 3. Roger Buchholz (Cedar Falls).

SECOND HEAT—1. Tom Moore (Waterloo); 2. Larry Schmidt (New Hampton); 3. Mike Krall (Waterloo).

SEMI-MAIN—1. Rick Forbes (Evansdale); 2. Jim Estle; 3. Wendle Baker (Shell Rock).

FEATURE—1. Kastli; 2. Moore; 3. Krall; 4. Schmidt; 5. Von Deest.

ROADRUNNERS

SEASON CHAMPIONSHIP—1. tie between Gary Eckvall (Marshalltown) and Roger Patterson (Cedar Falls); 3. John Strouble; 4. Dave Swarts (Cedar Falls); 5. Gary Kaune (Waterloo); 6. Walter Hersh.

Hansen drops back four rows, still wins at Tunis

By JIM FICKESS
Courier Sports Writer

Dropping four rows back in the starting order Sunday night didn't stop Dike's Curt Hansen from winning his sixth late model feature in seven Tunis Speedway programs.

Both Hansen and Ed Sanger, who earned first row starting positions with heat victories, agreed to promoter Claus Stricker's suggestion that they start back in the pack to avoid the possibility of having a two-car race between the two teammates.

Hansen moved up six spots to fourth by the second lap and third restart of the race. He was ...

... for causing the restart. Under the no-fault restart rule at Tunis this year, he should have been given his position back if someone had hit his car, causing Plum to lose control. Several observers thought Plum's car was tapped by another before the spinout.

He moved up five positions to seventh in the final four laps.

ROGER KLINGFUS, who broke Hansen's Tunis winning streak last week, finished fourth with Denny Osborn and Stan Stover fifth and sixth, respectively.

Greg Kastli was a triple winner in the sportsmen bracket. He scored convincing ...

Curt Hansen runs away with 50-lapper

By JIM FICKESS
Courier Sports Writer

Curt Hansen of Dike breezed to his third stock car track championship of the season Sunday night at Tunis Speedway.

Hansen, the Tunis late model regular season point leader, started the 50-lap title race on the inside first row, jumped out to a big lead early and was never challenged.

Runner-up Stan Stover of Reinbeck finished a full straightaway behind Hansen at the end of the race. Only five cars finished on the same lap as Hansen.

Hansen has also captured the track titles at Cedar Rapids' Hawkeye Downs and the State Fairgrounds in Des Moines. He's also the favorite to win the Oskaloosa championship, which hasn't been run yet.

Stover also finished second to Hansen in the Des Moines championship Saturday night.

SPORTSMAN POINT-LEADER Greg Kastli also won his class' season title Sunday night.

Hansen shouldn't have as easy a time of it when he goes for his eighth Tunis main event win of the season in Monday night's late model special.

Track promoter Claus Stricker says "a bunch" of new cars have indicated they'll be in Waterloo Monday night to compete for a $6,200 purse, including $1,200 plus lap money to win the 75-lap feature.

Also, a couple of the top track regulars who were missing Sunday night have told Stricker they'll be back for Monday night. Both Ed Sanger and Bill Zwanziger, the only repeat feature winners at Tunis this ...

See TUNIS
Continued on page 18, col. 1

LATE MODELS

[illegible]

SPORTSMEN

[illegible]

Karl Sanger fifth late model feature winner at Tunis Speedway

By LARRY CONRAD
Courier Sports Writer

The list of late-model feature winners at Tunis Speedway grows ever longer with Karl Sanger's name being added as Sunday night's victor.

Tunis has had five different winners in seven nights of racing. Ed Sanger and Bill Zwanziger have each won a pair of main events.

Waterloo's Roger Klingfus took an early lead in the 25-lap event and seemed to have a comfortable margin. But a four-car pack closed in on the leader in the 22nd lap and when the dust had settled it was Sanger on top, Dick Schiltz of Waterloo second, Dike's Curt Hansen third and Klingfus hanging on to fourth place. Ed Sanger finished in eighth.

The late-model main event went virtually unmarred compared to the ...

Cedar Falls' Roger Patterson captured the Tunis roadrunner crown for the fifth time in as many races. Gary Kaune of Waterloo led for the first eight laps of the 10-lap event but Patterson was not to be denied. Scott Braun of Cedar Falls finished second and Kaune ended up in third place.

Bob Hesse of Waterloo won the highly disputed, somewhat madcap, wheelbarrow race, an annual Father's Day event at Tunis.

It seems Hesse had the foresight to install a set of pedals on the front of his "wheelbarrow" so that he could aid his pusher. Hesse, of course, far out-distanced everyone on the track to cross the finish line amidst a chorus of "boos" from the delighted fans.

LATE MODEL

FIRST HEAT—1. Dick Schiltz (Waterloo); 2. Curt Hansen (Dike); 3. Carl Sanger (Waterloo).

SECOND HEAT—1. Jack Mitchell (Cedar Falls); 2. Dan Nesteby (Waterloo); 3. Ed Sanger (Waterloo).

THIRD HEAT—1. Bob Hilmer (Dysart); 2. Stan Stover (Reinbeck); 3. Bob Hesse (Waterloo).

SEMI-MAIN—1. Roger Klingfus (Waterloo); 2. Tom Bartholomew (Waterloo); 3. Dave Trower (New Hampton); 4. Jim Buhlman (Waterloo); 5. Tim McDonough (Cedar Rapids); 6. Jim Patterson (Cedar Falls).

FEATURE—1. Karl Sanger (Waterloo); 2. Schiltz; 3. Hansen; 4. Klingfus; 5. Denny Osborn (Cedar Falls); 6. Nesteby.

SPORTSMAN

LATE SATURDAY

At Independence

LATE MODEL

FIRST HEAT—1. Greg Kastli (Waterloo); 2. Dick Chapman (Dubuque); 3. Bob Hesse (Waterloo).

SECOND HEAT—1. Glen Martin (Independence); 2. Tom Fitzpatrick (Gilbertville); 3. Bob Schulte (Delhi).

THIRD HEAT—1. George Brasil (Albuquerque, N.M.); 2. Jim Burbridge (Delhi); 3. Joe Schaefer (Waterloo).

FIRST SEMI—1. Bob Hesse; 2. Larry Wasserfort (Waterloo); 3. Bob Kinsello (Dubuque).

SECOND SEMI—1. Bill Barthelmes (Troy Mills); 2. Dave Bentley (Fairbank); 3. Al Meyrer (Winthrop).

CONSOLATION—1. Mike Krall (Waterloo); 2. Jim Decker (Winthrop); 3. Jack Mitchell (Cedar Falls).

FEATURE—1. Bob Hesse; 2. Bill Barthelmes; 3. Bob Kinsello; 4. Al Meyrer; 5. Joe Schaefer; 6. Dave Bentley.

SPORTSMAN

FIRST HEAT—1. Dick Chapman II (East Dubuque, Ill.); 2. Ron Shafer (Waterloo); 3. Gary Trapp ...

Zwanziger wins at Tunis; sales pitch for his car

By JIM FICKESS
Courier Sports Writer

Bill Zwanziger earned some good advertising for his late model stock car Sunday night at Tunis Speedway.

He won both the feature and first heat races in a car which is up for sale. The car, owned by Al Frieden, will shortly be replaced by a new machine.

Zwanziger led all the way in both victories, scoring an easy victory in the heat then winning a dogfight with Karl Sanger in the main event.

The Waterloo veteran who's been racing stock cars for over 20 years jumped off to a sizable early lead in the feature and third much of the race, placed fifth while semi-main winner Curt Hansen sixth.

Both Zwanziger and Bartholomew notched easy wins while starting from the pole spot in the two late model heats.

Tim Swope of Raymond captured the sportmen's 15-lap feature race. He enjoyed a lead of over a straight away on the three-eighths mile track over his nearest competor.

Gary Kaune won the roadrunner race which saw the field cut down to four cars after a three-car pileup on the second lap.

LATE MODELS

1978
In the News

Hansen, Braun pole-to-pole victors

By JIM FICKESS
Courier Sports Writer

Tunis Speedway's mid-season championship stock car races Sunday night held true to form.

The drivers who have been dominating their classes recently at the Waterloo three-eighths mile track—Curt Hansen in the late models and roadrunner Scott Braun—scored comfortable victories in mid-year title races.

The sportsmen class, whose point list showed just $55 in earnings separating the top five men before Sunday, produced the most exciting championship race of the evening. Barry Schmidt of New Hampton came out on top of that 25-lapper.

Hansen breezed to his third straight Tunis checkered flag and ... first feature win of the season.

SUNDAY NIGHT also marked the second straight main event he's led from start to finish at Tunis. Hansen started last Tuesday's July 4 Special on Sunday due to his No. 1 position in the point standings.

He had a little trouble shaking off teammate Ed Sanger early, but was breezing to the victory by the end of 35 laps.

Sanger, second in the point standings, had to borrow John Weers' car to compete in the mid-season. He blew an engine for the second straight Sunday at Tunis while competing in the third heat.

Waterloo veteran Bill Zwanziger finished second to Hansen, with Dick Schiltz third and Tom Bartholomew edging out Ed Sanger for fourth. Karl Sanger was sixth.

SEVERAL OF the top cars were running well, but not good enough to catch up with Hansen, the feature winner at the State Fairgrounds in Des Moines Saturday night.

The first half of the sportsmen mid-season was a five or six car battle for first place.

Mike Krall, who won the mid-season championship at Midway Downs the previous evening, led the first 14 laps.

Then, Schmidt took the lead and the race remained a multi-car battle for first.

He held on for the rest of the 25-lap race, registering a two car-length victory over Gene Ehlers. Tim Swope, the race's pole sitter, wound up third with Craig Haupt of Sumner fourth and Krall fifth.

BRAUN'S margin of victory was more than a straightaway even though two restarts bunched up the field during the 15-lapper.

Braun came out with a new car last Tuesday and won after he refused to sell his old car for $350.

The $350 claim rule was designed to prevent roadrunners from putting too much money in their cars. It disqualifies a driver from running his car in Tunis roadrunner races if he's refused $350 for it from another competitor.

Laverne Lehman and Mike Paulus, running second and third at the time, collided and rolled their cars on the ninth lap of the roadrunner.

LATE MODELS

FIRST HEAT—1. Karl Sanger (Waterloo); 2. Bill Zwanziger (Waterloo), 3. Don Nesleby (Waterloo), 4. Duane Van Deest (Grundy Center).

SECOND HEAT—1. Dave Bedard (Waterloo), 2. Dick Schiltz (Waterloo), 3. Darrell Sells (Waverly).

THIRD HEAT—1. Bob Hilmer (Dysart), 2. Dave Plum (Waterloo); 3. Curt Hansen (Dike); 4. Stan Stover (Reinbeck).

CONSOLATION—1. Jack Mitchell (Cedar Falls), 2. Bob Hilmer (Dysart); 3. Tim McDonough (Cedar Rapids).

FEATURE—1. Hansen, 2. Zwanziger; 3. Schiltz; 4. Tom Bartholomew (Waterloo), 5. Ed Sanger (Waterloo); 6. K. Sanger, 7. Nesleby, 8. Van Deest, 9. Sells, 10. Plum.

SPORTSMEN

FIRST HEAT—1. Dave Wach (Evansdale), 2. Ed Jessen (Waterloo), 3. Rick Brinkema (Waterloo).

SECOND HEAT—1. Gary Keidel (Dysart); 2. Craig Haupt (Sumner), 3. Bob Hesse (Waterloo).

THIRD HEAT—1. Gene Ehlers (Independence), 2. Larry Schmidt (New Hampton), 3. Ken Hoeppner (Waterloo).

CONSOLATION—1. Jessen, 2. Wach.

FEATURE—1. Schmidt, 2. Ehlers, 3. Swope, 4. Haupt; 5. Mike Krall (Waterloo), 6. Greg Kastli (Waterloo).

ROADRUNNERS

FIRST HEAT—1. Dave Rice (Waterloo) 2. Walter Hirsh (Waterloo).

SECOND HEAT—1. Scott Braun (Cedar Falls), 2. Gary Kaune (Waterloo).

FEATURE—1. Braun, 2. Rice, 3. Ben Cunningham.

Roadrunners, demolition derby, horses at Tunis Sunday

Tunis Speedway's stock car season will end with a crash Sunday night.

In fact, a whole flock of crashes.

A roadrunner and demolition derby program is scheduled for the final evening of the Tunis season.

Both the demolition derby and roadrunner programs will consists of heat events and features.

The final Sunday evening program at Tunis will be preceded by a harness horse racing event which begins at 2 p.m. on the Tunis track.

Cars must weigh in at 2,800 pounds at Tunis

Jim Fickess

TUNIS SPEEDWAY promoter Claus Stricker hopes to have a set of scales installed at that stock car track before Sunday night's second program of the season.

Scales are becoming a common fixture at most Iowa stock car ovals because of new weight restrictions on cars.

Most promoters have put minimum weight limits of 3,000 pounds for small engine block cars and 3,200 for large blocks.

However, Stricker and Hawkeyes Downs promoter Al Frieden went with different rules, setting a 2,800 pound minimum for all late models.

The weight rules were enacted as a safety measure. Some drivers were sacrificing safety for a lighter, and therefore faster, car. Some cars were, reportedly, running as light as 2,400 pounds last year and were very flimsy.

Stricker maintains a safe car can be built at 2,800 pounds and says his rule will continue to work in the future.

"THE MANUFACTURERS are coming out with smaller cars all the time," says Stricker. "If cars are coming out with smaller engines, they won't be able to haul heavy bodies around the stock car tracks.

"I think the drivers can live with this 2,800 pound minimum for years to come and won't have to build a new car every year to fit new rules."

Stricker, who also promotes Saturday night races at Eldon, is hoping the weather will cooperate so he can get the electronic scales anchored in behind the Tunis judges' stand by Sunday night.

He's also may have a problem getting that accomplished since he's busy promoting the Pepsi-Mountain Dew Special for Tuesday night at Eldon. A $7,700 total purse, including $1,000 to win, is being offered for that race.

Stricker has been circulating around the Iowa tracks and says the state's top drivers have all indicated they'll be in Eldon Tuesday night. Time trials are set for 6:45 p.m. with races at 8 p.m.

MIDWAY DOWNS, located between Nashua and Charles City on old Highway 218, is scheduled to open its stock car racing season Saturday night at 8 p.m.

Independence, meanwhile, will be trying to get its second card run Saturday night. The Greater Iowa Racing Association, which manages races at both Independence and Sunday at Dubuque, was rained out twice last weekend.

Independence is running a special midget car show for Memorial Day, May 29, while Tunis has scheduled a Sunday-Monday stock car doubleheader for the holiday.

Sanger collision lets Hansen win Tunis title

By JIM FICKESS
Courier Sports Writer

Ed Sanger's collision with a lapped car Sunday night ended a brilliant two-car battle and gave Curt Hansen of Dike his second Tunis Speedway late model season championship race triumph.

Sanger, who started on the front row outside of Hansen, took the lead going into the first turn of the race and never relinquished it until a costly 25th-lap bump.

He went on the high side of the track when he tried to get around Gary Heuer going into turn No. 1. But, Heuer's and Sanger's cars struck, nearly forcing Ed off the track.

Hansen, driving nose-to-nose with Sanger several times during the 35-lap... couldn't get around," answered Hansen when asked if he thought he could have passed Sanger in the final 10 laps without the aid of the collision.

"We were really running kind of equal. He was high and having troubles with his front end while I was low and having problems with my rear end handling. It's really too bad it had to happen like this."

Hansen completed a championship sweep at the four tracks he races at weekly.

THE DIKE DRIVER has no claimed the season point and championship race titles at Oskaloosa, Cedar Rapids, Des Moines and, now, Tunis.

... ing victory.

Kaune finished second.

LATE MODELS

FIRST HEAT—1. Dave Bedard (Waterloo), 2. Denny Osborn (Cedar Falls); 3. Curt Hansen (Dike), 4. Roger Klingfus (Waterloo).

SECOND HEAT—1. John Weers (Readlyn); 2. Darrell Sells (Waverly); 3. Bill Zwanziger (Waterloo); 4. Stan Stover (Reinbeck).

THIRD HEAT—1. Ed Sanger (Waterloo); 2. Karl Sanger (Waterloo); 3. Don Nesleby (Waterloo); 4. Duane VanDeest (Grundy Center).

SEASON CHAMPIONSHIP—1. Hansen; 2. Stover; 3. E. Sanger; 4. K. Sanger; 5. Osborn; 6. Klingfus; 7. Bedard; 8. Sells; 9. Weers; 10. Nesleby.

SPORTSMEN

FIRST HEAT—1. Dave Trower (New Hampton); 2. Larry Schmidt (New Hampton); 3. Greg Kastli (Waterloo).

SECOND HEAT—1. ... Liddell (Cedar Falls); 2. Mike Krall (Waterloo); 3. Mike Fordice (Dysart).

THIRD HEAT—1. Craig Haupt (Sumner); 2. Lynn Ihde (New Hampton); 3. Gary Keidel (Dysart).

SEASON CHAMPIONSHIP—1. Gene Ehlers (Independence); 2. Schmidt; 3. Haupt; 4. Bob Hesse (Waterloo); 5. Kastli; 6. Liddell.

ROADRUNNERS

SEASON CHAMPIONSHIP—1. Scott Braun (Cedar Falls); 2. Gary Kaune (Waterloo); 3. Rickey Ott; 4. Mike Horton.

Osborn feature winner at Tunis

By LARRY CONRAD
Courier Sports Writer

Denny Osborn of Cedar Falls notched his first late model stock car feature victory of the season Sunday night at Tunis Speedway and he did it in a most convincing manner.

Osborn screamed out of the 20-car field from the initial lap and had the 25-lap main event all to himself from that point on. By the ninth lap, Osborn had built a half-lap lead on the pack and, at the 19th, he was three-fourths of a lap ahead of the second place car.

Meanwhile, a battle was going on for second place between Waterloo's Tom Bartholomew, Karl Sanger and the frequent winner at Independence, Gary Crawford.

Crawford was running third behind second turn of the 12th lap to nudge Liddell out of third place.

Coming out of turn four on the last lap, Schmidt swung high trying to overtake Haupt at the wire, but lost some traction in the lesser-packed part of the track and Ehlers breezed past him to take second place with Schmidt finishing third.

SCOTT BRAUN of Cedar Falls overtook the leader in the roadrunner feature race in the sixth lap and hung on to win the somewhat shortened eight-lap event.

A special "mechanics race" was an additional feature Sunday night with the race consisting of "eight laps or three red flags—whichever came first."

The winner—or survivor—of this special event was Kevin Tjebkes driving Scott Sells car No. 31.

Sanger, Hansen keep stock car titles in the family

By JIM FICKESS
Courier Sports Writer

Curt Hansen's current phenomenal late model stock car feature winning percentage fell slightly Sunday night at Tunis Speedway.

But, at least the man who broke the victory string was Ed Sanger, Hansen's teammate and car owner.

Sanger won the first late model feature of the evening, the main event that was rained out last Sunday night.

Later in the program, Hansen bolted from an 11th place starting spot to grab an early lead in the regularly-scheduled feature and sped to his ninth victory in his last 11 starts.

Hansen's .500 night lowers his recent late model feature batting average to .818, still an astounding figure.

Tom Bartholomew of Waterloo spun out while leading the 17th lap of the make-up ...

Sanger got by him two laps later anyway for the win. Bartholomew wound up second and Hansen third.

In the regular feature, Hansen moved from 11th to third but a by a fifth-lap red flag. He pulled away from the rest of the pack off the restart.

Sanger was the only driver to be anywhere near striking distance to Hansen the rest of the race.

Waterloo veteran Bill Zwanziger finished a distant second to those two.

The feature victories were the second of the Tunis season for both Hansen and Sanger. Hansen's other win was in Thursday night's 40-lap Coca-Cola Special.

Each also won a 10-lap heat race.

Zwanziger claimed the second preliminary while Duane Van Deest of Grundy Center won the semi-main and placed fourth in the regular feature.

Larry Schulte of Cedar Rapids totally dominated the sportsmen class, winning ...

Sumner's Craig Haupt placed second to Schulte in both features.

Scott Braun of Cedar Falls won the make-up roadrunner race. He was knocked out of the other roadrunner event on a first-lap multi-car accident.

Don Berg of Waterloo went on to win that race.

LATE MODELS

MAKE-UP FEATURE—1. Ed Sanger (Waterloo); 2. Tom Bartholomew (Waterloo); 3. Curt Hansen (Dike); 4. Darrell Sells (Waverly); 5. Bill Zwanziger (Waterloo); 6. Dick Schiltz (Waterloo); 7. Karl Sanger (Waterloo); 8. Stan Stover (Reinbeck); 9. Duane Van Deest (Grundy Center); 10. John Weers (Readlyn).

FIRST HEAT—1. E. Sanger; 2. Sells; 3. Stover.

SECOND HEAT—1. Zwanziger; 2. Bartholomew; 3. Schiltz; 4. Dave Bedard (Waterloo).

THIRD HEAT—1. Hansen; 2. Don Nesteby (Waterloo); 3. K. Sanger; 4. Dave Plum (Waterloo).

SEMI-MAIN—1. Van Deest; 2. Red Oralie (Evansdale); 3. Weers; 4. Jim Patterson (Cedar Falls); 5. Dave Maxson (Cedar Falls); 6. Rick Heuer (Waterloo).

FEATURE—1. Hansen; 2. E. Sanger; 3. Zwanziger; 4. Van Deest; 5. Stover. 6. Plum; 7. Sells; 8. Oralie; 9. Schiltz; 10. Weers.

SPORTSMEN

MAKE-UP FEATURE—1. Larry Schulte (Cedar Rapids); 2. Craig Haupt (Sumner); 3. Bob Hesse (Waterloo); 4. Ken Hoeppner (Waterloo). 5. Gary Keidel ...

1979

In the News

Tom Bartholomew in first Tunis feature victory since 1974

By JIM FICKESS
Courier Sports Writer

Tom Bartholomew's four and one-half season home track jinx ended Sunday night at Tunis Speedway.

Bartholomew, whose $32,000 earnings in 1978 rank him among the leading stock car drivers in Iowa, hadn't won a Tunis late model feature since the 1974 mid-season championship.

But he changed all that Sunday night when he led from start to finish in the 25-lap late model feature.

Bartholomew bolted away from the pack off the start from his inside second row position and led by a comfortable margin until a couple of accidents midway through the race bunched up the field.

He held off Ed Sanger, who owns Bartholomew's race car, at the end for first-place money.

Fuzzy Liddell of Cedar Falls claimed the 15-lap sportsmen main event on a dry, slick three-eighths mile dirt oval while Mike Grapp won the roadrunner race on the final lap.

"IT'S ABOUT TIME," said a grinning Bartholomew after the race. "I've led a lot of races here since the last one I won but when the checkered flag dropped someone else had already won and I was second or third."

Sunday night's brisk, cold winds dried most the moisture out of the track, leaving a tricky racing surface.

"It was a difficult track out there tonight, that's for sure," said Bartholomew. "The track was hard and there were some crumbs, too.

"If you got out of the groove you were in trouble. I slipped a little bit a couple of times and Ed almost got by me."

Sunday didn't start out as such a great day for Bartholomew.

He had had engine problems the night before and starting working on his car at 9 a.m. Sunday. The work continued almost until race time with Bartholomew arriving last at Tunis and missing the pre-race hot lap warm-ups.

"We did the right thing," said Bartholomew, stating the obvious, after he had outrun the rest of the late model field.

Bartholomew led by almost a straightaway before the first race-stopping wreck which came on the 13th lap. The red flag came out again on lap No. 15

See TUNIS
Continued on page 19, col. 4

Hansen wins last Tunis feature

By JIM FICKESS
Courier Sports Writer

Curt Hansen was able to get by slower traffic and Tom Bartholomew wasn't. As a result, Hansen won the final late model stock car feature of the season Sunday afternoon on a dry, slick Tunis Speedway track.

Hansen and Bartholomew started in the front row after winning the first and second heats, respectively, under the open competition format.

Bartholomew took the lead on the high side of the track right off the start. He led through the first 13 laps, then had to slow down when he got tangled with lapped cars.

Hansen was able to get around Bartholomew and the slow cars and didn't relinquish that lead.

Several of Tunis' regular late model competitors competed in the lucrative World 100 in Rosburg, Ohio.

Braun, the Tunis season champion, got by him on the 12th circuit before Sells gained back the top spot for the final three laps.

Vern Jackson claimed the roadrunner feature.

Hansen's victory was his fifth of the year at Tunis, one better than regular season champion Ed Sanger's four.

The three heat winners occupied the late model feature's top three spots as Greg Kastli placed third. Dave Plum was fourth and Rick Wendling fifth.

LATE MODELS

FIRST HEAT—1. Curt Hansen (Dike); 2. Rick Wendling (Hazleton); 3. Steve Auringer (Waterloo).
SECOND HEAT—1. Tom Bartholomew (Waterloo); 2. Darrell Zwiefel (Rochester, Minn.); 3. George White.
THIRD HEAT—1. Greg Kastli (Waterloo); 2. Dave Plum (Waterloo); 3. Bill Moyer (Des Moines).
SEMI-MAIN—1. Darrell Sells (Waverly); 2. Red Dralle (Evansdale); 3. Rick Heuer (Waterloo); 4. Jim Patterson (Cedar Falls).
FEATURE—1. Hansen; 2. Bartholomew; 3. Kastli; 4. Plum; 5. Wendling; 6. Sells; 7. Fitzpatrick; 8. Zwiefel; 9. Moyer; 10. Heuer.

SPORTSMEN

FIRST HEAT—1. Steve Mullahy (Burlington); 2. Fuzzy Liddell (Cedar Falls); 3. Mike Kroll (Waterloo).
SECOND HEAT—1. Willy Kilagfus (Cedar Falls); 2. Dean Wagner (Waterloo); 3. Ron Moyer (Riceville).
THIRD HEAT—1. Scott Sells (Waverly); 2. Keith Braun (Cedar Falls); 3. Mike Fordice (Dysart).

Tunis decides to halt Sunday night racing

By JIM FICKESS
Courier Sports Writer

For the first time in 32 years, there will be no regular Sunday night stock car racing program in Waterloo this summer.

Tunis Speedway owner Judd Tunis has decided to discontinue the weekly shows after 31 consecutive summers of Sunday night races at the dirt track located off University Ave. between Waterloo and Cedar Falls.

Tunis says there are several reasons why he decided to shut down the track.

"I'M GETTING along in the years," says the spry 83-year-old. "There's a lot of work to do around this place that is just too hard for me to get done any more."

Claus and Marlene Stricker, who promoted the Tunis stock car races for the past six years, told Tunis this past season would be their last.

However, lack of a contract with a promoter played no role in his decision, Tunis emphasizes.

"I won't rent it out to anybody," says Tunis, when asked if he'd be receptive to any last minute offers from promoters. "I've had plenty of offers, but I've turned them all down."

There is a possibility that a couple of special stock car races, as well as some horse racing events, could be run at Tunis this summer, he adds.

Tunis also cited declining attendance as one of the reasons he ended the weekly cards.

"OH, YOU can still make money out here, but it's not like it used to be," recalls Tunis. "In those early years, we were the only track around and used to draw a lot of people from out of town.

"Now, there's five race tracks between Webster City and Dubuque on Highway 20.

"It's hard to draw fans anymore."

During the track's glory days, Tunis says it averaged about 4,000 fans per Sunday night with as many as 6,000 for some programs. The current average is in the 2,000-3,000 range.

Track problems, such as neighbors' complaints about noise and dirt, weren't factors in his decision, says Tunis.

A longtime horseman, Tunis now hopes he can spend more time with his 25 head on the facility originally built for harness racing. He is still driving a harness every morning.

"After 31 years, I think it's time for a summer off," says Tunis with a chuckle.

In fact, it was because of one his horses that Tunis missed the only event in his track's history of weekly auto racing this past summer. "The damn horse kicked me in the leg and I couldn't walk for two or three days," recalls the active octogenarian.

THE CESSATION of Sunday night racing at Tunis brings to an end an era in Iowa sports history. The Waterloo facility is the longest-running in the state and a hotbed for the rapid growth of the sport in the post-World War II Midwest.

Eaker survives pileup to win

By JIM FICKESS
Courier Sports Writer

Verlin Eaker, involved in one of the evening's early crashes, bounced back Sunday to win his first Tunis Speedway late model stock car feature in over 13 seasons.

A brisk wind whipped up just before Sunday's program, drying out the top layer of the three-eighths mile dirt track. That turned the oval's surface into a slick condition which made it almost as slippery as ice. That helped cause 19 race-stopping accidents Sunday night.

Greg Kastli of Waterloo continued his mastery of ... tive barrier in front of the flagman's stand. Some sheet metal around the left rear tire was bent back and Eaker went on to finish second in that 10-lapper.

Eaker started the feature on the inside of the third row and was in the lead to stay by the 10th lap.

Pole-sitter Red Dralle led for the first seven laps before Em Fretheim of Decorah took over for the next two times around.

Fretheim, driving Ed Sanger's old No. 96 Camaro which is nearly a clone of Eaker's machine, ran second the rest of the race.

Bill Zwanziger of Waterloo finished third, with Dick Schiltz in fourth and Dralle fifth.

The sportsman class had the most spectacular accidents.

Larry Schmidt's car went over on its top between the first and second turns when his left front tire buckled in.

THE SPORTSMAN feature had a four-car pileup on the front straightaway before the green flag had been dropped. The chain reaction pileup came when a couple of drivers couldn't slow down in time after they saw the signal for one more preliminary lap.

Scott Braun, who's moved up to the sportsmen this year after dominating the roadrunner class last season, held off Kastli until the 12th lap of the fifteen lapper.

Braun finished second with earlier frontrunner, Bernie Juliar, third.

Venenga caught Snyder right at the end of the roadrunner race to finish in a tie for first.

Despite the frequency of pileups, no one was injured in Sunday's three and one-half hour program.

LATE MODELS

FIRST HEAT—1. Dan Nesteby (Waterloo); 2. John Weers (Readlyn); 3. Denny Osborn (Cedar Falls); 4. Em Fretheim (Decorah).
SECOND HEAT—1. Tom Bartholomew (Waterloo); 2. Verlin Eaker (Mechanicsville); 3. Red Dralle (Evansdale); 4. Dick Schiltz (Waterloo).
SEMI-MAIN—1. Curt Hansen (Dike); 2. Bill Zwanziger (Waterloo); 3. Darrell Sells (Waverly); 4. Karl Sanger (Waterloo); 5. Mike Mauer (Cedar Falls); 6. Larry Wasserfort (Waterloo).
FEATURE—1. Eaker; 2. Fretheim; 3. Zwanziger; 4. Schiltz; 5. Dralle; 6. Wasserfort; 7. Hansen; 8. Weers; 9. Sells; 10. Osborn.

SPORTSMEN

FIRST HEAT—1. Keith Zobel (Waterloo); 2. Tim Swope (Raymond); 3. Benjamin Dover (New Hampton).
SECOND HEAT—1. Fuzzy Liddell (Cedar Falls); 2. Bernie Juliar (Hudson); 3. Chuck Roberts.
THIRD HEAT—1. Duane VanDeest (Cedar Falls); 2. Greg Kastli (Waterloo); 3. Steve Weber (Dunkerton).
SEMI-MAIN—1. Scott Braun (Cedar Falls); 2. Mike Krall (Waterloo); 3. Mike Fordice (Dysart).
CONSOLATION—Keith Braun (Cedar Falls).
FEATURE—1. Kastli; 2. S. Braun; 3. Juliar; 4. Krall; 5. Liddell; 6. Weber.

ROADRUNNER

1. tie between Dan Snyder and Dave Venenga; 3. Todd McCombs.

Schiltz becomes first Tunis double winner of season

By JIM FICKESS
Courier Sports Writer

Darrell Sells' slip Sunday night helped Dick Schiltz become Tunis Speedway's first late model stock car feature double winner of the season.

Sells was leading Schiltz by a small margin on the next-to-last lap of the regularly-scheduled main event before he spun between turns No. 3 and 4. Schiltz was able to avoid Sells' car and drove on to victory in the thriller.

SUNDAY NIGHT'S program started with a make-up of last week's rained out card.

Drivers in loaned cars did well in that portion of the evening's action.

Red Dralle, driving Ed Sanger's old No. 96 Camaro, led from start to finish in that late model feature while Larry Schmidt won the sportsman make-up. Mike Krall claimed the second sportsman 15-lapper of the evening.

Dralle's main challenger in the first feature was Denny Osborn. Osborn was able to get close to Dralle, who started on the outside front row, but couldn't get around him.

Dralle is the third driver to race Sanger's old car at Tunis this season. Dralle opened the year the Camaro before his Ford Mustang was ready. Then it was raced by Em Fretheim and Sanger, himself, when his 1979 ride, a Zip LeKander-owned car, was out of commission.

TIM SWOPE led the early laps of both sportsman features.

Schmidt grabbed first on the ninth lap of the accident-shortened make-up feature.

The race was called at 14 laps when sportsman pole leader Greg Kastli slammed into a pole between the pit exit and the first turn.

Krall led from the fifth circuit on in the regular sportsman main event.

Both roadrunner races were both shortened by accidents. Gary Kaune was in the lead when the first roadrunner event was called at eight laps while Laverne Lehman captured the second race, which was half the scheduled distance of 10 laps.

Next Sunday is Kids' Night at Tunis with all children under 12 years old being admitted free.

MAKE-UP PROGRAM

LATE MODELS

SEMI-MAIN—1. Dick Schiltz (Waterloo); 2. Red Dralle (Evansdale); 3. Darrell Sells (Waverly); 4. Verlin Eaker (Mechanicsville); 5. Dave Bedard (Waterloo).
FEATURE—1. Dralle; 2. Denny Osborn (Cedar Falls); 3. Tom Bartholomew (Waterloo); 4. Schiltz; 5. Ed Sanger (Waterloo); 6. Bill Zwanziger (Waterloo); 7. Bedard; 8. Dan Nesteby (Waterloo); 9. Curt Hansen (Dike); 10. Karl Sanger (Waterloo).

SPORTSMEN

SEMI-MAIN—1. Keith Zobel (Waterloo); 2. Willy Kilangfus (Cedar Falls); 3. Larry Doherty (Marion); 4. Timm Jensen.
CONSOLATION—Duane Van Deest.
FEATURE—1. Larry Schmidt (New Hampton); 2.

April 25, 1985

1980s
In the News

METRO DEATHS

Judd L. Tunis

Services for Judd L. Tunis, 88, of 3715 University Ave., will be 1 p.m. Saturday at Memorial Park Chapel with burial in the Memorial Park Cemetery.

Waterloo Lodge 105 AF & AM will conduct public Masonic services at 7:30 p.m. Friday at O'Keefe & Towne-Carter

Judd Tunis

& Waychoff Funeral Home, where friends may call after 2 p.m. Friday.

He died at 12:35 p.m. Wednesday at Schoitz Hospice Unit.

Mr. Tunis was born May 2, 1896, at Independence, son of August and Charlotte Lorenz Tunis. He married Marie Fish in 1917.

At the age of 10, he was employed by Wittick Meats. In 1923 he and his wife opened a butcher shop in the location presently occupied by Con-Way Civic Center. In 1942, he opened a wholesale meat outlet in the family home on University Avenue.

Mr. Tunis developed and operated Tunis Speedway for 32 years, an enterprise begun in 1950. He sponsored or supported numerous entertainment events: horse racing, midget car racing, stock car racing, car stunt shows, circuses and parades.

He was an expert horseman.

He was active in Waterloo Masonic Lodge No. 105, served as an officer in the White Shrine Lodge of Jerusalem No. 9 of Cedar Falls, and a long-time member of the High 12 Club.

Survivors include his wife; a daughter, Lorene C. Higgins of Waterloo; a sister, Lois Tunis of Kansas City, Mo.; two grandchildren; and three great-grandchildren.

The family will receive friends at the funeral home from 7:15 to 9 p.m. Friday.

Memorials may be made to Shrine Crippled Children's Hospital or the Schoitz Hospice Unit.

Neith of Algona and Ge of Georgia.

Friends may call a home Friday from ! service time.

May 23, 1982

Harness racing returns and draws 500 to Tunis

By MARK THALACKER
Courier Sports Writer

Harness racing returned to Tunis Speedway Sunday before a modest crowd of 500 spectators.

Some braved the broiling sun because they were dedicated fans. Many others had never seen a harness race and may have had their interest piqued by the thought of parimutuel betting at future racetracks. But there was no parimutual betting Sunday. In fact no money officially changed hands because the program was admission free on the track built by Jud Tunis for racing and training horses but made famous by some 30 years of stock car racing.

The season's first race card (a stock car event is scheduled for Labor Day night) called for five events, three for pacers and two for trotters, with two heats of each.

The 90-degree temperatures eventually took their toll, and the crowd melted away after the first hour.

By the start of the five second heats only 150 people remained in their seats. The final two races were viewed by less than 60.

THE NINTH race was the most exciting of the day. It was the second heat of the Free-for-All Pace, with a 10-horse field.

The reason for the excitement was the speed of Cash's Lad, owned by Royal and Roger Roland of Grinnell and driven by Duane Roland. Fourth in the first heat, Cash's Lad took control on the first turn and pulled away from the rest of the field to lead by three lengths.

Although Fire Skipper closed the gap on the final straightaway, Cash's Lad set a new track record of 2:07.3 for the one-mile course and won by more than a length. It was exactly five seconds faster than the fourth event's first heat, which was the fastest of the first five heats.

WATERLOO'S Kevin Nanke drove two horses Sunday.

In the first event he drove his father Bernie's pacer, Melrick, to a pair of second-place finishes, almost catching winner Paint Your Wagon in the second heat.

In the third race Nanke drove his own trotter, Match Mat. Match Mat edged Hickory Nut by a nose for third in the first heat, but finished fifth in the second heat.

The first heat of that race was won by Noble Tuffet, owned by W.D. Card of Cedar Falls and driven by Dave Sertz.

Three horses won both heats of their events.

Paint Your Wagon, owned by Pat Smith of Oskaloosa and driven by Don Smith, took both firsts in the 750 Pace. St. Patrick, owned by R.D. Lewis of Cowley, Wyo., and driven by Dick McDanel, turned the 1500 Pace into Irish property. And Jubilie John, owned and driven by Sac City's Roger Owens, swept the Free-for-All Trot.

NON-WINNERS 750 PACE
FIRST HEAT—1. Paint Your Wagon 2. Melrick 3. Bommer Gano
SECOND HEAT—1. Paint Your Wagon 2. Melrick 3. Bommer Gano

NON-WINNERS 1500 PACE
FIRST HEAT—1. St Patrick 2. Miss Butty Tarheel 3. San Padro
SECOND HEAT—1. St Patrick 2. San Padro 3. Filth of May

NON-WINNERS 1000 TROT
FIRST HEAT—1. Noble Tuffet 2. Reddy Butler 3. Match Mat
SECOND HEAT—1. Zoom Along Hap 2. Q T Kaye 3. K K Daytime

FREE-FOR-ALL PACE
FIRST HEAT—1. Courier Babe 2. Marcie Mahone 3. Fire Skipper
SECOND HEAT—1. Cash's Lad 2. Fire Skipper 3. Marcie Mahone

FREE-FOR-ALL TROT
FIRST HEAT—1. Jubilie John 2. Danny 3. Burton Ernie
SECOND HEAT—1. Jubilie John 2. Danny 3. Loreli Sue

Stock car races return to Tunis Monday

Courier News Service

Waterloo stock car racing fans haven't had their hometown track, Tunis Speedway, running regular weekly programs for three summers now.

But, weather permitting, there should be plenty of racing action Monday night in the John Deery Memorial Day special on that banked three-eighths mile dirt oval.

Four classes of stock cars will run in the program which begins at 6 p.m.

The late models, racing for points in the NASCAR circuit, will compete in the evening's main event, a 50-lap feature which pays $600 to the winner.

IMCA modified, sportsmen and altered street stock cars will also run.

The modified races will count on the IMCA point totals.

The admission prices are $5 for adults in the main grandstand, $3 on the backstretch and $2 for children 6-12 years old.

Vinton's Keith Knaack, who's promoting the event, was optimistic earlier this week that the track will be ready for Monday's action. The fast majority of the preparations were completed before the latest round of rains.

Knaack also predicts he'll have an outstanding field of cars, including most the top names who ran Sunday night programs at Tunis before the track quit its weekly races.

Knaack says there should be plenty of parking for the

Permit sought to reopen Tunis Speedway for races

By NANCY RAFFENSPERGER
Courier Staff Writer

Two auto racers with 55 years of combined experience are proposing to reopen Tunis Speedway for weekly stock car racing.

Vic Frey and Bob Hilmer went before the city's Planning, Programming and Zoning Commission earlier this week seeking a special permit to reopen the speedway.

A public hearing was set for Nov. 18.

The speedway, located in the 3700 block of University Avenue, was the site of weekly stock car races for 31 years until 1979. Races were conducted periodically at the track through 1982 and then stopped altogether.

One of the problems has been citizen complaints about loud noise. In 1982, the City Council ordered that all stock cars be equipped with mufflers while racing at Tunis.

Frey said the plans to reopen the track are still in the preliminary stages and that several obstacles must be overcome before racing begins.

Plans call for Frey and Hilmer to be the promoters of the track. They plan to run Sunday shows, ending by 10 p.m., from May through Labor Day. The track would employ 15 to 20 part-time workers and the goal is to draw 2,000 spectators each week.

"We think we know what it takes to run a race track. The closest place anybody has to go around here for stock car racing is Independence. That's a lot of money leaving our area each week," Frey said.

He noted that the track could draw up to 75 racers each week, with each car bringing in a minimum of four people. In addition, many racers draw their owns fans.

"People from three to four counties will come in here and spend money. They all buy gas, eat and stay in motels. It's up to the people to make this work. This area has a bad economy, but we've got to keep the taxpayers in this town," Frey said.

He said he and Hilmer do not want to cause problems with residents, but they will not operate the track if the cars must be equipped with mufflers.

"Most racers don't run just one night a week. They will run several other tracks and no other track has to run mufflers in this area. If racers start placing makeshift mufflers on their cars for races here, you're going to have half of them laying all over the track. They won't get permanent mufflers because the cars don't run as well with mufflers and because they don't have to have them at other tracks," Frey said.

In the end, it will mean that fewer drivers will want to race at Tunis.

A major obstacle in their plans is obtaining the track itself. The track is owned by Marie Tunis, widow of Judd Tunis, who sponsored numerous entertainment events at the track for many years.

Details on whether the track will be leased or sold are being worked out, Frey said.

Fender Benders

1952

Stock Car Races

Sponsored by
Hawkeye Racing Association

"FENDER BENDERS" 1952

Edited and Published by
Morris L. Bailey, Dike, Iowa
at the
College Hill Print Shop
2016 College Street, Cedar Falls, Iowa
Letterpress and Offset Lithographers

Pictures in this Year Book are by
Ted Gallentine, Waterloo, and Morris L. Bailey, Dike

NOTE—Most information in this year book was submitted by the personnel of the organization and was compiled by the editor. Some of the material was left to the discretion of the writer, so, we neither accept nor reject any bouquets for our efforts. Some things may have been written which might better have been left out, but, on the other hand, some of the better things may have been left unsaid. We, the editors, wish to thank all who have helped make this year book possible, and hope to improve on it in the years to come with the Hawkeye Racing Association, Inc.

Copies of this year book may be obtained by sending $1.50, plus 6 cents postage to Morris L. Bailey, Dike, or to Ted Gallentine, Sherwood Park, Waterloo,

In September of 1951 after a season of much dissatisfaction among the drivers and owners of stock cars with the association that they were then running with Jim Krogh, Bob Piper and I had Mary Wolff mail out letters to all interested parties inviting them to attend a meeting at which would be discussed the possibility of forming our own association. This meeting was held September 10, 1951, at Boslough K-F Motors, 123 West Firist Street, Cedar Falls, Iowa, and at this meeting it was decided to form our own association.

Herman Wenzel, George Bass, Pearl Custard, Bud Carr, and I were appointed to draw up rules and by laws, set up stock car specifications, track regulations and dues and fees. The Association has been incorporated under the laws of the State of Iowa as a non-profit and charitable organization. The following officers were elected for the ensuing year:

President	Howard Boslough
Vice-President	Gordon Bentley
Secretary	Ted Leckbee
Treasurer	Ira (Speed) Chumley

We very soon signed a contract with Jud Tunis of the Tunis Speedway, which was to be known as our home track, and the Mohawk Speed Drome of Mason City, Iowa. We also have run a series of races at the Amusements, Incorporated of Marshalltown, Iowa. In addition, we have had engagements at the Benton County Fair, Vinton, Iowa, and at the Central Iowa Fair, Marshalltown, Iowa, the only half-mile track we ran on this year. The association has 250 members and 50 registered cars. There are seven non-member paid employees. The association has bought and paid for all necessary racing equipment.

In addition to our one night a week engagement at the Tunis Speedway, our Holiday Races, and our out-of-town engagements, we had a Polio Benefit race on September 10, 1952, at which 100% of the gate receipts and concessions were donated to the Polio Fund.

Some of the extra attractions are the Holiday Races, the Mid-Season Championship Race, the Season Championship Race, and the Open Competition State Championship Race, which we intend to make an annual feature.

I now wish to thank each and every member for their help and cooperation in putting this association over and making it a success. We are now concluding a very successful season and are looking forward to a bigger and better season in '53.

HOWARD BOSLOUGH,
Pres

J. L. TUNIS
Owner Tunis Speedway

Mid-Season Championship

Hal Schroeder
1952 Mid-Season Champion

Heat Winners

Season Championship

Feature Winner

Harry Petersen, Jr.
1952 Champion

Three 7s

Al Hanson - Jimmy Krogh

Car No. 777, the most beautiful on the oval, is owned by Al Hanson of Al's Automotive and handled by Jimmy Krogh. With Al's know how as a mechanic and Jim's ability as a driver the Three-7s has been one of the top cars of the assoiation the past season. Jim also proved himself a winner at love, taking unto himself a bride late in August this year.

AL'S AUTOMOTIVE
777

35A

No. 35A

Gordon Bentley - Bob Hilmer

35-A, sister stock to 35, one of the Benley creations, is also a top car in the association. Chauffered by Bob Hilmer of Dysart, this car can always be expected to take its share of honors anywhere it appears on the banked oval.

No. 35

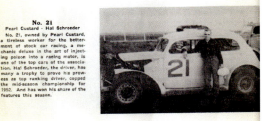

Gordon Bentley - Bill Zwanziger

No. 35, the top car of the association, at this writing, is owned by Gordon Bentley, master-mind of the Bentley racing teams and is driven by Bill Zwanziger, top-flight driver and at present point leader for the 1952 season. Always a good show from this team. On to the championship!

35

No. 245

LuVerne (Red) Droste

No. 245 sponsored by Don and Dels Service Station and a product of Red Droste, owner of Reds Auto Service, has been one of the crowd pleasers all season. The car, with Red behind the wheel, always gives a top performance.

245

Circle 245

LuVerne (Red) Droste

Circle 245, formerly the original 245, also known as "the Goat", and called a great many other things, is also owned by Red Droste. The most beat up car on the track, but still a top performer, originally driven by Roy Fangman, but now chauffered by Red.

No. 727

Bill Combs

No. 727 was owned and operated by Bill Combs before becoming completely demolished early in mid-season. The salvaged parts were put together to help make up another hot car, 5-9, a grand finish for a fine car.

121
MID-WEST MOTOR BEARING

No. 121

Pearl Custard

No. 121 is also owned by Pearl Custard, completing the duo that makes up one of the top racing teams in the organization. This car, at the start of the season, did a very neat roll at the hands of Jay Sharp on the Mason City track. Since then various drivers, such as Cal Swanson, Lloyd Thurston, Hal Shroeder, an deven Hal's dad, have chauffered the car around the ovals. Late in August a complete new car bearing this number was put on the track by this team.

No. 21

Pearl Custard - Hal Schroeder

No. 21, owned by Pearl Custard, a tireless worker for the betterment of stock car racing, a mechanic deluxe in the art of injecting poison into a racing motor, is one of the top cars of the association. Hal Schroeder, the driver, has many a trophy to prove his prowess as top ranking driver, copped the mid-season championship for 1952. And has won his share of the features this season.

21

AUTO
20

No. 20

John Collins - Dick Reisinger

No. 20, owned by John Collins and driven by Dick Roberts along with many of the other top notch drivers, was one of the hot cars on the track. After being taken thru the "mill" it finally succumbed to the battering and beating received at Marshalltown. Picture shows the new car.

199

No. 199

Al Warneke - Frank Lago

No. 199 is owned by Al Warneke and driven by Frank Lago and has provided some of the most spectacular entertainment at the speedway this season. Frank has one of the most thrilling end-over-end-flips on the track to think about this coming winter. All 199 needed was a new body, etc.

Circle 199

Al Warneke - Mark Kustic

Circle 199, also a Warneke production, met the same fate as 199 the same eevning, when Mark Kustic, the driver failed to negotiate the first turn and proceded to flip. However, the next week the car, and Mark, were both back in competition none the worse for their antics.

199

CITY MOTORS
141' KF

No. 141-J

Bob Ledtje

No. 141-J made its appearance on the oval in mid-season with Bob Ledtje of Gladbrook as owner and driver. Bob is employed as a mechanic and has helped build up several cars including 86 and 141. Bob had his first feature win at the Polio Benefit Show.

333
GENE A.D. BOIS
HOME
BUILDER

Three 3s

George Bass - Arnold Spore

The Three Threes has been the hard luck car of the season. Along with the regular driver, Arnold Spore, this team has been involved in almost every major crackup of the year. Hard driving Spore is one of the leaders of the association but has been dogged by Old Lady Bad Luck all the way.

No. 64

Leo Johnson - George Bass

No. 64, owned by Leo Johnson and chauffered by George Bass, has a record of slam bang racing. This team can always be depended upon for a fast time trial and as a feature competitor. Bass is a hard driver and is equally hard to beat.

64

222

No. 222

Vic Payton

No. 222 is owned and driven by Vic Payton of Waterloo. This team is a serious threat at all races at the Tunis oval as Vic pushes them all the way whether or no it ends in glory or disaster.

No. 86

Kenneth Kruger

No. 86, the Reinbeck Lincoln Special, is owned and driven by Kenny Kruger. Kenny has owned and helped build up several stocks all of which have been in the money and provided plenty of thrills and experience for both drivers and fans.

SPECIAL 86

V8

No. V-8

Kenny Bell - Claude Black

V-8 is owned and operated by Kenny Bell and Claude Black. On its initial appearance on the track the car was chauffered by Black, lately has been pushed by various other driver. The recently acquired chassis also became a victim of the Marshalltown mayhem.

Boxed 7

The Boxed 7 is owned by ______ Custard and has been driven for the better part of its short existence by the top drivers of the association. "The Little Jewel" has been involved in numerous crackups since its initial appearance, and has even taken a crack at getting into the stands, being stopped short by a light pole.

7

ENP
99

No. 99
Harry Petersen - Eugene Petersen

No. 99, the first of the Petersen cars, is driven by Eugene Petersen, Jr. As one of the racing Petersens has become outstanding on the local track.

No. 100
Harry Petersen - Babe Petersen

No. 100, driven by Babe Petersen, another of the Petersen team, also helps to keep the Petersen "stable" in the public eye. These lead-foot drivers make the sport the sensation it has become.

100

No. 113
Harry Petersen, Jr.

No. 113, driven by Harry Petersen, Jr., completes the trio of cars making up the Petersen racing team. These drivers have each carried the checkered flag during the season and have all given their best to help put the show over.

No. 177
Ray Barnhart - Dick Hinton

No. 177 was built up and owned by the combination of Ray Barnhart and Dick Hinton, with Dick as the driver. This car was replaced later in the season after taking a beating at the hands of fellow opponents.

177

177

Circle 177
Ray Barnhart - Dick Hinton

Circle 177, the first nighter, was owned by Ray Barnhart and driven by Dick Hinton. This team made its debut by flipping end-over-end, making a momentary nose stand on the first turn, first lap, first race of the evening — last appearance.

No. 44
John Cummings - Wayne Fox

The Two Fours, a late comer to the banked oval, is owned by John Cummings and was driven by Wayne Fox. The team, when present made a fine effort, but the appearances were few and far between.

HOOK'S RADIATOR
11

No. 11
Gene Hultman - Carroll Jensen

Car No. 11 is owned by Gene Hultman and Carroll Jensen and is driven by Carroll. Gene is a mechanic and Carroll a carpenter contractor. They are assisted in the pits by Harold Cox. Carroll had gained tenth place in the point standing at the mid-season championship point of the season.

No. 711
Gene Hultman - Carroll Jensen

Car No. 711 is owned by the same team. Gene is now driving 711 as Don Isley, former driver moved to another car. 711 was almost completely demolished and 11 was badly wrecked on the same evening in late August this season.

HOOK'S RADIATOR

555

Three 5s
Guy Rich - Glenn DeBower

555 is owned by Guy Rich and sponsored by DeBowers D-X station at Dike, Iowa. The car made its initial appearance on the track early in August and was an immediate success. Red Droste brot the car into the money the first night out and it has been a consistent money winner since. Glenn DeBower, after making a good try in the Polio Show, will chauffer the car after gaining more experience. Guy is proprietor of the Dike Body Shop.

No. 5
Bud Slater

No. 5 made regular appearances on the oval at the beginning of the season under the guidance of Bud Slater, but after a series of flips and crashes due to misguidance the car was retired to the local scrap heap.

5

5

Circle 5
Bud Slater

Circle 5, a hot number at the start of the season, was given a series of rolls, flips and crashes, and soon became obsolete as far as racing was concerned. The salvaged parts were used in building up No. 4, another Boslough sponsored car.

No. 87
Clarence DuToit - John Thede

No. 87, the only car out of Marshalltown was owned by Clarence DuToit and drven by John Thede. This team was a serious threat to the leaders at the start of the present season, but bad luck took its toll and has kept the car off the track the past few weeks.

87
QUINNS
RADIATOR
SHOP

No. 88
Gene Gunther

No. 88 is owned and driven by Gene Gunther of Waterloo. A relative newcomer to th track as a driver, Gene is in there trying hard. He gained his know-how as to the building of his cars by working with Red Droste in the pits in the past. His knowledge as a driver is being gotten the hard way.

88

No. 101
Johnny Barta

No. 101 was owned and driven by Johnny Barta of Waterloo. This was Johnny's third year of driving stocks but he has helped build several of the cars in the association, including his own. No. 101 was also a victim of the tangle at Marshalltown.

No. 109
Johnny Reider

No. 109 was owned and driven by Johnny Reider. At the start of the current season the white 109 was always a car to watch, both from the driver's angle and from the stands, as the unexpected was almost always sure to happen. This Deep Rock boys and now appears car was purchased by the Tyler on the track carrying the Blue and Cream colors of the Deep Rock firm as Circle 26.9.

109

No. 26.9
Harold Tyler - Al Runyan

26.9, a Tyler Deep Rock sponsored car is one of the leading contenders at all races. Driven by Al Runyan, the fugitive from 161, this team puts on a top show at all meets. Al is one of the more experielnced drivers in the organization, having started with the opening of the stocks at Tunis.

Circle 26.9

Circle 26.9, the old 109, is driven by Johnny Reider. Now owned by Howard Tyler of Tyler Deep Rock, the car is still being driven by Reider and makes good account of itself. This car, too, received an unmerciful beating at Marshalltown.

TRUCK
STOP

FELDMAN'S
36

Circle 36
Ed Wellner - Don Wellner

Circle 36 is owned by Ed Wellner of LaPorte City, garage mechanic, and driven by Don Wellner of Waterloo. Don is a member of both the Hawkeye Racing Association of Waterloo and Cedar Falls and the Championship Stocks of Cedar Rapids.

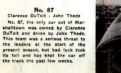

ENP
99

No. 99
Harry Petersen - Eugene Petersen

No. 99, the first of the Petersen cars, is driven by Eugene Petersen, Jr. As one of the racing Petersens has become outstanding on the local track.

No. 100
Harry Petersen - Babe Petersen

No. 100, driven by Babe Petersen, another of the Petersen team, also helps to keep the Petersen "stable" in the public eye. These lead-foot drivers make the sport the sensation it has become.

100

No. 113
Harry Petersen, Jr.

No. 113, driven by Harry Petersen, Jr., completes the trio of cars making up the Petersen racing team. These drivers have each carried the checkered flag during the season and have all given their best to help put the show over.

No. 177
Ray Barnhart - Dick Hinton

No. 177 was built up and owned by the combination of Ray Barnhart and Dick Hinton, with Dick as the driver. This car was replaced later in the season after taking a beating at the hands of fellow opponents.

177

177

Circle 177
Ray Barnhart - Dick Hinton

Circle 177, the first nighter, was owned by Ray Barnhart and driven by Dick Hinton. This team made its debut by flipping end-over-end, making a momentary nose stand on the first turn, first lap, first race of the evening — last appearance.

No. 44
John Cummings - Wayne Fox

The Two Fours, a late comer to the banked oval, is owned by John Cummings and was driven by Wayne Fox. The team, when present made a fine effort, but the appearances were few and far between.

HOOK'S RADIATOR
11

No. 11
Gene Hultman - Carroll Jensen

Car No. 11 is owned by Gene Hultman and Carroll Jensen and is driven by Carroll. Gene is a mechanic and Carroll a carpenter contractor. They are assisted in the pits by Harold Cox. Carroll had gained tenth place in the point standing at the mid-season championship point of the season.

No. 711
Gene Hultman - Carroll Jensen

Car No. 711 is owned by the same team. Gene is now driving 711 as Don Isley, former driver moved to another car. 711 was almost completely demolished and 11 was badly wrecked on the same evening in late August this season.

HOOK'S RADIATOR

555

Three 5s
Guy Rich - Glenn DeBower

555 is owned by Guy Rich and sponsored by DeBowers D-X station at Dike, Iowa. The car made its initial appearance on the track early in August and was an immediate success. Red Droste brot the car into the money the first night out and it has been a consistent money winner since. Glenn DeBower, after making a good try in the Polio Show, will chauffer the car after gaining more experience. Guy is proprietor of the Dike Body Shop.

No. 5
Bud Slater

No. 5 made regular appearances on the oval at the beginning of the season under the guidance of Bud Slater, but after a series of flips and crashes due to misguidance the car was retired to the local scrap heap.

5

5

Circle 5
Bud Slater

Circle 5, a hot number at the start of the season, was given a series of rolls, flips and crashes, and soon became obsolete as far as racing was concerned. The salvaged parts were used in building up No. 4, another Boslough sponsored car.

No. 87
Clarence DuToit - John Thede

No. 87, the only car out of Marshalltown was owned by Clarence DuToit and drven by John Thede. This team was a serious threat to the leaders at the start of the present season, but bad luck took its toil and has kept the car off the track the past few weeks.

87
QUINN'S
RADIATOR
SHOP

No. 88
Gene Gunther

No. 88 is owned and driven by Gene Gunther of Waterloo. A relative newcomer to th track as a driver, Gene is in there trying hard. He gained his know-how as to the building of his cars by working with Red Droste in the pits in the past. His knowledge as a driver is being gotten the hard way.

88

No. 101
Johnny Barta

No. 101 was owned and driven by Johnny Barta of Waterloo. This was Johnny's third year of driving stocks but he has helped build several of the cars in the association, including his own. No. 101 was also a victim of the tangle at Marshalltown.

No. 109
Johnny Reider

No. 109 was owned and driven by Johnny Reider. At the start of the current season the white 109 was always a car to watch, both from the driver's angle and from the stands, as the unexpected was almost always sure to happen. This Deep Rock boys and now appears car was purchased by the Tyler on the track carrying the Blue and Cream colors of the Deep Rock firm as Circle 26.9.

109

Nc. 26.9
Harold Tyler - Al Runyan

26.9, a Tyler Deep Rock sponsored car is one of the leading contenders at all races. Driven by Al Runyan, the fugitive from 161, this team puts on a top show at all meets. Al is one of the more experieinced drivers in the organization, having started with the opening of the stocks at Tunis.

Circle 26.9

Circle 26.9,the old 109, is driven by Johnny Reider. Now owned by Howard Tyler of Tyler Deep Rock, the car is still being driven by Reider and makes good account of itself. This car, too, received an unmerciful beating at Marshalltown.

TRUCK
STOP

FELDMAN'S

Circle 36
Ed Wellner - Don Wellner

Circle 36 is owned by Ed Wellner of LaPorte City, garage mechanic, and driven by Don Wellner of Waterloo. Don is a member of both the Hawkeye Racing Association of Waterloo and Cedar Falls and the Championship Stocks of Cedar Rapids.

No race meet can be a success without the certain "musts" that are present in the pits and infield. Two of the cooperators at all the races are the all purpose Jeeps owned by Chumley's Auto Market of Waterloo and Brown's Skelly Service of LaPorte City, used as push cars. Another, Hurley's Ambulance, a regular for the past three years, with Everett Delp in attendance. Mr. Delp has been on duty the past two seasons. Then there is the Colonial Petroleum Co. Tank Truck of Waterloo, operated by ________________, on hand to furnish gas for the boys. Then last, but not least, the cleanup squads, Bass Auto Repair tow truck and the Chumley Auto Market truck, both of Waterloo.

COLONIAL
PETROLEUM CO.
FUEL OIL

AUTO
MARKET

The Hawkeye Racing Association, Inc., would be unable to operate if it were not for certain officials whose duty it is to see that the racing program runs smoothly and these persons must be at every race meet.

Dale Randall, KWWL announcer, has been the master of ceremonies since the start of the 1952 season and is assisted by Warren Mead, KWWL program director. These men keep the fans informed of the happenings on the track, the names of the drivers and the numbers of the cars in the heat races. They also call the cars from the pits over the extension speaker.

Bud Meeker, Cedar Falls, is chief judge and timer. It is Bud's duty to operate the "eye", the electrical timer, during the time trials. He is assisted in the judges' stand by Kay Nabholz, bookkeeper at the Chumley Auto Market, Waterloo. These two, after the time trials have been recorded, must set up the heat races, keep the lap records and act as judges by making the decisions in case of close finishes, unlawful acts on the track, etc.

In case of an absence on the part of these regulars Cal Leckbee is ready to take over on the "mike" and Mary Wolff is an able assistant to the judge.

Our handsome young flagman, who in July took off time for a honeymoon, is Don Bashford of Cedar Falls. This is Don's first year as a flagman and he must be complimented for his magnificent job. Don rates as one of the best in these parts. Mrs. Bashford is also known as a very popular young lady for presenting trophies. It seems they all come back for seconds.

Bill DeLong and Irv Sassman, both of Waterloo, have the job of signing in the boys. The former being chief pit steward and the latter his assistant. Owners and drivers must sign waivers and pay into the benevolence fund at each race to these boys at the pit gate. They also notify cars and drivers of their positions in the heat races and get them out to the track in their turn.

20
M-M
AUTO

Dick Reisinger, Waterloo sign painter, has been interested in stock car racing since its inauguration at the Waterloo oval. Dick has driven the stocks at one time or another, and started out the season in No. 20. He has ceased participating in the sport as a driver and is now using his talents as a sign painter, decorator and cartoonist to beautify the cars of the association. Evidence of the fact that he is a master in the art can be found by looking over the new No. 20 recently put on the track.

64

11-7

DIKE BODY SHOP
555
DIKE
IA

V8

Fender Benders

1953

Stock Car Races

Sponsored by
Hawkeye Racing Association

Left to right: Ted Leckbee, Howard Boslough, "Speed" Chumley, and Gordon Bentley

HOWARD BOSLOUGH, JR., president of the Hawkeye Racing Association, Inc., became interested in racing in 1950 as the result of sponsoring Car No. 197 being built up by Bob Piper and Car No. 334 being built up by Gene Kaskaden. In 1951 cars No. 197, driven by Bob Piper, No. 28, handled by Piper, and No. 1, driven by Jim Krogh, were sponsored by Boslough's K-F Motors. The same year much of Howard's time was spent in the judges stand and in the pits doing as much as he could toward the betterment of stock racing. During the winter of 1951 and 1952, along with Bob Piper, Jim Krogh, Al Runyan, and Mrs. Russ Wolff, Boslough Motor's secretary, he helped organize the present association. This past season he has sponsored cars No. 1, 2, 3 and 4.

GORDON BENTLEY, vice-president, formerly a midget enthusiast, started building stocks in 1949, always as an owner and mechanic, never a driver. Besides having quarter mile stocks, he has also entered cars in 200 lappers at Des Moines, in Wisconsin, Nebraska and Missouri. He has raced cars on all the tracks in this vicinity, and in 1951 his car, driven by Mike Moody, was one of the top cars of the season, as have been the cars driven by Bill Zwanziger and Bob Hilmer this past season. Bentley owns and operates a garage at Fairbanks.

TED LECKBEE, secretary, became a car owner in 1950 and has given much of his time and effort the past two years in keeping a car operating at all times since. Ted has taken his cars to all tracks in the midwest and has made a good record for himself with his cars at all appearances. Wherever there is the white of stock motors, the squeal of tires biting the dirt, or the smell of oil fumes mingled with dust, there Leckbee can be found.

IRA (SPEED) CHUMLEY, owner and operator of the Chumley Auto Market in Waterloo, is treasurer of the association. A former midget operator, both as owner and driver, "Speed" started building stocks in 1948. Along with his son, Bill, and many succeeding drivers, "Speed" has set an enviable record on Iowa tracks. He has slowed down somewhat recently, but always has a car on the track and assumes the position of treasurer, track manager from the infield, traffic controller, etc., at the time of a mishap on the tracks, and aids as a mediator at misunderstandings after the mishaps occur.

To these four, Boslough, Bentley, Leckbee and Chumley, we dedicate this, the first edition of the Hawkeye Racing Association, Inc., year book, "FENDER BENDERS". May your cars continue to roll to the starting lines for years to come.

Stock Car Races — As Seen Through the Camera's Lens
by Morris L. Bailey, Dike, Iowa

Vol. 1 - Number 2 — Waterloo, Iowa, Saturday, May 16, 1953

1st Feature to Droste on Tunis Oval

Above: Red Droste carrying the flag for the "Winner's Lap" after the feature race at the Tunis Speedway Sunday, May 10. Red now has possession of the "Fender Bender" Trophy a traveling prize, presented to the feature winner each week.

NO. 10 GOES INTO A ROLL — The Chumley entry, driven by Johnny Proctor fails to make the first turn during the 3rd heat race at Tunis' on Sunday, May 10. Proctor's mount was righted and again run in the heat which was won by Bob Posekany, Dike.

Wins Season Opener In Circle 245

Sunday, May 10, 1953

Red Droste of Waterloo won the 20-lap main event in the opening stock car racing program of the season on the Tunis Speedway Sunday afternoon before 1,597 fans.

Droste won over a strong challenge by Bob Hilmer of Dysart when several of the lead cars were involved in a series of spinouts on the south curve during the 11th lap. The only accident of the day occurred in the third heat when Johnny Proctor turned over in the second lap but was not injured and continued in the race.

Bob Leidje of Gladbrook won over Droste in the first heat race. Other winners included Arnold Spore and Bob Piper, both of Waterloo; Frank Lago, Oelwein, and Bob Posekeny of Dike.

Another program is scheduled for Sunday afternoon with time trials at 1:30 and the first race at 2:30.

Summaries:

First heat (10 laps): 1. Bob Ledtje (Gladbrook); 2. Red Droste (Waterloo); 3. Russ Steffan (Waterloo); 3:77.

Second heat (10 laps): 1. Arnold Spore (Waterloo); 2. Bob Piper (Waterloo); 3. Carrol Jenson (Waterloo); 3:56.

Third heat (10 laps): 1. Frank Lago (Oelwein); 2. Bob Posekeny (Dike); 3. Arnold Spore (Waterloo).

Novelty (10 laps): 1. Bob Piper (Waterloo); 2. Red Broune (Waterloo); 3. Frank Lago (Oelwein).

Semi-main (10 laps): 1. Bob Posekeny (Dike); 2. Curt Madison (Waterloo); 3. Don Isley (Cedar Falls); 4. Herb Frye (Waterloo); 3:51.

Main event (20 laps): 1. Red Droste (Waterloo); 2. Bob Hilmer (Dysart); 3. Hal Schroeder (Bettendorf); 4. Red Broline (Waterloo); 6:53.

"Thru the Camera's Lens" To Be Issued Weekly

In this, the first issue of "Through the Camera Lens," we are submitting a few of the pictures taken from last year's "Fender Benders" and some of the pictures taken at last week's

The purpose of this pictorial is to help you to become better acquainted with the owners and drivers and to help to keep a more composite record of the year's action. Each week there will be photos of the Feature winner, accident shots and of the highlights of the week's racing both in Marshalltown and Waterloo, plus pictures of the owners, drivers and field men who help make stock car racing the sport it is.

In order that you may secure a copy each week, we are making a special offer which will entitle you to a copy of the paper at the track and at the termination of the racing season you will receive a bound copy of the season's editions under the title of "Fender Benders, 1953". This offer is being made to you at the price of $2.00. If you are interested in receiving this tabloid please fill out the blankand mail it to Morris L. Bailey, Dike, Iowa, with $2.00, or hand it to the program boys at the entrance to the stands.

If you want to receive the copies by mail add 50c for postage and your copy will be sent to you weekly.

Be Sure You Obtain Your Copy of

"Through the Camera's Lens"

At Each Race During the Season

Act Now - $2.00

10c per single copy

By paying $2.00 before the 1st of June you can receive a copy of "Through the Camera's Lens" each week at the track and at the termination of the racing season you will get a bound volume of the issues published. ..This publication will be known as the yearbook "Fender Benders," picturing activities ,cars, drivers, etc., of the Hawkeye Racing Association.

Fill in the blank below and hand it, with your remittance of $2.00, to the program salesmen or the staff photographers, or mail to Morris L. Bailey, Dike, Iowa.

SPORTS PUBLICATIONS
Morris L. Bailey
Dike, Iowa

Please enter my name on your list in order that I may receive a copy of "THROUGH THE CAMERA'S LENS" each week at the races of the Hawkeye Racing Association, Inc. Enclosed find $2.00 which will also entitle me to a 1953 copy of "FENDER BENDERS" at the close of the 1953 Season.

$2.50 by mail.

Name ....

Address ....

....

Bob Letje, 1st heat winner.

Arnold Spoor, 2nd heat winner

Bob Posekany, 3rd heat winner.
Also Semi-Main winner

Bob Piper, Novelty race winner

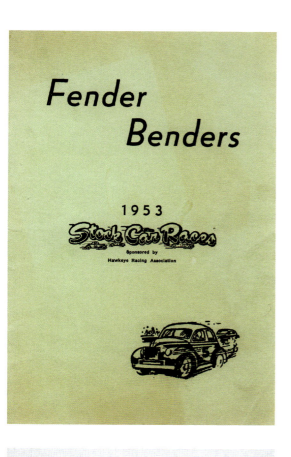

Stock Car Races As Seen Through the Camera's Lens
by Morris L. Bailey, Dike, Iowa

Vol. I - Number 3 May 23, 1953

Droste Tops Field at Tunis' Sunday

Rain Stops Final Two Stock Races

A sudden shower washed out the semi main and feature events at Tunis Speedway Sunday afternoon after an earlier shower had delayed the start of racing and slowed the track so much that the fastest time trial posted was 23.53 seconds by Arnold Spore of Waterloo.

This compared with 19.82 chalked up by Red Droste the previous week.

Five events plus the special trophy dash were completed before the racing was halted, with Red Droste picking up top honors in the trophy dash and the Australian pursuit race and copping second in the second heat for the most impressive record of the day.

A total of 1,286 paid customers were on hand for the racing.

The results:

Time trials—Arnold Spore, Waterloo; :23.53.

First heat (10 laps)—1. Bob Hilmer, Dysart; 2. Arnold Spore, Waterloo; 3. Russ Steffans, Waterloo; 3:95.

Second heat (10 laps)—1. Bob Posekeny, Dike; 2 Red Droste, Waterloo; 3. Cal Swanson, Cedar Falls; 3:87.

Third heat (10 laps)—1. Bud Slater, Cedar Falls; 2. Harry Peterson, Waterloo 3. Bob Roe, Waterloo; 3:88.

Trophy dash (10 laps)—1. Red Droste Waterloo; 2. Arnold Spore, Waterloo; 3 Cal Swanson, Cedar Falls.

Novelty event (10 laps)—1. Red Droste, Waterloo; 2. Carroll Jensen, Waterloo; 3. Bob Posekeny, Dike; 3:82.

ARNIE SPORE GETS 1st FEATURE OF CAREER AT MARSHALLTOWN

. . . Story on the Inside

33

FIRST FEATURE WIN — Arnold Spore, veteran driver from Waterloo carries the flag on the "Victor's Lap" after the first feature win of his carrer at Amusement's Inc. Race Track, where he captured the 20-lap main event on Saturday, May 16th. Arnie is now driving in his third year of competition.

"Volunteer" Aids Fire

Insult was added to injury Saturday night, May 10th, for Glen Stauffer of Brooklyn during the running of the feature event at the season's opener at the Amusements Inc., Race Track at Marshalltown.

An oily rag, left on the exhaust stacks of Stauffer's No. 47, became ignited during the course of the race and as a result a pit stop became necessary.

One of the pit men grabbed the first can handy and raced to the scene and tossed the contents on the blaze.

You're right - gasoline - resulting in a roaring blaze.

Stauffer made a hasty exit by way of a side window as the association fire extinguisher was pressed into service extinguishing the fire.

With a slightly damaged car under him, Stauffer re-entered the race only to lose a wheel to retire him for the evening.

Vukovich Does 138 To Lead Qualifiers

Bill Vukovich and Jack McGrath, who chased each other to new records in the opening laps of the 1952 Indianapolis 500-mile auto race, are all set to do it again in the 37th running on May 30th.

Vukovich, of Fresno, Calif., won the pole position, in the three-car front row, last Sunday by qualifying at an average speed of 138.392 miles an hour for the 10-mile trial.

McGrath, of South Sasadena, Calif., won the outside spot in the front row for the fourth time in five years, that's the best position for breaking into the lead on the first lap. He has done just that in the last two meets at Indianapolis. He qualified his new Hinkle Spec. at 136.602.

Fred Agabashian of Albany, Calif., who sat on the pole last year, won the middle spot in the front row in the new Granco-Elgin Spec. at 137.546.

Vukovich's qualifying mark was second only to the record of 139.034 made last year by Chet Miller, who was killed Friday, May 15th in a practice run.

Sports Car Races At Omaha July 5

Spectators at the National Sports Car Races at Offutt AFB July 5 will be the first sports car racing fans to sit in on a contest steeped in rivalry as keen as that which exists between Brooklyn's beloved Bums and Leo Durocher's boys from Coogan's Bluff across the river in New York.

Seems like sports car racers from the West coast and those who campaign out of the East differ in opinion as to whom are the greatest drivers, both sides having voiced publicly its friendly opinion. But up to now there has been no way for either side to qualify its statements.

Contestants in the races include drivers from both sections of the country. And the argument that has been raging since sports cars racing came into its own should be settled.

The winner will have his work cut out for him; it is already established that he will have to outrun the best cars and drivers in the world on one of the trickiest courses ever laid out on an airport. The hairpin turns and sharp curves offer a challenge that only the best drivers in the business can accept.

Proceeds from the races go to the Airmen's Living Improvement Fund

Gets Traffic Ticket

Pino Lella of Milan, Italy, received a traffic ticket while driving in an auto race.

He was on a trial lap during the Guardsmen's road race in Golden Gate Park, San Francisco, Sunday, when he mistook an emergency escape route for a continuation of the course.

He roared along a quiet residential street at 100 miles per hour.

Spore Grabs First Race in Thrilling Finish

from the Marshalltown Times-Republican

In a thrilling finish which saw less than two car lengths separate the first three cars, Arnie Spore of Waterloo sped to victory in the first stock car races of the season Saturday night at the Amusements Inc. track southwest of Marshalltown.

This was the first feature win of Spore's racing career.

Spore took over the lead on the eighth lap of the 15-lap feature from Gene Hultman of Hudson and was never headed thereafter, but was seriously challenged by Cal Swanson of Dike and Red Droste of Waterloo.

Swanson came up fast after starting in 12th position, took over second spot in the 11th lap and was barely nosed out by Spore. Droste was only a few feet behind Swanson. Hultman, who paced the field the first seven laps, finished fourth.

Don Graham of Waterloo received a gash over his eye when his car hit the retining wall in the feature.

Ted Denkolff of Bettendorf was an easy 40-yard victor in the semi-main driving Bentley's No. 35A. Hultman was a strong second.

Swanson topped the 27-car field of drivers from the Waterloo and Marshalltown areas in the time trials with a fast 22.34.

The large crowd in attendance got its biggest thrill n the second qualifying heat when Mark Taylor of Hudson and Bob Ledtje of Gladbrook collided on the No. 4 turn and performed a double roll. Neither driver was injured.

A local pilot, Floyd Needham, captured honors in the novelty event, while the winners of the three qualifying heats were Spore, Droste, and Bob Hilmer of Dysart.

Summary —

Time Trials: Swanson, Ledtje, Droste, Schroeder, Posekeny, Piper, Hilmer, Spore, Thede and Graham for the first ten money spots.

1st heat - Spore, Schroeder and Roe

2nd heat - Hilmer, Runyan and Jensen

3rd heat - Droste, Piper and Peterson.

Novelty - Needham, Reid and Stauffer.

Semi-Main - Denkolff, Hultman and Peterson.

Feature - Spore, Swanson, Droste, Hultman, Posekeny, Thede, Denkolff, Schroeder and Strohm.

Dust . . .

You can say that again! That's about the only thing that did get through the camera lens last Saturday night.

Were our faces red after the dust rolled away? All four of us had that beautiful crimson tint. My companions, Gallentine, Lindsey, and the Sports Photographer from the local daily, and myself, M. Bailey, all goofed off. Three shots too soon, and as for myself, musta cracked a flash bulb before using.

There was plenty of action. Taylor of Hudson high in the air over Ledtje of Gladbrook, and us caught with our shutters closed. As a result, no pictures of the most spectacular flip that has ever come within my camera's range.. We either wait too long, or not long enough, or somethin'.

Let's hope that in the coming events if we do continue to have these spectacular crashes and fine races that we also have Lady Luck riding in the seat beside us.

Fans, show your appreciation to the participants in these events by telling your friends of the type of shows you are witnessing. And, each time you come out to see them, bring along a new friend.

Next time more and better pictures, we hope!

Graham Injured

Donnie Graham, pilot of the Chumley No. 10 on the Marshalltown oval last Saturday night ran into a bit of difficulty comng out of the back stretch and zigged when he should have zagged and made straight for the fence which was backed up by a number of 12x12's.

The ensuing crash did niether Donnie or the car much good. Mr. Graham received a wound over the left eye which required three stitches to close, and the car suffered extensive front end damage. However, both were able to be on the track at Waterloo Sunday afternoon, Donnie being the more battered of the two.

First In Novelty - Marshalltown

35

1st in 2nd Heat - Marshalltown

HELP! I'm going blind!

1st in Novelty - Waterloo

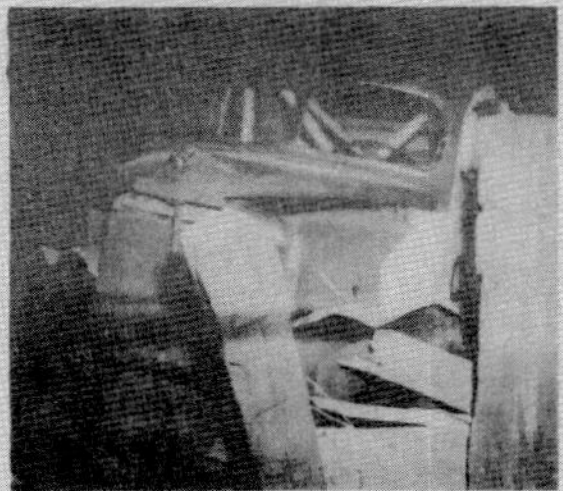

Sudden Stop!!

First in 3rd Heat - Marshalltown

555

Which Way??

First in 3rd Heat - Waterloo

First in 2nd Heat - Waterloo

Stock Car Races As Seen Through the Camera's Lens
by Morris L. Bailey, Dike, Iowa

Volume 1 - Number 4 Saturday, June 6, 1953

Action Galore the Past Two Weeks

Wha Hoppen?

Marshalltown Winner

Fer Go'ness Sakes!

Roe! Roe! Roe!

Him Too?

121

Muddy Ain't It?

Ledtje Scores 3 Wins At Marshalltown

After running in second spot most of the race, Bob Ledtje of Gladbrook moved to the front on the 13th lap and finally won the feature event in the second weekly stock car racing show at Amusements, Inc. track May 23rd.

His margin of victory was about four car lengths over runner-up Bob Reid of Cedar Falls.

Bill Zwanziger, on leave from the Army, led the pack most of the 15-lap race. The Waterloo speedster took over on the third lap and left the field eating his dust until Ledtje made the grade on the 13th.

Zwanziger developed engine trouble at the same time and was forced from the race the next lap, allowing the third place car, piloted by Reid, to gain second. Dysart's Bob Hilmer finished in the No. 3 slot with Toledo's Dewey Wilfong and Chelsea's John Thede next.

Besides winning the 15-lap feature in 5.73, Ledtje also paced the time trials with :22.17 and won the trophy dash of the six fastest cars, with Droste and Spore third.

Last week Ledtje rolled in his qualifying heat and was unable to enter the feature, won by Spore, who Saturday was sidelined early with engine trouble.

Hilmer copped the 10-lap semi-main event by some feet over Droste. Hilmer was also front-runner in the Australian pursuit, with Jim Krogh of Cedar Falls, also home on leave, the only other driver left after the fourth lap.

From the "crash-up, bang-up" standpoint, the third heat race was tops. That event was delayed five times when cars rolled, spun out or collided before the first lap could be completed. Reid was the eventual winner. Droste and Spore won the other heats.

Results:

Time Trials - Ledtje.

Trophy Dash - Ledtje, Droste and Spore.

First Heat - Spore, Ledtje and Zwanziger.

Second Heat - Droste, Thede and H. Petersen.

Third Heat - Reid, Droste and Warneke.

Australian Pursuit - Hilmer and Krogh.

Semi-Main - Zawnziger, Droste and Runyan.

Main - Ledtje, Reid and Hilmer.

Al Speth Dies At Des Moines

Many of the racing fans in this community will remember Al Speth.

He was not one of the top drivers that appeared at the Tunis Speedway when it first opened, with the midgets furnishing the excitement, but Al was there doing his part.

Speth graduated from the midgets to the big cars in the past few years and finally bought himself a car that all drivers dream of owning, an Offenhauser. The tops in race cars.

Al took his car to Des Moines last Sunday and entered in the races there. He was using, as the big boys say it, "hot metal", a 270 cubic inch motor. It proved too "hot". In event No. 4, the car got away from Al, climbed over his running mate, Fritz Tegtmeier and hit the cement retaining wall.

Al's brother Art accompanied him to the hospital where attendants said the driver had died just a few minutes after his arrival. His death was caused by internal injuries and multiple fractures.

Trophies . . .

The way those guys go after those golden trophies with the Hudson Hornet on top of them you'd think they were something that could be taken out on the track and raced, or that they'd pay a month's fuel bill for the stock they are driving. Did you ever see so much action in one race. Spore and Droste both had the idea that they should take home the bacon, but I guess they got too anxious. Those cars were certainly wedged together.

Trophy dash winners to date have been Droste, Ledtje, Graham, Spore and Petersen. Still no repeaters. Let's keep them moving.

Droste has now taken possession of the "Fender Bender" trophy. In this instance he won it by picking up three features in a row. The first time in the history of the association that this feat has been accomplished.

THROUGH THE CAMERA LENS
Edited and Published by
Morris L. Bailey, Dike, Iowa
at the
College Hill Print Shop
2016 College St.
Cedar Falls, Iowa

If you are interested in this type of paper and want to see it continue why don't you let us know at once by getting in touch with the program salesmen or the photographers at once. We must have a large subscription list in order to keep the publication going.

We are planning on going to 8 pages a week, too, so if there is anything you wish to advertise get in touch with the publisher and he will take care of you.

We will have news from the tracks at Marshalltown and Waterloo, along with pictures and other speed sport news. What better way is there for you to keep a complete record of all the doings of the association, the owners,drivers and other members, than to get it each week in such a way that it can be filed away to be brought out again next winter when the races are run all over again around the fireside.

If you have any choice bits of news about the racing fraternity just let us know, and it will be published in the columns of this periodical.

If you want a year book at the close of the season just mail $2.00 to Morris L. Bailey and a copy will be reserved for you.

Did You Ever

Sit down to a refreshingly cool glass of grapefruit juice and relax to the music of the juke box as you sipped the nectar.

Then in comes the salad with that, would you say heavenly, garlic dressing, mmm-mmm good.

Then top that off with fried spring chicken, piping hot, with a golden brown crust that melts in your mouth. This sided with french fries and Vienna bread and coffee good to the last drop.

Where do you get all this? Just stop in at the Dixie Chicken Basket and order "Chicken for Two." 1400 Falls Avenue, Waterloo, Iowa. Man! that's eating!

Droste Wins Four

May 24, 1953

Red Droste of Waterloo cleaned up on the field in the Sunday stock car racing program at Tunis Speedway by winning the final four events, including the 15-lap feature.

Droste also won the third heat race, the novelty and the semi-main event and missed winnng the trouphy dash when he locked wheels with Arnold Spore of Waterloo and both cars were forc-out of the race.

As a result of the wheel locking, the two drivers challenged each other and will drive in a special grudge race next Sunday.

Don Graham of Waterloo won the time trials in :24.58 and the Trophy Dash Sunday while driving a Droste car. Spore won the second heat race, while Cal Swanson of Dike won the first heat.

The official paid attendance was announced as 1,297.

Results:

Trophy Dash - Graham and Petersen.

First Heat - Swanson, B. Hilmer, H. Petersen.

Second Heat - Spore, Lago and Taylor.

Third Heat - Droste, Hilmer and Scroggins.

Novelty - Droste, Hilmer and Sanderson.

Semi-Main - Droste, Ledtje, and Lago.

Main - Droste, Posekany, H. Petersen, Swanson and Reid.

Notes . . .

Texas, Independence, Mo., Chevrolet convertible, Bill Zwanzigr, deer. That's the way my notes read.

Here's the story . . .

Seems that as he was on his way to Texas last week and was somewhere in the vicinity of Independence, Mo., while driving a Chevrolet Convertible Coupe, our good friend and associate, Bill Zwanziger managed to run into a deer.

That's all the dope I have. Don't know what happened to Bill, the car or the deer.

By the way, if any of you guys want these fancy satin jackets, just drop into the Iowa Sports Supply on College Hill at Cedar Falls

Droste Rolls 245 Goe On To Win In Circle 245

Drivers of the Hawkeye Racing Association still are wondering how they can beat Red Droste at Tunis Speedway here.

In the feature event on Sunday, May 31, his car rolled coming out o fthe second turn on the first lap. Droste, injured slightly, made a dash for the ambulance, received first aid, and then proceded to his second car, the Circle 245, and went on to win the feature for the third straight time on the Waterloo oval.

Droste placed first in the third heat, but lost the "grudge" race with Arnold Spore. This comedy of errors was something to see. Both men were driving 1936 model cars, old, but runable. After being flipped in the first turn by Droste, the Ford was put back on its wheels and Spore went on to win after Droste's Chevy lost its front end as it went into the far turn. Spore in crossing the finish line put his car into a neat roll for the benefit of the fans in the stands.

Several rollovers and pileups occurred during the regular heats and no injuries were reported. As a result, the crowd of 3,074 persons were well pleased with the show.

Bud Slater moved into the win column with a pair of firsts, one in the first heat, and one in the novelty. Droste had the other double win for the evening along with Eugene Petersen who copped the time trials and the trophy dash.

Results:

Time Trials - E. Petersen, :19.96.

First Heat - Slater, H. Petersen, Red Sanderson.

Second Heat - Swanson, Spore and Droste

Third Heat - Droste, Carpenter and Reid.

Trophy Dash - E. Petersen, Red Droste, Harry Petersen.

Novelty - Slater, Droste, Taylor.

Semi-Main - C. Hilmer, Droste, Posekany.

Main - Droste, Piper and Ledtje.

Contact any one of the photographers or program salesmen and start getting your copies at once. You'll not regret it.

Mud . . .

You can say that again, too . . .

The Marshalltown infield was a sea of the sticky stuff on Saturday, May 23. Picture taking is hard enough in the best of conditions, but try it when you don't know whether you're going to be able to stay on your feet when the going gets rough. In that mess there was less traction than the cars had on the track, in fact, I started getting out of the way as the cars went into the first turn so that I'd be in motion by the time the cars got to where I was.

There was plenty of action. In fact, there was too much. The ruts on the west end got so deep the rear ends of the cars were dragging, and brother that's deep!

First it was No. 30 coming into the far turn, up and over the wheels of the car beside it and finally nose first into the mud, then, end over end.

Where was I . . .

On the far side of the track with another car between myself and the action. That's right, no picture.

Then when the action had died down (we thought), on the same turn what did I gaze upon?—Not 50 feet away lay No. 1 on it's side. What I'd like to know is how it happened. Neither my camera nor I saw that one.

Then after four or five restarts we got a beautiful race going . . . another flip. This time 555. Seems that between getting bumped, a few deep ruts and a broadside, the car just wouldn't stay put.

. . . Me? Nah, I didn't get that either. Ted Galelntine did. He was almost close enough so you could recognize the car.

The Big Ten

Bill Vukovich
Fred Agabashian and Paul Russo
Art Cross
Sam Hanks and Duane Carter
Jack McGrath
Jimmy Daywalt
Jim Rathman and Eddie Johnson
Ernie McCoy
Tony Bettenhausen, Chuck Stevenson and Gene Hartley
Duke Nalon

The above named are the first ten in the recent Memorial Day Classic held at Indianapolis May 30, in the order in which they finished.

Stock Car Races As Seen Through the Camera's Lens
by Morris L. Bailey, Dike, Iowa
Volume 1 - No. 5 Waterloo, June 13, 1953

142 Three Rolls; Cal Three Trophies

Once in the Feature

Saturday Night - Trophy Dash

In the Novelty

Sunday Night - Trophy Dash, Waterloo.

Twice in the Feature

Saturday Night - Traveling Trophy

Sports Cars?

What is a sports car? What will spectators at the National Sports Car Races at Offutt Air Force Base July 5 see as cars burn up rubber at speeds up to 150 miles per hour?

The French have 50,000 words to describe a sports car. The Federation d'Automobile of Paris — the great grandfather organization that controls all international racing and defines all sports cars — wrote a whole book on the subject.

But for Americans a better definition mght be a ltttle bucket of bolts with a few hundred horsepower. It accelerates like a rocket, handles like a dream, and costs like everything.

Its main stock in trad is that it can be used for everyday driving as well as all out racing. Its handling characteristcs have to be experienced to be believed.

A driver can blast into a curve at a hundred miles per hour with perfect safety, yet a standard car would upset trying to make it at 60. By shifting into an acceleration gear a driver can pass three trailer-trucks on a highway in less time than it takes your family car to pass one.

Despite the fact it weighs half as much and has twice the horsepower of a standard American car, it holds the road far better, and can be controlled at practically any speed even on a rough road. When the oversize brake pedal is hit, the car responds almost like it hit a brick wall.

The low center of gravity keeps the car on the road when your family car would be in a nearby field with its wheels spinning in the air. Steering is delicately balanced so that a slight flick of the wrist controls the car.

Sports cars are designed to please the eye, with low, sweeping lines, and an ovrall sleek appearance to delight the ladies.

A MAN was driving his wife and her girl friend home from a shopping trip. The girl friend asked, "Why does your husband always keep his hand out when he's driving?"

The wife answered, "The worm is probably getting ready to turn."

STOCK CAR SUSPENSIONS LIFTED

The indefinite suspension meted out April 24th to stock car drivers Pat Kirkwood of Ft. Worth and E. T. (Preacher) Durr, Shreveport, and car owner J. W. Gentry of Shreveport, have been lifted.

The trio has been elegible to enter sanctioned meets since May 29th. They were suspended for refusal to submit ther machnes to teardown checks after a meet on April 19th in Shreveport.

Three In a Week End

As of Saturday night, June 6, at eight o'clock in the eevning, Cal Swanson had spent a lot of time and driven a lot of miles on these dirt tracks without much to show for it but a lot of hard earned experience. Three years of racing, in fact.

Sunday night, June 7th, at 8:30, Cal was looking for a carpenter to get bids on a trophy case. By that time he needed one.

At Marshalltown Saturday nite Cal practically walked away with Trophy dash. Well, almost. He was running third with a quarter of a lap to go when the front runners, Graham and Spore got a little over anxious, tangled, spun and slithered off the track momentarily. Cal saw his opportunity and squeezed by for a photo finish win over Arne.

Then, while still thinking himself top man on the totem pole, Swanson went out in the feature to let the boys know that it was no accident. That's right, 5-9 was in the grove. Cal took home the beautiful traveling trophy presented by the Marshalltown Times-Republican.

Sunday night he really thought he was good. In fact, I guess he proved that point. He not only drove the fastest time for the evening, but went out and took the trophy dash again.

Congratulations, Cal. You're the first to take two trphy dashes, but did you have to make 'em two in a row.

Arne Spore decided he needed something to brighten up his mantle piece, also, so went out and grabbed first place in the feature to take home the Iowa Sports Supply Traveling Trophy and gain the advantage over the other drivers.

Swanson and Spore Top Stock Field

Cal Swanson of Dike and Arnold Spore of Waterloo topped the field Sunday night, June 7, in stock car races at Tunis Speedway as Red Droste failed to win an event in the fifth 1953 racing session of the Hawkeye Racing Association.

Spore took the main event, while Swanson won the trophy dash and the second heat. Droste won three previous features. This time he was third behind Spore and Carroll Hilmer in the feature.

Red Sanderson of Gladbrook was rolled twice in the feature event, once in the first lap and again in the sixth and went on in the same car. Bob Ledtje also rolled the aforementioned car in the novelty. A crowd of 2,025 was on hand despite the threatening weather.

Summary:

Time Trials - Cal Swanson, 20.35

First Heat - Reid, Swanson, Bob Hilmer

Second Heat - Swanson, Payton and Carroll Hilmer

Third Heat - Lago, Kustic and Hultman

Novelty - Reid, Sanderson and Arne Spore

Trophy Dash - Swanson, Ledtje & Graham

Semi-Main - Isley, Corwin and Roe

Main - Spore, C. Hilmer, and Red Droste

142 Rolls . . .

Three rolls for one car . . .

That's a lotta rolls, especially in one evening. To make matters even worse, two in the same race. And, to top that off, the BOSS did it the first time.

In the novelty, the car was rolled by Ledtje, himself. Did you notice how tenderly he laid it over on its side. He couldn't have been more gentle. And besides that, he used a tractor tire as a buffer.

I don't think he planned on Bob Posekany using the top as a bang-board though. Bob did remove some of the paint as he went by.

Then Red Sanderson and 333 (I don't know who was driving it) became tangled on the east end. Yep, they flipped. 333 was scratched (for the evening, that is) but Red tried the car and found it roadworthy until the sixth or seventh lap and then tried to make the west end bottomside up. Again he went on in the race, only the car looking the worse for the beatings of the evening.

I believe Red thought somebody was after him, er somethin'.

Swanson won the feature last week and took the first leg on the new feature trophy. Droste retired the first trophy by winning the three Sundays previously in succession.

A MAN DRIVER is one who, after seeing an accident, drives carefully for several blocks.

Move Over

Marshalltown Car Wins

Out'a Stock

Also A Novelty Winner

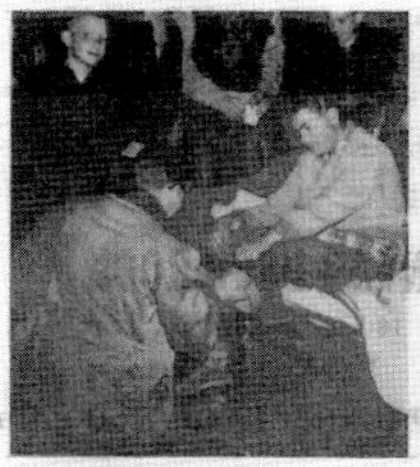

Emergency Treatment

Battered Ain't It?

Swanson Starts 15 Wins Feature

Though he started in a 16-car field, Cal Swanson of Cedar Falls feature on the stock car racing card capped off a big night of driving to a four-lenght victory in the 15-lap at Amusements, Inc., Saturday nite, June 6.

Swanson moved up steadily after the bunched start, taking the lead on the sixth lap by passng front-running Carroll Jensen, a Waterloo car pilot. Jensen was forced from the race a lap later by a flat tire.

Making Swanson hustle all the way were Donnie Graham and Arny Spore, veterans from Waterloo, and Chelsea's John Thede. Graham stayed close in the runner-up spot from the eighth lap on, and Spore took over third from Thede on the final turn around the oval.

Swanson added the trophy dash his heat race and second in time trials to his feature win. Graham topped the trials with a 23.78 clocking.

The 12-lap hemi-main event resulted in a 30-yard triumph for Gladbrook's Red Sanderson over Red Droste of Waterloo, with Thede again showing well in grabbing a third. A local driver, Dick Davis, won the novelty in a 10-lap pursuit race, with Slim Doonan of Brooklyn the only real challenger. Winning heats with Swanson were Spore and Graham.

Despite lots of sliding, spinning and bumping due to the muddy condition of the track, only one serious accdent occurred. Bob Posekany of Dike, driving 121 for Pearl Custard, escaped injury even though the car was badly dabmaged in a roll during the feature.

Summary —

Time Trials - Graham, Swanson, Spore

Trophy Dash - Swanson, Spore and Rowe.

First Heat - Graham, Reid and Corwin.

Second Heat - Swanson, DuToit and Roe.

Third Heat - Spore, Ledtje and Davis

Novelty - Davis, Doonan, DeWalter

Semi-Main - Sanderson, Droste and Thede

Main - Swanson, Graham and Arne Spore.

Droste Leads in Pts

Red Droste of Waterloo held his lead in the current stock car racing standings this week despite a winless Sunday last weekend, the Hawkeye Racing Association announced Friday.

He is followed in order by Cal Swanson of Dike, Arnold Spore of Waterloo and Bob Ledtje of Gladbrook.

The point standings as of June 7 are as follows:

1.	Red Droste	144
2.	Cal Swanson	124
3.	Arnold Spore	120
4.	Bob Ledtje	89
5.	Don Graham	73
6.	Bob Reid	56
7.	Bob Hilmer	54
8.	John Thede	51
9.	Harry Petersen	50
10	Bob Posekany	40
11	Bob Piper	39
12	Bud Slater	39
13	Carroll Hilmer	28
14	Hal Schroeder	27
15	Bob Roe	27
16	Eugene Petersen	27
17	Gene Hultman	23
18	Don Isley	19
19	Carroll Jensen	20
20	Al Runyan	12

Droste has at this time won one trophy dash and the Fender Bender Trophy.

Swanson has one trophy dash at Waterloo, one at Marshalltown and the first leg of the Times-Republican trophy.

Spore has a Marshalltown trophy dash and one leg of the Iowa Sports Supply trophy.

Graham has a trophy dash at Tunis.

Ledtje has a trophy dash at Marshalltown .

Eugene Petersen a trophy dash at Tunis.

Points are figured on a basis of

Time Trials:
10-9-8-7-6-5-4-3-2-1 for the first ten places in the time trials with the 10 points going to the fastest, etc.

Heat Races:
5-3-2, with the five points going to first place winner, etc.

Novelty:
No points.

Semi-Main:
6-4-3-2, with six going to the first place wnner, etc.

Main Event:
12-9-7-5-4-3, with the 12 points going to the winner, etc.

THROUGH THE CAMERA LENS
Edited and Published by
Morris L. Bailey, Dike, Iowa
at the
College Hill Print Shop
2016 College St.
Cedar Falls, Iowa

Set Futurity for Auto Racers

A new, revolutionary idea for big car auto racing on dirt tracks was announced in Des Moines on Thursday, June 4, by the operations managers of National Speedways, Inc., Al Sweeney and Gaylord White of Chicago.

They are introducing the futurity idea to auto racing and have scheduled the history-making inaugural for the Iowa state fair grounds half-mile dirt track Sunday, June 5, 1955.

Distance will be for 100 laps, with a 25-lap consolation race for non-starters in the feature field of 16 cars.

A purse of $10,000 is expected for this initial futurity race, named the "Hawkeye Futurity."

$6,000 Guaranteed

National Speedways, Inc., is guaranteeing a total of $6,000 in prize money should the purse fall short of expectations.

Entries are open to the auto racing world, according to Sweeney and White. There is no maximum limit on entries.

The entry deadline has been set for July 1, 1953. No entries will be accepted after that.

The size of the purse depends entirely upon the number of drivers and owners who enter. The purse could, with enough entries, go as high as $25,000 or more.

Entry fees will be paid in six deposits with the money being held in escrow at a bank in Des Moines.

Match Money

Dollar for dollar, National Speedways, Inc., will match the entry deposits of drivers and owners, this money also going into escrow with the same bank.

Hot rod chauffeurs and owners as well as those from present big car, sports car, midget, hard-tops, standard stock and other racing ranks are eligible to enter now.

Owners have until May 1, 1955, to officially nominate their cars and drvers. Drivers don't have to nominate their cars until May 1, 1955.

Drivers Must Be 21

All drivers must be 21 years of age on race day. Thus a youth of 19 training now to become a race driver is eligible to enter.

Here's the way the purse deposit breaks down. The first deposit s $5.00 to accompany the entry blank which must be filed at the Hawkeye Futurity headquarters at the Iowa state fair board office in Des Moines not later than July 1, 1953.

The second payment of $5.00 is due on October 1, 1953. The payments are increased to $10.00 in 1954, with the deadlines set for June 1 and Oct. 1. On May 1, 1955, when cars and drivers must be nominated officially, a $20,00 payment will fall due.

Stock Car Races
As Seen Through the Camera's Lens
by Morris L. Bailey, Dike, Iowa
Volume 1 - No. 6
Waterloo, Iowa, June 20, 1953

Newcomers Cop Stock Car Victories; Ledtje Wins Main

The Tunis Speedway stock car racing program wound up with a series of upsets after starting with veteran drivers copping the time trials and the first two heat races Sunday evening.

Bob Ledtje of Gladbrook, ranked fourth in the season's point standings going into Sunday night's card, won the main, while Arnold Spore of Waterloo, last week's winner, finished second.

Red Droste, Waterloo, a three-time winner of the main early in the season, copped the trophy dash and second heat, but failed to place in the main.

Al Runyan of Waterloo won the semi-main.

Two newcomers, turning in their first victories of the season, won the novelty and third heat. Bill Corwin of Cedar Falls was the novelty winner, while Curt Madison of New Hampton won the third heat.

Cal Swanson won the time trials.

A crowd of 2,331 saw the races.

Next Sunday's card will feature a spectator's race, Howard Boslough, Cedar Falls, president of the Hawkeye Racing Association, announced.

Time trials—Cal Swanson, Cedar Falls; 20.11.

First heat (10 laps)—1. Bob Hilmer, Dysart; 2. Bob Posekeny, Dike; 3. Bob Reid, Cedar Falls; 2.60.

Second heat (10 laps)—1. Red Droste, Waterloo; 2. Carrol Hilmer, Dysart; 3. Harry Peterson, Waterloo (no time because of roll over).

Third heat (10 laps)—1. Curt Madison, New Hampton; 2. Mark Kustic, Waterloo; 3. Harry Peterson, Waterloo; 3.54.

Trophy dash (six laps)—1. Red Droste, Waterloo; 2. Bob Reid, Cedar Falls; 3. Cal Swanson, Cedar Falls.

Novelty (10 laps)—1. Bill Corwin, Cedar Falls; 2. Dewey Wilfang, Toledo; 3. Don Graham, Waterloo; 3.53.

Semimain (15 laps)—1. Al Runyan, Waterloo; 2. Carrol Hilmer, Dysart; 3. Mark Kustic, Waterloo; 4. Red Droste, Waterloo; 5.24.

Main event (20 laps)—1. Bob Ledtje, Gladbrook; 2. Arnold Spore, Waterloo; 3. Bob Hilmer, Dysart; 4. John Hill, Marshalltown; 5. Carrol Hilmer, Dysart (no time because of roll over).

2 Car Racers Burn to Death Before 4,000

READING, PENN., (UP)—Two racing drivers burned to death in their wrecked stock cars before 4,000 screaming spectators at the Reading fairgrounds Sunday.

Dead are George Lloyd, 27, and Robert Rolland, 26, both of Reading. Hospitalized with a possible skull fracture and other injuries is David Haldeman of Boyertown, Penn.

As 31 races jockeyed in the 50-lap race over the half-mile dirt track, Haldeman's car hit a guard rail and bounced across the track.

Some 10 cars crashed as they swerved to avoid the accident. Rolland's auto rammed the base of a 50-foot light standard. Lloyd's car struck Rolland's and the two burst into flames.

Firefighters tried to battle through the flames but were turned back. It took 15 minutes to squelch the fire. Pit crews needed 30 minutes to pry out the bodies.

Two years ago, Lee Wallard, fresh from winning the 500-mile Indianapolis classic, suffered serious burns in a crash at the track. Wallard was driving a speedway-type car.

About Spinouts

"The race will be stopped after a spinout in the first turn of the first lap." That's what it says in the rules.

So, if you sometimes wonder why a race is not stopped when a car spins in the first lap it's because from the flagman's viewpoint, and from the judges' stand, the car has left the track after reaching the straightaway in the backstretch.

In conferring with Don Bashford on the subject, he says, "I calls 'em as I sees 'em." And after looking at the situation from his angle, we'll just have to agree that's as it has to be.

I still say that even though Don is young in experience, he has gained a place among the flagmen in the middlewest as one of the most efficient and consciencious members in that business. I've seen lots of them in my days with the stocks, midgets, big cars and chuck wagons (horses).

Spore's Loss Ledtje's Gain

Those trophies certainly are elusive. First you have one, then you don't.

That's the experience Arnold Spore had this past week end. He already had the Iowa Sports Supply trophy in his possession and was going strong in the feature toward grabbing the second leg. Then, (how do you make a noise like a motor going to pieces) kerflooey, it was all over. Spore had to drop out, letting our good friend Bob Ledtje go on for the win and take home the trophy.

Droste captured the trophy dash Sunday night in the car timed by Donnie Graham. Cal Swanson, the holder of the fast time for the evening, was forced out of the dash with transmission trouble.

Swanson still has the Times-Republican trophy in his possession, mostly due to the fact that the races were rained out in Marshalltown Saturday, June 13.

Fireworks - Tunis Speedway -July 5th

THE LESS FOR BEST
TYLER'S DEEP ROCK
East 6th and Franklin
Our Premium Products are a Main Event
At Our Fair Prices
Regular - 24.9 Premium 26.9

DIKE BODY SHOP
Rebuilding and Painting of Wrecked Automobiles
Refinishing Household Appliances
Phone 4371 — Dike, Iowa
Hours: 8 to 5 Except Saturday 8 to 12 Noon
GUY RICH (Owner of 555) Proprietor
Have You Purchased a "Fender Bender"

My Chat With The President

Gordon Bentley, vice president of the Hawkeye Racing Assn., was on the track again last Sunday and as a token of good luck, or something, one of his cars came through for the first win since Gordon was stricken with his kidney ailment.

Three new cars are about to make their appearance with the Hawkeye Racing Assn. The owners and drivers have not yet been determined, but the cars will be No. 19 of Oelwein, 66 of Waverly, and 666 of Waterloo.

A big week is coming up starting June 28 when the Hawkeye Racing Assn. will make its regular Sunday evening appearance on the Tunis Oval, then on the 4th of July in the afternoon at the Vinton Fair Grounds on the new short track. The same evening they will make ther regular scheduled appearance on the Amusements, Inc. track at Marshalltown, and then back to Tunis' on Sunday for a full evening of entertainment and fun. This will include fireworks by the management, the appearance of the Soap Box Derby winner and other contestants, and a program of race events. The winner of the Soap Box Derby appearaing here goes direct to Akron for the National event.

Don't forget that the OFFICIAL T-SHIRTS can be bought at the judges' stand at each race meet. There are sizes for all, kids, big kids and adults. I'm not supposed to mention the fact that I have a few of the unofficial brand. I promise not to get any more.

Howard says that if there are any questions or complaints about the races to please jot such down on a piece of paper and hand to someone in the judge's stand and he will answer it to the best of his ability in this column. Lets deluge him with questions, at least.

Rain . . . ?

First dust, then mud, and now RAIN . . ? So they said at 4 p.m. Saturday, June 13th, at Marshalltown. But according to reports from reliable sources the track was in perfect condition at race time.

But, that's the way it goes. Posekany, Spore and others who weren't notified soon enough, had their cars at the track and reported a good, fast oval. Must'a been something else there, too, as they came through Dike after midnight on their way home.

THE BEST FOR LESS
RUNYAN DEEP ROCK
18th and Williston
Waterloo, Iowa
The STOP . . that keeps you going

When Your Appetite Craves a Change - It's
BOUSKA'S TAYSTRYT CAFE
PHONE 194 - NEW HAMPTON
Steaks - Chicken - Ribs - Sea Foods
Serving Excellent Foods Is Our Hobby
Draft Beer At Its Best
Served Thru KOLD DRAFT - Taste the Difference

Stock Car Races

As Seen Through the
Camera's Lens
by Morris L. Bailey, Dike, Iowa

Volume 1 - Number 7 Waterloo, Iowa, June 27, 1953

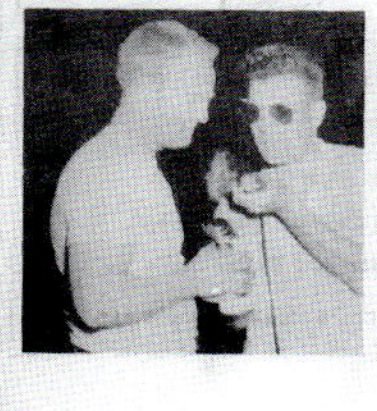

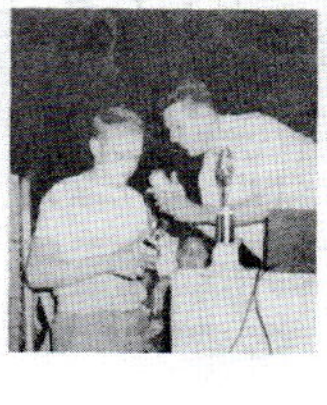

I DOOD IT!...

Had to go to Marshalltown to do it, but I finally came through. I was on the scene, had a good flash bulb in the camera, pulled the slide and tripped the shutter at the proper time. That's right, I got a fairly good picture of the best piece of action this year. I am speaking of the picture on the top half of the front page. It has no title, but at the time of the action it was called plenty of things.

The only thing that I didn't do right was to run out of film before I had taken all the picaures I thought were necessary to record the event. I don't believe the fellows will do it over again for me so that I can get the pictures either. We certainly are thankful that everyone could walk away from that one.

Now let's go through the rest of the pictures starting at the left, going across and down to the next row, etc.

The mixup in which Bob Roe was injured involved Bill Corwin, Frank Lago and Bob. After a trip to the hospital and an x-ray examination Roe was released.

Arnie Spore in the 777 carries the checkered flag in one of the wins he recorded in that car at Marshalltown Saturday night.

The next three: Droste, in the TD win at Marshalltown; Hultman holding the traveling trophy supplied by the Iowa Sports Supply in his feature win at Tunis Speedway Sunday, and Cal Swanson with his trophy for his third TD win of the season.

Top tow, back page: Aftermath of the Marshalltown pileup showing 87 with the Boslough No. 1 on its top. Next to it is DuToit beside his pride and joy.

Don Heideman, the only victim of a mishap in the spectator race when he piled into the fence on the three-quarter turn.

711, 113, 94 and 89, driven by Hultman, Harry Petersen, Mark Taylor and Hill, respectively, for their first flag carrying trips of the season.

That's all the pictures for this week, but I sure had fun takin' them. Herb Frey gave me the only scare of the week and I didn't have to think up an excuse of any kind for failures.

Stock Car Driver Injured at Ottumwa

From Ottumwa comes the report that Dick, Santee, 27, prominent Southern Iowa stock car driver from Fremont, was seriously injured in a crackup at the Sports Arena near Ottumwa last Sunday night.

The hospital Monday listed Santee's injuries as a broken neck and severe head injuries but said he appeared to be making satisfactory progress.

Santee was injured in the fifth lap of the feature event of the evening. His car rolled after coming in contact with another driven by Johnny Baker of Batavia.

After coming to a stop on its side three closely bunched machines piled into the Santee car. Santee was the only driver hurt.

Dick was the championship driver on the Chariton and Oskaloosa tracks last season.

My Chat With the President

Arrangements have been completed for racing every other Friday night on the West Pnion half-mile track. The first race will be held there under the lights on the evening of the 3rd of July.

Don't forget next weekend! Friday nite, West Union, Saturday afternoon, the 4th, at Vinton; the same evening on the Marshalltown oval; and Sunday evening back to Waterloo for a full night of racing and fireworks.

Besides the regular scheduled affairs the following dates have been booked:

August 5 - Benton County fair at Vinton, an afternoon show.
August 6 - Delaware County Fair at Manchester, an afternoon show.
August 6 - Grundy County Fair at Grundy Center, evening show.
Aug. 11 - Hardin County Fair at Eldora, afternoon show
Sept. 12 - Marshall Co. Fair at Marshalltown, afternoon show.

With the taking on of new tracks we will be seeing new cars and drivers at the races in the near future. Several new cars are expected from the West Union area.

Pictures . . .

Copies of all pictures used in this and other issues of the paper, can be obtained from Ted Gallentine or Morris L. Bailey. If you are interested in getting some of the shots contact either of the above two at the judges stand between events or have a call sent out and we will put in an immediate appearance.

Would like to get some more reservations for year books. It takes a little more of that folding stuff to keep getting out a paper like this than I figured. $2 will keep putting it out to you at the track and also reserve a year book for you at the close of the season.

While on the subject of the paper I would like to mention the fact that there is advertising space available and also that you should patronize the advertisers now cooperating as they are the ones who make it possible for you to receive one of the thousand copies distributed at the track each week.

To be sure of obtaining a copy each week, pay your $2, get it from Morris L. Bailey at the track. Or, $2.50 with your name and address will bring it to you by mail.

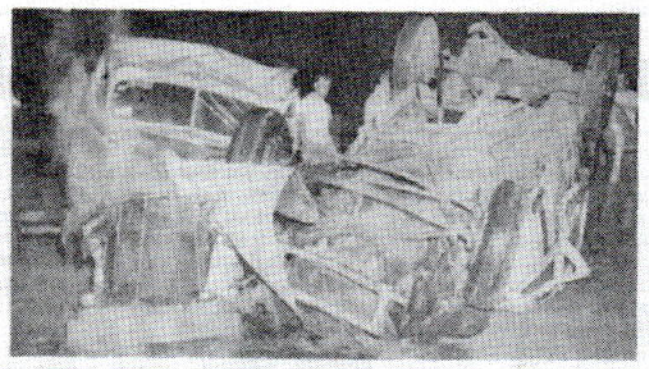

5-Car Pile-Up at Marshalltown Oval

Marshalltown, Iowa, June 20 — A series of crashes cut the field of cars in the stock car races at Amusements, Inc., Saturday night from 19 at post time to five cars in the wind-up of the feature event four hours later.

Although the accidents slowed the running of the races considerably, there were few spectators who left before the checkered flag was dropped for the final time.

Several cars were damaged but got back into later races. Others were loaded on their trucks and hauled away. Several drivers received minor injuries but none required hospitalization.

The most spectacular crash of the evening was in the three-quarter turn on the first lap of the main event. Twelve cars were entered and five failed to survive that crash.

Don Graham of Waterloo was eventual winner, with Red Droste of Waterloo second and Cal Swanson, Dike, third.

It was reported that the right front wheel of the car driven by Clarence DuToit of Marshalltown came off as he was leading the others in the speeding pack. When his car went out of controll and into a roll it was hit by several other cars and practically demolished. DuToit was shaken up but unhurt otherwise.

Arne Spore of Waterloo was behind DuToit's car and in an effort to avoid hitting the rolling auto, broadsided his mount, leaving it wide open for a crash by John Thede who in turn was piled into by Don Graham. In the meantime Bob Reid, in an effort to miss the congested area, rolled and landed on his top tangled with the DuToit car. Reid was scalded and cut on the arms, but the other drivers escaped with a shaking up and various bruises.

Spore was the hardluck driver of the evening. In the first turn of the first lap of the third heat, he locked wheels with another car. His car did a complete flip in the air and turned over without scratching the top. Spore complained of rib and neck injuries but in the next race he drove another car until it threw the rods.

Spore was again driving his first car when it was involved in the main event crash that finished it for the evening. The car was too badly damaged to be put back on the track again. Spore, however, copped the semi-main, with Don Graham next.

In the novelty race, run the wrong way around the track for 12 laps, the field of nine cars was cut to only one by mechanical trouble. Spore's car threw its rods in the 11th lap and yet placed for a third.

The second place went to Floyd Needham who lost a wheel in the 11th lap but managed to finish that lap. Vern DuToit was the only other driver to complete the race and he got first place money.

The second attempt to run the third heat had to be called off when Red Sanderson of Gladbrook hit the outside rail on the three-quarter turn and rolled his car. He was not injured.

Results:

Time Trials - Red Droste
First Heat - Ledtje, Droste and DuToit.
Second Heat - Swanson, Graham and Hinton
Third Heat - Spore, Reid and Corwin
Novelty — Vern DuToit, Needham and Spore
Semi-Main - Spore, Graham and Clarence DuToit
Main Event - Graham, Droste and Swanson
Trophy Dash - Red Droste

THROUGH THE CAMERA LENS
Edited and Published by
Morris L. Bailey, Dike, Iowa
at the
College Hill Print Shop
2016 College St.
Cedar Falls, Iowa

Gene Hultman in First "Main" Win

Waterloo, Sunday, June 21 — Gene Hultman of Waterloo scored his first major victory of the season here Sunday night when he won the main event of the stock car races at Tunis Speedway before 3,043 fans.

He beat out Carroll Jensen, his co-driver and helper who drives the other of the team's cars, in the feature to finish a night of racing that included four crashes.

One of the accidents sent Bob Roe to the hospital, but he was released after x-ray examinations. He was shaken up in a tangle of cars on the second turn of the second lap of the semi-main event.

Bob Ledtje of Gladbrook, last week's main event winner, piled up in an end-over-end flip in the 14th lap of the same race.

Don Heideman, one of the drivers in the spectator's race, ripped into the fence in the home stretch but escaped injury. His car was badly damaged.

Bob Hilmer rolled in the final lap of the main, but he was not hurt. Both Hilmer and Ledtje placed despite their rollovers. The Hawkeye Racing Association rules are that when an accident occurs in the closing lap of a race, the race shall be considefed complete at the finish of the last completed lap prior to the mishap.

Cleo Bedard of Evansdale won the spectators' race.

The results:

Time trials - Cal Swanson, Dike.
Trophy Dash - Cal Swanson, Dike
First Heat - Hilmer, Runyan and Gene Petersen
Second Heat - Hill, Ledtje and Swanson
Third Heat - Harry Petersen, Jensen and Graham
Novelty - Taylor, Spore and Runyan
Semi-Main - Reid, Posekany and Harry Petersen
Spectator's Race - Bedard, Heidman and Osborn
Main Event - Hultman, Jensen and Harry Petersen

There will be no issue printed next week as the platemaker, the man who makes the printing plate for the front page, is going on vacation. So, will see you in Marshalltown July 11th, I hope.

Fireworks - Tunis Speedway -July 5th

Stock Car Races

As Seen Through the Camera's Lens

by Morris L. Bailey, Dike, Iowa

Volume 1 - Number 8 Waterloo, Iowa, July 11, 1953

Tunis Speedway Wrecked by Wind

It's Swanson Again at Marshalltown

. . . See Story Inside

Hilmer Wins 1st Round at W. Union

. . . See Story Inside

Tournament of Thrills at Tunis'

. . . See Story Inside

Bob Posekany Takes 1st Feature

. . . See Story Inside

DIKE
BODY
SHOP 555

Spore Rolls; Swanson Wins

A full evening of racing at Marshalltown was highlighted by the triple roll executed by Arnie Spore as he went into the first straightaway in the first lap of the evening's first heat race, in which Arnie was taken to the hospital for treatment and immediate release. The 333 was badly damaged, and Spore was cut and broused. Arnie was heard to tell Droste, after his flip of the night before, "Anything you can do, I can do better." Unquote!

Cal Swanson grabbed the second leg of the Marshalltown Times-Republican trophy when he came from behind to overtake a long lead by Dewey Wolfang in the final event of the evening. Cal also holds the same claim on the Iowa Sports Supply Trophy at Waterloo. Only needs one more feature at each track to take permanent possession.

Clarence DuToit and Dewey Wolfong, both of the Marshalltown area, put on a good showing Saturday night when both drivers ran in front in the races in which they were entered for the evening. Du Toit winning two events and placing third in the main and Dewey winning his heat race and placsecond, behind Swanson in the main.

Results:

Time Trials- Swanson

1st Heat - DuToit, Swanson and Ledtje.

2nd Heat - Graham, Thede and Krogh

3rd Heat - Gene Petersen, Hultman and Reid.

Novelty - DuToit - Gene Petersen and Hinton

Semi - Wilfong, DuToit and Jensen

Main - Swanson, Wilfong and Du Toit

Stunt Men Show Here July 15

Being catapulted through space from an inclined rampway while another car passes underneath is one of the stunts to be staged at the Tournament of Thrills Wednesday, July 15, at Tunis Speedway, when top daredevils of the nation compete in a contest sanctioned by International Stuntmen's Associaton, Hollywood, Cal.

Teams in the contest will represent the Chitwood Daredevils, the Canadian Aces, Scottish Krashmen, Texas Tornadoes and Hollywood Thrill Drivers.

Points will be awarded the contestants toward the national seasonal championships.

The ramp to ramp catapult, a feature of the Chitwood Daredevils, will be a special feature on the pro gram. Dive bomber crashes, precision driving and motorcycle stunts will comprise the two-hour program of daredeviltry.

There will be no advance sale of tickets. Admission will be paid at the track the night of the performance.

Tunis Speedway Hit by Wind

Tunis Speedway was badly damaged by the high winds that visited the Waterloo area Sunday afternoon and forced cancellation of the evenings stock car races.

The winds ripped out the bleacher seats, hanging seats and brackets on the fences and light wires. Twisted lights and fixtures and knocked down the wrestling ring mounted in front of the west end bleachers.

The winds also tore up one large tree in the barnyard area of the Tunis property, causing a large amount of damage to the horse barn on which it came to rest. Many more of the beautiful trees in his home yard were badly damaged as the winds whipped through the tops.

Judd was working on the track preparing it for the evening when the storm struck. Upon being asked if he was scared, he commented: "Didn't have time to get scared, I just dove for the basement and let her blow."

Spore Injured

One serious injury in races last weekend was reported to the association. Arnold Spore was cut about the face and received a badly bruised left arm when his car went into a triple roll at Amusement, Inc. track at Marshalltown last Saturday night. He was hospitalized, treated and released.

Posekany Wins At Vinton

Bob Posekany came through at Vinton for his first feature win of the season after being threatened for fifteen laps by Hilmer, Krogh and Jensen, in that order.

Bob started on the pole and was never headed in the full fifteen lap feature. Hilmer, Krogh and Jensen came from the rear but were unable to make the grade. Krogh took over second spot in the 13th lap, but lost it again to Hilmer as he went wide in making his bid for the lead in the last turn coming in for the checkered flag.

The first heat was delayed by a spinout and roll by Don Isley as the cars went into the stretch as the race was started. After a few minor adjustments were made on Mammy Yokum, Don went out and finished in first place in that heat.

The Semi also saw action when Isley became tangled with another car, and in trying to avoid a collision, No. 30, driven by Carroll Hilmer went into a roll. The race was won by Bob Hilmer of Dysart.

Results:

Time Trials - Droste

1st Heat - Isley, Krogh and Droste

2nd Heat - Lago, Bob Hilmer, and Krogh

3rd Heat - Jensen, Davis and Ledtje

Novelty - Lago, Corwin and Slater

Semi - Bob Hilmer, Reid and Sanderson

Main - Posekany, Bob Hilmer, Krogh and Jensen

Stock Cars Race at West Union

The Hawkeye Racing Association members made their first appearance of the season on the fair grounds track at West Union last Friday night, July 3. A bang up show was presented before the rather small crowd who came out to see the array of iron assembled there.

The evening was highlighted by a rather nasty roll when Droste attempted to pass four other cars on the fifth lane of a four lane track. The result was the loss of the Circle 245 and a collection of bumps, bruises and abrasions by Red. He couldn't have been too badly abused as he had already put in a phone call for spare bodies, wheels and such needed parts at 2:00 a.m. with the thought in mind of having another car on the track at race time when the boys assembled at Vinton the next afternoon.

A visiting driver from Tacoma, Washington, whose name we did not learn, found the ditch rather deep on the east side of the track where Droste had his trouble when he went over the embankment on the head of the back stretch in the same race. He was hospitalized with a broken nose and severe back injury. No report as to his condition has been sent in at this time.

The feature event of the evening was won by Bob Hilmer in the No. 30, being pushed hard all the way by Donnie Graham in the 245.

Results:

Time Trials - Graham

1st Heat - Crinklow, Spore and Ladeberg.

2nd Heat - Bob Hilmer, Harry Petersen and Taylor

3rd Heat - Droste, Gilbertson and Swanson

Novelty - Crinklow, Bass and Taylor

Semi - Crinklow, Ladeberg and Harry Petersen

Main - Bob Hilmer, Graham and Swanson.

Gregory to Victory

Masten Gregory, a 21-year-old rookie driver from Kansas City, out speeded some of the nation's top race car pilots to win the 200-mile feature event of the National Sports Car Races at Offut Air Force base last Sunday, July 5.

Gregory covered the distance over the three-mile closed course at an average speed of 76.6 miles an hour as a crowd estimated anywhere from 50-thousand to 65-thousand looked on. He was clocked at 131 miles per hour on the long straightaway.

The favorite, Jim Kimberly of Chicago, did not finish the race because of engine trouble.

James Simpson, of Wadsworth, Ill., won the 100 mile race, and Carroll Shelby, of Dallas, Texas, took the 75 mile event.

The 50 mile opener for novices was won by E. Tom Newcomer of Overland Park, Kansas.

WORLD CHAMPIONSHIP
STUNT CONTEST
TOURNAMENT OF THRILLS
7 CHAMPIONSHIP STUNT TEAMS 7
See attempt to break the world's record Ramp to Ramp Jump!
WITH CHITWOOD DAREDEVILS
TEXAS LONESTARS
HOLLYWOOD STUNTMEN
CANADIAN ACES
Indianapolis Daredevils
& many others
See 22 of the World's Greatest Daredevil Champions competing for $25,000 in Season Cash Prizes
The World's Greatest Thrill Show
STUNTING BIG NEW '53 FORDS
7 GREAT SHOWS!

TUNIS SPEEDWAY

WED JULY 15th

Swanson Now Leading Association In Total Points for Season; Droste to 2nd

Cal Swanson is the new point leader of the Hawkeye Racing Association, President Howard Boslough of Cedar Falls announced Thursday. Boslough said Swanson's victory in Marshalltown Saturday night earned him enough points to pass Red Droste in the stock car standings.

Droste, three time winner of the main, had, at the time of this writing racked up a total of 202 points to Swansons 192. Cal has won the main twice and has been timetrials winner five times thus far this season.

Officials of the speedway on Highway 218 between Waterloo and Cedar Falls said recently that Swanson has been coming up rapidly in the past few weeks and stands a good chance of passing Droste, which he did last Saturday

Started in 1949

Formerly of Cedar Falls, Cal Swanson began racing almost by accident. In 1949 Swanson happened to be at the track in Cedar Rapids when one of the drivers failed to show up. Still in his teens, Cal volunteered to take over the driverless car.

He had never raced before but turned in a good performance and has been racing ever since. He is employed as a truck driver.

The drivers of the association race again at Tunis Speedway on Sunday night, and Owner Jud Tunis has rescheduled the fireworks display that was rained out last Sunday. The fireworks will follow the feature event.

Follow the Hawkeye Racing Association

STOCK CAR RACES

Friday Night, July 17 - West Union
Saturday Night, July 18 - Marshalltown
Sunday Night, July 19 - Waterloo
Aug. 5, Aft. - Benton Co. Fair, Vinton
Aug. 6, Aft. - Delaware Co. Fair, Manchester
Aug. 6, Eve. - Grundy Co. Fair, Grundy Center
Aug. 11, Aft. - Hardin Co. Fair, Eldora
Sept. 12, Aft. - Marshall Co. Fair, Marshalltown

Hawkeye Racing Association